Trading Places?

VAT and Customs Treatment of Imports, Exports, Intra-EU Transactions, and Cross-border supplies of Services in the Digital Age

Andrew Rimmer

"VAT Needn't Be Vexing"

First published in December 2010

Second edition May 2016

by

Spiramus Press Ltd
102 Blandford Street
London W1U 8AG

Telephone +44 20 7224 0080

www.spiramus.com

© Spiramus Press Ltd

ISBN 978 1910151 32 7

All rights reserved. No part of this publication may be reproduced in any material form (including photocopying or storing it in any medium by electronic means and whether or not transiently or incidental to some other use of this publication) without the prior written permission of the copyright owner except in accordance with the provisions of the Copyright, Designs and Patents Act 1988 or under the terms of a licence issued by the Copyright Licensing Agency Ltd, 90 Tottenham Court Road, London W1P 4LP.

British Library Cataloguing-in-Publication Data.

A catalogue record for this book is available from the British Library.

The right of Andrew Rimmer to be identified as the author of this work has been asserted by him in accordance with the Copyright, Designs and Patents Act, 1988.

Printed and bound in Great Britain by Grosvenor Group (Print Services) Ltd.

Attributions and acknowledgments

The author acknowledges use of material relating to the subject matters included in this book as published by H M Revenue & Customs in its Website, Guidance Manuals and printed Notices and as licensed under the terms of the Open Government Licence which can be accessed at:
(www.nationalarchives.gov.uk/doc/open-government-licence/version/3)
and accessed by the author between September 2015 and March 2016.

The author acknowledges use of the material that is set out by the European Commission on the Europa websites that comes within its European Union, 1995-2016 copyright notice and as promulgated in COMMISSION DECISION of 12 December 2011 on the reuse of Commission documents (2011/833/EU), also accessed by the author between September 2015 and March 2016.

The Author also acknowledges the use of the Inco Terms® as provided by International Chamber of Commerce (ICC) at:
www.iccwbo.org/products-and-services/trade-facilitation/incoterms-2010/the-incoterms-rules/

The text in Palatino font 10 point is the author's commentary, interpretation and paraphrasing of HMRC's and the Commission's text as appearing in their guidance. The text in Calibri font 10 point is transcribed from HMRC's and the Commission's text as appearing in their guidance.

Author's Disclaimer

Nothing in this book constitutes advice or can be deemed to constitute advice provided to any person reading the text. Any person wishing to receive advice on any matter set out in this book should consult with a VAT and Indirect Tax specialist or other legal adviser. The text represents the law and HMRC's and the Commission's policy on the matters contained herein at March 2016.

Contents

1 Introduction ... 1
1.1 Purpose of this book ... 1
1.2 'EU' not 'EC' ... 1
1.3 The complexities ... 1
1.4 Future of VAT in the EU ... 2
1.4.1 VAT principles ... 4
1.4.2 Import duty ... 4
1.4.3 Intra-EU trading ... 5
1.4.4 International services ... 5
1.5 Definitions and meanings ... 6
1.6 The Extent of the "Territories" of the EU ... 9
1.6.1 VAT Territory ... 9
1.6.2 The Customs Territory ... 10
1.6.3 The Excise Territory ... 10
1.6.4 The Intrastat Territory ... 10

2 Imports ... 13
2.1 Background ... 13
2.2 Imports and "Acquisitions" ... 13
2.3 Import VAT ... 13
2.4 Importer's responsibilities and "EORI" numbers ... 14
2.5 "Authorised Economic Operator" status ... 15
2.5.1 AEOC status ... 16
2.5.2 AEOS status ... 17
2.5.3 "Union Customs Code" ... 17
2.6 Import duty and import VAT deferment ... 18
2.7 "Simplified Import VAT Accounting" (SIVA) ... 19
2.8 Importation methods ... 19
2.8.1 "Import Control System" (ICS) ... 19
2.8.2 Air ... 21
2.8.3 Imports by Sea ... 22
2.8.4 Imports through the Channel Tunnel ... 22
2.8.5 Imports across the Northern Ireland Land Boundary ... 22
2.8.6 Imports by Pipeline ... 22
2.8.7 Imports through the UK Post Office ... 23
2.9 Import procedures ... 23
2.9.1 Classification ... 24
2.10 Community/common transit procedures ... 28
2.11 Suspending or delaying import charges ... 30
2.11.1 Temporary storage ... 30
2.11.2 Declaring the goods ... 35
2.11.3 Declaring "Community Goods" ... 36
2.11.4 The import entry – the "Single Administrative Document" (SAD/C88) ... 36

CONTENTS

    2.11.5 The UK's import system – "CHIEF" (Customs Handling Imports Exports and Freight) 38
    2.11.6 Managing freight logistics – "Customs Freight Simplified Procedures" (CFSP) 39
  2.12 The Customs debt 40
    2.12.1 Who is the "Declarant"? 41
    2.12.2 Post-presentation of the import entry 42
    2.12.3 Warehousing 44
    2.12.4 Excise goods 44
    2.12.5 "Free zones" 44
    2.12.6 "Non-Union goods" 45
    2.12.7 Merchandise In Baggage (MIB) 46

3   **Reliefs from import duty** 49
  3.1 Inward Processing Relief (IPR) 49
  3.2 Processing Under Customs Control (PCC) 52
  3.3 End-Use Relief 53
  3.4 Returned Goods Relief (RGR) 53
    3.4.1 VAT Returned Goods Relief (VAT RGR) 55
  3.5 Goods transferred to other Member States 56
  3.6 Outward Processing Relief (OPR) 57
    3.6.1 OPR and VAT 58
  3.7 Rejected imports 59
    3.7.1 Goods not in accordance with contract 60
    3.7.2 Rejected imports and VAT 60
    3.7.3 Goods in "special situations" 61
  3.8 Temporary admission 63
    3.8.1 Goods eligible for relief of import duty under the TA regime 64
    3.8.2 Discharging a liability to import duty under the TA regime 66

4   **Valuation – valuing the goods for customs *ad valorem* duty** 69
  4.1 Method 1 – the transaction value 70
    4.1.1 "Earlier sale" value 70
  4.2 Additions to the transaction value 74
    4.2.1 Delivery costs 75
    4.2.2 Commissions 75
    4.2.3 Royalties and licence fees 75
    4.2.4 Proceeds of resale 76
    4.2.5 Export duty & taxes paid in the country of origin or export 76
  4.3 Items that can be excluded from the transaction value 77
    4.3.1 Delivery costs within the EU 77
    4.3.2 EU duties or taxes 77
    4.3.3 Discounts 77
    4.3.4 Dividends 79
    4.3.5 Marketing activities related to the imported goods 79
    4.3.6 Buying commission 79

4.3.7	Export quota and licence payments	80
4.3.8	Interest charges	80
4.3.9	Rights of reproduction	80
4.3.10	Post-importation work	80
4.3.11	Management fees	81
4.4	Method 2 – the value of identical goods	81
4.5	Method 3 – the value of similar goods	81
4.6	Method 4 – the selling price of the goods in the EU	82
4.6.1	Subtractions from the unit price	82
4.6.2	Evidence to support the valuation (and deductions)	83
4.7	Method 5 – the cost of producing the goods	84
4.8	Method 6 – the "fall-back" method	85
4.9	Simplified Procedure Values (SPVs)	85
4.10	Frozen meat in "round sets"	85
4.11	Value of goods imported free of charge	86
4.12	Value of imported "replacement" free of charge goods	86
4.13	Value of used goods	86
4.14	Goods used after purchase and before entry into the EU	86
4.15	Valuing rented or leased goods	87
4.16	All Methods – additional considerations	87
4.16.1	Transport costs	87
4.16.2	Surcharges and currency adjustments	89
4.16.3	Insuring the goods in transit	90
4.16.4	Rates of exchange	90
4.17	Valuation declarations and statements	90
4.18	"Season Ticket" valuation statements	91
4.19	Valuation rules for other Customs procedures	91
4.19.1	Customs warehousing	91
4.19.2	Outward Processing Relief (OPR)	92
4.20	Imported replacement products	93
4.20.1	Where a charge is made for the replacement products	93
4.20.2	Where no charge is made for the replacement products	93
4.20.3	Inward Processing Relief	93
4.20.4	Valuation rules for import VAT	93
4.20.5	Special VAT valuation rules	95
4.21	Special VAT valuation rules for Customs Suspensive arrangements	100
4.21.1	Continental shelf goods	102
4.21.2	Onward Supply Relief	102
4.21.3	Goods imported under Temporary Admission Relief and "ATA Carnets"	103
4.21.4	Customs warehousing	104
4.21.5	Tables showing the treatment of goods for Customs and VAT purposes (import VAT and Supply VAT) for goods received into a UK Customs warehouse	107

CONTENTS

4.21.6	End Use Relief	112
4.21.7	Outward Processing Relief	113
4.21.8	Processing Under Customs Control	115
4.21.9	Inward Processing Relief	115
4.21.10	External and Internal Transit	116
4.22	Valuation rules for trade statistics	117

5   Import duty and import VAT reliefs 119

5.1	Aircraft ground and security equipment	119
5.2	Animals for scientific research – Notice 365	120
5.3	Antiques – Notice 362	121
5.4	Blood grouping, tissue typing and therapeutic substances – Notice 369	121
5.5	Capital goods – Notice 343	122
5.6	Chemical and biological substances for research – Notice 366	123
5.7	Commercial samples – Notice 372	124
5.8	Decorations and awards – Notice 364	126
5.9	Donated medical equipment – Notice 341	127
5.10	Duty and VAT-free allowances	129
5.10.1	Arrivals from EU Member States	129
5.10.2	Imports from outside the EU	129
5.11	Food and plants	130
5.12	Gold	130
5.13	Goods for disabled persons – Notice 371	131
5.14	Electricity and natural gas	133
5.15	Fuel, animal fodder and feeding stuffs, and packing for use during transportation	133
5.15.1	Fuel and lubricants	133
5.15.2	Fodder and feeding stuffs	134
5.15.3	Packings	134
5.16	Goods imported for onward dispatch to another Member State – Notice 702/7	134
5.17	Goods for use by a charity – Notice 317	134
5.18	Goods for test – Notice 374	136
5.19	Goods related to war graves	137
5.20	Inherited goods – Notice 368	137
5.21	Miscellaneous documents and other related articles – Notice 342	139
5.22	Museum and gallery exhibits – Notice 361	140
5.23	Sailing "pleasure craft" to the EU – Notice 8	141
5.23.1	Change of Residence relief	143
5.23.2	Use within EU waters	144
5.23.3	Pleasurecraft Temporarily Admitted (TA)	144
5.24	Scientific instruments – Notice 340	145
5.25	International science projects	145
5.26	Private gifts (postal packages) – Notice 143	146

- 5.26.1 Procedures 147
- 5.26.2 De minimis limits 147
- 5.26.3 Charges 149
- 5.26.4 Regular importers 151
- 5.26.5 Packages received from other Member States 151
- 5.26.6 Receiving Alcohol and tobacco from other Member States 151
- 5.27 Returned Goods Relief (RGR) – Notice 236 152
  - 5.27.1 Import duty relief 152
  - 5.27.2 Import VAT 153
- 5.28 Visiting forces – Notice 431 154
  - 5.28.1 Supplies to US visiting forces 154
  - 5.28.2 Supplies to NATO International Military Headquarters (IMHQ) 155
  - 5.28.3 Motor vehicles 156
  - 5.28.4 American cemeteries 156
- 5.29 Visitors to the UK – Notice 3 156
  - 5.29.1 Personal effects 157
  - 5.29.2 Private motor vehicles 157
  - 5.29.3 Pet animals 157
  - 5.29.4 Guide dogs and assistance dogs 158
  - 5.29.5 Transfer of residence 159
  - 5.29.6 Items bought under "Duty and tax-free" regimes 160
  - 5.29.7 Personal possessions and motor vehicles retuning to the EU 160
  - 5.29.8 "Marriage relief" 161
- 5.30 Visual and auditory materials – Notice 373 162
- 5.31 Zero-rated articles including printed matter 163

6 Accounting for import duty and import VAT 167
- 6.1 Determining the VAT amount due 167
- 6.2 Amendments to Declarations and of the sums due to HMRC 168
- 6.3 Postal Imports 169
- 6.4 Unregistered importers 170
- 6.5 Duty Deferment 170
  - 6.5.1 Security 172
  - 6.5.2 Simplified Import VAT Accounting (SIVA) 173
- 6.6 Recovery of import VAT 175
  - 6.6.1 "Postponed Accounting System" (PAS) for imports by post – VAT recovery 178
  - 6.6.2 Merchandise In Baggage (MIB) – Evidence of VAT paid 179
- 6.7 Goods imported into the UK by a third country/territory supplier 179
  - 6.7.1 UK agents 180

7 Remission of import duty and import VAT 181
- 7.1 Goods "not in accordance with contract" 181
  - 7.1.1 Goods "not in accordance with contract" – Import VAT 182

CONTENTS

    7.1.2   Goods "not in accordance with contract" – excise duty...............182
  7.2   Goods imported in "special situations" – import duty and import VAT..................183
  7.3   Offences...................183
    7.3.1   Customs Civil Penalties (CCP) 184
    7.3.2   Customs Civil Evasion Penalties (CCEP).......................185

8   Exports 187
  8.1   Background.....................187
  8.2   Types of export........................189
    8.2.1   Direct exports and VAT.........................189
    8.2.2   Indirect exports and VAT.........................190
    8.2.3   Agents 191
  8.3   Customs procedures relating to exports of goods......................191
    8.3.1   National Export System (NES) 192
  8.4   Community Transit and the New Computerised Transit System (NCTS).........................194
  8.5   The Transport International Routiers (TIR) procedure 194
  8.6   Admission Temporarie – Temporary Admission (ATA) Carnet 194
    8.6.1   Types of Export Declarations.....................195
    8.6.2   Merchandise In Baggage (MIB) 197
  8.7   Excise goods..................198
    8.7.1   Excise Movement Control System (EMCS)......................199
    8.7.2   Warehousing For Export (WHE) 200
  8.8   European Community export preferences 200
  8.9   Proof of export...................201
    8.9.1   Official evidence 201
    8.9.2   Commercial evidence.......................202
    8.9.3   Supplementary evidence 202
    8.9.4   Tertiary legislation – HMRC Notices having the "force of law" 203
    8.9.5   Goods supplied "Ex-Works" (EXW)......................203
  8.10   Evidence of export under New Computerised Transit System........204
  8.11   Goods exported via another Member State........................206
  8.12   Ports or airports without access to NES.........................206
  8.13   Goods exported to the Channel Islands........................206
  8.14   Particular types of export – proof required......................207
    8.14.1   "Groupage" 207
    8.14.2   Goods exported by post......................208
    8.14.3   Courier and fast parcel services......................209
    8.14.4   Exports by rail......................209
    8.14.5   Exports by auctioneers......................209
  8.15   Time limits for exporting the goods and for obtaining proof of export........................211
  8.16   "Time of supply" and "tax point" for exports 212
  8.17   Particular types of exports......................213

- 8.17.1 Goods delivered to a non-UK branch of the same legal entity ... 214
- 8.17.2 Goods that are lost, stolen or destroyed before leaving the UK . 215
- 8.17.3 Goods for "supply and install" contracts 215
- 8.17.4 The temporary export of goods for exhibition or processing 216
- 8.17.5 Goods supplied on "sale or return" terms 216
- 8.17.6 Supplies to "overseas persons" 216
- 8.17.7 Racehorses (Notice 700/57/14) 217
- 8.17.8 Supplies to the Ministry of Defence and overseas military establishments 217
- 8.17.9 Certain supplies in connection with the management of defence projects 217
- 8.17.10 Supplies to Government Departments other than the Foreign and Commonwealth office (FCO) 218
- 8.17.11 Supplies to regimental shops 218
- 8.17.12 Goods exported after process or incorporation into other goods 218
- 8.17.13 Goods exported following several chain transactions 219
- 8.17.14 Exports by members of VAT groups 219
- 8.17.15 Freight containers – see Notice 703/1 220
- 8.17.16 Ships and aircraft stores 221
- 8.17.17 Stores delivered direct to shipping companies and airlines 222
- 8.17.18 Stores for sale on-board ships etc 223
- 8.17.19 Supplies of mess and canteen stores for HM ships 223
- 8.17.20 Exports by British Forces Post Office (BFPO) 224
- 8.17.21 Exports of goods to oil rigs, gas rigs and "continental shelf" installations 224
- 8.17.22 Machine tools used in the UK to manufacture goods for export (see Notice 701/22) 225
- 8.17.23 Goods exported by a charity 226
- 8.17.24 Supplies to persons departing from the EU under the "Retail Export Scheme" ("tax-free shopping") 226
- 8.17.25 Exports of motor vehicles 230
- 8.17.26 The "Personal Export Scheme" for motor vehicles 231
- 8.17.27 Sailaway boats 232
- 8.17.28 Supplies of "marine fuel" 234
- 8.17.29 Hydrocarbon oils 234
- 8.17.30 Supplies at "Duty and Tax-Free" shops 235
- 8.17.31 Computer software 235
- 8.18 Trade Associations and contact details 235

9 Intra-EU Transactions 237
- 9.1 Background 237
- 9.2 Introduction to cross-border movements 238
- 9.3 Dispatches 239
  - 9.3.1 Goods removed after process or incorporation 242

CONTENTS

9.3.2	Time limits for removing the goods	243
9.3.3	Evidence of removal	243
9.3.4	Goods not removed	247
9.3.5	Invoicing	247
9.4	"B2C" supplies and "Distance Selling"	248
9.4.1	Goods removed to the UK under distance selling	250
9.5	"New Means of Transport"	250
9.5.1	Removing an NMT from the UK – private persons	251
9.5.2	Removing an NMT from the UK – UK VAT-registered supplier	252
9.6	Acquiring NMTs in the UK – unregistered persons	253
9.6.1	NMTs relieved from Acquisition VAT	254
9.6.2	Acquiring NMTs in the UK – VAT-registered persons	255
9.7	Arrivals and Acquisitions	256
9.7.1	Value of the Acquisition	258
9.8	Transfer of an entity's own goods to another Member State	259
9.9	Temporary movement of goods	260
9.9.1	Supplies of services in the Member State of Arrival	260
9.9.2	Goods for temporary use in the Member State of Arrival	261
9.9.3	Changes in circumstances	261
9.9.4	Register of own movements	261
9.10	Goods for installation or assembly in another Member State	261
9.11	Goods removed for process or repair	262
9.11.1	Work performed on goods before being removed to another Member State	263
9.12	"Triangulation" and "Chain Transactions"	264
9.12.1	Simplified procedure	264
9.12.2	Non-EU goods	266
9.12.3	"Chain transactions"	266
9.13	Supplies to diplomats, "international organisations" etc.	266
9.14	"Call-off" stocks	268
9.15	"Consignment" stocks	268
9.16	Excise goods	268
9.17	Goods removed under "sale or return" arrangements	270
9.18	Goods sold on "intra-EU transport"	270
9.19	Samples	271
9.19.1	General	271
9.19.2	Samples given to the general public via an intermediary	271
9.20	Goods sent for testing	271
9.21	Record-keeping requirements	271
9.21.1	VAT returns	272
9.21.2	EC Sales Lists (ESLs)	273
9.21.3	"Intrastat"	276
9.22	Tables of VAT liabilities for Intra-EU movements	280

| 10 | Recovery of VAT "Cross-Border" | 295 |

- 10.1 Introduction ... 295
- 10.2 EU Scheme ... 295
  - 10.2.1 Eligibility criteria ... 295
  - 10.2.2 Applications ... 296
  - 10.2.3 Applications by UK businesses to other Member States ... 298
  - 10.2.4 Refunds in the UK for EU businesses ... 298
- 10.3 Non-EU scheme ... 299
  - 10.3.1 Eligible goods and services ... 300

| 11 | Intra-EU Transactions – Supplies of Services | 303 |

- 11.1 Introduction ... 303
  - 11.1.1 Nature of the supply ... 305
  - 11.1.2 "Place of Belonging" ... 306
  - 11.1.3 Meaning of "business establishment" ... 306
  - 11.1.4 Meaning of "fixed establishment" ... 306
  - 11.1.5 Meaning of "usual place of residence" ... 307
  - 11.1.6 More than one place of establishment ... 308
  - 11.1.7 Contradictory evidence ... 309
  - 11.1.8 Request for a "Non-Statutory Clearance" by HMRC ... 310
- 11.2 The General Rules ... 311
  - 11.2.1 B2B General Rule ... 311
  - 11.2.2 B2C General Rule ... 312
  - 11.2.3 "Relevant Business Person" ... 312
  - 11.2.4 Special POS rules ... 314
  - 11.2.5 General exception for "land services" ... 315
  - 11.2.6 Special rule for "passenger transport services" ... 324
  - 11.2.7 Special rule for the "hiring of a means of transport" ... 326
  - 11.2.8 Special rule for the "hiring of any goods other than a means of transport" ... 329
  - 11.2.9 Special rule for "cultural, artistic, sporting, scientific, educational or entertainment services" and "ancillary services" relating to them – "Where Performed" services ... 331
  - 11.2.10 Admission to Where Performed services ... 335
  - 11.2.11 Special rule for "restaurant and catering" services ... 336
  - 11.2.12 Special rule for EU "on-board" restaurant and catering services ... 336
  - 11.2.13 Special rule for the "Tour Operators' Margin Scheme" (TOMS) ... 337
  - 11.2.14 Special rules for the transport of goods ... 341
  - 11.2.15 Ancillary transport services ... 343
  - 11.2.16 Special rule for "Broadcasting", "Telecommunication services" and "Electronic Services" ("Electronically Supplied Services") ("BTE" services) ... 344
- 11.3 "Mini One Stop Shop" or "VAT MOSS" schemes ... 363
  - 11.3.1 Non-Union MOSS ... 364

CONTENTS

- 11.3.2 Accounting for Non-Union VAT MOSS 366
- 11.3.3 Union MOSS 366
- 11.3.4 Pricing services and VAT 371
- 11.3.5 POS tables for Broadcasting, Telecommunications and Electronic (BTE) services 372
- 11.4 Specific exception for 'B2C' "intellectual-type" services and other "intangibles" 376
  - 11.4.1 Transfers and assignments of copyright, patents, licences, trademarks and similar rights. 378
  - 11.4.2 The acceptance of any obligation to refrain from pursuing or exercising (in whole or in part) any business activity or any rights relating to an intangible service 379
  - 11.4.3 Advertising services 379
  - 11.4.4 Services of consultants, engineers, consultancy bureaux, lawyers, accountants and other similar services; data processing; and the provision of information 379
  - 11.4.5 Banking, financial and insurance services (including reinsurance), other than the provision of safe deposit facilities 383
  - 11.4.6 The provision of access to, and transport or transmission through, natural gas and electricity distribution systems and the provision of other directly linked services 385
  - 11.4.7 Supplies of staff 385
  - 11.4.8 The letting on hire of goods 386
  - 11.4.9 BTE services 387
- 11.5 "Emissions Allowances" 387
- 11.6 Agency services ("intermediary services") 388
- 11.7 Valuations services and "work on goods" 389

12 Tax invoices, Reverse Charge and Reverse Charge EC Sales Lists ... 391
- 12.1 Introduction 391
- 12.2 Sales 391
  - 12.2.1 UK VAT invoices for Sales to EU Customers 392
  - 12.2.2 Reverse Charge EC Sales Lists ("ESLs") 392
  - 12.2.3 Agreement with VAT returns 393
- 12.3 Purchases or "imported services" 393
  - 12.3.1 Accounting for Reverse Charges 394
  - 12.3.2 Reverse Charge VAT not accounted for 395

13 "Best Practice" and Planning 397
- 13.1 Imports 397
- 13.2 Exports 398
- 13.3 Arrivals 398
- 13.4 Dispatches 399
- 13.5 International services 400
- 13.6 Summary 400

13.6.1	Imports	401
13.6.2	Exports	401
13.6.3	Intra-EU supplies of goods	401
13.6.4	Declarations	402
13.6.5	International services	402

Appendix A: Terms of Trade **403**
   Using the correct "Incoterms®" 403

Appendix B: Useful addresses **406**

Glossary **408**

Index **417**

CONTENTS

1 Introduction

1.1 Purpose of this book

The book sets out to guide readers through the highly complex VAT and import duty issues for importers, exporters and businesses transacting across the EU. There is a distinct technical and commercial language ascribed to imports, exports and intra-EU transactions and a definitions table is provided in section **1.5** for reference.

Secondly, with the advent of widespread changes to the supply of international services in a "digital age" this second edition has incorporated commentary on the VAT treatment for such transactions.

However, this book is not, and cannot be, an exhaustive guide to all the transactions and circumstances that businesses become involved in, which can create a VAT or import duty exposure or liability. Readers should therefore seek expert help where they require advice on the VAT and import duty issues for any aspect of their international trading.

1.2 'EU' not 'EC'

The *Treaty of Lisbon (Changes in Terminology) Order* 2011 (SI 2011/1043) amended UK legislation to reflect changes in terminology referring from 22 April 2011 to the "EU" rather than the "EC". The term EC is reserved for the Commission itself and all of the politico-legal inferences and bodies encompassed in that organisation.

The EU now has 28 Member States and, on behalf of the European Commission, each is tasked with controlling the movement of goods, capital and people both into and out of the EU. Ensuring that duties and taxes are collected, whilst allowing the free movement of goods, is a vital objective both to the Commission and each Member State. Import duties are uniform across all Member States, being collected on behalf of the Commission, whilst each Member State levies and retains its own import VAT. In the UK, HM Revenue & Customs (HMRC) are required by the Commission to protect the EU's borders and to prevent smuggling, avoidance and abuse. *Whilst not wishing to hamper the international movement of goods, HMRC will always place their 'policing' duties above the commercial interests of any business.*

1.3 The complexities

Successfully managing the import duty and import VAT issues affecting international trade requires a great deal of knowledge and expertise. The advent of the "Single Market" in 1993, which dictates how VAT on intra-EU transactions is to be accounted for, has added to this burden. The VAT and Customs Regulations relating to international trade are constantly evolving with such regimes as the "Authorised Economic Operator" ("AEO") being introduced in the geo-political arena, i.e. world governments and the Commission are using fiscal measures to tackle international security issues

INTRODUCTION

post "9/11". Essentially, the Commission, in response to the US Government's "CPAT" initiative, are looking for businesses to be as compliant as possible, adopting AEO status where feasible to do so, and penalising poor compliance. The stated aim is to keep HMRC and other tax authorities 'on-side'.

The book introduces the main concepts and trade facilitation reliefs that businesses must understand if they are to trade internationally with the least intervention and disruption from the tax authorities. The worst-case scenario is for an importer to have their goods still within a Customs authority's control, instead of being where they are needed because the correct procedures have not been followed or the goods are liable to forfeiture. Allied to this is the need for businesses to utilise all available reliefs to minimise the amount of duty and import VAT payable - whilst import VAT is recoverable by most businesses it is still a major cash-flow cost, which has to be funded, whereas customs duty is an absolute cost so importers must review all available means to reduce or remove the duty payable (see section **4.1.1**). Something as simple as using incorrect "Incoterms" (see **Appendix A**) may result in expensive mistakes and the goods left on the quayside at the place of importation or arrival in a third country/territory. Alternatively, it would be a major issue for a business if goods that were meant to be in transit in an export movement were still in the UK because of a lack of an appropriate export licence or correct documentation.

The book highlights the means of importing goods and arriving at the value for import duty on which both import duty and import VAT are computed. It also provides commentary on export procedures and the VAT treatment of intra-EU transactions, including potential fiscal barriers to exploiting non-UK markets.

Equally, in the digital age, the Commission has struggled to keep abreast of the fast-paced changes in the market economy especially with multi-channel retailing. It has introduced measures to combat fraud and to insist on VAT being brought to account in the place of consumption by, for example, requiring non-EU suppliers to register for VAT somewhere in the EU and non-EU suppliers to account for VAT on 'downloadable products" in a chosen Member State. These developments are discussed in **1.4**.

1.4 Future of VAT in the EU

Regarding intra-EU transactions, because the Commission is working on a "transitional" system there are a number of regimes and measures that have been introduced to prevent avoidance of VAT and evasion, but as with all taxation systems they have their limitations. Goods can also move 'cross-border' without being sold and these movements also need to be recognised for VAT purposes.

On 1st December 2010, the Commission adopted a Green Paper on *The future of VAT - Towards a simpler, more robust and efficient VAT system*. This Green

Paper was followed by a six-month public consultation in which the Commission received 1,700 contributions from businesses, academics, citizens and tax authorities. The European Parliament, the European Economic and Social Committee and the Tax Policy Group consisting of the personal representatives of the finance ministers welcomed the Green Paper and confirmed the need to reform the EU VAT system. In parallel, the European Commission carried out an economic evaluation of the VAT system.

The Single Market Act stressed the fundamental importance of establishing a definitive VAT regime applicable to cross-border transactions. The Green Paper provided an ideal opportunity to examine whether the commitment made in 1967 to establish a definitive VAT system operating within the EU in the same way as it would within a single country, based on the principle of taxation in the country of origin, is still relevant. However, recent discussions with Member States confirmed that this principle remains politically unachievable. This deadlock is even recognised by the European Parliament – until now a fierce defender of the principle of origin – which has called for a move towards the destination principle. Also, stakeholders acknowledge that the origin system, which is in theory the most attractive choice for them, will not be achievable in the foreseeable future. They therefore promote a properly functioning system based on taxation at destination as a pragmatic and politically achievable solution.

Under the 'destination system' goods are liable to VAT in the country to which they are dispatched. Thus goods sent from the UK to France are liable to French VAT and vice versa. The French recipient of the goods accounts for VAT on the "Acquisition" (or "Arrival") of the goods in France, the country of destination of the goods.

Given the difficulties mentioned by businesses trading in several Member States, the One-Stop-Shop (OSS) – a measure proposed in the Commission's plan to reduce the administrative burdens and supported by the High Level Group of Independent Stakeholders on Administrative Burdens – is still a high priority.

The supply of a mini OSS for the EU providers of telecommunications, broadcasting and electronic services provided to final consumers within the EU came into force in 2015 – see **Chapter 11**. Some businesses exposed to cross border trade do not understand why their activities have been excluded from this facility, despite the fact that they are confronted with the same difficulties.

The implementation of the mini OSS is seen by many Member States and by business as a major milestone. The Commission hopes that its smooth functioning should pave the way for a more general use of this concept. However, given the lack of experience of an OSS for intra-EU trade, Member States appear to be somewhat reluctant to consider broadening its scope at such an early stage. The Commission remains convinced that, in a VAT system

INTRODUCTION

based on taxation at destination, an OSS is a crucial instrument to facilitate access to the single market, in particular for SMEs. So, the "jury is still out" on this concept and driver for change.

1.4.1 VAT principles

At its simplest definition, VAT is a tax on "consumption", being levied as a percentage of the price of the goods or services charged to the "consumer" by the supplier. The principal VAT Directive is now Directive 2006/112/EC, which replaced the EC Sixth Directive 77/388/EEC, and the principal UK legislation is the VAT Act 1994 and the Value Added Tax Regulations 1995. A number of other statutory instruments apply to the import, export and intra-EU supply of goods and a number of public notices also have the "force of law" which means they are tertiary legislation which must be complied with, for example VAT Notice 703: *export of goods from the UK*[1], which are referred to throughout this book.

Because VAT is levied at all stages of the "production cycle", it applies to every entrepreneur or business operating within the cycle, from manufacturers and growers to wholesalers, traders and retailers. Additionally, and as a means of ensuring that consumers inside the EU are unable to purchase goods from outside the EU at 'VAT-free' prices, thereby potentially damaging the competitiveness of a supplier sourcing goods that originate within the EU, VAT is also levied on goods that are imported into the EU. There are wide-ranging exceptions where certain goods are relieved of import VAT or where qualifying persons or businesses can import goods free of import VAT, for example, charities and the Armed Forces.

The amount of import VAT that is chargeable on an importation of goods is based on the Customs valuation of the goods, including all charges, levies, and the import duty itself at the point of import i.e. where the goods land at a designated port or airport within the EU. Immediately, it can be seen that agreeing the correct valuation for the goods for import VAT purposes is important. That value in turn rests on the valuation applying to the goods for import duty purposes, and so it is vital to ensure that the valuation declared for duty purposes is itself the lowest value possible. Ensuring that import duty, if any, and the import VAT, are calculated on the lowest possible valuation is a specialist area. Importers and their agents must take note of how the valuation has been calculated and a large number of factors within the supply chain must be examined to ensure the least amount of import duty and import VAT are due.

1.4.2 Import duty

The main difference between import VAT and import duty is that the "importer" is able to recover the import VAT in his business, provided that the

---

[1] www.gov.uk/government/publications/vat-notice-703-export-of-goods-from-the-uk

goods have been imported for business use, subject to his VAT return cycle, whereas import duty is an absolute cost to the business as the importer is unable to recover it, even where the goods are used fully in his business (there are a large number of duty reliefs according to the business and trade that the importer is engaged in).

1.4.3 Intra-EU trading

A major distinction lies between imports of goods into the EU and goods that are traded within the EU ("Intra-EU"). The advent of the Single Market in 1993 revolutionised the VAT and import duty implications and responsibilities for Intra-EU trading. The continuous development of cross-border taxation has, if anything, complicated matters rather than achieving the simplification desired; the Commission states otherwise, but most VAT and duty practitioners as well as businesses would argue that the degree of administration can outweigh the fiscal relief introduced by the measures.

The advent of the Single Market has also narrowed the scope of "Exports" from the EU by differentiating an Intra-EU "Dispatch" of goods from an export of goods to countries and territories outside the EU, referred to in this book as "Third countries/territories".

1.4.4 International services

The advent of the "digital age" and advancements in technology that have enabled the cross-border supply of electronic services (and "intellectual-type" services that can now be provided by electronic means) has resulted in a worldwide marketplace for all suppliers and customers. Both suppliers and customers can now trade across the world with very few barriers. This has and will continue to test global tax authorities to the limit as they seek to manage national tax revenues and for the Commission to manage its wider taxation receipts.

Geo-political interest groups now proliferate and businesses wish to see "level playing-fields" where all businesses are treated fairly. This requires robust taxation systems with bodies such as the "G20" countries collaborating to minimise "tax leakage" as much as possible, such as that exploited by certain multi-national companies choosing to locate in particular jurisdictions that have low-rates of taxation.

In the VAT arena, the Commission has introduced detailed legislation to tax relevant international services in the places where the businesses and the consumers "consume" the actual services, rather than relying on suppliers to continue to account for VAT in the places where they are established or have chosen to establish their companies.

INTRODUCTION

1.5 Definitions and meanings

The following definitions and meanings are used throughout the book and should be read as a means of understanding the text:

"**Acquisition**" means the "Arrival" of goods in a Member State that is different from the Member State of "Dispatch".

"**Acquisition VAT**" means VAT that is due to be accounted for and declared to the tax authority by the person who acquires the goods in the Member State of Arrival, as though he had supplied the goods himself. The Acquisition VAT can also be reclaimed as an input tax provided the goods are to be used in the business of the Acquirer to make taxable supplies or other supplies that qualify for VAT recovery.

"**By way of business**" means the supplier and/or the recipient are acting in a business-like manner and the activities being pursued are for the purposes of a business conducted on a reasonable scale on a regular or semi-regular basis. The absence of profit or a profit motive is generally seen as indicative that the activity is not for a business or carried on in a business-like way although many activities and businesses do not systematically aim to make a profit.

"**Commission**" means the European Commission.

"**Consideration**" means:

> a payment in money or by non-monetary means such as a payment in kind, including the netting off of inter-company debits and credits in management or annual accounts etc., **or**

> the amount paid or payable by a customer to a supplier in return for the supply of goods and services. Consideration can be non-monetary as well such as in a barter arrangement.

"**customs**" means Customs Community Import Duty

"**Customs Authority**" means the Member State tax authority responsible for controlling the importation, exportation and removal of goods into, out of and within Member States.

"**Dispatch**" means the removal of goods from one Member State to another Member State for sale.

"**Directive 2006/112/EC**" means Council Directive 2006/112/EC of 28 November 2006 on the common system of Value Added Tax, which replaced Directive 77/388/EEC (the Sixth Directive).

"**EU**" means the European Union.

"**EU Trader**" means a "Taxable Person" (legal or individual) that is in business (in the UK the definition of taxable person is of a person who is or is required to be VAT registered) and who supplies goods from a place within the EU, whether or not that person is resident or established within the EU.

"**Export**" means the removal of goods from a place within the EU to a Third Country or Third Territory that is outside the EU by either the supplier or a person on behalf of the customer.

"**Exporter**" means the person (legal or individual) who either supplies or owns goods and exports them or arranges for their export to a place outside the EU, or supplies goods to an "Overseas Person" who arranges for the goods to be exported to a place outside the EU.

"**Free circulation**" means when the goods imported are able to move freely throughout the EU after all Customs import duty and import VAT has either been paid to HMRC/EU Customs authority or guaranteed in favour of HMRC/EU Customs authorities.

"**Fixed establishment**" means an establishment that is not the business' "Permanent Establishment" (see below in "**Place of Belonging**") but is a place that has sufficient legal and technical resources, for example staff and/or an office, from where strategic or commercial decisions are taken on behalf of the business.

"**HMRC**" and "Customs" means H M Revenue & Customs.

"**Import**" means goods that are brought into the EU from a "Third Country" and/or a "Third Territory".

"**Importer**" means the person (legal or individual) who is liable to make the import declaration and pay any import duty and import VAT due on the imported goods.

"**Import Duty**" means Community Customs Duty and, except where the context otherwise requires, includes any agricultural levy, tax or charge provided for under the "Common Agricultural Policy" ("CAP") or under any special arrangements which, under the EU Treaty art 23 (as renumbered), are applicable to goods resulting from the processing of agricultural products. Customs import duty is predominantly an *ad valorum* duty, being levied at a percentage based on the "value" of the goods.

"**Import VAT**" means VAT that is charged and payable on the importation of goods into the UK/EU as if it were a duty of customs. The rate of VAT is the same as if the goods had been supplied in the UK/EU and whether or not the person importing the goods is actually registered for VAT.

"**Intra-EU**" means the removal of goods from a place within the EU to another place within the EU even though the goods may not be the subject of a sale or other disposal where title passes, so includes all transfers of an owner's own goods between Member States e.g. "call-off" stock.

"**Member States**" means the 28 member countries of the EU.

"**Non-Taxable legal person**" means a legal person or a natural person that has a legal identity, but for the purposes of VAT is not making supplies by way of business and cannot be treated as a **Relevant Business Person** (see below).

INTRODUCTION

"Overseas Person" means the person (legal or individual) that is not resident or registered for VAT in the UK (and other EU countries where the goods in question are located in that other EU Member State(s)), has no business establishment in the UK from which they make taxable supplies, or is an overseas authority.

"Place of belonging" means the physical place i.e. the country where a business is legally constituted or has its head office referred to as its "Place of Establishment" or "Permanent Establishment". A business can have other establishments as well as its Permanent Establishment and these are referred to as **"Fixed establishments"** (see above).

"Place of import" means the Member State into which the goods enter the EU. If goods are entered into a permissive suspension regime, for example "Temporary Importation", then the place of import becomes the EU Member State where they are located when those suspension arrangements cease.

"Place of export" means the place within the EU from which the removal takes place.

"Place of residence" means the physical place where a natural consumer, in this book referring to a private consumer, usually lives or has their main or permanent home (usually taking the direct tax treatment as the final determining factor).

"Place of Supply of Services" means the place where services supplied by a supplier to a customer are treated as supplied and are liable to VAT.

"Removal" means the transfer of goods from one Member State to another.

"Relevant Business Person" means a legal or a natural person e.g. a sole trader, that is a "Taxable Person" (see below) who is actively engaged in business activities and who is either registered for VAT in their own EU Member State or if not VAT-registered still makes supplies that can be classed as business supplies. Non-EU legal or natural persons can also be treated as Relevant Business Persons as can Government departments and Charities.

"Relevant Services" mean services that fall within specified headings and categories stipulated under the European VAT Directives that can be treated as supplied in a Member State that is different from the supplier's Member State or outside the EU entirely.

"Reverse Charge" means a charge to VAT in the customer's EU Member State on services supplied from a person or business in another Member State.

"Taxable person" means a legal or natural person that the EU Directives treat as a person that is making **"Taxable supplies"** (see below) by way of business and rendering that person liable to be registered for VAT. In the UK legislation a Taxable Person is a legal or natural person that is or is liable to be registered for VAT.

"Taxable supplies" means the sale of goods or the provision of any services or any other activity such as refraining from doing something on behalf of

INTRODUCTION

another person, by a Taxable Person acting as such, in return for "Consideration" (see above).

"The Tariff" means the Community Customs Tariff used by all Member States to classify imported goods and for Intrastat purposes.

"Third Country" and **"Third Territory"** mean a country or a territory that is outside the EU and all Member States' dependent territories that are treated as part of the EU.

"Used and Enjoyed" means the place where Relevant Services (see above) supplied by a supplier in a Member State or from outside the EU are actually consumed or put to use in another Member State or outside the Member States entirely and without this provision there could be distortions of VAT by either double-taxation or non-taxation of the Relevant Services.

"Value" and **"Valuation"** mean the cost of the goods that are sourced in a Third Country or Third Territory when they are "sold for export" from that country or territory to the EU.

"VATA 1994" means the Value Added Tax Act 1994.

1.6 The Extent of the "Territories" of the EU

Currently there are 28 Member States as listed below. All 28, and certain of their territories, are part of the EU. However, not all Member States' territories are part of the Customs Territory, although included within the VAT Territory.

1.6.1 VAT Territory

The table below sets out the current VAT Territory of the EU:

Member State	Territories Included	Territories Excluded
Austria		
Belgium		
Bulgaria		
Croatia		
Cyprus	the British Sovereign Base Areas of Akrotiri and Dhekelia	The UN buffer zone and the part of Cyprus to the north of the buffer zone where the Republic of Cyprus does not exercise effective control
Czech Republic		
Denmark		the Faroe Islands and Greenland
Estonia		
Finland		the Aland Islands
France	Monaco	Martinique, French Guiana, Guadeloupe, Reunion and St Pierre and Miquelon
Germany		Büsingen and the Isle of Heligoland

INTRODUCTION

Greece		Mount Athos (also known as Agion Oros)
Hungary		
Italy		Campione d'Italia, the Italian waters of Lake Lugano and Livigno
Ireland		
Latvia		
Lithuania		
Luxembourg		
Malta		
Netherlands		the Antilles
Poland		
Romania		
Portugal	the Azores and Madeira	the Canary Islands, Ceuta & Melilla
Slovakia		
Slovenia		
Spain	the Balearic Islands	
Sweden		
United Kingdom	the Isle of Man	the Channel Islands and Gibraltar

1.6.2 The Customs Territory

The Customs Territory of the EU consists of the VAT territory, plus:
- Andorra (but only concerning the importation of goods that are within Chapters 25 onwards of the "Community Customs Tariff");
- The Aland Islands (dependant of Finland);
- The Channel Islands (dependant of the UK);
- The Canary Islands (dependant of Portugal);
- The overseas departments of the French Republic (Guadeloupe, Martinique, Reunion and French Guiana);
- Mount Athos (Agion Oros) (dependant of Greece); and
- San Marino.

1.6.3 The Excise Territory

The Excise Territory of the EC consists of the VAT territory, plus San Marino (dependant of Italy) only.

1.6.4 The Intrastat Territory

For the purposes of compiling and reporting EC **"Trade Statistics"** (the Intrastat Territory) to the Commission, the following EU countries and dependent territories are included:
- Austria;
- Belgium (excluding all dependent/associated territories);
- Bulgaria;
- Croatia

10 TRADING PLACES

INTRODUCTION

- Cyprus (including the British Sovereign Base Areas, but excluding Northern Cyprus (see below);
- Czech Republic;
- Denmark (excluding the Faroe Islands);
- Estonia;
- Finland (including the Aland Islands);
- France (including Monaco, but excluding all French Overseas Departments and territories (see note below));
- Germany (including Heligoland, but excluding Büsingen);
- Greece (including Mount Athos);
- Hungary;
- Ireland;
- Italy (excluding Livigno, Campione d'Italia, San Marino, the Italian Waters of Lake Lugano, and The Vatican) - Livigno is part of the statistical territory of Italy;
- Latvia;
- Lithuania;
- Luxembourg;
- Malta;
- Netherlands (excluding all dependent/associated territories);
- Poland;
- Portugal (including the Azores and Madeira);
- Romania;
- Slovakia;
- Slovenia;
- Spain (including the Balearic Islands, but excluding Ceuta, Melilla, and the Canary Islands (see note below));
- Sweden;
- United Kingdom (including the Channel Islands and the Isle of Man, but excluding Gibraltar).

Notes:

a) The French territories of French Guiana, Guadeloupe, Martinique and Reunion are now part of the statistical territories of France; and
b) The Canary Islands are now part of the statistical territory of Spain.
c) However, as customs documentation is still required for trade with these territories, HMRC continue to collect trade statistics from these territories using the SAD/C88.
d) The EU *acquis* (the body of European law) is currently only applicable in the Government Controlled Area of the Republic of Cyprus.
e) Andorra and Liechtenstein are both outside the Customs Territory, and therefore the statistical territory, of the EU.
f) For trade with the territories that are outside the VAT, Customs, Excise and Trade Statistics Territories, there has been no change to the treatment

INTRODUCTION

of imports etc. as applied before the introduction of the Single Market. Accordingly, all such territories are treated in the same way as any other Third Country.

g) For trade with the Azores, the Balearic Islands, Madeira and Monaco (which are within the VAT, Customs, Excise and Trade Statistics Territories), the same procedures apply as for trade with other EU countries. This also applies to trade between the Isle of Man and EU countries other than the UK.

h) Where goods are imported into the EU from any of the additional territories within the Customs Territory, there is no liability to import duty, but import VAT may still be payable, according to the nature of the goods and any import VAT relief that is available. For example, there are special schemes for goods such as cut flowers which enter the UK from the Channel Islands. Excise duty may also be payable, again depending upon the nature of the goods in question, but is not payable on any goods imported from San Marino, which is inside the Excise Territory.

2 Imports

2.1 Background

The advent of global trade has meant that businesses are much more likely to source goods and raw materials from countries outside of their own country. Goods can often only be sourced from overseas countries or can be bought at more favourable prices, compared to the business' own marketplace, and for traders in the 'Eurozone', exchange-rate differences are no longer a factor that need to be considered.

2.2 Imports and "Acquisitions"

Goods entering the Member States are, in principle, subject to VAT. As explained above, only goods that are sourced from a third country/territory are classed as imports with all movements of goods between Member States classed as "Dispatches" (formerly exports) and "Acquisitions" (formerly imports). The importer must declare the goods as entered into the EU, accounting for any import duty and import VAT. The import duty and import VAT can either be paid at the time the goods are cleared through HMRC's control or deferred under the import agent's or the importer's own duty deferment account. Acquisition VAT on the other hand is accounted for on the Acquirer's own VAT return as an "output tax" entry and can also be reclaimed as an "input tax" entry provided the goods are used are to be used in the Acquirer's business and subject to the normal rules on recoverability, etc. The commercial invoice issued by the supplier in the Member State of Dispatch acts as evidence to support the reclaim of the input tax.

2.3 Import VAT

Import VAT is due on the imported goods at the point when they are entered for "free circulation". Free circulation, in essence, means when all import VAT and import duty has been paid or lodged with the appropriate Customs Authority. This means that import VAT could become due either when goods arrive in the UK directly from a third country/territory or when they arrive from another Member State.

The goods are not treated as imported at any time before an EU customs debt would be incurred, which is treated as the time of acceptance of the relevant Customs declaration. Where the Customs debt is relieved, for example if the goods are entered under a Customs suspension arrangement, the charge to import VAT still arises unless the relief extends to VAT. If an EU customs debt is incurred in the Member State to which the goods are initially imported, import VAT is due in that Member State and any subsequent removal of goods to the UK would be potentially liable to VAT in the UK as an Acquisition.

IMPORTS

Although the Channel Islands are part of the Customs Territory of the EU, they are not part of the territory of the UK or the EU for VAT purposes, so goods removed from the Channel Islands to the UK are subject to import VAT.

The "Importer" is the person who is liable to discharge any EU customs debt, being in most circumstances the person who makes the Customs declaration. Where the person making the Customs declaration is acting on behalf of another person then that other person is also liable to discharge the Customs debt.

2.4 Importer's responsibilities and "EORI" numbers

The person acting as the importer has a number or responsibilities and may not be the person who actually ordered the goods or paid for them, and must:
- deliver an import declaration (referred to as an "import entry" to the Customs Authority; and
- pay "Customs duty" (which includes import VAT) or defer the duty and VAT by use of a deferment account, guaranteed by a bond.

All business that are involved in the import, export or movement of goods under a transit procedure or where they need to provide 'pre-arrival'/'pre-departure' information for goods require an EORI number.

New security laws mean that importers and exporters must declare goods arriving or leaving the EU within set time limits. Persons who supply normal import or export declarations will be covered. However, if not declaring imports or exports in the usual way businesses will need an EORI number to complete an Entry Summary Declaration or an Exit Summary Declaration.

The EORI number is unique to a business and is to be used in all communications with any EU Customs authority. In the UK, the EORI number replaced the "Trader Unique Reference Number" ("TURN") which was in use until 30 June 2009. In the UK the EORI number comprises the letters "GB" followed by the importer's VAT registration number, plus a three-digit suffix. The importer must identify their EORI number on the import entry to enable the import VAT to be recovered as an input tax on their VAT return. The Application form and details of the EORI Scheme are online.[1]

Only legal business entities e.g. sole proprietors, partnerships or companies can be assigned an EORI number. Branches or divisions of a company cannot have their own number as this is allocated to the head office.

The EORI number is also used by Customs authorities to exchange information and, where appropriate, to share information with other government departments and agencies. It is also used to analyse and exchange risk information between Customs authorities and the Commission.

---

[1] www.gov.uk/guidance/economic-operator-registration-and-identification-eori-scheme

UK VAT-registered businesses can check to see if they have EORI status by prefixing the 9 digit VAT number with 'GB' and suffixing with '000', e.g. GB123456789000 (no spaces between the digits) and accessing the EC's Europa database.[2]

EORI numbers are held on both a national and Commission database and data is exchanged between Member States and the Commission. Member states may also share the information with their Customs, veterinary, sanitary, statistical and tax authorities, as well as authorities for trade policy, the 'fight against fraud' or authorities responsible for border control. The general public can also access limited data via a searchable website, but when a business is notified of its EORI number HMRC ask whether the business has any objections to this data being published on the site.

Computer-produced VAT Certificates (Form C79) are sent to the importer whose VAT registration number is shown on the import entry. Since Form C79 constitutes evidence of entitlement to input tax recovery, the use of the correct EORI number is essential to ensure that the import VAT appears on the correct certificate. See **Chapter 6** to understand how HMRC issues C79s and how they are to be used by importers to reclaim import VAT.

2.5 "Authorised Economic Operator" status

Large businesses that regularly import goods are being encouraged to apply for "Authorised Economic Operator" (AEO) status as a means of securing less onerous control by Customs authorities. Originally intended by the Commission as a means of simplifying the Customs control of international trade, an AEO would be entrusted with policing its own affairs, be subject to minimal control and would be ignored by the Customs Authority, save for periodic verification of its continuing high standards. By contrast, it was intended that all other traders would experience significantly enhanced control, both at the ports and inland, as HMRC targeted their resources, based exclusively on the use of EU-wide risk-assessment techniques.

However, the extant AEO is now seen as a means of safeguarding and securing international trade as a response to the '9/11' attacks on New York and there are few, if any, simplification benefits afforded to AEO importers compared to any other importer. Continuous review both by the Commission and other world Customs authorities (for example, the US) are likely to overhaul the extent and purpose of AEO status. Both importers and HMRC report very little change in the exacting requirements to manage the import process. The move to AEO status has, however, been seen by importers as a

---

[2] ec.europa.eu/taxation_customs/dds2/eos/eori_validation.jsp?Lang=en&redirectionDate=20110411

IMPORTS

means of enhanced credibility in international trade, albeit administratively intensive.

Businesses can apply for AEO status for customs simplification ("AEOC"), AEO status for security and safety ("AEOS") or both.

The EU AEO database[3] allows anyone to check who holds an AEO status, what type it is, and the date and country of issue. Whichever authorisation is held, the business will benefit from recognised status across the EU and an industry 'kite mark'.

Any business involved in the international supply chain that carries out customs related activities in the EU can apply for AEO status irrespective of the size of their business. This includes:

- manufacturers;
- exporters;
- freight forwarders;
- warehouse keepers;
- customs agents;
- carriers;
- importers; and
- others (for example, port operators, secure freight parking operatives, airline loaders).

2.5.1 AEOC status

AEOC status is issued to any business that fulfils the specified criteria of having:

- good tax and customs compliance history;
- good commercial and transport record-keeping standards;
- financial solvency;
- professional qualifications or demonstrating practical standards of competence in the activity they're involved in.

Businesses that hold AEOC status could benefit from:

- a faster application process for customs simplifications and authorisations; and
- reductions or waivers of comprehensive guarantees.

Businesses need to be a holder of an AEOC if they wish to qualify for:

- moving goods in temporary storage between different Member States;
- a notification waiver when making an entry in a declarant's records ("EIDR");

---

[3] ec.europa.eu/taxation_customs/dds2/eos/aeo_consultation.jsp?Lang=en&holderName=black&aeoCountry=&certificatesTypes=AEOC&certificatesTypes=AEOF&certificatesTypes=AEOS&Expand=true&offset=1&range=25

- a 70% reduction in a business's deferment account guarantee;
- undertaking centralised clearance (when available); and
- completing self-assessment (when implemented).

2.5.2 AEOS status

AEOS is issued to any business that fulfils all of the above criteria with the exception of professional qualifications and practical standards of competence, which is only applicable to AEOC. The business must also have appropriate security and safety standards to protect the international supply chain. These should include:
- physical integrity and access controls;
- logistical processes and, if appropriate, the handling of specific types of goods; and
- personnel and identification of business partners.

Additionally, businesses need to be a holder of an AEOS if they would like to benefit from arrangements under mutual recognition agreements with third countries.

A holder of AEOS will benefit from:
- a lower risk score – used to determine the frequency of customs physical and documentary checks;
- consignments being fast-tracked through customs control;
- reduced requirements for the mandatory pre-arrival/pre-departure Entry Summary Declarations or Exit Summary Declarations (EXS); and
- reciprocal arrangements and mutual recognition with countries outside the EU – for example, USA or trading partners that adopt the World Customs Organisation safe framework.

Full details and links to the HMRC web pages enabling Application for AEO status are at:

www.gov.uk/guidance/authorised-economic-operator-certification.

2.5.3 "Union Customs Code"

With the increasing reliance by tax authorities on businesses to operate legally and professionally and international co-operation between tax authorities in the Customs field, the Union Customs Code is being introduced.

The Union Customs Code (UCC) was adopted on 9 October 2013 as Regulation (EU) No 952/2013 of the European Parliament and of the Council. It entered into force on 30 October 2013 and repealed the Regulation (EC) No 450/2008 of the European Parliament and of the Council of 23 April 2008 laying down the Community Customs Code (OJ L 145, 4.6.2008, p.1). Its substantive provisions will apply only on 1 May 2016, once the UCC-related Commission Acts (Delegated and Implementing Acts) are adopted and in force.

IMPORTS

The UCC is part of the modernisation of customs and will serve as the new framework regulation on the rules and procedures for customs throughout the EU. The UCC and the related delegated and implementing acts shall:
- streamline customs legislation and procedures;
- offer greater legal certainty and uniformity to businesses;
- increase clarity for customs officials throughout the EU;
- simplify customs rules and procedures and facilitate more efficient customs transactions in line with modern-day needs;
- complete the shift by Customs to a paperless and fully electronic environment; and
- reinforce swifter customs procedures for compliant and trustworthy economic operators (Authorised Economic Operators).

The use of electronic data-processing techniques and electronic systems will support the application of the UCC.

The UCC introduces a new standard of practical competence or professional qualification directly related to customs activities. Training which provides recognised customs qualifications is currently limited in the UK, so the focus will be on evidence and demonstration of practical competence over the previous three years. This standard only applies to AEOC.

Because the UCC will be implemented in the UK on 1 May 2016 there is a transitional period for AEO authorisations issued before then. This will mean that all AEOs must meet the new requirements by 1 May 2019. The reassessment work will be managed over this three-year period and AEOs will be given more information on how and when this will be done.

2.6 Import duty and import VAT deferment

To import goods into the UK from outside the EU or remove them from another EU Member State businesses must:
- find the correct commodity code for the goods;
- pay VAT in some cases;
- fill in a VAT return if VAT registered;
- register with the CHIEF system for importers if importing from outside the EU;
- declare the goods imported using the CHIEF system;
- pay duty in some cases; and
- check if the goods are banned from being imported into the UK or require an import licence.

The exact rules for importing depend on whether the goods are being removed from another EU Member State or are being imported from outside the EU. Many businesses appoint freight forwarding agents to help them with their import procedures. Full details are set out in **7.4**.

2.7 "Simplified Import VAT Accounting" (SIVA)

As a means of securing the amount of import duty and import VAT deferred by the importer, in the UK, HMRC requires the importer to guarantee the duty and VAT should any mishap befall the importer and they are subsequently unable to meet that liability. However, because the importer is able to reclaim the import VAT as input tax (where the goods are imported for the importer's business), HMRC will allow "approved" importers to only have to guarantee the amount of import duty. This facility is only awarded to businesses that have a good 'track record' with HMRC in terms of paying all liabilities when they fall due and not having failed to submit all their VAT returns on time etc.

Where approved for SIVA, the business will be able to reduce the amount of guarantee in favour of HMRC and therefore lower the charges levied by their bank or insurance agent etc. for the facility. However, if the importer fails to continue to keep up to date with their VAT affairs, HMRC will withdraw the approval for SIVA resulting in the requirement for a full guarantee. Details of the SIVA arrangements are set out in **6.4.2**.

2.8 Importation methods

As soon as goods arrive at a nominated entry point in the EU Customs Territory they become subject to the rules of the "Community Customs Code" (CCC). The Code requires that from the time of their entry, the goods are subject to Customs supervision, meaning that:
- they may be subject to Customs controls;
- they remain under such supervision for as long as may be necessary to determine their Customs status or until their Customs status is changed;
- they enter a free zone or free warehouse;
- they are re-exported; or
- they are destroyed.

All goods destined for free circulation in the EU must be conveyed for the attention of the relevant Customs authority by an approved route. These can be all of the following:
- air;
- sea;
- rail;
- road;
- pipeline; and
- post.

In the UK these are designated as Air, Sea, the Channel Tunnel, the Northern Ireland land boundary, Pipeline and the Post Office – see **2.8.2 to 2.8.7**.

2.8.1 "Import Control System" (ICS)

New safety and security laws in force since 1 January 2011 mean that goods destined to arrive in the EU must be declared to the Office of First Entry to the

IMPORTS

EU – that Member State's Import Control System or ICS – within set time limits. ICS is the first phase implementation of the EU-wide "Automated Import System" (AIS). ICS implements the EU safety and security legislation which requires carriers, or their authorised representatives, to provide pre-arrival information, in a specified format, for all cargo entering the EU regardless of the eventual destination of the cargo.

However, ICS does not replace the need to make a customs import declaration that is ordinarily submitted, in the UK, to the "Customs Handling of Import and Export Freight" (CHIEF system). ICS Phase 1 does not impact on fiscal customs declarations as the submission of an Entry to ICS is a totally separate process from the handling of the import customs declaration submitted to CHIEF.

The legal onus is on the carrier of the goods to make the ICS declaration. However, the carrier may, with its explicit knowledge and consent, delegate this activity to the importer and/or its agent. As such, an "Entry Summary Declaration" (ENS) must be made for the goods.

The UK ICS will provide the carrier, or delegated declarant, with a "Movement Reference Number" (MRN) for the goods. The MRN is an ICS system-generated number that is automatically allocated by the Member State which, after successful validation, accepts and registers the received ENS. The MRN will be notified to the declarant and, where different, the carrier.

This information is submitted on the ENS to the first port/airport of entry into the EU, the Office of First Entry (OoFE), and will include, amongst other things, details which identify the cargo, the traders involved in the movement, the vessel/aircraft and the envisaged route into and across the EU.

ICS information will be assessed against a set of common EU risk criteria and will also allow for messages to be passed onto subsequent ports or ports/airports in other Member States' "Offices of Subsequent Entry" (OoSE), about any positive risks identified at the first port/airport of entry into the EU.

All ICS messaging must be fully electronic. An ENS is an electronic declaration of goods being carried into the Customs territory of the EU. The declaration is made to the customs OoSE in the EU and will be required for all goods carried on-board the means of transport, including: goods to be discharged at the port/airport in the EU and those remaining on board and destined for a port/airport outside of the EU.

The operator of the active means of transport on or in which the goods are brought into the Customs territory of the Community (e.g. the vessel, aircraft, train or road vehicle), commonly known as the carrier, is responsible for ensuring an ENS is filed. The operator is the person who brings, or who assumes responsibility for the carriage of the goods into the Customs territory.

In the case of maritime or air traffic where a vessel sharing or contracting arrangement is in place, the obligation lies with the person who issues the bill of lading/air waybill for the actual carriage of the goods on the vessel / aircraft. For a deep sea container vessel, there may be several such ocean carriers.

Someone other than the carrier may lodge an ENS. However, as it is the carrier's responsibility to ensure that it is submitted within the legal time limits, it must only be done by a representative with the carrier's knowledge and consent.

2.8.2 Air

An "aerodrome" is an area of land or water designed, equipped, set apart or commonly used for affording facilities for the landing and departure of aircraft and, in the UK, an aerodrome is referred to as a "Customs and Excise airport" if it is designated for the time being as a place for the landing or departure for the purposes of the Customs and Excise Acts. An "examination station" is a place at a Customs and Excise airport approved for the loading and unloading of goods and the embarkation and disembarkation of passengers.

In the UK, the following are all designated as Customs and Excise airports:

Aberdeen	Leeds/Bradford
Belfast Aldergrove/International	Liverpool
Biggin Hill	London City
Birmingham International	London Gatwick
Blackpool	London Heathrow
Bournemouth	London Luton
Bristol Filton	London Stansted
Bristol Lulsgate	Lydd
Cambridge	Manchester
Cardiff	Newcastle
Coventry	Prestwick
Durham Tees	Newquay
Edinburgh	Norwich
Exeter	Nottingham East Midlands
Farnborough	Plymouth
Glasgow	Shoreham
Heathrow	Southampton
Humberside	Southend
Isle of Man	Sumburgh
Kent International (Manston)	

2.8.3 Imports by Sea

Essentially all parts of the UK coastline and tidal waters are within the limits of an appointed port. There are also a number of inland ports for example London and Manchester including the Manchester Ship canal. The limits of a port are set out in Statutory Instruments and (strictly speaking) relate solely to the waterways concerned. However, land adjacent to a port is included extending to an area separated from the main port by the width of a single road. Dock territory entirely separate from the quay area, such as a separate storage compound in the general district of a port, but separated from it by an area of industrial or domestic buildings, is not considered to be land adjacent to the port.

"Transit shed", added to the list in June 2002, is defined as a place which has been approved by HMRC for the storage of goods in temporary storage, no matter where that place is located.

HMRC may appoint boarding stations in any port for the boarding or disembarkation of Officers. A report must be made of every ship arriving at a port from a place outside the UK or carrying uncleared goods brought from a place outside the UK.

A ship is deemed to have arrived at a port at the time when the ship comes within the limits of that port and the time of importation of any goods brought by sea is the time when the ship carrying them comes within the limits of a port. However, in certain cases, the time of importation can be deferred to the time when the goods are discharged.

Goods imported by sea must be landed at an approved wharf, with all major UK ports having such wharfs. HMRC can advise importers of all approved wharfs should the importer not be using a major port, for example Felixstowe, Liverpool, Southampton etc.

2.8.4 Imports through the Channel Tunnel

HMRC may approve places within the Channel Tunnel system for the purposes of the control of persons, goods or vehicles in relation to the operation or use of the Tunnel or any part of it and any such place is referred to as a "Customs Approved Area".

2.8.5 Imports across the Northern Ireland Land Boundary

HMRC may appoint places, known as "Customs and Excise stations", for the examination and entry of goods imported by land and goods are deemed to be imported when they are brought across the boundary into Northern Ireland.

2.8.6 Imports by Pipeline

HMRC may approve a pipeline for the importation of goods and goods must not be imported, and uncleared goods must not be moved, by an unapproved

IMPORTS

pipeline. For goods imported by pipeline or similar means, the importer must arrange the procedures through the local HMRC Control Officer.

2.8.7 Imports through the UK Post Office

Goods imported by post may only be imported in a "postal packet" with an attached customs declaration. If these provisions are not complied with the goods are liable to forfeiture. The addressee is required to make an entry, or a full and accurate account, in respect of a postal import when so required by an HMRC Officer and the postal packet may be returned to sender, delivered to the 'proper officer' of HMRC or destroyed if the required entry or account is not delivered within 28 days or such longer period as HMRC may allow.

A full import declaration on a "Single Administrative Document" (SAD), using Form C88A, is required for all postal imports exceeding £2,000 declared to 'home use' i.e. to be retained in the EU and in 'free circulation'. For imports declared to one of the customs procedures with economic relief, temporary importation, customs warehousing, returned goods relief over £600 and processing under customs control or end-use relief, a full import declaration on a SAD is required where the potential duty liability exceeds 10 Euros (£7).

Form C87 *Notice of Arrival of Goods by Post*, must also accompany the C88A. This advises the importer that the goods have arrived in the UK, but that they cannot be delivered until the C88A is completed and returned to HMRC. It also gives a Customs reference number associated with the package which must be quoted if the importer needs to speak to HMRC about the package.

Individual C88As and C87s must be used for separate postal packages.

This additional evidence must be included when submitting the C88A:
(a) the commercial invoice and any other documents in support of the declared value of the goods;
(b) any work sheets used to calculate import VAT;
(c) an import licence (for goods subject to licensing);
(d) documentary proof of origin (where required);
(e) a preference certificate, where applicable, for goods from countries that has a preferential trade arrangement with the EU;
(f) any other certificate required for particular kinds of goods;
(g) packing slips for multi-package consignments, giving details of the contents of each package;
(h) evidence of export such as an invoice or approval note for returned goods relief; and
(i) any other documents in support of the importation and/or required by HMRC.

2.9 Import procedures

Imports from overseas are treated differently depending on whether the goods come from countries within the EU or from elsewhere. Within the EU, most

IMPORTS

goods can be imported with minimal customs control and, mostly, no import duty or VAT to pay.

Within the EU most goods are in free circulation. Importing goods from the EU is usually not termed as 'importing' – this is often referred to simply as a 'movement' of goods, or as an 'acquisition'. The term 'importing' is often used with the implied meaning that the goods have come from outside the EU.

Goods can be moved freely within the EU, although VAT and excise within Member States should be taken into consideration. Goods in free circulation in the EU can be moved from country to country with minimal customs control. Unless the goods are subject to excise duty, e.g. alcohol, or licence requirements such as agricultural goods, they generally cross borders without any special taxes and minimal import paperwork.

The SAD/C88 is also used to declare goods that are moved from one part of the EU to another. This form can be completed manually or electronically although manual submissions may well take longer to process. Importers can register for electronic declarations via the government Gateway website.

Imported goods must arrive at a designated place and be presented to Customs by the person who brought the goods into the EU. Presentation means informing Customs in the required manner that the goods have arrived. Goods are declared to Customs using form SAD/C88; that in most cases is presented in an electronic format. Import VAT is dealt with in the same way as a Customs duty.

SADs can be submitted either electronically using the "Customs Handling of Import and Export Freight" (CHIEF) system (see **2.11.5**), or manually (although manual submissions may take longer to process) (see **2.11.2**). Importers can use an agent, such as a freight forwarder, to make the declaration on their behalf. This can make importing simpler and faster if the importer is not authorised to make electronic declarations themselves.

To make the declaration the correct customs classification is required i.e. the nature of the goods must be described using a "Commodity Code" to which Customs import duty is levied at applicable rates. Because the rate of duty can vary widely based on the manufactured "ingredients" of the products being imported it is vital to ensure that the correct commodity code is used.

2.9.1 Classification

HMRC uses commodity codes found in the "UK Integrated Trade Tariff" (the Tariff) to classify individual products. Classification of commodities is necessary for import and export declarations as well as Intrastat returns. Other government departments also rely on Tariff classification for licences and other documents.

IMPORTS

The Tariff is based on the EU TARIC ("TARiff Integre Communautaire"). Member States hold commodity codes in the TARIC. Commodity codes and other regulations are updated daily which ensures that importers and exporters can rely on the same standards and treatment throughout the EU. The UK Trade Tariff uses the daily updates of the TARIC directly so that Tariff users have access to consistently accurate information.

The commodity code is a ten digit number although an additional four digits may apply to certain products. For imports from outside the EU it is necessary to provide the full Tariff classification. For exports the first eight digits are sufficient.

Tariff classification in the EU is based on the harmonised system which defines the first six digits. Although many countries subscribe to the same Tariff classification system, actual classifications may differ.

Incorrect classification can lead to delays in clearing goods, overpayment of duty and possible penalties. HMRC uses classification information to collect data and trade statistics. Classifying the goods correctly will help to ensure that the importer:

- pays the correct amount of duty and VAT;
- knows if duty is suspended on any of the goods;
- knows if any preferential duty rates can be applied;
- knows whether they need to obtain an import or export licence – for plant and animal products on health and conservation grounds or for firearms and hazardous materials;
- knows whether excise or anti-dumping duties apply ('dumping' relates to goods that are exported from one country to another at a lower than normal price);
- avoids paying interest on back-payments for incorrect classification; and
- avoids the goods being seized or delayed.

Many goods are subject to specific controls such as those falling under the EU's "Common Agricultural Policy" (CAP) or those subject to 'anti-dumping' duties or tariff quotas. The correct classification of these products will enable such controls and duty to be handled correctly.

To find the correct commodity code for the goods, importers should use the General Rules contained in the Tariff. There are six rules which should be applied in order:

1. covers the main headings under which goods are classed;
2. covers incomplete or unfinished articles and articles of mixed materials or substances;
3. covers goods which can be classified under more than one description – it also covers composite goods of different materials and sets for retail;
4. covers goods which can't be classified using the first three rules;
5. covers packaging items that come with the goods; and

IMPORTS

6. covers subheadings under which goods are classed.

In order to apply these rules correctly importers and their agents need to be able to describe the goods accurately. Many manufactured items are made up of several parts. Importers trading in foodstuffs or domestic products, for example, need to know what they contain before consulting the Tariff. This will help make classification as accurate as possible.

HMRC provides the following example of how to classify a bicycle:

Classification	Description
Chapter 87	vehicles, other than railway or tramway rolling-stock and parts and accessories thereof
Subheading 871200	bicycles and other cycles (including delivery tricycles), not motorised
CN Code 8712 00 30	Bicycles, with ball bearings
CN Code 871200 70	Other

Occasionally correct classification relies on supporting resources such as HMRC industry-specific classification guides, Harmonised System Explanatory Notes and Combined Nomenclature Explanatory Notes.

Once the commodity code matching the description of the goods has been determined it is entered in box 33 of the SAD/C88 – a copy of which can be found in Volume 3 of the Tariff. Alternatively, it can be downloaded from the HMRC website.[4]

As well as the correct commodity code importers also need to enter in box 37 of the SAD/C88 the "Customs Procedure Code" e.g. import to free circulation or use of one of the customs procedures such as temporary admission. Together with the commodity code, this helps determine what rate or type of import duty is to be charged and how the goods are to be treated. Together, these two entries determine how the goods will be treated by Customs officials in the country of importation.

The UK Trade Tariff is available online for most of the information required when importing or exporting goods and there are helpful tools for managing Tariff information at www.gov.uk/trade-tariff. Volume 1 of the Tariff provides much of this information. In Part 1, there is a list of other publications which are available to help with classification, including:

- "Harmonised System Explanatory Notes" (HSENs). These give useful guidance on the scope of Tariff chapters, headings and sub-headings. These can be purchased on the World Customs Organisation (WCO) website;[5]

---

[4] www.gov.uk/government/publications/import-and-export-single-administrative-document-full-8-part-set-c88-1-8#forms

[5] wcoomdpublications.org/explanatory-notes-harmonized-system-2012.html

- "Combined Nomenclature Explanatory Notes" (CNENs). These are supplementary to the HSENS and are available on the Commission website,[6] and are updated once a year;
- the "Compendium of Classification Opinions". These deal with decisions taken by the Harmonised System Committee which confirm classifications which were in doubt. These can be purchased from the WCO website.[7]

If importers still have difficulty in classifying the goods then HMRC can be contacted by email at: **classification.enquiries@hmrc.gsi.gov.uk**. To ensure the enquiry is dealt with efficiently, HMRC ask that all of the following information is included in the email request:
- what the product is;
- what it is made of;
- if it's made of more than one material please explain the breakdown of the materials;
- what it's used for;
- how the product works / functions; and
- how it's presented / packaged.

The products listed below will require additional information.
- Footwear – include the type (shoe, boot, slipper etc.), upper material details, outer sole material details, the heel height and the purpose for men or woman;
- Food – include precise composition details by percentage weight of all the ingredients to 100% and the method of manufacture or process undergone e.g. fresh, frozen, dried, further prepared / preserved etc.;
- Chemicals – include the "Chemical Abstracts Service" (CAS) number, whether the product is a liquid/powder/solid and include the percentages of the ingredients;
- Textiles – the material composition, how it is constructed (knitted /woven) and the name of fabric' and
- Vehicles – the age, the engine type (petrol or diesel), the engine size, whether the vehicle is new or used, whether the vehicle is over 30 years old and whether it is in its original condition. Is the vehicle going to be for everyday use?

A HMRC Classification Officer will respond to the enquiry by providing a ***non-legally binding*** classification advice based on the information supplied. This will not debar HMRC from potentially raising assessments for duty and import VAT should they later determine that the commodity code applied has been applied incorrectly because, for example, the product was misdescribed by the enquirer.

---

[6] eur-lex.europa.eu/homepage.html?locale=en
[7] wcoomdpublications.org/catalogsearch/result/?q=Compendium+of+Classification+Opinions

HMRC can be asked to make a ***binding decision*** on correct classification of the imported goods. If this is required an application for a "Binding Tariff Information" (BTI) ruling can be submitted electronically. Importers should complete a separate application form for each type of item they need classifying.

This BTI will be legally binding throughout the EU for up to six years after the date of issue. Applying for a BTI is usually free. However, the importer will have to pay the costs incurred such as laboratory analysis and testing, obtaining expert advice and returning the samples.

However a BTI will provide the importer with:
- the correct commodity code for the goods;
- a detailed description of the goods, enabling any customs regime to identify them;
- legal justification for the decision reached; and
- a unique reference number.

A BTI can only be obtained before any customs procedures take place. Therefore HMRC may refuse an application altogether if the importer:
- does not plan to import or export the goods in question;
- has made a similar application in another EU Member State; and
- is unable to provide complete information about the goods.

If the importer is unhappy with a BTI decision they can lodge an appeal with HMRC. They also have 45 days in which to request an independent review of the decision. If they remain dissatisfied with the HMRC review, they then have a further 30 days to apply for a Tribunal (Tax Chamber) hearing.

Once a 'satisfactory' BTI ruling is obtained, the BTI reference number must be entered in Box 44 of the SAD/C88, which must accompany the goods throughout the EU.

2.10 Community/common transit procedures

Community Transit (CT) is a customs procedure which allows customs and excise duties and VAT on imported goods to be suspended until the goods either reach their point of destination in the Community or are exported out of it. The CT procedure can also be used for movements to and from the "European Free Trade Association" (EFTA) countries, and is then known as common transit. The EFTA countries are Switzerland, Liechtenstein, Norway and Iceland.

The external transit procedure (T1) allows the movement of mainly non-Union goods within the Customs territory of the EU without them being subject to import duties and other charges or to commercial policy measures. Community goods that are subject to a Community measure involving their export to third countries may also have to move under external transit. The external procedure ends and the obligations of the holder are met when the goods placed under the procedure and the required documents are produced at the office of destination in accordance with the provisions of the relevant customs procedure.

The internal transit procedure (T2 or T2F) allows the movement of Community goods from one point to another within the Customs territory of the EU to pass through the territory of a third country without any change in their customs status. In the case of internal Community transit this is also sometimes used in other circumstances.

External transit must be used for movements of both:
- Non-Union goods that have not been put into free circulation or another customs procedure which permits movement within the Union; and
- Union goods which have been placed under the common transit procedure and are travelling to or via an EFTA country and subject to a Union measure involving their export to a third country, e.g. Common Agricultural Policy (CAP) goods – see Notice 800.[8]

Internal transit must be used for movements of Union goods when they are:
- travelling from one point in the EU Customs territory to another through one or more EFTA countries. Use of the T2 procedure for direct transport by air or sea to or from an EFTA country is not required;
- travelling to, from or between the 'special territories' of the Community except for direct movements between the UK and the Channel Islands; or
- goods in Chapters 25-97 of the Harmonised System (HS) which are travelling to or from the Principality of Andorra. Although Andorra is not part of the EU, a special Customs union exists with the EU for the above-mentioned goods. Goods in Chapters 1-24 of the HS are treated as non-Community goods.

Internal transit may also be used for Community goods when they are travelling to or from San Marino. Although San Marino is not part of the EU, a special Customs union exists with the EU, but it excludes goods coming under the Treaty establishing the European Coal and Steel Community, (Chapters 72 and 73). These goods are treated as non-Community goods when arriving in the Community from San Marino.

Further information on the CT procedure can be found in the Commission Transit Manual.[9]

The "New Computerised Transit System" (NCTS) must be used for all community/common transit declarations (except for private travellers (with

---

[8]www.gov.uk/government/publications/notice-800-common-agricultural-policy-export-procedures/

[9]ec.europa.eu/taxation_customs/customs/procedural_aspects/transit/common_community/index_en.htm

goods in excess of their allowances) and for some authorised simplifications. Any potential taxes and duties on the goods must be guaranteed. Use of NCTS does not normally preclude use of other customs procedures such as customs warehousing.

Traders who are approved as Authorised Economic Operators (see **2.5**) can gain access to certain simplifications in customs procedures such as guarantee waivers and approval to start NCTS movements at their own premises (*"Authorised Consignors"*) or end the movements there (*"Authorised Consignees"*) without having to produce the goods to Customs.

If the journey begins outside the EU, the "Transport Internationaux Routiers" (TIR) procedure can be used for movements to and from countries that are contracting parties to the TIR Convention. The goods must travel by road in approved vehicles or containers under customs' seal, accompanied by a TIR carnet document. The importer, or their freight forwarder, must be authorised to use TIR and the potential taxes and duties on the goods must be guaranteed.

All businesses moving goods across the EU under TIR are required to submit a declaration using NCTS when the consignment reaches the frontier of the EU.

2.11 Suspending or delaying import charges

There are a number of customs procedures that can be used to help delay or suspend paying duty. Imported goods are not normally released by Customs until the importer has paid any duty and any import VAT. These procedures are set out in **Chapter 3**. However, goods destined for importation may be placed into temporary storage before the time at which the importation is practically completed and this is described next.

2.11.1 Temporary storage

The term 'temporary storage' applies to the status of goods imported from outside the EU from the time that they are presented to Customs until the time that they are assigned to a "customs-approved treatment or use".

After presentation, goods have the status of being in temporary storage until they are assigned to a Customs-approved treatment or use. While in temporary storage, goods may not be removed, opened or examined without Customs permission and may only be handled in a way which preserves them without changing them. They may only be stored in places which Customs has approved.

The goods may only be unloaded after presentation and with Customs permission at the places they have approved. In emergencies, goods may be unloaded for safety reasons without obtaining Customs permission. However Customs must be informed immediately of their arrival once the goods have been unloaded. The goods must also be unloaded if Customs require this so that the goods and the means of transport may be examined.

IMPORTS

The breaking up of individual packages in temporary storage is not permitted except for essential examination or preservation purposes. This means that all goods covered by a Summary Declaration, whether unloaded or not, must be re-presented intact and can only be unpacked after goods have been cleared to a customs approved treatment or use such as Free Circulation or customs warehouse.

EU legislation requires that goods that are not in free circulation and moving from one point in the Community to another may only do so under Customs control. Therefore goods being removed to, from, and between temporary storage facilities must be entered to the Community Transit procedure using the New Computerised Transit System or the Community Systems Providers National Transit simplification.

Where goods move between the 28 EU Member States and the EFTA countries – Iceland, Norway, Liechtenstein and Switzerland – the common transit procedure must be used.

The term also applies to the special customs-approved premises or facilities that are used to store such goods – whether situated inside or outside the approved area of a sea or airport – during the time that the goods have the *'status of goods in temporary storage'*.

The term 'customs approved treatment or use' covers the following:
- the placing of goods under a customs procedure;
- the entry of goods into a free zone or free warehouse;
- the re-exportation of goods from the Customs territory of the community;
- the destruction of goods; and
- the abandonment of goods to the Exchequer.

The term *'customs procedure'* used in the first point above covers the following procedures:
- release for free circulation;
- transit;
- customs warehousing;
- inward processing;
- processing under Customs control;
- temporary admission;
- outward processing; and
- exportation.

Goods imported from outside the EU must be presented to Customs by using an approved computerised trade inventory system linked to HMRC or lodging form C1600A (presentation of Third Country Goods) at the designated customs office, the address of which will be advised by the port or airport concerned.

IMPORTS

The goods must be presented within three hours of their arrival at the place of unloading – and be followed by a *"Summary Declaration"* within 24 hours of presentation of the goods. The Summary Declaration may be on an approved computerised trade inventory system linked to HMRC or by lodging form C1600 (goods arrived from non-EU countries) at the designated HMRC office at the port or airport concerned. A full customs declaration must be made immediately or shortly after the Summary Declaration. The full customs declaration assigns the goods to a customs-approved treatment or use. Payment of the relevant duty and taxes is made at the time of the full declaration or soon after.

However, where imported goods are put into temporary storage, only the presentation and Summary Declaration will need to be completed within the relevant timescales. The full customs declaration and payment of the relevant duties and taxes do not need to take place until the permissible time limit for temporary storage has expired.

All importers can use temporary storage facilities, but only certain types of traders can apply to have their premises approved as a temporary storage facility. They are:
- freight forwarders;
- customs agents;
- warehousekeepers; and
- transport companies.

All of these businesses must be involved in the movement of non-Community goods.

Goods in temporary storage must be cleared to a Customs-approved treatment or use within:
- 45 days from the date of the Summary Declaration – in the case of goods brought in by sea; and
- 20 days in the case of goods brought in by any other means such as air or road.

If the importer cannot arrange for the goods to be assigned to a Customs-approved treatment or use within the period allowed, they must apply in writing to the HMRC office for the place where the goods are stored for an extension of time. The application must give the reason for the request and the following information:
- the name and address of the applicant;
- the location of the goods;
- the number of the summary declaration, or indication of previous customs procedures, or the means of identifying the means of transport on which the goods are located; and
- all other information necessary for identifying the goods.

When an application is granted, HMRC will write to the importer giving a date by which the goods must be entered. The importer must pass a copy of this letter to the operator of the temporary storage facility.

Temporary storage facilities must be approved by Customs. The premises in question must meet the criteria and conditions laid down by them. For example:
- such facilities must meet the national health and safety at work legislation;
- they must be suitable for storing, loading, examining and sampling of goods;
- the facility must be physically secure and maintained in good repair; and
- proper stock records must be kept.

Temporary storage facilities may be situated inside or outside the approved area of a sea or airport. There are five main types of temporary storage facilities:
- a *"transit shed"* – an approved place situated within the appointed area of an approved port or airport, but outside the Customs-approved area;
- a *"remote transit shed"* – an approved place within the boundaries of the appointed area of an approved port or airport;
- an *"enhanced remote transit shed"* – an approved place situated outside the appointed area of the approved port or airport;
- an *"inland clearance depot"* – an inland site usually made up of individual transit sheds, where goods arrive in containers or vehicles; and
- an *"inland rail depot"* – as described above but in a rail environment.

In some cases, temporary storage facilities may also include tanks and 'unshedded' areas.

An approved depository serves the same function as a temporary storage facility and is subject to the same rules and regulations; however, an approved depository can only be used for the storage of personal effects, whilst temporary storage facilities are generally used to store commercial third country/territory goods.

There is a restriction on the forms of processing or handling that is allowed on goods whilst they are in temporary storage. EU legislation restricts forms of handling in temporary storage to that which is necessary to ensure preservation of the goods in an unaltered state without modifying their appearance or technical characteristics.

Certain goods cannot be moved to a temporary storage facility from their place of importation until they have undergone physical and documentary checks. For example:
- veterinary products;
- endangered species of wild fauna and flora; and
- plants and fresh produce.

IMPORTS

2.11.1.1 *Veterinary products*

The "Trade Control and Expert System" (TRACES)[10] is an online system that makes it easier for importers and exporters to provide health certification and track consignments of animals or animal products.

TRACES aims to make the paperwork for trading in animals and animal products easier by generating the necessary documents and sending copies to the appropriate authorities inland and abroad, saving businesses time and effort.

The system allows businesses to obtain export health certificates and movement notifications of their dispatches. It helps the authorities to meet health regulations and businesses' needs. This information is aimed at those who trade within the EU and at importers who import from outside the EU.

Specific guidelines for trading animals and products of animal origin, including health certificates and licences, and the general system of declarations and checks for importing or exporting can be found online.[11]

2.11.1.2 *Endangered Species*

Goods subject to control under the "Convention on International Trade in Endangered Species of Wild Fauna and Flora" (CITES)[12] must have a licence.

2.11.1.3 *Plants and fresh produce*

The "Procedure for Electronic Application for Certificates" (PEACH) is an online tool for fulfilling a number of important requirements when importing into the UK from outside the EU plants or fruits and vegetables that are subject to Specific Marketing Standards.[13]

Imports of plants and plant products must be accompanied by a phytosanitary certificate to confirm their health and importers must provide advance notice through PEACH that a consignment is about to enter the UK.

Two distinct sets of EC Marketing Standards stipulate quality and labelling requirements for consignments of fresh produce being imported into the UK from any non-EU country. Details of the marketing standards can be found on the Rural Payments Agency (RPA) website.[14]

PEACH applies to England and Wales but not Scotland or Northern Ireland. However, it does apply to Scottish and Northern Ireland businesses, whose imports arrive from either England or Wales. Scottish importers should contact the Scottish Government Rural Payments and Inspections Directorate

---

[10] www.gov.uk/guidance/using-traces-to-trade-in-animals-and-animal-products
[11] www.gov.uk/guidance/animal-products-import-and-export
[12] whitehall-admin.production.alphagov.co.uk/government/admin/detailed-guides/3882
[13] www.gov.uk/guidance/using-the-peach-system-to-import-plants-and-fresh-produce
[14] www.gov.uk/guidance/comply-with-marketing-standards-for-fresh-fruit-and-vegetables

on 08457 741 741. Those from Northern Ireland should contact the DARD Helpline on 028 9052 4999.

2.11.2 Declaring the goods

The "Customs Handling of Import and Export Freight" (CHIEF) system (see **2.11.5**) records the declaration to HMRC of goods imported by land, air and sea. It allows importers, exporters and freight forwarders to complete customs information electronically, and automatically checks for entry errors. CHIEF connects with five "Community System Providers" (CSPs), these being independent trade systems that directly serve hundreds of carriers, transit sheds and freight forwarders.

CSPs record and track the movement of goods within ports and airports, enabling them to operate more efficiently. CHIEF is also part of HMRC's risk assessment process, by identifying which consignments, or goods within a consignment, will need to be physically examined, or have their documentation examined. This allows legitimate goods, and those deemed to be of a low-level risk, faster passage when they are directly imported from non-EU countries, or exported to them from the UK.

Businesses can submit import/export/transit or pre arrival declarations to HMRC by a variety of methods:

- "CSPs" – Customs-approved third party service providers offering access to inventory controlled ports around the UK;
- the "Excise Movement Control System" (EMCS) – the EMCS is aimed at all Excise businesses who are currently involved in the movement of goods in/under duty suspense;
- the "Import Control System" (ICS) – ICS is provided for the use of carriers responsible for bringing goods into the EU that require Safety and Security checks;
- the "New Community Transit System" (NCTS) – a basic, free to use service, suitable for low volume NCTS users;
- the "National Export System" (NES) – for businesses to submit Export Declarations to the CHIEF system; and
- "Hard copy declarations" – HMRC permit the submission of manually completed customs declarations under agreed circumstances – completed hard copy declarations should be submitted to the HMRC "National Clearance Hub".

The EC is considering changing the European Union Customs Code with the result that HMRC are rethinking the future of CHIEF. Information about these changes can be found online in an HMRC Consultation.[15]

---

[15] www.gov.uk/government/publications/customs-information-paper-3-2014-draft-proposals

IMPORTS

2.11.3 Declaring "Community Goods"

The importation of Community goods i.e. goods that have been imported from certain countries within the EU "Customs Territory" (but not the VAT Territory of the EU), must be presented to HMRC under EC Regulations. The parts of the Customs Territory concerned are as follows:

Aland Islands	Guadeloupe
Canary Islands	Martinique
Channel Islands	Mount Athos (Agion Oros)
French Guiana	Reunion

These goods travel to the UK under the internal Community Transit Procedure referred to as "T2" status, and the 'Office of Destination' copy of the T2 will act as the Summary Declaration.

There are also certain circumstances where Community goods must have their status established. This applies unless the goods are carried by air between two Community airports under the cover of a single transport document, or are carried by sea on an authorised regular shipping service. The affected goods are usually either:
- in temporary storage in a free zone or a free warehouse; or
- placed under a suspension procedure when they have been brought into the Customs Territory of the Community.

If the status document is not available at the port or airport of destination, the goods will be treated as goods of third country/territory origin until their status is established.

2.11.4 The import entry – the "Single Administrative Document" (SAD/C88)

The SAD/C88 is recognised by Customs authorities throughout the world and is essential for trade outside the EU, or of non-EU goods and it details both the goods and their movement.

The SAD/C88[16] was introduced to control goods arriving from outside the EU and goods being exported outside of the EU. For trade within the EU single market the SAD/C88 is not necessary. The SAD/C88 also covers the movement of non-EU goods within the EU.

The SAD/C88 is harmonised in line with other European versions of the form and is largely restricted to instances when computer systems are not working and customs resort to manual processing, or as an advice to shipping agents. SAD/C88 box numbers refer to the electronic system field numbers respectively.

---

[16] www.gov.uk/guidance/declarations-and-the-single-administrative-document

IMPORTS

New security legislation requires advanced information for goods arriving in or leaving the EU (see **2.8.1**). Using a SAD when importing or exporting goods will enable many of these security requirements to be met. Importers will need an Economic Operator Registration and Identification (EORI) number (see **2.4**) to complete an Entry Summary Declaration or an Exit Summary Declaration.

A completed SAD must detail:
- what the goods are;
- the movement of the goods;
- the goods' commodity code - also called Tariff heading, Tariff code, classification code or harmonisation code (see **2.9.1**); and
- the customs procedure code (CPC) - which determines how Customs treat the entry.

The SAD breaks down into 54 boxes and the full version comes in eight parts for use at different points in the trading process. Parts 2 and 3 are for export, parts 6, 7 and 8 are for import, and parts 1, 4 and 5 are for transit. Businesses should use Volume 3 of the Tariff (see **2.9.1**) to complete the required boxes.

However, two of the most important pieces of information required on the SAD/C88 are the "Commodity Code" (also called the Tariff Heading, Tariff Code, Classification Code or Harmonisation Code) and the "Customs Procedure Code" (CPC). Both have significant impact on how much duty is due and how the consignment is to be treated for Customs import duty purposes – see section **2.9.1**.

Most businesses now submit their SAD/C88 online although when systems are down it can still be submitted on paper. Software can be bought from freight software suppliers and is designed to simplify submitting electronic declarations. As changes to the SAD/C88 are often given through software updates the software used to connect to the CHIEF system (see **2.11.5**) may require amending or updating; the freight software supplier should ensure that SAD/C88 information is updated and is always compatible.

For goods that are liable for duty a full declaration to CHIEF or a paper SAD/C88 declaration is required whereas for duty free goods a copy of an approved standard commercial document, such as a commercial invoice or a partly completed SAD/C88 is sufficient. The SAD/C88 can also be used to declare imported goods allocated to customs procedures with economic impact such as:
- "Inward Processing Relief" (IPR) or "Outward Processing Relief" (OPR);
- "End-Use relief"; or
- "Customs warehousing".

For "Merchandise in your own baggage" (MIB), such as goods or samples, a SAD/C88 must be completed where the good are:
(a) valued at less than £867;
(b) they weigh less than 1,000 kilograms;

IMPORTS

(c) they do not need an export licence; and
(d) they are not subject to export duty.

In such cases a commercial invoice or an electronic declaration is made instead.

2.11.5 The UK's import system – "CHIEF" (Customs Handling Imports Exports and Freight)

The importer may either complete the SAD/C88 themselves or arrange for an agent to act for them. If either the importer or their agent has approval from HMRC, they can input the data directly to CHIEF, this being referred to as "Direct Trader Input" ("DTI").

The SAD/C88 is input to CHIEF which interfaces with six independent trade systems, in turn directly serving hundreds of carriers, transit sheds and freight forwarders to record and track the movement of goods within ports and airports. Using Electronic Data Interchange ("EDI") inter-system messages, CHIEF checks that the data on the SAD/C88 matches the inventory maintained on each trade system. All of these systems notify CHIEF as soon as goods arrive, whereupon they are promptly validated, cleared or selected for examination. Despite the fact that the independent trade systems are all based on different technologies, CHIEF handles each interface seamlessly.

CHIEF provides all of the following services:
- direct trader access to electronic processing of imports and exports – including the calculation of duties, currency and quantity conversions – and the automatic clearance of consignments;
- identification of goods which require documentary or physical examination making use of a highly sophisticated risk profiling system;
- information for the production of the UK's external trade statistics;
- a means of electronic communication between HMRC and business users;
- validation of the accuracy of data input by advising the users of any errors; and
- recording, monitoring and accounting for duties and taxes incurred by individual importers.

CHIEF facilitates three key functions for HMRC:
- the collection of £34 billion of revenue each year;
- the accurate collection of international trade and transport statistics; and
- the protection of society by controlling the import and export of restricted goods, and detecting the smuggling of prohibited goods.

CHIEF also facilities three, separate, key functions for UK international trade:
- the efficient passage of legitimate goods into and out of the UK, allowing importers, exporters and freight forwarders to complete the necessary Customs formalities with the minimum of manual intervention;

- it enables major ports and airports in the UK to operate more efficiently and effectively; and
- it helps maintain the attractiveness of the UK as a major international trading centre.

The CHIEF system is supported by detailed user guides[17] for trade users and the more technically minded which address technical questions about CHIEF functionality.

2.11.6 Managing freight logistics – "Customs Freight Simplified Procedures" (CFSP)

EC legislation allows Member States to make available "Simplified Procedures" for handling and managing the importation of goods, both from a risk basis and a trade facilitation basis. Customs Freight Simplified Procedures, or CFSP, is a control methodology that is designed to provide greater flexibility to businesses engaged in third country/territory importations by moving fiscal and statistical controls inland. Importers gain a greater certainty of clearance, because administrative controls at the border are minimised. The procedures rely on the development of commercial software and the use of EDI messaging facilities, linked to the CHIEF system.

Most imported third country goods are eligible for CFSP. HMRC's main objective under CFSP is to achieve enhanced compliance by improved targeting and greater use of systems-audit techniques. For the vast majority of goods imported using CFSP, HMRC will exercise control of the imported goods under 'post-clearance' regimes at an inland facility, for example the importer's premises, rather than on entry at the port or airport.

CFSP offers a variety of procedures which may be operated in isolation or combined to best meet the importer's particular needs. The importer can opt to use either the "Simplified Declaration Procedure" ("SDP") or "Local Clearance Procedure" ("LCP"). In both cases the declaration is submitted in two stages. The initial declaration provides HMRC with a minimum amount of data which effects the release of the goods. The importer can provide this either at the frontier in the form of a simplified SAD/C88 (SFD) or as an entry in their own records. The SFD is then followed up with an electronic SAD/C88 which contains the full fiscal and statistical data. HMRC provide guidance on these processes in Notice 760: *Customs Freight Simplified Procedures (CFSP)*.

The import duty and any import VAT must be paid using a duty deferment account. This is because CFSP is an electronic declaration method using CHIEF processing procedures. Therefore other payment methods such as cash or the "Flexible Accounting System" (FAS) are not acceptable.

---

[17]www.gov.uk/government/collections/customs-freight-simplified-procedures-message-specifications

IMPORTS

The deferment account used may be the importers or may belong to a third party, as long as HMRC has received written permission from the owner of the account for the account to be used. The deferment account(s) to be used for payment will be noted in the authorisation for CFSP. The level of the deferment account used must be sufficient to cover the actual duty and VAT liability for one calendar month.

Under EC law the importer must provide security against any potential debts arising from the release of goods to a customs procedure. The security takes the form of a blanket authority to debit the duty deferment account should the debt fail to be met. The deferment account(s) to be used for security will be noted in the CFSP authorisation.

The deferment security level must be sufficient to cover the actual duty and VAT liability for one calendar month unless the importer is approved for Simplified Import VAT Accounting" (SIVA) (see **2.7**) or the "Excise Payment Security System" (EPSS) (see **2.12.4**).

VAT Notice 760 gives full details of CFSP accounting methodologies.[18]

2.12 The Customs debt

The phrase 'Customs debt' is used to refer to import duties (customs duties, anti-dumping duties, CAP charges) which become payable upon importation of goods into the Community. HMRC must ensure that the correct import duties are paid on imports into the UK, by the person who is liable to pay them.

The charge to import VAT arises when HMRC accept the entry. An entry must be made within 45 days of the date on which a Summary Declaration is made of the arrival of goods by sea and within 20 days of the date on which a Summary Declaration is made for all other methods of arrival. The goods should be presented to HMRC within three hours of the arrival of the ship or aircraft, and the Summary Declaration must be made within 24 hours of the goods being presented.

For imports where no import declaration is required, the charge to tax arises at the time of importation and this varies according to the method of arrival of the goods, as follows:
- goods arriving by air – the earlier of the time when the aircraft lands in the UK or the goods are unloaded;
- goods arriving by sea – the time when the ship comes within the limits of a designated Customs and Excise port;
- goods arriving by the Channel Tunnel – the time when they cross the frontier (with certain exceptions);

---

[18] www.gov.uk/government/publications/vat-notice-760-customs-freight-simplified-procedures/

- goods arriving via the Irish land boundary – the time when they are brought across a Customs and Excise Station; and
- goods arriving by post:
  - for datapost parcels of less than £2,000 in value payment is required when the package is delivered;
  - for datapost parcels of more than £2,000 in value an import entry is sent to the consignee, which must be returned to HMRC with evidence of the value. Payment must be made immediately unless approval for deferment has been obtained; and
  - for non-datapost parcels delivered to VAT-registered businesses, the "Postponed Accounting System" (PAS) may be used. Under PAS the importer must account for the import VAT on the VAT return covering the importation, but he may also treat that import VAT as input tax where the goods are used for the purposes of his business, subject to any disallowance that might be applicable, for example, for partial exemption.

2.12.1 Who is the "Declarant"?

The "declarant" is the legal person such as a company, partnership, or public body, or an individual who makes the declaration in his own name, or the person in whose name a declaration is made. Often this is not the same as the individual who signs the form. Since legal persons other than individuals cannot themselves sign forms, officers must be employed to do this for them, but such an officer signing on behalf of a legal person is not the declarant.

A declaration may be made by any person who is able to present the goods and all the relevant documents and who is established in the EU. Individuals who are normally resident in the EU are regarded as established in the EU, as is any company which has a genuine permanent place of business, its central headquarters or its registered office in the EU. However, any person making a declaration for transit or temporary admission, or who declares goods on an occasional basis is not required to be established in the EU.

Warehousing entries made by authorised schedulers on behalf of their principals for goods for free circulation can only be made by way of indirect representation. The declarant has to be the person who is authorised and because of this, if the authorised person is doing this on another person's behalf, it is being done indirectly.

If the acceptance of a declaration imposes obligations on a particular person, then the declaration must be made by that person or on that person's behalf.

Debts and enforcement

The person to be pursued for the customs debt depends upon whether representation is involved and the type of representation agreed between the parties concerned.

Where a person acting as a direct representative, makes a customs declaration on behalf of a principal in their name, the principal is the declarant and liable for the customs debt.

Where a person is acting as an indirect representative, that is they are making a customs declaration on behalf of a principal in the agent's own name, they are treated as the declarant. However, both the representative and the principal are jointly liable for the customs debt. If either of these parties is insolvent, the debt will be claimed by HMRC in the insolvency. And, if only one of the parties is established in the EU, HMRC will pursue that party.

A person that makes a declaration in their own name and on their own behalf is the declarant and is liable for the customs debt. In a VAT Group, the debtor will be the member company that made the customs declaration.

HMRC will charge interest on the customs debt if it is not paid by the due date, that being 10 days from the date of issue of the demand on Form C18. Interest will, however, be waived if payment is received within five days of the due date. The rate of interest charged is the same as that charged for all UK departmental duties and taxes, and is subject to a minimum charge of £25.

2.12.2 Post-presentation of the import entry

Following presentation to HMRC, the goods must be assigned to a Customs-approved treatment or use. These are:
- the placing of goods under a Customs-approved procedure;
- their entry into a free zone or free warehouse;
- their re-exportation from the Customs Territory of the Community;
- their destruction; and
- their abandonment to the Exchequer.

Customs-approved procedures are:
- release for free circulation;
- transit;
- customs warehousing;
- inward processing;
- processing under Customs control;
- temporary admission;
- outward processing; and
- re-exportation.

If the importer is unable to arrange for the goods to be assigned to a Customs-approved treatment or use within the period allowed, they must apply in writing to the Customs office for the place where the goods are stored for an extension of time.

The application must give the reason for the request and the following information:
- the name and address of the applicant;

- the location of the goods;
- the number of the Summary Declaration, or indication of previous customs procedures, or the means of identifying the means of transport on which the goods are located; and
- all other information necessary for identifying the goods.

When an application is granted, HMRC will write to the importer giving them a date by which the goods must be entered. The importer must pass a copy of this letter to the operator of the temporary storage facility.

If the goods are not assigned to a Customs-approved treatment or use within the time allowed, including any extensions granted, HMRC are required without delay to take measures, including the sale of the goods, to ensure that they are properly disposed of, including depositing them in a "Queen's Warehouse" (an authorised repository). All storage charges are the responsibility of the person in possession of the goods, unless the goods have been formally seized. In the latter case, HMRC are not responsible for accrued charges prior to seizure.

To declare goods for free circulation or another Customs-approved procedure the importer or their agent must make a declaration on the SAD/C88 when the goods to which it relates have arrived. HMRC may allow a declaration to be lodged before the arrival of the goods, but they will only accept it when the goods have actually arrived and have been presented.

To place goods under a transit procedure the importer should present the goods, together with the appropriate transit document, to HMRC at the office of departure where the transit movement will start.

If, for any reason, goods are to be destroyed, the importer must make a written application to HMRC. The application must be signed by the owner of the goods and include the following details:
- the name and address of the applicant;
- the location of the goods;
- the number of the Summary Declaration, or indication of previous Customs-approved procedures, or the means of identifying the means of transport on which the goods are located; and
- all other information necessary for identifying the goods.

A copy of HMRC's authorisation, which will set out the conditions which must be met, must be passed to the operator of the temporary storage facility. Destruction of the goods must not entail any expense to the UK Treasury.

Should the imported goods be subject to any special conditions or controls such as the carrying out of veterinary or other health checks these will be completed before temporary storage status ends. The production of import licences, certificates etc. may also be required when the goods are entered.

2.12.3 Warehousing

Warehousing is a Customs-approved regime that enables any import duty, import VAT and/or CAP charges to be suspended on goods originating from third countries/territories. The import duty and any import VAT only become due when the goods leave the warehousing regime for free circulation. These facilities are also available for excise goods and for CAP goods imported from other Member States, which are liable only to positive Monetary Compensatory Amounts (see HMRC Notices 232: *Customs warehousing*; 197: *Receipt into and removal from an excise warehouse of excise goods*; 702/9 *VAT: Import Customs Procedures*; and 780: *Common Agricultural Policy import procedures and special directions for goods*). Further details on the valuation for VAT purposes and supplies made within the warehouse are in **4.23.4**.

2.12.4 Excise goods

Excise goods can only be moved by authorised traders and warehouse-keepers. The "Excise Movement and Control System" (EMCS) has been introduced to control the international movement of goods that are liable to excise duty and where, particularly, the goods move whilst the duty is suspended. Further details of EMCS are explained in section **8.7.1.** in this book and Notice 197 details HMRC's guidance on these matters.[19]

In order to receive excise goods that have been imported from a non-EU country and which are to be stored free of all duties, the importer/warehouse must hold both an excise warehouse and customs warehouse approval for the premises. A Registered Consignor is a natural or legal person approved by HMRC who, in the course of their business and under the conditions set by HMRC, dispatches excise goods under excise duty suspension arrangements to persons authorised to receive duty-suspended goods upon their release to free circulation.

Registered Consignees are liable for the duty on all consignments of excise goods that are correctly consigned to them, regardless of where the goods are actually delivered to or which deferment account is used.

2.12.5 "Free zones"

Before 2013 imported goods could be moved into a free zone without paying import charges. However, all of the free zone designation orders have expired. Customs Information Paper (10) 48 *Free zones – non renewal of designation orders* (2 July 2010) announced that:

> with the implementation of the Modernised Customs Code, scheduled for June 2013, the option of a type II free zone, a free zone based upon the record-keeping requirements of customs warehousing, will cease to exist. This change applies to all the free zones operating in the UK.

---

[19] www.gov.uk/government/publications/excise-notice-197-receipt-into-and-removal-from-an-excise-warehouse-of-excise-goods/

Thus, the designation orders were not renewed. All free zone managers and free zone operators should have received a letter from their supervising office explaining the options available following the expiry of the free zone designation orders.

2.12.6 "Non-Union goods"

"Non-Union goods" have the status of goods in temporary storage from the time they are presented to Customs at the frontier until they are assigned to a Customs-approved treatment or use.

A temporary storage facility is a place situated inside or outside the approved area of a sea or airport, where non-Union goods may be placed in storage prior to being assigned to a Customs-approved treatment or use. These facilities were previously known as Transit Sheds at the frontier and Enhanced Remote Transit Sheds inland.

There are two ways of referring to these premises depending on their location. These are:
- "Internal Temporary storage Facility" (ITSF), which is inside the Customs controlled area of the frontier (air/port); or
- "External Temporary storage Facility" (ETSF) which is outside the Customs controlled area of the frontier (air/port)

In order for an application for a temporary storage approval to be accepted the applicant must be one of:
- an air/port operator;
- a freight forwarder;
- a Customs agent;
- a warehouse keeper; or
- a transport company.

They must also be:
- established in the UK; and
- involved with the movement of non-Union cargo.

The operator of the proposed temporary storage facility is responsible for the physical acceptance and release of the goods into and out of the actual temporary storage facility, for the collection of data into the temporary storage stock account record on the physical arrival of the goods into the premises.

The applicant must provide a written Deed of Undertaking, in the appropriate format, to cover any Customs duty and taxes which may arise for the goods held in temporary storage. HMRC may also require some additional financial security, the form of a guarantee for particular types of high duty goods or in particular circumstances such as a bad debt liability, non-compliance etc. This guarantee will be calculated in the same way as a normal Transit guarantee and will be reviewed annually.

IMPORTS

Full details of the accounting requirements and classes of goods that may be temporarily stored in such warehouses is provided by HMRC in Notice 199A.[20]

2.12.7 Merchandise In Baggage (MIB)

MIB refers to goods which are not in free circulation in the EU or are goods that are in free circulation prior to export. They are goods that are carried by passengers either in accompanied baggage or in private vehicles and are required for trade or business use; they are not recorded on the ship or aircraft manifest as freight and are not the personal property of the passenger.

MIB includes goods acquired for a company or other business, goods for sale, spare parts, trade samples, etc. whether or not they are permanently or temporarily imported/exported, in transit or liable to customs charges.

All commercial goods carried in a traveller's baggage or private vehicle must be declared in the red 'Goods to Declare' channel. If there is no separate Red Channel, the traveller should use the red point phone in the customs area. MIB goods are not allowed to form part of the traveller's passenger allowances. Failing to use the Red Channel or use the red phone point may result in the forfeiture of the goods and being liable to prosecution or fined.

The requirement to complete a SAD/C88 is dependent on the value of the goods and the Customs regime that the goods are being entered to. A SAD/C88 is only required if the goods are valued at over £750, or if below that value any one of the following customs procedures is being used:

- Inward or Outward Processing Relief;
- Processing under Customs Control;
- Requesting clearance under Tariff Quota;
- requesting relief from duty under duty-free direction, or certificate of re-importation;
- Temporary Admission;
- End Use relief;
- customs warehousing; or
- using the Community/Common Transit.

Customs will require the completed SAD/C88 to be accompanied by documentary evidence of the value of the goods, for example the supplier's invoice. If the value is more than £750, it will be retained so if the traveller requires a copy they are advised to take a photocopy before presenting the entry.

Where applicable the following documents will also be required:
(a) a movement certificate or Certificate of Origin;
(b) proof of origin for textiles;

---

[20]www.gov.uk/government/publications/notice-199a-temporary-storage-and-approved-depositories/

(c) import licences or restrictions; and
(d) a comprehensive guarantee certificate/individual guarantee. The guarantee may be either:
- an individual guarantee covering a single transit operation in the form of a cash deposit, voucher(s) or an individual guarantee by a guarantor; or
- a comprehensive guarantee covering a number of transit operations. The need for a guarantee may be waived if the duties and VAT is below 500 euros.

When due, any duties and VAT must be paid before the goods are released. If the goods are entered on a SAD/C88, all charges must be paid at the (air)port. For goods valued at less than £750, that are cleared in the Red Channel or at the Red Point phone, the charges will be assessed and collected and the traveller will be issued with a receipt.

Import duty and import VAT due on goods declared in the Red Channel or by the Red Point phone against a duty slip receipt, can be paid by any one of an approved debit card, subject to the normal conditions of acceptance, uniform euro cheques supported by a uniform euro cheque card, a banker's sterling draft or sterling cheque, guaranteed by an approved bank, an approved credit card, subject to the normal conditions of acceptance and limited to £1,000, travellers cheques in UK sterling, or euros issued by an approved bank, or cash in UK sterling or euro.

Where a form SAD/C88 is required, the traveller may prefer to use a Customs clearance agent to deal with the formalities; however, they will make a charge for their services.

Using an agent can save time if the agent is provided with prior notification of the goods being carried and the traveller can arrange for the agent to meet them when they arrive. At most locations, agents are able to input the declaration direct into the Customs computer and arrange payment of any duty and VAT due there and then.

Travelling to another Member State

The import procedures differ depending upon whether the MIB is in the traveller's cabin or hold baggage. If it is in the hold of the aircraft and is in transit to another EU airport, it cannot be declared in the UK and must be dealt with at the final destination.

If it is in a cabin and the traveller is in transit to another EU Member State, it should be declared at the final destination. If the MIB is in cabin baggage, and the passenger is travelling on to another EU airport on a different aircraft, the goods must be declared in the UK. The traveller then has the option of either paying any customs charges in the UK or completing a Community Transit (CT) declaration for the MIB to be cleared at the final destination.

IMPORTS

HMRC advise that to avoid transfer delays travellers are strongly advised to carry MIB goods in their hold baggage for clearance at their final destination.

3 Reliefs from import duty

Not all goods that arrive in the EU are subject to import duty or import VAT. Some goods benefit from relief from both import duty and import VAT whilst others may only benefit from one or the other. There are a number of reliefs from import duty, these being:

- Inward Processing Relief ("IPR") – **3.1**;
- Processing Under Customs Control ("PCC") – **3.2**;
- End-Use Relief – **3.3**;
- Returned Goods Relief ("RGR") – **3.4**;
- Goods sent to other Member States – **3.5**;
- Outward Process Relief ("OPR") – **3.6**;
- Rejected imports - **3.7**; and
- Temporary Admission – **3.8**.

3.1 Inward Processing Relief (IPR)

Inward Processing is also known as a "Customs Procedure with Economic Impact" (CPEI). Under this procedure, payment of Customs import duties and import VAT may be suspended (or later repaid) when goods imported from outside the EU for processing are then re-exported/exported from the EU. To benefit from IPR or any other CPEI, the legal requirements of the procedure must be met by the person/company that holds the IP authorisation.

There are currently two types of IP facility allowed for in EU law, "IPR suspension" and "IPR drawback". The IP drawback facility will be removed when the Union Customs Code (UCC) (see **2.5.3**) is implemented in 2016. A business currently using IP drawback may wish to consider transferring to the IP suspension facility before the UCC is implemented.

IPR suspension allows Customs duties (including "Anti-Dumping Duty" (ADD) and "Common Agricultural Policy" (CAP) duties), import VAT and excise duty on third country goods imported to the EU for processing to be suspended on condition that there is an intention to re-export the goods at the end of processing and that all the requirements of the procedure are met. It is intended to assist EU established processors to compete on an equal footing in the world market without harming the essential interests of EU producers of similar goods.

For businesses that plan to re-export or transfer only a percentage of their processed products, IPR suspension may be used for the percentage of imports based on a reasonable estimate. If the majority of the goods are to be re-exported, the importer may enter all of the goods to suspension, but if the re-export figure falls below 80%, the importer will be required to apportion future imports. Importers must liaise with HMRC if they need to agree this apportionment.

RELIEFS FROM IMPORT DUTY

If more goods are imported under IPR suspension than are actually required for re-export (or other eligible IPR disposals) the importer will need to divert the surplus goods to free circulation with full payment of Customs duties, import VAT and compensatory interest.

Prior authorisation is required from HMRC to use IPR. The authorisation holder is responsible for the duty and associated charges on all goods entered to IPR under the authorisation, whether or not the authorisation holder owns them, until they are put to an eligible method of disposal.

IPR authorisation holders will need to consider whether or not to arrange for a form of indemnity to cover any ineligible entry, processing or disposal by other operators named on their authorisation or by agents acting on authorisation holders behalf.

"Processing" can be anything from re-packing or sorting goods to the most complicated manufacturing. Some of the simplest processing types such as receiving and re-packing goods may come under "Usual Forms of Handling" (UFH) rules. UFH is restricted to a three month 'throughput period'.

Almost any type of goods may be processed under IPR provided there is a proven economic need. Economic codes are used to identify the reason the IPR authorisation has been agreed. Some goods are restricted to being processed under IPR suspension (not IPR 'drawback') and some cannot be processed under a simplified authorisation. Some goods also require an economic test to be performed by The Department for Environment, Food and Rural Affairs (DEFRA).

If the imported goods are not re-exported after processing (or discharged to an eligible method of disposal) the importer will have to pay the suspended duties (at the rate the good first entered IPR) and import VAT and will also be charged compensatory interest on all goods diverted to free circulation.

The calculation for compensatory interest is made from the date the goods were imported into the EU. It is charged to make sure that IPR is not used by some traders to gain an unfair advantage over others who pay Customs duties and import VAT on the way in and later reclaim the VAT under normal input tax rules.

To use IPR, the importer does not need to be the owner of the goods, but they must be:
- a 'natural', or 'legal' person established in the EU;
- the person carrying out the processing (or arranging for it to be carried out);
- authorised by HMRC to use the procedure (or be eligible to use IP with a simplified authorisation for you goods); and
- have an Economic Operator Registration and Identification (EORI) number – see section **2.4**.

A 'natural' person is any person normally resident in one of the Member States and a 'legal' person is a business such as a partnership or a limited company, which has a permanent business establishment in the EU.

The actual importer may name other processors on its application for authorisation that will carry out the processing on its behalf. However, as IPR authorisation holder, that person is responsible for paying any duty or other charges which become due on the imported or processed goods.

A person not established in the EU cannot be authorised for IPR unless the imports are of a non-commercial nature (meaning the goods are privately owned by that person). However, an authorisation can be issued to a person established in the EU who acts on behalf of a person established outside the EU provided that person either:
- actually carries out the processing on the goods; and
- arranges for the processing to be carried out.

Agents are not eligible for IPR authorisation if they do no more than complete import and re-export declarations (either for a person established in the EU or a non-established EU trader).

The Applicant needs to provide information on all the products expected to be obtained from the goods imported/received under IPR. "Compensating products" are all the products resulting from processing operations under IPR including by-products. The applicant should include details of both the "Main Compensating Products" (MCPs) and "Secondary Compensating Products" (SCPs) that will be produced by the processing. They will also need to include details of how the goods entered to IPR will be identified in the processed product(s).

Additionally, the applicant should provide details of both the commodity code and a description of the goods. Descriptions of goods should be complete and accurate (the common trade description not just the Tariff classification heading), as terms such as 'various' will not be accepted by HMRC and any application showing this will be rejected unless supplementary documentation with the required information is provided to them.

For goods free of import duty liability 'VAT only' IPR may be authorised. Under IPR drawback the import VAT must be paid at the time of entry to the EU. However, under IP suspension, the payment of import VAT is suspended and only becomes due if the goods are subsequently diverted to free circulation.

While the goods are held under Customs suspensive procedures the import VAT remains suspended. All relevant Customs legislation, including EU Regulations, applies for import VAT purposes. This includes any authorisation, transfer, discharge, or security requirements as detailed in your authorisation for the procedure concerned.

RELIEFS FROM IMPORT DUTY

The Regulations relating to IPR are complex. HMRC has issued detailed guidance in Notice 221.[1]

3.2 Processing Under Customs Control (PCC)

In most cases, imported goods carry higher rates of Import Duty than the raw materials or components used in their manufacture. There are instances however, where processed products attract a lower rate of duty than the materials or components used in their manufacture. These anomalies can make it more economical to import finished products from a third country, than to import the raw materials and manufacture the products within the EU.

PCC is a procedure intended to encourage processing in the EU by allowing the importation of certain raw materials or components under a duty suspension arrangement. After processing in duty suspension, the finished products can usually be declared to free circulation at the rate applicable to the finished goods rather than the higher rate applicable to the raw materials.

Goods only subject to import VAT may not be entered to PCC or goods whose duty rate is zero. Once processing of the goods has finished they should be declared to free circulation. Goods may not be stored under PCC after processing has been completed.

Using the PCC arrangements, importers are able to:
- import goods from outside the EU with all customs charges suspended;
- process them in their own premises, or have them processed on their behalf; and
- pay duty and import VAT at the rate and value which applies to the processed products (rather than the imported goods) when they are entered into free circulation.

Importers will normally save money if the rate of duty on the processed products is less than the rate on the imported goods. If the duty rate on the imported goods and processed products are the same there is no duty advantage. Therefore, PCC should not be used.

Importers may import goods directly to the PCC arrangements, or transfer goods into PCC from another customs procedure, such as customs warehousing. Before entering goods to PCC the importer must be authorised to use the arrangements and must be able to identify specific goods. Duty suspended goods cannot be mixed (comingled) with duty paid goods.

Full details of PCC are set out in HMRC Notice 237.[2]

---

[1] www.gov.uk/government/publications/notice-221-inward-processing-relief/
[2] www.gov.uk/government/publications/notice-237-processing-under-customs-control/

RELIEFS FROM IMPORT DUTY

3.3 End-Use Relief

End-Use Relief is available on certain goods imported into the EU that are to be processed or put to a specific use. To be eligible for End-Use Relief, products must meet defined criteria and be identified in the Tariff. End-use goods include:
- shipwork goods;
- aircraft and parts;
- hydrocarbon oil;
- marine propulsion engines;
- military equipment;
- fish;
- cheese; and
- casein (used in the cheese industry).

Importers who import such goods will be able to claim this relief if:
- they are authorised by HMRC;
- the goods are eligible for end use; and
- the goods are put to a prescribed use within a certain time.

End-Use Relief means that the importer pays either a reduced rate of import duty or none at all. However, it doesn't remove the obligation to pay any other importation charges such as VAT, excise duty or Anti-Dumping Duty.

Different types of authorisation are available, depending on the size, frequency and nature of the business and its operation. Importers need to consult the Tariff to find out if the goods being imported qualify for End-Use Relief (the footnotes in the Tariff explain whether the goods are eligible).

In order to claim the End Use Relief the importer (or its agent) must complete and submit the SAD/C88 (see **2.11.4**) and must supply:
- a description of the goods;
- a preference code;
- a customs procedure code; and
- the end-use authorisation number.

Full details on the authorisation process and control for End Use Relief are provided by HMRC at www.gov.uk/guidance/end-use-relief.

3.4 Returned Goods Relief (RGR)

RGR allows goods which were previously exported from the Customs Territory of the EU, plus Turkey, San Marino and Andorra to be re-imported in the same condition without having to pay some, or any, import duty and import VAT when declared for free circulation. Import duty, CAP charges, VAT and excise duty may all be relieved, although there are different

RELIEFS FROM IMPORT DUTY

conditions for each (see HMRC Notice 236: *Importing returned goods free of duty and tax*).[3]

The conditions for relief are different for each type of duty or tax, and if relief is claimed from more than one, the importer must meet the conditions for each. It should be noted however that claims to RGR do not override any import prohibition, restriction or licensing requirements which may be in force for the goods intended to be re-imported.

To qualify for RGR the goods must:
- have been in free circulation with all duties and taxes paid when they were exported from the EU;
- where the goods or any components were previously imported into the EU any Customs Duty suspended or relieved at the time of import must have been paid prior to export;
- any refunds obtained on export from the EU must be repaid;
- the goods must be re-imported in an unaltered state, apart from any work that may have been required to maintain the goods in working order;
- any work done must not have upgraded the goods to a higher specification or increased their value;
- the goods must not have been exported for the purpose of repair or process (however, if they are being returned unaltered relief may be available); and
- the goods must be re-imported within three years of the date of the original export.

All of the following types of goods are eligible for RGR, subject to the strict conditions for each type:
(a) personal effects, sports equipment or a vehicle brought back into the EU by any person;
(b) goods that have been hired, leased or loaned outside the EU;
(c) any goods which were exported under the OPR procedure (see **3.6**) and which remain unprocessed on re-import and which remain in the same state as they were when originally exported;
(d) goods originating outside the EU which are non-free circulation goods and which were previously entered to the IPR procedure in the EU;
(e) goods previously entered to free circulation in the EU, with relief from duty and or import VAT, under the End Use procedure (see section **3.3**);
(f) goods temporarily exported from the EU using an ATA or CPD carnet;
(g) re-imported pallets and containers; and
(h) exported pallets and containers.

RGR is not limited to goods moving solely between the UK and countries outside the EU. Importers can claim customs duty and CAP RGR (and VAT

---

[3] www.gov.uk/government/publications/notice-236-returned-goods-relief/

RGR) on 'triangulation' goods which were exported from one Member State and re-imported to another.

Triangulation is the exportation of goods from one EU Member State to a third country, followed by their re-importation into another EU Member State, for example, France to the USA and then back to the UK (and should not be confused with *"Triangulation"* for intra-EU removals as set out in section **9.12**). Importers of such goods can claim Customs Duty and CAP RGR as long as they meet the conditions.

3.4.1 VAT Returned Goods Relief (VAT RGR)

To be eligible for VAT RGR the importer must:

(a) be shown on the original export declaration as exporter and the re-import declarations as the importer; and

(b) the goods must be re-imported in an unaltered state, apart from any work that may have been required to maintain the goods in working order.

Any work done must not have upgraded the goods to a higher specification or increased their value.

To remain eligible for VAT RGR the goods must not have been exported for the purpose of repair or process. However, if they are being returned unaltered, relief may be available. Additionally, the goods must be re-imported within three years of the original export. However HMRC will consider longer periods on the full eligibility requirements for waiver of the three year time limit.

Additionally:
- any VAT refunds obtained on export from the EU must be repaid;
- the rules on end use also apply;
- goods are also eligible for VAT RGR where they only represent a proportion of the goods exported; and
- any VAT or equivalent turnover tax had been paid on them in the EU and not refunded when they were taken outside the EU.

VAT-registered persons may choose to pay the VAT. For a VAT-registered person, RGR saves the business having to pay and reclaim VAT several times on, for example, goods taken outside the EU on approval and brought back unsold, or tools and equipment which are returned to the EU after being hired, loaned or leased for use in a place outside the EU.

However, VAT-registered businesses can still choose as an alternative to claiming VAT RGR, to pay or defer the VAT due on re-importation and, subject to the normal rules, deduct it as input tax on the next VAT return. In this case HMRC will issue the usual VAT certificate (Form C79) or VAT copy of the declaration.

Most goods are liable to VAT at the rate of 20%, but certain works of art, antiques and collectors' items are entitled to an effective VAT rate of 5%. Full details and conditions of these rules are provided in Notice 702 *VAT Imports*.[4]

For VAT purposes, HMRC treat goods returned to the UK from the Special Territories and countries which have customs unions with the EU as imported goods. That is because these areas are outside the VAT fiscal territory of the Community. Importers who wish to claim VAT RGR on such goods must declare them on the Single Administrative Document (SAD), and use Customs Procedure Code "CPC 49 23 F01".

3.5 Goods transferred to other Member States

Where goods have been imported into the UK, but are to be dispatched to another Member State under the "intra-EU" rules, they are relieved from import VAT. The goods must be dispatched to a "taxable person" in another Member State and the goods must be removed from the UK within one month of the date of importation, i.e. the date the goods enter free circulation, but HMRC may approve a longer period. The importer may be required to pay security to HMRC until satisfying HMRC that the goods have in fact been removed from the UK.

Instead of accounting for import VAT on their Arrival in the customer's country, the customer accounts for local country VAT as an "Acquisition" in their own country (see section **9.7**). The relief can be used by freight/forwarding agents provided they will be making a zero-rated supply of the imported goods, not merely dispatching them, to a taxable person in another EU country.

The UK importer in this example must issue a VAT invoice to the EU customer and must record the dispatch on an EC Sales List. Where appropriate, an "Arrival" "Supplementary Statistical Declaration" ("SSD") or "Intrastat Arrival" is also to be completed and submitted to HMRC.

Relief under these provisions cannot be claimed for goods imported for process and supply to a customer in another Member State.

Details of the relief are provided in Notice 702/7.[5]

Importers talking advantage of this relief should use Customs Procedure Code "CPC 63 23 F01" on the declaration and complete Form C1314. Importers should also apply for a waiver of the three-year time limit if they need further time in which to complete the removal.

The Single Market concept also means that VAT RGR does not apply to goods returned from another EU Member State. Goods sent to or from a trading

---

[4] www.gov.uk/government/publications/vat-notice-702-imports
[5] www.gov.uk/government/publications/vat-notice-7027-import-vat-relief-for-goods-supplied-onward-to-another-country-in-the-ec/

RELIEFS FROM IMPORT DUTY

partner in another Member State are neither imports nor exports for VAT purposes. For a taxable person, the VAT rules on Acquisition apply to goods returned from within the EU for the purposes of a business. Further, a non-taxable person need pay no further VAT on goods returned from another Member State as long as that person had acquired the goods VAT paid.

3.6   Outward Processing Relief (OPR)

OPR provides duty relief on imports of goods from third countries which have been produced from previously exported EU goods. It allows businesses to take advantage of cheaper labour costs outside the EU, while encouraging the use of EU produced raw materials to manufacture the finished products. Goods may also be temporarily exported to undergo processes not available within the Community. The procedure also allows faulty goods to be returned to a third country for repair, or for replacement with equivalent goods under the "Standard Exchange System" (SES).

When goods are first imported from outside the EU normally duty on the full customs value of the goods plus any import VAT has to be paid. When EU goods are exported outside the Customs territory of the EU they lose their EU status. If they are later re-imported they are treated in the same way as non-EU goods and are liable to duty on the full customs value.

By using the OPR procedure businesses are permitted to claim relief from import duty on the EU goods which have been exported for process, as long as the importer can show that the exported goods were used to produce, or are incorporated into, the products now being re-imported. The business must be authorised to use OPR before claiming duty relief. Individuals, partnerships or corporate bodies established within the EU, acting on their own behalf or representing a non-EU body can use OPR.

To qualify for duty relief under OPR arrangements, the exported goods must be EU goods, or Turkish goods that have free circulation status in the EU. EU goods are goods which either originate in the EU or have been imported to free circulation within the EU with all customs formalities completed and customs charges having been paid.

Most goods in free circulation in the EU are now also treated as being in free circulation in Turkey and vice versa since the EU and Turkey formed a Customs union in 1996. Importers can therefore export Turkish goods under the OPR arrangements and claim duty relief on them when re-importing the compensating products either to the EU or to Turkey.

Because Turkey is not a Member State of the EU and a separate Turkish OPR authorisation is required to export the goods for process direct from there, the importer will not need to apply for a single Community authorisation, but will need to apply for an OPR authorisation using Form C&E 1153.[6]

When the business exports the goods under the OPR arrangements it may not claim any refund or remission of import duties or any refunds or other financial benefits under the "Common Agricultural Policy". The business must also pay any export levies or other amounts in full.

OPR relief does not extend to excise duties. Any Excise Duty due on OPR compensating products must be paid in full at importation. However, agricultural component (EA) additional charges can be relieved under OPR.

Any goods that have been entered into the EU under IPR (see section **3.1**) which are to be exported temporarily for further process or for repair, can qualify for duty relief on the costs of the process when they are re-imported, by exporting them under the OPR arrangements. However, to be eligible for OPR when re-imported the processed goods must be re-entered under IPR – they may not be re-entered to free circulation or OPR. In order to do this the importer will need to be authorised for both OPR and IPR or hold an integrated authorisation.

OPR-authorised businesses must comply with the normal requirements of EU and UK export and import prohibitions and restrictions.

3.6.1 OPR and VAT

OPR is a customs procedure that relieves re-imported goods only from Customs Duty. Importers may be able to pay VAT on a reduced value for goods that have previously been exported where they can satisfy the conditions. If the exported goods are normally free of duty, the importer does not need to use the OPR arrangements, but may still be able to claim relief from VAT by using Customs Procedure Code "CPCs 22 00 000" on export and "CPC 40 00 065" on re-import.

Providing ownership of the goods was not transferred to any other person when they were exported or during the time they were outside the EU, VAT is due on the following value at the time of re-importation to the UK:

- the price charged for the process, repair or services including any charge made for parts and materials; plus
- any freight and other charges, except insurance, paid for the transport of the goods to and from the processor's premises; plus
- any Customs or Excise Duty or other import charges payable in the UK.

If the process has been carried out free of charge, for example, because the goods are covered by a warranty, guarantee or service agreement, no VAT is due on re-importation.

---

[6]www.gov.uk/government/publications/import-and-export-application-for-outward-processing-relief-ce1153

RELIEFS FROM IMPORT DUTY

Where the repair was carried out under a service contract agreement HMRC state:
> Some companies have arrangements with a repairer outside the EU which allow them, for payment of a regular service charge, to send goods for repair. When such goods are returned after repair, the accompanying documentation may not indicate that any payment has been made for the repair facility. However, for our purposes these service charges are regarded as part of the value of the goods when they were originally supplied, and are therefore liable to import duties. Similarly, an extended warranty for which a 'one off' payment is made is liable to duty as the charge for this type of warranty is regarded as part of the original price of the goods. If you have goods repaired under arrangements similar to these, you will not be able to account for the customs charges on individual consignments. You must however, declare to us that you are being charged for the repair facilities, and make arrangements with your supervising office to pay the duty and VAT charges when you make payments to the repairer for the service facilities.

All replacements of old goods for new goods are regarded as importations of new goods and are chargeable with VAT in accordance with the normal valuation rules. This applies whether or not any duty relief can be claimed.

Full guidance about paying VAT on a reduced value for goods imported after process or repair is provided by HMRC in VAT Notice 702: *imports*.[7]

Full details about OPR are provided by HMRC in Notice 235.[8]

3.7 Rejected imports

The "Rejected Imports" regime allows for the repayment or remission of import duty on imported goods which the importer rejects because one or more of the following apply:
- they are not in accordance with contract;
- they are defective;
- they were damaged in transit before Customs clearance; or
- they fall within a defined range of "special situations".

The regime covers imports from:
- third countries/territories;
- countries having a Customs Union with the EU; and
- the "Special Territories".

The conditions for repayment or remission of import duty, CAP charges, import VAT and excise duty differ as explained in HMRC Notice 266: *Rejected imports: repayment or remission of duty and VAT*.[9]

---

[7] www.gov.uk/government/publications/vat-notice-702-imports
[8] www.gov.uk/government/publications/notice-235-outward-processing-relief/
[9] www.gov.uk/government/publications/notice-266-rejected-imports-repayment-or-remission-of-duty-and-vat/

RELIEFS FROM IMPORT DUTY

The method of claiming the duty and the import VAT is set out in section **7.7**.

3.7.1 Goods not in accordance with contract

Claims for remission of duty must be made within twelve months of the date the Customs charges became due (for example when declared for free circulation) and for an amount exceeding 10 Euros.

The goods must be disposed of in one of the following ways:
- by exporting them outside the customs territory of the EU;
- by destroying them; or
- by placing them in a customs warehouse.

HMRC then treat the goods as non-Community goods, and they can subsequently be declared to free circulation or another customs procedure, or be re-exported.

Claims can also be made where only part of an article is defective, and all the other conditions for relief are met. The claim must be for the difference between the duty charged on the complete article as imported and the duty which would have been charged on that article had it been imported separately without the defective part. The rate of duty applying at the time of the original Customs declaration involving duty payment should be used.

Claims can also be made for remission of duty on goods which are being rejected and are currently located in another Member State awaiting disposal. Equally, if the importer now holds goods which are being rejected after having been originally imported into another Member State, the person in the other Member State who paid or is liable to pay import duty and VAT may make the claim.

There are special procedures for dealing with rejected imports under these 'triangulation' arrangements. Claims can also be made for Common Agricultural Policy goods.

3.7.2 Rejected imports and VAT

Importers can claim repayment or remission of import duty and import VAT on goods imported if:
- they have been rejected because at the time of declaring them to a customs procedure involving payment of charges (such as release for free circulation), they:
  - are defective;
  - do not comply with the terms of the contract under which they were imported; or
  - were damaged originally declared; and
- they have not been used more than was necessary to establish that they were defective or did not comply with the contract; and
- they have not been sold after finding them to be defective or not to comply with the contract.

RELIEFS FROM IMPORT DUTY

Where the goods have been imported by a "fully taxable" VAT-registered person i.e. a person who can reclaim all of the VAT they incur (subject to the normal rules) for business purposes, they can deduct the tax as input tax.

Where the goods have been imported by an unregistered business or the VAT-registered business is "partially exempt for VAT" i.e. unable to reclaim all of the VAT it incurs), they may apply to HMRC for a special refund using form C&E 1179 in time to reach HMRC at least 48 hours before the goods are packed or destroyed.

The form should be sent to:

The National Rejected Imports Team
HM Revenue and Customs
Excise and International Trade
Sapphire Plaza
Reading
RG1 4TE

The following documents should all be attached, as appropriate:
- a copy of the import invoice;
- documentary proof of entitlement;
- a copy of the VAT certificate for a direct repayment of VAT; and
- a worksheet showing how the amount to be repaid or remitted has been calculated if your claim relates to only part of the imported consignment.

HMRC may attend to see the goods being packed for export or to witness their destruction.

The importer must supply HMRC with all relevant documents substantiating the basis for the claim. For example, if the goods were damaged in transit, this could be an insurance report showing that the damage happened before customs clearance.

Similarly, if it applies to the importer's goods, they must provide proof that they were defective, or not in accordance with the contract under which they were imported, when they were declared to the Customs procedure involving payment of charges (for example, release for free circulation). This would normally be in the form of confirmatory correspondence from the overseas supplier.

3.7.3 Goods in "special situations"

There are a wide range of "special situations". HMRC state that claims for repayment or remission of import duty and import VAT can be made on the goods imported when they are:
(a) stolen after entry to a system of duty relief, as long as the goods are recovered promptly and returned to the same duty relief system in the state they were in when stolen;

(b) inadvertently withdrawn from a system of duty relief, but only if, as soon as the error is found, they are returned to the same duty relief system in the state they were in when withdrawn;

(c) in a means of transport which it is impossible to open on arrival at its destination after the goods have been released for free circulation, as long as they are immediately re-exported;

(d) after release for free circulation, returned to the non-EU supplier under outward processing arrangements to eliminate faults or bring them into line with contract, which the supplier then decides to keep because the defects cannot be remedied or it is uneconomic to do so;

(e) now liable to charges, but originally allowed duty relief and re-exported without Customs supervision, as long as repayment would have been allowed at the time of export if the charges had been collected at import;

(f) forbidden to be marketed by a judicial body, and are re-exported from the EU or destroyed under Customs supervision, but only if they have not been used in the EU;

(g) entered by a declarant empowered to do so on their own initiative and which, through no fault of this declarant, cannot be delivered to the consignee;

(h) addressed to the consignee in error:
- e.g. wrongly labelled, not ordered by the consignee, or received in excess of the quantity ordered, but only if the consignee refused the goods immediately the excess was discovered (no claim may be made if the consignee accepts excess goods, as such action is considered to amend the original contract, even if the goods are subsequently rejected); and
- the goods are re-exported to the original supplier or to an address specified by them;

(i) found to be unsuitable because of an obvious factual error in the consignee's order – e.g. wrong goods received due to quoting an incorrect reference number;

(j) found not to have complied, at the time of entry to free circulation, with the rules in force concerning their use or marketing and cannot therefore be used as the consignee intended;

(k) unable to be used because of official measures taken after the date of entry for free circulation – e.g. new safety or hygiene laws prevent the goods from being used for their intended purpose;

(l) entered to a system of duty relief which is refused through no fault of the consignee – e.g. where relief under a tariff quota is claimed but refused because the quota has been exhausted;

(m) delivered to the consignee after a fixed delivery date – e.g. because of shipping delays;

(n) unable to be sold in the EU and are to be donated to charities. The goods must be either:

RELIEFS FROM IMPORT DUTY

- exported and given free of charge to a charity operating outside the EU, provided that the charity is also represented in the EU; or
- delivered free of charge to a charity operating within the EU, provided that the charity is eligible to import similar goods free of import duty under Notice 317: *Imports by Charities free of duty and* VAT or Notice 371: *Importing goods for disabled people free of duty and VAT*; and

(o) liable to customs charges for reasons other than entry to free circulation, for example by failure to meet post import conditions, but where Community transit or other documentation can be produced to prove entitlement to nil or reduced rates of charge.

These situations do not represent the full range of circumstances under which HMRC could repay or remit import duty and VAT. Importers are advised by HMRC to contact a Customs' business centre if they consider their situation justifies repayment or remission. HMRC will decide the case on its merits, but HMRC will not repay or remit the duty if:
- the only reason for re-export of the goods is failure to sell them in the EU, and the goods are not being donated to a charity outside the EU; and
- the only grounds are that the goods have been destroyed after release for free circulation.

Additionally, the goods must not have been sold after being imported, but claims can be made for goods located in another Member State.

3.8 Temporary admission

Relief from import duty can be claimed under the 'Temporary Admission' ("TA") regime if the goods are imported from outside the EU only for temporary use in the UK/EC. The general conditions for relief are that:
- the goods must be imported for specific use;
- be intended for re-export after use within a specified time; and
- not be altered or changed.

If goods are imported for process or repair or simply to be stored without use before re-export, alternative reliefs may be available under IPR or Customs warehousing. However, TA does not remove the need for the goods to comply with any import/export prohibitions or restrictions, for example for drugs, counterfeit/pirated goods or endangered species, including derivatives such as ivory, furs and goods made from skins.

TA relief can only be claimed by the person who actually uses the goods or arranges for them to be used on their behalf. In most cases this will usually be the person shown as the 'consignee' for the goods on arrival in the UK. If the consignee is not the user or the person on whose behalf the goods will be used, the person claiming relief must be clearly identified when the goods are declared. Depending upon the type of goods and use, they may need to be owned and/or used by a person resident outside the EU.

RELIEFS FROM IMPORT DUTY

Agents, freight forwarders or fast parcel operators who complete Customs entries on behalf of an importer or deliver goods to the place where they will be used, cannot claim relief in their own name if they are not responsible for using the goods or arranging for them to be used on their behalf.

An HMRC authorisation to claim TA relief is required and in most cases this can be applied for at the time of import. There is a wide variation in the list of goods that qualify for TA. If the goods are not 'listed goods' or, if listed but not all of the conditions for TA relief can be met, the importer may be able to claim partial relief; however, an application for full TA still needs to be made. For most goods, HMRC require security for the full amount of import duty and import VAT that is potentially due. The security can be reclaimed when the goods have been re-exported or put to another allowable disposal, subject to production of satisfactory documentary evidence.

Security is normally provided by cash deposit or a bank guarantee. Regular importers can lodge a single guarantee which HMRC will adjust as imported goods are diverted to TA. A reduced value for security can be applied for works of art and second-hand goods (see VAT Notice 702: *imports*), but HMRC will require to see certificates of antiquity and evidence of authenticity.

To reclaim the sum secured or guaranteed, the importer will need to provide evidence to HMRC that they have:

- re-exported the goods;
- transferred the goods to another person authorised for TA;
- declared them to IPR, Customs Warehousing, Free zone procedures or sent them to another person who has declared them to these procedures;
- diverted the goods to free circulation; or
- for goods imported for a specific purpose, met any conditions attached to their import. For example, for tools and instruments evidence that 100% of the goods manufactured using them have also been exported or, for moulds, dies, blocks, drawings, sketches, measuring, checking and testing equipment and other similar articles, that at least 75% of the production resulting from their use has also been exported.

3.8.1 Goods eligible for relief of import duty under the TA regime

Each of the following headings depicts the types of goods that can be entered to TA. HMRC's Notice 200: *Temporary Admission*[10] provides full details of the types of goods that can be entered to TA, the conditions for relief, whether security is required and how long the goods can remain under TA. HMRC remind readers of section 4 of Notice 200 that the lists of goods contained within it are illustrative only.

---

[10] www.gov.uk/government/publications/notice-200-temporary-admission/notice-200-temporary-admission

Headings:

- radio and television production and broadcasting equipment and vehicles specially adapted for use for the above purpose and their equipment imported by public or private organisations;
- instruments and apparatus necessary for doctors to provide assistance for patients awaiting an organ transplant;
- traveller's personal effects reasonably required for a journey;
- goods for sports purposes;
- welfare material for seafarers;
- disaster relief material;
- medical, surgical and laboratory equipment;
- activities carried out using animals (except those imported for transport);
- saddle or draught animals;
- sound, image or data carrying material;
- publicity material;
- professional equipment;
- pedagogic (educational) material and scientific equipment;
- packings;
- moulds, dies, blocks, drawings, sketches, measuring, checking and testing equipment and other similar articles;
- special tools and instruments;
- goods subjected to tests, experiments or demonstrations;
- goods subject to satisfactory acceptance tests;
- goods used to carry out tests, experiments or demonstrations;
- samples;
- replacement means of production;
- goods to be used or exhibited at a public event;
- goods for approval;
- works of art, collectors' items and antiques (see section 12 of HMRC Notice 200 for details of what artefacts qualify as works of art, collectors' items and antiques);
- goods, other than newly manufactured ones, imported with a view to sale at auction;
- spare parts, accessories and equipment; and
- other goods or conditions for TA not met provided the goods are to be used in the UK and re-exported and they are imported occasionally and for a period not exceeding three months, or the value of the goods is less than €10,000.

Applications for retrospective approval for TA can be made and HMRC will treat all requests on an individual basis. The applicant needs to produce records to support their application and demonstrate that the goods in

RELIEFS FROM IMPORT DUTY

question were, or are, eligible for TA relief. For an application to be successful, all of the following criteria must be met:
- the application must be made within 12 months of the date of entry;
- exceptional circumstances must apply – retrospection cannot be used as a regular or recurring form of authorisation;
- there is no obvious negligence or attempted deception;
- the maximum periods of use of the goods must not have been exceeded;
- evidence is available to show that all the requirements to claim relief are satisfied; and
- any relevant documents and declarations can be amended.

'Obvious negligence' is defined by the Commission as being any situation where the applicant has failed to comply with the conditions of granting an authorisation, although they must have been aware of those requirements or had previously been in a similar situation and, therefore, must have been aware of the need to obtain an authorisation prior to importation.

Goods entered to TA can also be transferred to another person. The transfer is effected by making a declaration on the SAD/C88. The 'consignor' will need to advise the 'consignee' of their original SAD/C88 entry number and the date of entry. The consignee should then complete a SAD/C88 entry in their own name and in box 40 state the consignor's original SAD/C88 entry number/date by entering 'Z/ZZZ/' (followed by the date of the consignor's previous entry in the format yy/mm/dd, followed by the entry number).

Goods can also be transferred under TA status to another Member State using a "Simplified Single Authorisation". Full details of the transfer declarations and forms to be used are set out in Notice 200 sections 3 and 6.

3.8.2 Discharging a liability to import duty under the TA regime

To discharge a liability to import duty, the importer can:
- re-export the goods from the EU (for TA goods liable to import VAT only, the re-export of the goods to a Special Territory will also discharge the import duty liability);
- transfer the goods to another person authorised to use TA or to a person who will declare the goods to another Customs procedure in the UK or in another Member State;
- declare the goods to another authorisation held by the declarant or by another person for IPR relief, Customs Warehousing;
- divert the goods to free circulation; or
- destroy the goods under HMRC's supervision.

Full details of the particular SAD/C88 data fields are shown in section 7 of HMRC Notice 200.

RELIEFS FROM IMPORT DUTY

If goods are defective, contaminated, obsolete or otherwise unsuitable and the importer wishes to destroy them, they must write to their HMRC supervising office for approval before the goods are destroyed. The importer will need to explain:
- why they need to destroy the goods;
- where they would intend to destroy them; and
- what waste/scrap would result from destruction.

If the waste/scrap resulting from destruction has any commercial value, import duty and import VAT will be due on the value and at the rate applicable to the waste/scrap. If the goods are destroyed without obtaining HMRC's permission, the importer may be charged import duty and import VAT on the full value and at the rate applicable to the goods when they were entered to TA.

Import duty and/or import VAT that has been relieved under TA will be due to HMRC if:
- a condition for placing the goods under TA was not fulfilled at the time they were declared for the regime;
- an obligation that is a requirement under the TA relief was not met;
- the goods are removed from official control such as using an incorrect export Community Procedure Code; and
- the goods are not re-exported, or put to an eligible disposal where the Customs debt is incurred at the time the goods are diverted.

A fiscal penalty called "compensatory interest" is charged by HMRC to prevent the diversion of goods by importers, which would enable them to gain a financial advantage over those who import directly for use in free circulation, and who will not have had the benefit of deferring the payment of import duty due on the same goods at import. Compensatory interest is calculated from the first day of the month following the date goods were entered to TA in the EU, to the last day of the month in which the goods are diverted. The minimum charging period is one month with no interest due for periods of less than one month. In some circumstances compensatory interest will not be charged (see section 8.5 of HMRC Notice 200).

Interest for late payment will also be charged on any import duty debt that is not paid within five days of the due date. Interest for late payment will be calculated on a daily basis from the due date and is subject to a minimum charge of £25 (see HMRC Notice 199: *Customs procedures and Customs debt*).

RELIEFS FROM IMPORT DUTY

4 Valuation – valuing the goods for customs *ad valorem* duty

Customs duty is often charged as a percentage of the value of the goods when they arrive in the EU, defined as "*ad valorem* duty". The amount of duty due to the Commission (and collected by HMRC on its behalf) depends on the value of the landed goods for import duty purposes. The rules for arriving at the Customs value are based on the World Trade Organisation "Valuation Agreement" (previously known as the "GATT Agreement"). Import VAT is also due at importation and is treated as a duty of Customs. The amount of import VAT due on the importation of the goods also depends on the value attributed to the landed goods (VAT Act 1994, section 21).

HMRC also has to collect and compile trade statistics for the UK (the balance of payments) and for EU purposes. A value of the goods must always be declared for trade statistics on the import entry or the removal document from Customs warehousing. This value must be declared in the value for duty box whether or not *ad valorem* duty is to be paid or the goods are to be entered to a Customs warehouse.

Importers can ask for release of their goods by paying the undisputed charges outright (a "deposit") and securing the balance by cash or cheque. When the value is agreed with HMRC, the importer may be asked to pay more duty or may obtain a refund. If the deposit equals the amount of duty due HMRC will bring the deposit to account. As an alternative to a cash deposit, the importer may be able to use a guarantee, underwritten by a bank.

There are six ways or "Methods" that can be applied to value the goods for customs import duty. The six Methods are:
- Method 1 – the transaction value (see section **4.1**)
- Method 2 – the value of identical goods (see section **4.4**)
- Method 3 – the value of similar goods (see section **4. 5**)
- Method 4 – the selling price of the goods in the EU (see section **4.6**)
- Method 5 – the cost of producing the goods (see section **4.7**)
- Method 6 – the "fall-back" method (see section **4.8**.)

Method 1 must be tried before going on to Method 2 etc. Importers must be able to justify to HMRC why a hierarchical earlier method cannot be used or is unsuitable. The only exception to the order of applying the Methods is that Method 5 can be tried before Method 4.

Method 1 is the normal Method of valuation and is to be used wherever possible; over 90% of importations liable to *ad valorem* customs import duty are computed under Method 1. It is important to remember that the buyer of the imported goods need not necessarily be established in the country of importation and will need to rely on their import agent to correctly value the goods.

VALUATION DECLARATIONS AND STATEMENTS

4.1 Method 1 – the transaction value

The transaction value is the price paid or payable by the buyer to the seller for the goods when sold *for export to the EU*, adjusted in accordance with specific rules. This may also cover situations where goods are imported from a processor. The "transaction value" may be built up or constructed by reference to the cost of processing, plus any items to be added, commonly referred to as "assists".

The "price paid or payable by the buyer to the seller" means the total payment made or to be made by the buyer to or for the benefit of the seller for the imported goods. It includes all payments made or to be made as a condition of sale of the imported goods by the buyer to the seller or by the buyer to a third party to satisfy an obligation of the seller. Thus periodic payments or "one-off" payments by the buyer to the seller for the imported goods must be taken into account, for example tooling charges, engineering fees, development costs etc.

Where goods are sold only once, the fact that they are declared for free circulation in the EU can be taken as confirming that the goods were "sold for export to the Community". Where the goods are sold to one or more subsequent buyers before entry into free circulation, this also applies to the last sale in the commercial chain prior to the introduction of the goods into the Customs Territory of the EU.

4.1.1 "Earlier sale" value

A fundamental planning point when determining the "correct" valuation for import duty (and hence the value of the imported goods on which import VAT is charged) is to identify and apply a valuation for the earliest sale when the goods were "sold for export to the Community". Where an earlier sale has taken place involving the imported goods, the earlier sale may be used as the basis for the import duty valuation. However, an earlier sale may not be used as the basis for import VAT where the import declaration is made in the name of a final consumer or a retail customer.

Buyers can only use an earlier sale where it can be demonstrated that there are specific and relevant circumstances which led to export of the goods to the Customs Territory of the Community. The ways to achieve this include the following:
- the goods are manufactured according to EU specifications, or are identified according to, for example, the marks they bear or the packaging is clear that they have no other use or destination;
- the goods in question were manufactured or produced specifically for a buyer in the EU; or
- specific goods are ordered from an intermediary who sources the goods from a manufacturer and the goods are shipped directly to the EU from that manufacturer.

VALUATION DECLARATIONS AND STATEMENTS

Section 28 of HMRC Notice 252: *Valuation of imported goods for Customs purposes, VAT and trade statistics* (June 2009) provides examples of transactions where the earlier sale principle can and cannot be used and are reproduced here:

Example 1

Facts:

Company 'A' of London orders 1,000 shirts from Company 'B' of Brussels at a price of £7.20 each, delivered to London.

Company 'B' has 8,000 shirts in stock in a warehouse in Taiwan which were originally purchased from a manufacturer there for £4.50 each.

Company 'B' arranges for the goods to be shipped from the warehouse to Company 'A' which imports the goods.

Comments:

The sale with price of £4.50 does not satisfy the "last sale in a commercial chain" test, nor can it be demonstrated that the corresponding sale took place for export to the EU.

Example 2

Facts:

Company 'A' buys hand-carved wooden coffee tables in India and stores them in a Bombay warehouse awaiting orders.

After a visit to the UK, Company 'A's sales manager believes that there is a market for these products and ships ten samples of eight types of table on speculation to Tilbury via sea freight.

The eight types of table cost Company 'A' on average 2,000 rupees each. While the ship is at sea, Company 'A' sells all eight coffee tables to Company 'B' of London for £6,400, Free-On-Board Bombay. Before the goods arrive at Tilbury, they are re-sold by Company 'B' to a customer in Birmingham for £7,200.

Comments:

The declarant cannot use the price of 2,000 rupees per unit, because it is not the last sale in a commercial chain. Also, it cannot be shown that the sale in question was for the export of goods to the Community.

The sale with the price of £6,400 is also not the last sale in the chain. However, it is possible to demonstrate that the goods while in transit were sold at this price to the Community.

Example 3a

Facts:

Company 'A' with a head office in Malta, buys petroleum products from Company 'B', a company in a Third Country, and stores them in facilities located in Malta. The goods conform to the standards which apply in the markets of both EC and Malta.

After 3 weeks, Company 'A' sells the products in question to Company 'C' a UK company, and consigns the goods from Malta to the UK.

Comments:

VALUATION DECLARATIONS AND STATEMENTS

The goods are not purchased by Company 'A' in the context of a sale for export to the EU.

Although the goods as designed are suitable for the EC marketplace, they cannot be regarded as sold for export to the EC. They are sold by Company 'B' with a destination in Malta.

Consequently, the Customs value cannot be based on the earlier sale.

Example 3b

Facts:

Company 'A', a firm established in a Third Country, buys (in a Third Country) a petroleum product which is designed as suitable for the EC market. These purchases are made subsequent to receipt of specific orders by Company 'A' from a UK firm, Company 'B'.

Due to limitations in its storage facilities in the UK, Company 'B' requests that Company 'A' holds the goods in its facilities for a three-week period before shipment to the UK.

The goods are subsequently shipped to the UK.

Comments:

The purchase by Company 'A' is not the last sale in a commercial chain.

However, the goods (which meet the required EC standards) have been bought in the context of prior arrangements for re-sale and shipment to the EU.

The intervention, before shipment by Company 'A', of a period involving the actual storage in a Third Country on behalf of Company 'B' does not invalidate the requirements for a sale for export to the Community.

Example 4

Facts:

Company 'A' is a US company engaged in the marketing of various types of perfumes, cosmetics, creams, etc, which it sources from various manufacturers throughout the world (Price A).

The European operations are directed from Company 'A''s head office in Syracuse, New York and consist of rented offices in London, out of which sales persons visit the purchasing offices of EU pharmacies etc. negotiate prices, take orders and send them for processing (shipping products, invoicing and collection of accounts) to Syracuse. Products are sold to EU customers on a "Delivered Duty Paid" basis (Price B). Although the sales persons have the authority to negotiate prices and sales contracts they do not have a general authority to contract on behalf of Company 'A'.

Comments:

The declarant cannot use Price A as it does not arise from "the last sale in a commercial chain".

Price A would be acceptable only where additional elements exist (for example, direct shipment by the producer and the goods bear marks or specifications indicating they are destined for the E- market).

VALUATION DECLARATIONS AND STATEMENTS

Example 5

Facts:

The President of Company 'A' of London, during a visit to Thailand, is offered a "close-out" deal on 10,000 metres of assorted silk fabrics at a job-lot price of £20,000 Free-On-Board Bangkok. He purchases the whole 10,000 metres and arranges for the fabric to be sent to the UK by ship on 4 April.

While attending a convention on 8 April, he meets the President of Company 'B', a silk blouse manufacturer from Manchester, who agrees to buy the 10,000 metres of silk now en-route to the EU for £39,000, delivered to Liverpool.

Comments:

The lower price sale is not "the last sale in a commercial chain", but it does arise from a sale for export to the Community so that lower price can be used as the customs import duty valuation.

Example 6

Facts:

Company 'A' of London enters into an agreement to buy 100 food mixers from Company 'B', a US entrepreneur at a price of £22.50 each.

Company 'B' negotiates with Company 'C' of Detroit to manufacture the food mixers for a price of £20.75 each, Company 'C' being responsible for shipping the goods to Company 'A' in London.

Comments:

The lower price sale could not be claimed by the importer. It is not the "last sale in a commercial chain".

However, it remains to be demonstrated that the sale to which the lower price corresponds was already a sale for export to the EU, taking account of the requirement of direct supply by the manufacturer. This proof is complete if the products when sold by the manufacturer bear specifications or marks showing their destination for the EU market in which case the lower price can be used.

Example 7

Facts:

Company 'A' is a multinational hotel chain with hotels in several countries, including the UK. Each UK hotel is incorporated as a separate limited liability company. At the beginning of every year, each hotel submits purchase orders to the New York head office for its supply needs for the following twelve months. The head office then submits purchase orders to various suppliers in the US with instructions to send the goods either to each hotel directly or to the New York head office for subsequent shipment to each chain hotel. The suppliers invoice the head office in New York which then bills each hotel in the chain.

Comments:

The same conclusions as for example 6 apply, i.e. if the goods are sent to each hotel directly from the supplier. If the goods are sent to the head office before being shipped to the UK, then the sale for export test can be positive only if other elements of proof are demonstrated, for example that the goods correspond to Community specifications or bear marks which indicate their destination for the EU market.

VALUATION DECLARATIONS AND STATEMENTS

Example 8

Facts:

Company 'A' produces perfumes, cosmetics etc. which it sells to distributors in the EU and the US.

In order to maintain differential pricing on the two markets, Company 'A' requires its distributors not to re-sell the goods outside of their respective territories.

In a particular case, a UK firm buys products from the US distributor and ships the goods to the Netherlands.

Comments:

The first sale does not satisfy the sale for export to the EC requirement.

4.2 Additions to the transaction value

The cost of containers and packaging that relates directly to the goods must be included in the customs value, for example bottles and cartons in which the product rests (the cost of freight containers and pallets etc. is part of the transportation costs). Where containers are for repeated use, for example, reusable bottles, their cost can be spread over the expected number of imports. If a number of the containers may not be re-exported, this must be allowed for.

The following additional services must be added to the manufactured cost:
- delivery costs;
- commissions;
- royalties and licence fees;
- goods and services provided free of charge or at reduced cost by the buyer;
- materials, components, parts and similar items incorporated in the imported goods including price tags, kimball tags, labels;
- tools, dies, moulds and similar items used in producing the imported goods, for example, tooling charges;
- materials consumed in producing the imported goods, for example, abrasives, lubricants, catalysts, reagents etc. which are used up in the manufacture of the goods but are not incorporated in them;
- engineering, development, artwork, design work and plans and sketches carried out outside the EU and necessary for producing the imported goods - the cost of research and preliminary design sketches is not to be included;
- Containers and packing including:
    i. the cost of containers which are treated for customs purposes as being one with the goods being valued (that is not freight containers the hire-cost of which forms part of the transport costs); and
    ii. the cost of packing whether for labour or materials.
- proceeds of resale; and
- export duty & taxes paid in the country of origin or export.

VALUATION DECLARATIONS AND STATEMENTS

4.2.1 Delivery costs

The costs of transport, insurance, loading or handling connected with delivering the goods to the EU border must be included. Delivery costs are:
- the cost of transport;
- the cost of insurance (including global or blanket policies);
- loading and handling charges;
- container charges (for example when hired for transportation of the imported goods);
- terminal charges being charges for a variety of services in connection with the handling/storage of freight containers at container depots; and
- any other charges involved in carrying the goods from one place to another.

More details are provided in **section 4.16.1**.

4.2.2 Commissions

Certain payments of commission and brokerage, including selling commission, must be included, but, if any buying commission is shown separately from the price paid or payable for the goods it can be excluded.

If a selling agent takes orders from customers in the EU on behalf of a third country/territory seller and then imports to fulfil those orders, Method 1 can usually be used. The customs value will be based on the selling price, inclusive of that selling agent's commission, to the EU customer. This also applies where:
- the contract provides for a supply of pre-ordered goods to be delivered to the customer at certain intervals to meet production requirements; and
- the selling agent holds the customer's pre-ordered stock for delivery on demand.

Where a selling agent imports goods to sell later from stock held in the UK on behalf of the third country/territory seller, Method 1 cannot usually be used and Methods 2 to 6 must be tried.

4.2.3 Royalties and licence fees

The value of royalties and licence fees must be included when they relate to the imported goods and are paid as a condition of the sale of those goods. A royalty or a licence fee is usually a payment made to a person for use of that person's patent or design rights, processes, trade-marks, copyrights or for "know how". Manufacturers and other businesses often have to pay for the right to manufacture, use or sell the licensor's goods or for technical knowledge and assistance. Royalty or licence fees payable to the seller are to be included in the customs value as long as they both:
- relate to the imported goods; and
- are paid as a condition of the sale.

VALUATION DECLARATIONS AND STATEMENTS

However, payment of royalties and licence fees do not have to be included in the customs valuation where such payments are made for the right to reproduce the imported goods. In addition, a royalty or licence fee for the right to use a trade mark is only to be included in the customs value where:
- the royalty or licence fee relates to goods which are resold in the same state or which are subject to only minor processing (such as diluting or packing) after importation;
- the goods are marketed under the trade mark, affixed before or after importation, for which the royalty or licence fee is paid; and
- the buyer/importer is not free to obtain such goods from other suppliers unrelated to the seller.

If the royalties and licence fees relate partly to the imported goods and partly to other ingredients or component parts added, or services related to the goods after their importation, the royalty payment can be apportioned between dutiable and non-dutiable elements. The basis for the apportionment of the total payment can sometimes be found in the licence agreement or be obtainable from the licensor. HMRC invite importers to approach them where this is not the case or cannot be ascertained from the commercial documentation to arrive at an acceptable valuation.

If the importer cannot arrive at a value for an item that must either be added to the price paid or payable or left out of the customs value HMRC will agree with them a Method for arriving at an appropriate amount to add or exclude at the time of entry. This could involve the use of average values or a percentage addition or deduction and be subject to periodic reviews. If apportionment is not possible, say because of a lack of relevant information, Method 1 cannot be used and the importer must try Method 2.

4.2.4 Proceeds of resale

If the importer/buyer is to share with the seller, either directly or indirectly, the profit on resale, use or disposal of the imported goods, the seller's share of such profit must be added to the price paid, but excluding dividends from the financial performance of a company. For example, if the seller is to have 30% of the profit which the importer derives from the transaction, then 30% additional value is to be added to the price paid or payable for the goods at importation. If the amount of profit is not known or cannot be computed at the time of importation, the goods can only be released to free circulation against a deposit or a guarantee in favour of HMRC.

4.2.5 Export duty & taxes paid in the country of origin or export

These taxes, when incurred by the buyer, are dutiable. However, if tax relief or repayment of these taxes is afforded to the importer, they may be left out of the customs value. It is incumbent on the importer to prove to HMRC that such taxes have been relieved in the exporting country.

4.3 Items that can be excluded from the transaction value

A number of items that can actually be quite expensive can be excluded from the customs valuation, these being:
- delivery costs within the EU;
- EU duties or taxes;
- quantity or trade discounts;
- cash and early settlement discounts;
- dividends;
- marketing activities related to the imported goods;
- buying commission;
- export quota and licence payments;
- interest charges;
- rights of reproduction;
- post-importation work; and
- management fees.

4.3.1 Delivery costs within the EU

An inclusive charge by the seller for carriage and delivery beyond the EU place of importation can be deducted providing they are shown separately in the commercial documents and invoices from the price paid or payable for the goods. For allowable delivery costs see section **4.2.1** above.

4.3.2 EU duties or taxes

If any EU duties or taxes have been incurred in the purchase cost of the goods, they can be deducted from the price paid. To find the amount of duty included in the invoice price, HMRC provide the following formula:

$$\text{Duty inclusive price} \times \frac{\text{duty rate}}{100 + \text{duty rate}}$$

For example, if the duty inclusive invoice price is £1,100 and the rate of duty is 10% the duty included in that invoice price is:

$$£1,100 \times \frac{10}{100 + 10} = \frac{£1,100 \times 10}{110} = £100$$

Therefore the included duty is £100.

4.3.3 Discounts

These can only be left out where they relate to the imported goods being valued and there is a valid contractual entitlement to the discount at the material time for valuation. Discounts such as contingency or retroactive discounts related to previous importations cannot be claimed in full on the current importation and have to be apportioned between importations.

4.3.3.1 Quantity or trade discounts

The importer can exclude these discounts when they are earned. If the importer is related to the seller, the discounts will also be allowed if that relationship has not affected the price of the goods. For related persons or

legal entities, HMRC have instigated a number of comparative "tests" that must be applied to ascertain if the relationship has affected the price, these being:
a) the price paid by the importer to the seller is close to one of the following:
   - the transaction value of identical or similar goods exported to the EU, in sales between buyers and sellers who are unrelated;
   - the Customs value of identical or similar goods arrived at under Method 4; or
   - the Customs value of identical or similar goods arrived at under Method 5.
b) alternatively, to demonstrate that either:
   - the importer and the seller trade with each other as though they are unrelated;
   - the price paid is the same as that for unrelated buyers in the EU operating at the same commercial level and purchasing similar quantities of the goods; or
   - the price paid is fully costed, i.e. it is an "arm's length" price.

It is important to note that HMRC must have accepted the "test" values at or about the same time as the importation of the goods that are to be valued. HMRC also state in section 30.1 of HMRC Notice 252 that they may also decide to examine the circumstances surrounding the sale to determine whether the transaction value is acceptable. HMRC add in their Notice that, in practice, they are seeking assurance that the importer does not receive preferential treatment under the inter-company pricing arrangements because of their relationship with the seller. If HMRC conclude that the relationship has influenced the price then Method 1 cannot be used and the importer must try Method 2.

4.3.3.2 Transfer pricing

Multi-National Enterprises (MNEs) normally transfer physical goods and intangible property or provide services to related enterprises at "favourable" (below market value) prices. UK taxation regulations and EU Customs law require the prices within a MNE to be set, for both corporation tax and customs valuation purposes as if group members were not related. A transfer price may be used as the basis of a Method 1 value only where it fulfils the criteria of Article 29 of the Community Customs Code and all relevant costs are included in the dutiable value if paid separately from the transfer price of the imported goods.

4.3.3.3 Cash and early settlement discounts

Importers can also leave out cash and early settlement discounts on the following basis:
- when the payment reflecting the discount has been made at the time of entry to free circulation;

- if the payment has not been made at the time of entry to free circulation, it will be allowed at the level declared provided it is a discount generally accepted within the trade sector concerned; and
- if the discount is higher than is generally accepted within the trade sector concerned it will only be accepted if the importer can demonstrate, where required, that the goods are actually sold at the price declared as the price actually paid or payable and the discount is still available at the time of entry to free circulation.

For some reasons, an importer may never take advantage of a cash discount and always pay the gross contract price for the goods. If so, the discount sum not taken may become liable for inclusion in the customs value at the time of entry to free circulation.

4.3.4 Dividends
Dividends accrued in a company's balance sheet and remitted to the seller can be excluded from the customs value.

4.3.5 Marketing activities related to the imported goods
The following activities carried out at the importer's own expense can be excluded from the customs value:
- advertising;
- promotion; and
- guarantee or warranty services.

Additionally, any payments made towards general marketing support which are not related to imported goods should also not be included. However, the cost of marketing activities borne by the seller must be included in the customs value even if they are charged separately from the invoice price for the goods.

4.3.6 Buying commission
Fees or brokerage paid to the importer's agent for representing them outside the EU in buying imported goods can be excluded, provided that the commission is shown separately from the price paid or payable for the goods.

The services usually provided by a buying agent for the importer include:
- locating suppliers;
- informing the seller of what goods are required;
- collecting samples of the goods;
- inspecting the goods;
- purchasing the goods on the importer's behalf; and
- arranging insurance, transport, storage and delivery of the goods from their place of origin to the EU.

The commission paid to a buying agent can be excluded from the customs value so long as the payment is shown separately from the price actually paid

VALUATION DECLARATIONS AND STATEMENTS

or payable for the goods. *However, buying commission must always be included in the value of the goods for import VAT purposes.*

4.3.7 Export quota and licence payments

Payments for buying export quotas and licences can be excluded from the customs value, except payments for certificates of authenticity for meat and meat products.

4.3.8 Interest charges

If interest is charged under a finance agreement for buying the imported goods it can be excluded from the customs value, provided that:
- the charges are shown separately from the price paid or payable for the goods;
- the financing arrangement has been made in writing; and
- it can be demonstrated that:
  a) such goods are actually sold at the price declared as the price actually paid or payable (net of the interest charge), and
  b) the claimed rate of interest does not exceed the level for such transactions prevailing in the country where, and at the time when, the finance was provided.

These provisions apply to all of Methods 1 – 6. The charge for interest must be shown separately from the price for the goods on the documentation, for example the invoice or the valuation declaration accompanying the SAD/C88 entry to free circulation. HMRC may call for further evidence in support of any claim to exclude the interest charges from the customs value, such evidence being:
- a copy of the finance agreement; or
- a copy of the contract of sale of the goods if it contains the financing clause; and
- information to show that the claimed rate of interest is not excessive.

4.3.9 Rights of reproduction

Payments for these rights may be excluded if they are shown separately from the price paid or payable for the goods.

4.3.10 Post-importation work

All of the following charges may be excluded from the Customs value:
- construction work;
- erecting;
- assembling;
- maintaining; or
- giving technical help for goods such as industrial plant, machinery or heavy equipment.

VALUATION DECLARATIONS AND STATEMENTS

The work may be carried out before or after importation so long as it is carried out as part of the installation of the imported goods and the charge must be shown separately from the price paid or payable for the goods.

4.3.11 Management fees

Any management fees that the importer pays to the seller can be excluded from the customs value. This includes general service fees for administration, marketing, accounting, etc. that are not related to the imported goods. Again, HMRC may request evidence to support any claim to exclude any of these items.

4.4 Method 2 – the value of identical goods

Method 2 is based on the customs value of identical goods exported to the EU at or about the same time as the goods to be valued. Identical goods are goods produced in the same country as those being valued. They must also be the same in all respects, such as physical characteristics, quality and reputation. Minor differences in appearance do not matter. If the producer of the Method 2 goods does not produce Method 1 goods, another producer's goods may be used for comparison. If there are no identical goods then Method 2 cannot be used and the importer must go on to try Method 3 *ad seq*.

The value for Method 2 is based on a customs value of identical goods already accepted by EU Customs authorities under Method 1. Where there is a sale at the same commercial level and in the same quantity this must be used and if more than one value is available the importer can use the lowest value.

If there are no sales at the same level or in the same quantity the importer must take into account any effect these differences have on the price. The importer must also take account of differences between the costs of delivering the identical goods and delivering the goods to be valued.

The importer must produce a copy of, or the necessary data to enable Customs to trace, an import entry (with supporting documents) for identical goods where Method 1 has been accepted by us or another EU Customs administration.

4.5 Method 3 – the value of similar goods

Method 3 is based on the customs value of similar goods exported to the EU at or about the same time as the goods to be valued. Similar goods are goods which differ in some respects from the goods being valued, but they:
- are produced in the same country;
- can carry out the same tasks; and
- are commercially interchangeable.

Where similar goods are not made by the producer of the goods to be valued, the importer can use similar goods produced by a different person. If there are no similar goods Method 3 cannot be used and Method 4 or Method 5 must be tried.

The conditions for using Method 3 are the same as for using Method 2 (see section **4.4** above).

4.6 Method 4 – the selling price of the goods in the EU

There are two variations of Method 4, Method 4(a) and Method 4(b). It should also be remembered that Method 5 can be tried before Method 4. If there are no sales to unrelated persons or companies Method 4 cannot be used and Method 5 should be tried, if not already examined. If Method 5 is unsuitable, then the next and probably only available method is Method 6 (see section **4.8**).

Under Method 4(a) the importer must be able to produce details of the sales in the greatest aggregate quantity at the time of entry into free circulation. Alternatively, Method 4(b) values the goods on the unit price of the actual sales of the imported goods that take place up to 90 days after importation. Because the importer cannot establish the customs value until the goods have been sold they must request the release of the goods against a deposit.

The unit price must relate to sales in the "greatest aggregate quantity" at or about the time of the importation of the goods to be valued. To arrive at the "sale in the greatest aggregate quantity" the number of items sold at each price is totalled and the largest number of items sold at one price is the greatest aggregate quantity.

The unit price can be based on:
- the imported goods;
- identical imported goods; or
- similar imported goods.

If the goods are not sold in the EU in the condition as imported, the customs value can be based on the price at which the goods are sold after processing. This cannot be done, however, if the goods:
- lose their identity (unless the value added by the processing can be easily established); or
- keep their identity, but form a minor part of the goods sold.

4.6.1 Subtractions from the unit price

A number of subtractions must be made from the unit price to arrive at the customs value under Method 4. These are as follows:
- *either* the commissions usually paid or agreed to be paid or the addition usually made for profit and general expenses in connection with sales in the EU of imported goods of the "same class or kind"; *or*
- the usual costs of transport, insurance and associated costs incurred within the EU, *and*
- EU Customs duties and internal taxes payable in the country of importation.

VALUATION DECLARATIONS AND STATEMENTS

"Goods of the same class or kind" refers to goods which fall within a group or range of goods produced by a particular industry or sector of industry. It includes "identical" and "similar" goods. The goods need not have been imported from the same third country/territory as the goods that are being valued.

The value added to the goods by the processing carried out in the EU can also be deducted if the goods are sold after processing. Also, any actual profit and general expenses can be deducted provided these are typical for the sale in the EU of imported goods of the same class or kind, but exaggerated figures will be challenged by HMRC.

HMRC strongly recommend that importers have available and can produce information to show that the deduction they have made is "usual" by comparison with importers within the relevant trade sector. They admit that this is a complex matter and advocate that importers contact the National 'Helpline' to agree a deduction before the importation of the goods begins (see HMRC Notice 252 section 6.9).

4.6.2   Evidence to support the valuation (and deductions)

HMRC set out in Notice 252 at section 6.11 the evidence it expects importers to produce to prove the customs value they have computed. This varies between Method 4(a) and 4(b).

4.6.2.1   Method 4(a)

The following evidence must accompany the SAD/C88 to show the unit price in the greatest aggregate quantity:
- a sales invoice;
- a price list current at the time of importation (for importations of sheepmeat carcases from Australia and New Zealand special valuation rules apply as agreed with the International Meat Trade Association Inc (IMTA)) – see Notice 252 section 40); or
- other evidence as agreed with HMRC.

4.6.2.2   Method 4(b)

There are two distinct aspects to valuing goods under Method 4(b). These are at the time of importation and at the time of adjusting the deposit.

At the time of importation

The importer must give a reasonable estimate of the final sales value for deposit purposes, supported by a pro-forma invoice, statement of value or other evidence. For importations of fresh fruit and vegetables and cut flowers HMRC provide a full methodology in Notice 252 section 41.

At the time of adjusting the deposit

There is no need to wait until all the goods imported in the consignment have been sold to establish the customs value. Once enough units have been sold to arrive at the unit price, the importer must send copies of the sales invoices and

VALUATION DECLARATIONS AND STATEMENTS

a copy of their calculations to HMRC. Unless an overall percentage deduction has been agreed with HMRC, they will also need details of the actual deductions claimed and duty will either be taken to account, refunded or called for. In the fresh fruit and vegetable and cut flowers trade the "Account Sales Procedure" may be used as a basis for arriving at the customs import duty payable (Notice 252 Section 41 refers).

4.7 Method 5 – the cost of producing the goods

Method 5 is based on the costs of producing the goods and is usually only used where the importer and supplier are related. The customs value is a built-up value and is based on the sum of the following:

- the cost or value of materials and fabrication or other processing used in producing the imported goods, including all of the items below if supplied by the buyer, directly or indirectly:
    i. materials, components, parts and similar items incorporated in the imported goods including price tags, kimball tags, labels;
    ii. tools, dies, moulds and similar items used in producing the imported goods, for example, tooling charges;
    iii. materials consumed in producing the imported goods, for example, abrasives, lubricants, catalysts, reagents etc which are used up in the manufacture of the goods but are not incorporated in them; or
    iv. engineering, development, artwork, design work and plans and sketches carried out outside the EU and necessary for producing the imported goods. The cost of research and preliminary design sketches is not to be included. [Even if this work is carried out in the EU it must be included in the value of the work for the customs value if it is charged to the producer of the goods]; and
    v. containers and packing (see section **4.8**).
- an amount for the producer's profit and general expense; *plus*
- the cost of transport, insurance and loading or handling connected with delivering the goods to the EU border.

Importers must be able to get information about the cost or value of these items, which must be based on the producer's commercial accounts and which must follow the general principles of accounting applying in the country where the goods are produced. Importers must also be able to present information about the producer's profit and general expenses. Again, the amount to be added must be in line with the usual figures for profit and general expenses for producers in the country of exportation of the goods, being:

- of the same class or kind; and
- for export to the EU.

VALUATION DECLARATIONS AND STATEMENTS

If the importer is unable to obtain this information they cannot use Method 5. If they have tried, unsuccessfully, to use Method 4 the importer must now use Method 6.

4.8 Method 6 – the "fall-back" method

Method 6 is the final Method and the customs value is computed by using reasonable means consistent with the World Trade Organisation (WTO) valuation principles. This is achieved where possible by adapting Methods 1 to 5 flexibly to fit unusual circumstances, for example:

- applying Methods 2 or 3 where the customs value could be based on the transaction value of identical or similar imported goods produced in a country other than the country of exportation of the goods being valued;
- in applying Method 4(b) the 90 day limit for sales could be extended; or
- the customs value could be based on the price that would have been paid for the goods if they had been purchased (perhaps by reference to the export price list for sales to the EU issued by the supplier), being consistent with WTO valuation principles.

The evidence that the importer should produce to support the valuation will vary according to the flexibility of the chosen or adapted methods being used. It is likely to be as much evidence of the actual or realistic prices and costs as possible.

4.9 Simplified Procedure Values (SPVs)

SPVs are customs values derived from prices realised on sales in specified marketing centres within the EU. A variety of deductions are made from these prices to arrive at an average sterling value per 100kg net for each product covered by the scheme. The scheme is specifically for the import of fruit and vegetables and flowers and details can be found in Notice 252 section 9.

A uniform basis of valuing fruit and vegetables called the "Entry Price System" is in place throughout the EU. For each product covered by the system the Tariff indicates a scale of entry prices per 100 kg net (the "Standard Import Value"). At the highest point on the scale the Tariff indicates an ad valorem rate of duty only. Proceeding down the scale, specific charges are introduced. Thus, the lowest entry price generates the highest specific charge in addition to the ad valorem duty. Guidance on deciding what Entry Price applies is given in Section 10.2 of Notice 252.

4.10 Frozen meat in "round sets"

Frozen meat is often imported in what is commercially described as "frozen round sets", which consist of several different cuts of meat invoiced at a unit price per ton. The cuts differ in value, but this may not be shown on the invoice. Importers must try Method 1, based on the alternatives outlined in section 43 of Notice 252.

VALUATION DECLARATIONS AND STATEMENTS

4.11 Value of goods imported free of charge

There can be occasions where goods are imported free of charge or for no sale, for example, where they could be part of promotional material. Importers cannot normally use Method 1 because there is no price paid or payable to the supplier. However, it may be possible to use Method 1 where:

- the goods have been the subject of an earlier sale (perhaps to the supplier); *or*
- they are being imported 'pre-sold'; *and*
- in both cases evidence of that sale can be produced.

If Method 1 cannot be used, then either Method 2 or Method 3 can be tried if imports of identical or similar goods are made under Method 1, or the importer at least has knowledge of such imports. Alternatively, Method 4 can be used where the goods or identical or similar goods are sold to unrelated customers in the EU. Method 5 can be used where the importer can obtain the detailed costings.

If none of Methods 1 to 5 can be used, the importer must use Method 6 and the customs value can be based, for example, on the price the importer would have paid the supplier if the goods had been bought. The additions and subtractions set out in sections **4.2** and **4.3** above must be made as appropriate. In the case of having to use Method 6, a copy of the supplier's current export price list for goods sold to the EU should be produced, or a statement from the supplier of the value of the goods, or other suitable evidence as agreed with HMRC.

4.12 Value of imported "replacement" free of charge goods

If the supplier includes in the *same shipment* a quantity of "free of charge" items as replacements for goods likely to be defective or damaged in transit, the contracted sale price is regarded as covering the total quantity of items shipped. For replacement goods imported in a *subsequent shipment*, the customs value is determined in accordance with the rules set out in section **4.11** above. On application, HMRC can amend the customs value of the original shipment in accordance with the contractual arrangements.

4.13 Value of used goods

No special treatment is required for valuing used goods imported into the EU. The rules set out here and in Notice 252 for new goods apply.

4.14 Goods used after purchase and before entry into the EU

If, after their purchase, the goods have been used in the country of origin or another third country/territory and the period and extent of use between being acquired and entered into free circulation results in the goods being worth less at the time of entry than when acquired, Method 1 does not have to be used. Alternatively, the importer can try either of Methods 2 or 3 if identical or similar goods of the same age and in the same condition are imported under Method 1. If Methods 2 or 3 are unsuitable then Method 4 can be used if identical or similar goods are sold to unrelated customers in the EU. If all of Methods 2, 3 and 4 cannot be used, then the importer must use Method 6 and the customs value can be based on the value of the goods when acquired, less an amount for loss of value due to the usage.

4.15 Valuing rented or leased goods

For the import of goods that are to be rented or leased, there will usually be no sale between the supplier and the importer in which case Method 1 is not possible. In the first instance, the importer should try any of Methods 2 to 5, but it is usually the case for such transactions that Method 6 will be appropriate. If, however, prior to being rented or leased, the goods were the subject of a sale, it may be possible to use Method 1.

It may be the case that a cash price for the goods is quoted in the rental or leasing agreement, should the importer/buyer wish to purchase the goods at a later date. However, this cash price may be artificially high to encourage the renting or leasing of the goods. Alternatively, it may be an option to buy when the goods are effectively second-hand. Therefore, HMRC will not allow such a cash price to be used as the transaction value under Method 1.

HMRC normally expect importers to use Method 6 for such goods. To arrive at the customs value the annual rental or leasing cost should be multiplied by the expected economic life of the imported goods. Interest charges should be excluded to arrive at the "cash" price of the goods using one of two formulae provided by HMRC. The formula to be used depends on whether payment is made in advance or arrears. Detailed guidance about the formulae is provided in Notice 252, section 44. As this is a complex area, importers are advised to contact the HMRC National Helpline where it is difficult to determine the expected economic life of the imported goods.

4.16 All Methods – additional considerations

The following rules apply for all of the valuation Methods.

4.16.1 Transport costs

Where the transport costs for the journey cover both EU and Non-EU territories in an inclusive charge, the costs cannot be apportioned. However, where separately distinguishable, the freight charge can be apportioned between non-EU and EU freight costs to arrive at the proportion that relates to reaching the EU border.

For goods transported by sea the freight charge is that which would have been paid to the place of introduction and rates shown in rate books or otherwise advertised by the shipping line or other carrier are usually acceptable.

For goods transported by rail or road the freight charge is to be apportioned using reasonable means for example by the distances covered both outside and inside the EU – Notice 252, section 45 provides other examples.

VALUATION DECLARATIONS AND STATEMENTS

The percentage of the air transport costs shown on the air-waybill to be included in the Customs value is set out in an EC Regulation (Annex 25 to Regulation (EEC) No. 2454/93 as amended by Commission Regulation (EC) No. 881/2003). The percentages are listed in Notice 252 Section 46. Also, importers connected to CHIEF can obtain details from the relevant data files.

It is important to note that locally agreed rates for EU transport costs for VAT purposes must not be used for *ad valorem* import duty calculations.

Where the transport costs are included in the total cost of the goods, a deduction for the transport costs may be made from the total price paid, provided they can be distinguished and evidence can be produced to support them – Notice 252, section 45 provides examples.

HMRC will accept all the following types of evidence:
- the amount shown separately on the seller's invoice;
- a certified statement or telex from the supplier;
- an invoice or certified statement of the actual freight amount charged by the carrier to the buyer, seller or agent;
- an invoice or certified statement establishing the total cost of transport, split to show the proportion of actual distances covered both inside and outside the EU;
- a statement from the buyer referring to a schedule of freight rates normally applied for the same mode of transport; or
- in the case of goods imported by air, a statement on the invoice confirming that the cost of freight included in the price is the same as that stated on the air-waybill.

If the transport is provided free of charge or is provided, say, from "own resources", the importer must include in the customs value an amount for transport costs to the EU border. This can be calculated by using the freight rates tariff for the type of transport used, for example "IATA" rates for air transport costs, or conference rates for sea freight.

For goods transported by air, but where the importer does not have access to or knowledge of the air freight tariffs, sea freight tariffs can be used where the contractual arrangements between the buyer and the seller determine that:
- the contract was in force at the time of entry of the goods concerned;
- they require the seller to have the goods transported by air to ensure agreed delivery deadlines are met; and
- the seller has to bear the additional costs.

In this case, the following treatment will apply:
- if the terms of the original order were 'CIF' (Cost, Insurance and Freight) or 'post CIF', then the terms change to 'CIP' (Carriage & Insurance Paid To) and the air transport cost is considered to be included in the CIP price. No further addition for transport and associated costs is required;

- if the terms of the original order were 'FOB' (Free On Board), those terms change to CIP or 'CPT' (Carriage Paid To). The CIP or CPT price is considered to include the air transport cost. No further addition for transport and associated costs is required unless any further costs are incurred by the buyer, for example, for insurance or if the buyer makes a contribution towards the additional air transport costs (by paying an amount equal to what it would have cost to transport the goods by sea), in which case those costs have to be included in the Customs value.

(Details of and an explanation of the use of Incoterms are provided in **Appendix A**).

In either case, the cost of transport within the EU can be excluded from the customs value in accordance with Article 166 and Annexe 25 of Commission Regulation 2454/93 (apportionment of airfreight costs), provided the airfreight costs are shown separately on the invoice, or can be evidenced by alternative satisfactory means.

The costs of containerisation and for a container terminal in the EU can be excluded from the Customs value where they are separately charged for. Similarly, a charge made for demurrage[1] as a result of a delay after arrival of the goods at the place of introduction can be excluded, but charges for delay before arrival of the goods at the place of introduction are to be included.

4.16.2 Surcharges and currency adjustments

Surcharges known as "bunker adjustment factors" are raised by shipping lines to take account of fluctuations in the price of marine fuel. A similar "fuel surcharge" is applied where goods are transported by air to compensate for fluctuations in the price of aviation fuel. Neither type of surcharge can be excluded from the customs value. All of the following surcharges are also considered to be part of the cost of transporting the goods to the place of introduction in the EU and must be included in the customs value:

- "Peak season" surcharge;
- "Security" surcharge;
- "War risk" surcharge; and
- "UK Port Congestion" charge.

In addition, any other payment or surcharge charged by the shipping line, airline or carrier of the goods, which does not relate to a cost incurred, or an activity or operation taking place after the arrival of the goods at the place of introduction must be included. Where the surcharge is made in connection with transport by air, it may be already be included in the total air transport costs declared for apportionment purposes so importers should check their commercial documents with this regard.

---

[1] The detention of a ship by the freighter beyond the time allowed for loading, unloading, or sailing.

VALUATION DECLARATIONS AND STATEMENTS

If an agent, rather than the shipping line/carrier of the goods, bills a "currency adjustment factor" it may be left out of the customs value, subject to evidence being produced to substantiate the actual total cost of transporting the goods. In all other situations the charge is dutiable.

Foreign currency amounts must be converted to sterling in arriving at the customs value. This must include the charges for freight or insurance.

4.16.3 Insuring the goods in transit

The cost of insuring the goods up to the place of importation in the EU against loss or damage in transit is to be included. However, if the insurance premium covers the whole journey, only the cost of insurance cover for the journey up to the EU border has to be included, but only where this element can be separately distinguished (the cost of any separate cover for the journey after the EU border can be excluded). Importers should note that if their insurance covers more than one importation, or relates to other items as well as the imported goods, the cost of that insurance must be apportioned and the appropriate amount included in the customs value. HMRC provide examples of how to apportion a periodic insurance premium to individual consignments in Notice 252, section 45.

4.16.4 Rates of exchange

If all or part of any amount to be taken into account in arriving at the customs value, including freight or insurance, is shown in a foreign currency then it must be converted to sterling. A fixed rate of exchange is to be used when:
- the contract of sale specifies this; and
- the seller is to receive payment in sterling.

Where the supplier requires payment in a foreign currency and the invoices are priced in sterling at a fixed rate of exchange (quoted in the contract of sale), then that rate of exchange must be used. The resulting foreign currency amount must be reconverted to sterling at the HMRC "official" rate of exchange applicable at the time of importation. HMRC publishes "Period rates of Exchange" for such purposes which are available from HMRC by contacting the National Helpline.

Where the contract does not stipulate that a fixed rate of exchange is to be used (see above) then the importer must use the rate of exchange published by HMRC at the time the entry to free circulation is accepted. However, for periodic declarations, the importer may ask HMRC to accept a single exchange rate based on the rate applicable on the first day of the period covered by the declaration in question.

4.17 Valuation declarations and statements

A "Valuation Declaration" is a form that provides HMRC with information about the value declared on the SAD/C88. Importers need only complete a

valuation declaration when asked to do so by HMRC, most likely only on a post-importation audit. Two forms are to be used:
- form C105A when using Method 1; and
- form C105B when using any of Methods 2 – 6.

Forms C105A and C105B can be signed by any person (natural or legal) who:
- resides or has a place of business in the EU, and
- who has the information needed to answer the questions on the forms.

Where the forms are completed for a company, the person signing must be a responsible representative of the company (for example, a director, company secretary, or a manager). Any of these persons may authorise an employee to sign on the company's behalf. Clearing agents may also sign these forms on behalf of the importer when authorised to do so.

Importers should note that the person signing a valuation declaration is responsible for the accuracy and completeness of the particulars given on the form and must be in possession of all the facts relating to the sale upon which the declared Customs value is based.

4.18 "Season Ticket" valuation statements

An individual valuation declaration should normally accompany the import entry for goods liable to import duty where the value of the goods exceeds £6,000. However, if dutiable goods are regularly imported, the importer can save time by completing and registering a general valuation statement (form C109A). This statement can last for up to three years, provided that the terms and conditions of supply in that period do not change.

Form C109A must be signed by the importer or someone authorised by the importer to do so, such as a director, company secretary, manager, partner, or sole proprietor. A form signed by an authorised employee must be accompanied by the letter of authority, signed by one of the accepted signatories. If there are any changes to the importer's registration details or terms of trading, they must notify the HMRC General Valuation Registration Unit that will advise whether a new application form is required; otherwise, a reminder will be issued to the importer three years after the date of registration.

4.19 Valuation rules for other Customs procedures

The following variations apply when determining the customs value for a number of Customs-approved procedures.

4.19.1 Customs warehousing

The importer must declare a value for statistical purposes, which will also be used for warehouse stock control purposes. When the goods are finally removed to free circulation any of the six Methods or SPVs and SIVs for fresh fruit and vegetables can be used. If Method 1 is used it does not have to be based on the last sale before entry into the warehouse and can therefore be based on any of the prices paid by any buyer in a series of sales before entry of the goods into free circulation. This includes any sales in the warehouse. However, the rules on completing valuation declarations set out above must be borne in mind.

The customs value of goods removed from warehouse to free circulation is to be computed at the time the goods are physically removed from the customs warehouse. This means that any elements making up the value for duty, for example price, freight and insurance charges, which are invoiced in a foreign currency will have to be converted to sterling at the Customs period rate of exchange in force at the time the goods are entered for removal from the warehouse.

There is a fundamental difference, however, where goods are entered to a "type D" Customs warehouse. In this case, the customs value is established at the time of entry of the goods to the warehouse. The importer has the option to use the rate of exchange applicable when the goods are removed from the Customs warehouse at the time when the customs debt is incurred. The actual cost of warehousing can be excluded from the customs value.

4.19.2 Outward Processing Relief (OPR)

As explained in section **3.6** above, OPR is a regime in which the import duty on goods that have been exported from the EU for a process to be performed on them and for their re-importation from a third country/territory, is only due on the added value of the processing. Determining the value for customs import duty purposes of the processing is as follows:

4.19.2.1 *Where the processor charges for the cost of the process*

Method 1 must be tried (see section **4.1**) where the customs value will be based on the cost of the process. All of the following items must be included in the customs value if not already in the processor's charge:
- the value of the exported goods (where the goods are purchased from an unrelated person, the cost of acquisition is to be used. Where the goods are produced by the importer or a related person, the cost of production is to be used);
- the value of any material rejected, lost or wasted before, during or after the process; and
- any third country/territory import duty or similar levy.

Outward freight and insurance are not to be included in the built-up value. The exception to this is when the temporarily exported goods are invoiced "CIF" and the outward freight and insurance is not separately distinguishable, in which case the outward freight and insurance is to be included in the built-up value.

4.19.2.2 *Where the processor does not charge for the cost of the process*

As no payment is made, Method 1 cannot be used. The importer must try:

VALUATION DECLARATIONS AND STATEMENTS

- Methods 2 or 3 if they import identical or similar processed goods under Method 1;
- Method 4 if they sell the processed goods or identical or similar processed goods to unrelated customers in the EU;
- Method 5 if they can obtain the detailed costings of the processed goods; *or*
- Method 6 if none of these Methods can be used. The customs value can be based on the charge that would have been made for the process. In this case, the additions detailed in **4.19.2.1** above have to be made.

For further details refer to HMRC Notice 235: *Outward Process Relief*.

4.20 Imported replacement products
The customs value of the imported replacement products is determined as follows:

4.20.1 Where a charge is made for the replacement products
Method 1 must be tried where the customs value will be based on the charge made for the replacement products. If this charge has been reduced to take account of the value of the exported goods, the amount of the reduction must be added back to arrive at the customs value. If the amount of the reduction is unknown, the importer must include in the customs value the 'FOB' export value of the exported goods.

4.20.2 Where no charge is made for the replacement products
No duty is due on goods which have been repaired or replaced free of charge under warranty or similar arrangements. Relief is also allowed on all costs involved, including outward and return freight and insurance – see HMRC Notice *235 Outward Process Relief*.

4.20.3 Inward Processing Relief
The customs value of the goods is determined at the time the goods are entered to the relief by using one of the six valuation Methods. Details are found in HMRC Notice 221: *Inward Processing Relief*.

4.20.4 Valuation rules for import VAT
The value of imported goods for VAT purposes is based on the customs valuation even where no import duty is due on the goods. In order to calculate the value for VAT all of the following costs must be added to the customs import duty valuation, unless already included:
- all incidental expenses such as commission, packing, transport and insurance costs incurred up to the goods' first destination in the UK, i.e. not just to the place of importation;
- all such incidental expenses where they result from transport to a further place of destination in the EU, if that place is known at the time of importation;
- any customs import duty or levy payable on importation into the UK; plus

- any Excise duty or other charges payable on importation into the UK (except the VAT itself).

Unlike for import duty where buying commission can be excluded from the duty calculation, it must be included in determining the value for import VAT. However, for imported works of art, collectors' items etc. "buyer's premium" is not to be included – see section **4.20.5.1**.

Payments to exploit 'intellectual property' such as royalties and licence fees can also be excluded as VAT is self-assessed within the business' VAT accounts under the "Reverse Charge" procedure – see HMRC Notice 741A: *VAT Place of Supply of Services*[2], and section 12.

Any discount offered for prompt payment is also excluded, provided that the discount is still available at the date of import.

If the price paid or payable is shown in a foreign currency, it must be converted into sterling. This includes any other part of the value shown in foreign currency for example transport, insurance etc. The rules set out in section **4.16.4** above should be followed.

HMRC has provided three methods for importers to value the incidental expenses for import VAT valuation purposes when importing goods. These are by using the actual costs ("Method One"), using nationally agreed rates ("Method Two") and by individual agreement with the HMRC "Entry Processing Unit" (EPU) ("Method Three").

4.20.4.1 Method One
This requires the actual costs to be declared at the time that the goods are imported, being the time when the Customs debt is incurred or would have been incurred if the goods were subject to customs import duty. In cases where the costs are later found to be incorrect, for example if additional storage costs are incurred, the amount(s) paid will need to be adjusted after importation.

4.20.4.2 Method Two
HMRC has agreed with trade bodies the following nationally agreed rates to estimate the value of all incidental expenses that are to be included in the import VAT value. The rates, however, are intended only for the international movement of goods that terminate in the UK and represent the average costs of handling, storage, submitting the SAD/C88 and transport to their final UK destination. Therefore, where the goods are moving to another Member State, the import value should be based on either Method One or Method Three.

A major benefit of Method Two is that post-importation adjustments are not required. Additionally, HMRC will not seek to collect the arrears of import VAT if it is found that the actual costs of the movement exceed the average

---

[2] www.gov.uk/government/publications/vat-notice-741a-place-of-supply-of-services

rates that have been used in Method Two, unless the importer is either not registered for VAT, or is unable to recover all of its input tax because it is partially exempt or makes both "business" and "non-business" supplies using the imported goods, for example a charity or a Health Authority etc.

The rates as at March 2016 are:

Group	Rates
Group A airfreight	40 pence per chargeable kilo or a minimum amount of £100 to be added to the value at the time of importation, whichever is the greater.
Group B Surface freight groupage/consolidation consignments by trailer, rail wagon or container	Delivery and handling combination of £90 per gross weight tonne plus a flat 'other ancillaries' rate of £80 per consignment, minimum £170, to be added to the value at the time of importation.
Group C Surface freight full load consignments by trailer, rail wagon or container	£550 per full load consignment to be added to the value at the time of importation.

4.20.4.3 Method Three

Where either Method One or Method Two are considered inappropriate or impractical to use, the importer can negotiate their individual valuation agreement with the local HMRC EPU or local "Excise and Inland Customs Office". Details of EPUs and ICOs can be obtained from the HMRC National VAT Helpline. Again, once the importer has agreed an individual valuation method with HMRC, post-importation adjustments are not required.

4.20.5 Special VAT valuation rules

A number of import VAT valuation rules apply for specific goods, as set out below:

- Hydrocarbon oils and certain racehorses – standard values have been agreed for certain goods, such as racehorses imported for auction and hydrocarbon oils and complete details are available from the relevant Trade Associations.
- Certain imported works of art, antiques and collectors' items – these are entitled to a reduced valuation at importation, giving an effective VAT rate of 5%. Details of how to calculate the reduced valuation are given in VAT Notice 702: *imports*[3] and in section **4.20.5.1** below.
- Computer software – details of how to value computer software are given in VAT Notice 702: *imports* and in section **4.20.5.2** below.

---

[3] www.gov.uk/government/publications/vat-notice-702-imports/

VALUATION DECLARATIONS AND STATEMENTS

- Goods re-imported after process or repair abroad – details are given in VAT Notice 702: *imports* and in **section 4.20.5.3** below.

4.20.5.1 *Works of art, antiques and collectors' items*

Certain works of art, antiques and collectors' items are entitled to a reduced valuation at importation, which is obtained by:
- calculating a value for import duty using the appropriate duty method (see above Methods 1 to 6);
- adding any additional costs (see section **4.2**);
- multiplying the total by 25%; and
- applying the 20% rate to this value (standard rate of VAT at March 2016).

The result is an 'effective VAT rate' of 5%. An imported work of art, antique or collectors' item will be eligible for the reduced rate provided that it had not been exported from the UK less than 12 months before the date of importation.

As set out in section **4.20.4**, commissions connected with an importation of goods are normally included as part of the overall value of goods for import VAT purposes. However, this general rule no longer applies in respect of certain imports of works of art, antiques and collectors' pieces.

Where works of art, antiques and collectors' pieces are temporarily admitted into the UK and sold by auction while subject to the TA regime (see section **3.8** above), the auctioneer should charge commission to the buyer, known as "buyer's premium". Until 1 September 2006, the VAT treatment was that, following their sale by auction, where the auctioned goods were removed from the TA regime and imported into the UK, the buyer's premium was included in the value of the goods for import VAT purposes. That meant, however, that because the goods attracted an effective reduced rate of VAT (equivalent to 5%), the buyer's premium was also taxed at this effective reduced rate of VAT. This was challenged in the Court of Justice of the European Union (CJEU) which ruled that the commission should be taxed at the standard rate of VAT.

Therefore, following the CJEU's ruling and for all imports after 1 September 2006, buyer's premium is not included in the value for import VAT purposes for works of art, antiques and collectors' items sold at auction under the TA regime and when subsequently imported into the UK. Alternative treatment for such imports has been agreed across the EU with the auctioneer/purchaser treating the transaction as a standard-rated "domestic" supply. Full details are provided to auctioneers and other purchasers in Notice 718: *The VAT Margin Scheme and global accounting*.[4]

The following articles are treated as works of art, antiques etc. and subject to the reduced value for VAT valuation rules:

---

[4] www.gov.uk/government/publications/vat-notice-718-the-vat-margin-scheme-and-global-accounting

VALUATION DECLARATIONS AND STATEMENTS

Articles	Tariff heading
Works of art	
• Pictures, collages and similar decorative plaques, paintings and drawings, executed entirely by hand by the artist, other than plans and drawings for architectural, engineering, industrial, commercial, topographical or similar purposes, hand-decorated manufactured articles, theatrical scenery, studio back cloths or the like of painted canvas.	9701
• Original engravings, prints and lithographs, being impressions produced in limited numbers directly in black and white or in colour of one or several plates executed entirely by hand by the artist, irrespective of the process or of the material employed by him, but not including any mechanical or photomechanical process.	9702 00 00
• Original sculptures and statuary, in any material, provided that they are executed entirely by the artist, sculpture casts.	9703 00 00
• Tapestries and wall textiles, made by hand from original designs provided by artists, provided that there are not more than eight copies of each.	5805 00 00
• Individual pieces of ceramics executed entirely by the artist and signed by him/her.	
• Enamels on copper, executed entirely by hand, limited to eight numbered copies bearing the signature of the artist or the studio, excluding articles of jewellery and goldsmiths' and silversmiths' wares.	
• Photographs taken by the artist, printed by him or under his supervision, signed and numbered and limited to 30 copies, all sizes and mounts included.	
Antiques	
• Objects other than works of art or collectors' items, which are more than 100 years old.	9706 00 00
Collectors' items	
• Postage or revenue stamps, postmarks, first-day covers, pre-stamped stationery and the like, franked or if unfranked not being of legal tender and not being intended for use as legal tender.	9704 00 00
• Collections and collectors' pieces of zoological, botanical, mineralogical, anatomical, historical, archaeological, palaeontological, ethnographic or numismatic interest. Also included as collectors' pieces of historical interest are: a) motor vehicles, irrespective of their date of manufacture, which can be proved to have been used in the course of an historic event; and b) motor-racing vehicles, which can be proved to be designed, built and used solely for competition and have scored significant sporting successes at prestigious national or international events.	9705 00 00

Items of historical significance[5]
- Postage stamps issued by a country to mark its independence;
- Motor vehicles which:
    - Possess a certain scarcity value;
    - are not normally used for their original purpose;
    - are the subject of transactions outside the normal trade in similar utility vehicles;
    - are of high value; and
    - illustrate a significant step in the evolution of human achievements or a period of that evolution.

This includes such motor vehicles as:
- Vehicles in their original state, without substantial changes to the chassis, steering or breaking system, engine etc, at least 30 years old and of a model or type which is no longer in production; and
- All vehicles manufactured before 1950, even if not in running order.

(The above notes and criteria also apply to motorcycles).

Products designed by famous historical craftsmen, such as:
- De Morgan or William Morris tiles and ceramics;
- Peter Waals desks and tables;
- Mcintosh and William Morris home furnishings (for example, carpets, curtains, vases, clocks, chairs); and
- decorative glassware produced by Galle, Lalique and Tiffany.

Medals (Military)
- All military medals awarded up to and including World War 1;
- medals awarded after World War 1 which are inscribed with the recipient's name; and
- individual military medals awarded after World War 1 for an act of gallantry, outstanding service etc whether or not they bear the recipient's name.

Medals (Civilian)
- All civil medals awarded individually which bear the recipient's name.

Militaria
- General military items up to and including World War 1 such as weapons, badges etc, items of militaria which belonged to, or were used by, a famous person who won a gallantry award.

4.20.5.2 *Computer software*

Software is normally understood to be defined as "off the shelf" or "bespoke". The customs value of imported software has to be determined according to the

---

[5] An article which is not 100 years old may be eligible for the scheme under this heading if it is of historical significance because of its uniqueness, or by having a direct association with an historical person or event, or is a rare example marking an important change in technical or artistic development in a particular field. Items, which were mass-produced or are merely the products of a bygone age, are unlikely to be eligible. The list of examples provided by HMRC is by no means exhaustive, but gives general guidelines on the types of articles that are eligible under this heading.

VALUATION DECLARATIONS AND STATEMENTS

normal valuation rules. HMRC use the phrases "Normalised" for off-the-shelf software and "Specific" for bespoke software. Under Method 1, the customs value should be based on the price actually paid or payable for both the carrier medium and the data and instructions (the software) on it. No distinction is drawn between normalised and specific software for customs import duty valuation purposes.

Normalised software is comprised of a coherent set of programs and support material and often includes the service of installation, training and maintenance. Packages such as personal computer software, home computer software and games are classed as normalised. The category also includes standard packages adapted at the supplier's instigation to include security or similar devices.

Conversely, specific or bespoke software is tailored to the customer's special requirements, either as a unique program or an adaptation from a standard program. It is also inter-company information data and accounts, enhancements and updates of existing 'specific' programs, and enhancements and updates of existing 'normalised' programs supplied under contractual obligation to customers who have bought the original program.

The VAT value of imported computer software is determined as follows:
- **Normalised software**. Import VAT is due on the customs value of the software, for example, the total value of the carrier medium and the data and instructions (the software) on it, adjusted where appropriate in accordance with VAT Act 1994, Section 21 (2).
- **Specific software**. No import VAT is due. The total amount of the value of both the data and the instructions (the software) and the carrier medium is treated as the consideration for a supply of services and is subject to VAT on the value of those imported services, normally under the "reverse charge" mechanism in the Member State where the customer normally resides or is established.

To value imported goods for VAT purposes that have been removed from a Customs warehouse, importers need to follow the rules set out in section **4.19.1** above. Some treatment or processes performed in a Customs warehouse, an Excise or a Customs and Excise warehouse may affect the declared VAT value. In these cases, the importer is advised by HMRC to refer to Notice 702: *imports*,[6] and Notice 702/9: *VAT - import Customs Procedures*.[7]

4.20.5.3 *Goods re-imported after process or repair abroad*
The value for import VAT purposes is the aggregated value of the original goods less the value of the goods when exported for process or repair abroad,

---

[6]www.gov.uk/government/publications/vat-notice-702-imports/vat-notice-702-imports#importing-computer-software
[7]www.gov.uk/government/publications/vat-notice-7029-vat-import-customs-procedures

VALUATION DECLARATIONS AND STATEMENTS

i.e. the value of the actual process or repair work added to the goods. Businesses are required to produce evidence of the value of the goods when exported and the value added in the processing or repair.

4.21 Special VAT valuation rules for Customs Suspensive arrangements

Notice 702/9: *VAT – import Customs Procedures* explains the VAT valuation rules for a range of customs suspensive reliefs, these being goods which are:
- entered into and removed from customs suspensive regimes;
- supplied within Customs Warehouses;
- entered into and removed from end-use relief;
- re-imported under OPR after process/repair or replacement; and
- placed under transit.

For import VAT purposes goods are generally treated as imported when they arrive in the UK and are entered to free circulation. This can be either by direct import (from a place outside the Customs territory of the EU) or indirect import (removal to the UK via another Member State within the EU).

However, if goods are placed under one of the following suspensive arrangements, duty and import VAT will only become due when they are removed to free circulation in the UK.

The suspensive arrangements are:
- IP-Suspension;
- temporary admission with total relief from customs duties;
- processing under customs control;
- customs warehousing;
- external transit (T1) arrangements or internal transit (T2) arrangements (although internal transit is not a customs suspensive procedure it is included here as import VAT may become due if the goods are subsequently removed to free circulation); and
- temporary storage (although such goods are not strictly under customs arrangements, goods arriving from outside the EU have the status of temporary storage until they are entered and cleared to free circulation or another procedure)

Suspension of import VAT does not apply to goods entered to:
- IP Drawback;
- TA with partial relief from customs duty;
- end-use relief other than goods for the continental shelf; and
- outward processing relief.

Any non-Community goods imported from outside the Customs territory of the EU which are not subject to a positive duty rate may be placed under IP (suspension), TA (total relief), customs warehousing or under external transit for import VAT purposes only. Any goods imported which are liable for import VAT only are not entitled to be entered for relief under OPR, TA partial relief or IP (drawback).

Any goods imported from one of the special territories outside the Customs territory of the EU may be imported to a Customs suspensory relief/end-use relief for import VAT purposes. Goods can be transferred from one suspensive regime to another, for example customs warehousing, to IP without the payment of import VAT.

Where a UK business receives from a taxable person in another Member State goods that have been held in one of the suspensive arrangements VAT must be accounted for on the acquisition in accordance with the normal rules, even though the import VAT remains suspended. Further, VAT is to be charged and accounted for in the UK where the acquirer supplies the goods to another person, subject to the following rules:

Goods in temporary storage.
Goods supplied to a purchaser who is required to make the import entry and between the arrival of the goods in the UK but prior to a customs entry being made may be zero-rated.

Goods under Temporary Admission
The supply of goods to a person established outside the EU may be disregarded where the goods remain eligible for TA arrangements.

Second-hand goods and works of art
The supply of second-hand goods and works of art held under Temporary Admission may be disregarded where they were imported with a view to their sale by auction or the works of art were imported with a view to a possible sale.

The sale of the second-hand goods by auction or the works of art may also be disregarded provided the sale occurs whilst the goods are still subject to Temporary Admission relief. A supply involving a change of ownership may also be disregarded.

Any services relating to such supplies e.g. auctioneers' charges, can be similarly disregarded, but these costs must be included in the value for VAT at importation.

In order to reclaim the import VAT as input tax the importer must hold proof of importation and the payment of the VAT. This is usually the import VAT Certificate, Form C79.

The certificates are sent to the VAT-registered person whose VAT registration number, plus a three-digit suffix, is shown in Box 8 of the import entry. The whole number is known as the Economic Operator Registration Identification Number (EORI) – see section **2.4**. Extreme care to use the correct EORI is required because if an incorrect number is used the VAT paid may not appear

VALUATION DECLARATIONS AND STATEMENTS

on the importer's own certificate and may even end up on another person's certificate. Similarly, importers could find another importer's import VAT on their certificate.

VAT Certificates cover accounting transactions made in each calendar month and are issued on or about the 12th day of the following month. For example, October certificates (certificates covering transactions with accounting dates in October) are issued on or about 12 November. Even where security for VAT has been provided, this action itself does not entitle the recovery of the VAT. VAT can only be reclaimed when it has been paid to release the goods to free circulation. Section **6.6** provides more details about the recovery of import VAT and Import VAT Certificates.

4.21.1 Continental shelf goods

Certain goods imported for the continental shelf, are eligible for end-use relief. Import VAT is also relieved for these goods under Regulation 120 of the VAT Regulations 1995.

Goods eligible for shipwork end-use relief for the Continental Shelf include offshore fixed drilling or production platforms within sub heading 8430 49 and floating or submersible drilling or production platforms of Tariff sub heading 8905 20, irrespective of whether the fixed or floating platforms are located within or outside UK territorial waters and tubes, pipes, cables and connection pieces linking drilling or production platforms to the mainland.

They cover goods intended for:
- incorporation in offshore drilling or production platforms/workpoints for the purpose of their construction, repair, maintenance, fitting out, conversion;
- equipping those platforms/workpoints;
- downhole well construction;
- subsequent shipment to a platform/workpoint which are required to be tested before use; and
- training, provided that at the end of the programme, the goods are shipped to a platform/workpoint.

For such eligible use import VAT can be relieved under Regulation 120 of the VAT Regulations 1995.

4.21.2 Onward Supply Relief

Goods imported for processing and supply to a customer in another Member State under IP suspension or processing under customs control may claim onward supply relief once the imported goods are entered to free circulation in the UK and dispatched to the Member State unprocessed or unaltered. See section **5.16** for further details.

The removal of non-Community goods entered into free circulation in the course of an onward zero-rated supply to another Member State may qualify for onward supply relief subject to meeting the conditions set out in and Notice 702/7.[8]

Further details of Onward Supply Relief are set out in section **5.16**.

4.21.3 Goods imported under Temporary Admission Relief and "ATA Carnets"

Import VAT is suspended for goods entered to TA total relief. However, under TA partial relief, import VAT must be paid at the time of entry. Therefore, goods which are free of customs duty and subject only to import VAT cannot be entered to TA partial relief. The supply of goods held under TA to persons established outside the EU may be disregarded for VAT purposes.

Duty, import VAT and compensatory interest are due when the goods are entered TA to free circulation in the UK. However, compensatory interest is not applicable to the import VAT liability of such diversions and is not applicable to:

- works of art, collectors' items and antiques diverted to free circulation – Commission Regulation 2454/93 Article 576 (3a);
- personal effects – Commission Regulation 2454/93 Article 563;
- disaster relief material – Commission Regulation 2454/93 Article 565;
- sound image or data carrying media / publicity material – Commission Regulation 2454/93 Article 568;
- goods subject to satisfactory acceptance tests – Commission Regulation 2454/93 Article 573 (b);
- goods for exhibition or use at a public event – Commission Regulation 2454/93 Article 576 (1); and
- goods for approval – Commission Regulation 2454/93 Article 576 (2), or
- goods other than newly manufactured imported with a view to sale by auction – Commission Regulation 2454/93 Article 576 (3b).

For certain works of art, antiques and collectors' items reduced valuation rules can apply which, in effect, reduces the VAT rate applicable to the goods – see **4.20.5.1**.

Compensatory interest is also not due when:
- the period for interest is less than one month;
- the amount of interest that would be due is less than €20;
- duty was secured by cash deposit at least equal to the amount of duty due;
- goods are imported to TA with partial relief from import duties;
- the TA goods are diverted to free circulation to allow export preference to be claimed (for example on products produced using TA goods); and

---

[8] www.gov.uk/government/publications/vat-notice-7027-import-vat-relief-for-goods-supplied-onward-to-another-country-in-the-ec/

- the goods being diverted to free circulation are waste and/or scrap from the destruction of TA goods or it can be proved that it has become impossible or uneconomic to re-export TA goods.

A SAD/C88 must be completed when diverting the goods in the normal way and the amount of compensatory interest that will become due must be placed on deposit. Written evidence to support the claim, for example a note of confirmation from the supplier refusing to accept the goods on return, should accompany the diversion entry. The supporting evidence must demonstrate that the circumstances did not arise from negligence or deception and that to re-export the goods would be impossible or uneconomic. Further, the claimant must also explain how the circumstances have changed since the goods were imported.

ATA Carnets

An ATA Carnet is an internationally recognised booklet of vouchers which replace the normal customs declarations. It avoids the need to provide security for customs duty when import goods are imported temporarily and they simplify the customs formalities for goods temporarily exported or imported.

In the UK, Chambers of Commerce and Industry issue ATA Carnets. As the Chambers provide a guarantee to cover any customs duty and other charges that become payable on the goods covered by the ATA Carnet (through the International Guarantee Chain), they may make a charge for the issue of an ATA Carnet and require the ATA Carnet holder to provide them, in turn, with a guarantee or other security for the duty and charges. Any goods imported on an ATA carnet will not be liable to either customs duty or import VAT providing they are re-exported prior to expiry of the carnet.

HMRC provide information on ATA Carnets in Notice 104.[9]

4.21.4 Customs warehousing

In the UK there are three kinds of warehouses, "Customs warehouses", "Tax warehouses" and "Fiscal warehouses". HMRC has provided in Notice 232[10] the following table of what classes of goods can be warehoused in each type:

Warehouse regime	Goods	Customs Duty (inc CAP charges)	Import VAT	Supply VAT	Excise Duty
Customs Warehouse	Third country goods of any kind whether subject to a positive rate of duty or not.	Suspended	Suspended	Suspended	Suspended

---

[9] www.gov.uk/government/publications/notice-104-ata-and-cpd-carnets.
[10] www.gov.uk/government/publications/notice-232-customs-warehousing/

Tax Warehouse (includes both manufacturing premises and storage premises)	Third country goods on which customs duty has been paid; Community goods; UK goods – mineral (hydrocarbon oils), alcohol and alcoholic beverages, manufactured tobacco	Paid	Paid	Suspended	Suspended
Fiscal Warehouse	Certain specified goods that are in free circulation (see Notice)	N/A	N/A	Suspended	N/A

No import VAT is due when goods are placed in a Customs warehouse. Import VAT only becomes due when they are removed from the warehouse to free circulation and it is normally payable together with any customs or excise duty suspended by the person removing the goods. Goods removed from Customs warehouses are subject to the normal valuation rules.

Supplies of goods within a Customs warehouse are treated as taking place outside the UK. Therefore, all such supplies are usually disregarded for VAT. Again, import VAT only becomes due when they are removed from the warehouse to free circulation and it is normally payable together with any customs or excise duty suspended by the person removing the goods.

However, VAT will be due if warehoused goods are sold to unregistered distributors who retail the goods on to the final consumers, or use the goods themselves. In these circumstances, the VAT due on such supplies is levied in addition to the import VAT, which remains due when the goods are removed from the warehouse.

When 'non-Community' goods are removed from a Customs warehouse to free circulation import VAT will become due and is normally payable by the person who removes the goods. The VAT due will be based upon the import value of the goods.

When imported goods are removed from a Customs warehouse to free circulation in the UK any import VAT/customs duty due or deferred is

VALUATION DECLARATIONS AND STATEMENTS

controlled by the importer completing a SAD/C88 unless any of the following apply:
- they have also been warehoused for excise duty in a customs warehouse, in which case excise duty may be suspended if the goods are now to be placed in a tax warehouse, but any duty and VAT must be paid when the goods are removed from the Customs warehouse;
- they qualify for relief from import VAT;
- the goods are removed to another Member State and Onward Supply Relief is claimed; and
- the goods are ex IP drawback and import VAT has already been paid.

While goods are under the respective warehouse regime none of Customs duty, Excise duty or Import VAT must be paid.

The supply of goods for export or their supply to a taxable person in another EU Member State where the goods move outside the Customs warehouse arrangements may be zero-rated whereas goods moving directly to a Customs warehouse in another EU Member State under the Customs warehouse transfer arrangements are disregarded as a UK supply.

However, in both cases the supplies must be included in EU Sales lists (Form VAT 101) covering the time of removal and also in Box 8 of the corresponding VAT return (Form VAT 100).

Storage charges and usual forms of handling carried out on goods under the Customs warehouse arrangements can be zero-rated, but services such as brokerage, agent's fees and transport between warehouses are excluded. Services which are exempt from VAT when supplied outside the warehouse remain exempt.

Any VAT or customs duty due in respect of previously zero-rated services should be accounted for together with any import VAT and customs duty payable when the goods are removed from the warehouse using a Form C88. The value of the services to be taxed should be entered in Box 47 of the Form C88.

To obtain zero-rating of handling within the warehouse the importer must issue the supplier with an eligibility certificate before the services are actually supplied. The Certificate is set out in Section 12 of Notice 702/9.[11] A certificate is not required to zero-rate warehousekeeper's storage charges. Such supplies of services are normally automatically zero rated. The invoice issued by the warehouse keeper to allow zero rating should include the words *'in accordance with Section 18C (1) VAT Act 1994'* and no VAT should be charged. Surprisingly, HMRC allow warehousekeepers to standard-rate their charges if

---

[11] www.gov.uk/government/publications/vat-notice-7029-vat-import-customs-procedures/vat-notice-7029-vat-import-customs-procedures#goods-imported-under-temporary-admission-relief-ta-and-ata-carnets

VALUATION DECLARATIONS AND STATEMENTS

the customer asks them to do so. In which case, the customer should notify the warehouse keeper in writing.

Any deficiencies of warehoused goods are deemed to be removed from the Customs warehousing regime. Where deficiencies of imported goods are charged with duty, import VAT not already paid on the imported goods will also become due. Similarly, any Acquisition VAT on goods from other Member States which has not been accounted for will also be payable. However, the importer may deduct the VAT as input tax subject to the normal rules.

4.21.5 Tables showing the treatment of goods for Customs and VAT purposes (import VAT and Supply VAT) for goods received into a UK Customs warehouse

In Notice 702/9 HMRC provides the following tables of the treatment of goods for Customs and VAT purposes using Customs warehousing

Table 1 Receipt of goods into a UK Customs Warehouse and their removal to free circulation in the UK

	1. Non-Community goods received direct from a third country placed in a customs warehouse	2. Non-Community goods received direct from a third country or via another Member State on which there is a nil rate of customs duty – VAT only Customs Warehousing	3. Non-Community goods received from a third country via another Member State	4. Goods imported from special territories
Customs duty	Suspended on entry into Customs warehouse. To be paid on removal	N/A	Suspended on entry into Customs warehouse. To be paid on removal	N/A
Excise duty	Duty not due and suspended whilst in warehouse.	Duty not due and suspended whilst in warehouse.	Duty not due and suspended whilst in warehouse.	Duty not due and suspended whilst in warehouse.

VALUATION DECLARATIONS AND STATEMENTS

Import VAT	Suspended on entry to customs warehouse. To be paid on removal	Suspended on entry to customs warehouse. To be paid on removal. Any VAT due in respect of zero-rated services should be paid on removal	Suspended on entry to customs warehouse. To be paid on removal.	Suspended on entry to customs warehouse. To be paid on removal. Any VAT due in respect of zero-rated services should be paid on removal.
Acquisition VAT	N/A	N/A	If the goods are the subject of an acquisition on arrival in the warehouse VAT is to be accounted for on the acquirer's VAT return for the period in which the acquisition tax point falls.	N/A
Supply VAT				
Extra-EU Trade Statistics	Due on arrival in the UK, and on removal from the warehouse to UK free circulation	N/A	Due on arrival in the UK, and on removal from the warehouse to UK free circulation	N/A
Intrastat Declaration	N/A	N/A	N/A	N/A
EU Boxes on VAT Return	N/A	N/A	N/A	N/A

VALUATION DECLARATIONS AND STATEMENTS

Table 2 Receipt of goods into a UK customs warehouse and their removal other than to free circulation in the UK

	1. Non-Community goods for direct export to a country outside the EU	2. Non-Community goods for indirect export to a country outside the EU	3. Goods transferred to another Member State under a duty suspensive regime
Customs duty	Not Paid	Not paid, Goods must move under CPEI arrangements or transit.	Not paid, Goods must move under CPEI arrangements or transit.
Excise Duty	Not Paid	Not Paid	Not Paid
Import VAT	N/A	Any VAT which would be due on removal to UK free circulation is not payable.	Any VAT which would be due on removal to UK free circulation is not payable. Otherwise outward movements of goods may be zero-rated subject to the normal conditions for intra EU trade.
Supply VAT	Supplies of goods removed from the UK may be zero-rated as exports (subject to the normal rules)	Supplies of goods removed from the UK may be zero-rated as exports (subject to the normal rules)	Supplies direct into a customs warehouse in another Member State are outside the scope of UK VAT.
Extra-EU Trade Statistics	Export declaration.	Export declaration.	Export declaration.
Intrastat	N/A	N/A	N/A
EU Boxes on VAT Return	N/A	N/A	N/A
EC Sale Listings	N/A	N/A	Completion required
	4. Non-Community goods moved to another Member State on which customs duty is paid on removal	5. Non-Community goods transferred to IP suspension in the UK from a customs warehouse.	6. Non-Community goods transferred to IP drawback in the UK from a customs warehouse
Customs duty	Paid on removal from customs warehouse.	Continues to be suspended to be paid on final removal from IP if IP if not discharged.	To be paid on removal from warehouse.
Excise Duty		Continues to be	To be paid on removal

VALUATION DECLARATIONS AND STATEMENTS

		suspended if IP is not discharged.	from warehouse.
Import VAT	VAT is payable but may be relieved. If the goods are removed in the course of an onward zero-rated supply, import VAT is relieved using CPC 42 91 000.	Any import VAT due is to be paid with the customs duty.	Any import VAT due is to be paid with the customs duty.
Supply VAT		Supplies of goods under IP are subject to domestic VAT rules.	Declaration of goods under IP are subject to domestic VAT rules.
Extra -EU Trade Statistics	Declaration required on removal from customs warehouse	Declaration required on removal from customs warehouse	Declaration required on removal from customs warehouse
Intrastat	Declaration required.	N/A	N/A
EU Boxes on VAT Return	Boxes 6 & 8	N/A	N/A
EC Sale Listings	Completion required.	N/A	N/A

VALUATION DECLARATIONS AND STATEMENTS

Table 3   Goods requiring a guarantee when transferred

Note: Where no figure appears in the minimum rate of guarantee column (column 5), security should be taken on basis of the actual customs charges that may become due.

1	2	3	4	5
CN code	Description of goods	Minimum Quantity Guarantee required only when the quantity exceeds the minimum quantity shown	Sensitive goods Code Where the CN code is insufficient to identify goods concisely the CN code and sensitive goods code should be used	Minimum rate of guarantee (Euro/tonne)
0207 12 0207 14	Meat and edible offal, of the poultry of heading 0105, of fowls of the species Gallus Domesticus, Frozen	3000 Kg		
1701 11 1701 12 1701 91 1701 99	Cane or beet sugar and chemically pure sucrose in solid form	7000 Kg		
2208 20 2208 30 2208 40 2208 50 2208 60 2208 70 ex2208 90	Spirits, liquors, other spirituous beverages	5hl		} } } €2,500/hl } pure } alcohol }
2402 20	Cigarettes containing tobacco	35000 pieces		€120/1000
2403 10	Smoking tobacco, whether or not containing tobacco substitutes in any proportion	35Kg		

4.21.6 End Use Relief

End Use Relief is described in section **3.3**. End-use relief does not affect a liability to incur import VAT, which must be paid or accounted for in the normal way, unless one of the reliefs listed in Notice 702 applies – see **Chapter 5**. End-use relief does not give relief from Excise or antidumping duties which, if due, must be paid.

Aircraft

Schedule 8, Group 8 of the VAT Act 1994 allows zero-rating of aircraft or their parts providing those items are only applied to 'qualifying aircraft'. A 'qualifying aircraft' is any aircraft which is used by an airline operating for reward chiefly on international routes.

Any import VAT due must be paid at the time of importation along with the customs duty on the SAD/C88. The relief does not apply to any parts and equipment supplied to a Government Department unless either:

- they are installed or incorporated in the course of a supply which is treated as being made in the course or furtherance of a business carried on by the department; or
- the parts and equipment are to be installed or incorporated in ships or aircraft used for the purposes of providing rescue or assistance at sea.

Ships

Schedule 8, Group 8 of the VAT Act 1994 allows zero-rating of ships or their parts providing those items are only applied to 'qualifying ships'. A 'qualifying ship' is any ship of a gross tonnage of not less than 15 tons which is neither designed nor adapted for use for recreation or pleasure.

Any import VAT due must be paid at the time of importation along with the customs duty on the SAD/C88. Again, the relief does not apply to any parts and equipment supplied to a Government Department unless either:

- they are installed or incorporated in the course of a supply which is treated as being made in the course or furtherance of a business carried on by the department; or
- the parts and equipment are to be installed or incorporated in ships or aircraft used for the purposes of providing rescue or assistance at sea.

Goods for the UK "Continental Shelf"

Any imported goods that are intended for use or incorporation in UK Continental Shelf installations (oil rigs etc.) are eligible for shipwork end-use relief. This covers offshore fixed drilling or production platforms within sub heading 8430 49 and floating or submersible drilling or production platforms of Tariff sub heading 8905 20 irrespective of whether the fixed or floating platforms are located within or outside UK territorial waters and tubes, pipes, cables and connection pieces linking drilling or production platforms to the mainland.

Eligible goods are relieved from import VAT under Regulation 120 of the VAT Regulations 1995.

Goods eligible for this relief include any for:
- incorporation in offshore drilling or production platforms/workpoints for the purpose of their construction, repair, maintenance, fitting out, or conversion;
- equipping those platforms/workpoints;
- downhole well construction;
- subsequent shipment to a platform/workpoint which are required to be tested before use; and
- training, provided that at the end of the programme, the goods are shipped to a platform/workpoint.

Military end-use scheme
EU Council Regulation No EU 150/2003 lays down the conditions for the suspension of import duties on certain weapons and military equipment when they are used by, or on behalf of, the military forces of a Member State, for defending the territorial integrity of the Member State or participating in international peace keeping or support operations or for other military purposes. Import VAT which, if due, must be paid at the time of importation unless relief under Outward Processing is available – see section **3.6**.

4.21.7 Outward Processing Relief

Details of Outward Processing relief are set out in section **3.6**. Import VAT is normally due on the full value of re-imported goods unless relief is available under Regulation 124, 125 or 126 of the VAT Regulations 1995. However, the amount of import VAT chargeable on goods imported from outside the EU may be reduced if the goods have been previously exported for process or repair from the UK or any other Member State. All of the following conditions must be met:
- the goods were temporarily exported from the EU;
- at the time of exportation the goods were intended to be re-imported after completion of the treatment or process outside the EU;
- the goods are re imported after having undergone repair, process or adaptation outside the EU or having been made up or re-worked outside the EU;
- ownership of the goods was not transferred to any other person at exportation or during the time they were outside the EU; and
- a declaration is made at the time of re-importation that the above conditions have been fulfilled.

Where the eligibility criteria are met (as above) import VAT can be calculated on the following value:

VALUATION DECLARATIONS AND STATEMENTS

- the price charged for the process, repair or service, including any charge made for parts and materials; plus
- any freight and other charges (excluding insurance) paid for the transport of the goods to and from the processor's premises; plus
- any customs or excise duties or other import charges payable in the UK.

Import VAT must be paid on the full VAT value of the compensating products unless the conditions for claiming VAT relief are satisfied.

The import VAT paid by the importer can be reclaimed as input tax, subject to the normal rules. However, if the importer is unable to reclaim input tax, for example, because they are not registered for VAT, they should contact HMRC at the point of importation as soon as it is known that the goods are to be replaced. If this cannot be ascertained until after the goods have been imported the importer should contact HMRC on its VAT helpline on **0300 200 3700** (or from outside the UK on **+44 2920 501 261**) and ask for Notice 266[12] and Form C&E 1179.

Processing charges and VAT
If the process is carried out free of charge, for example because the goods are covered by a warranty, guarantee or service agreement, or where the compensating products are zero-rated in the UK, no import VAT will be due on re-importation of the compensating products.

If the supply of the goods themselves is normally zero-rated they are not liable to import VAT on return from any repair or process carried out whilst outside the EU.

All replacement goods are considered to be new imports and import VAT is therefore payable in accordance with the normal valuation rules. This applies regardless of whether any duty relief can be claimed under OPR.

Triangulation movements between Member States normally involve a change in title to the exported goods and therefore the compensating products will not normally qualify for VAT relief.

Any goods re-imported after process or repair on which VAT relief only will be claimed are not eligible for OPR authorisation and are not under OPR relief. However, VAT relief under Regulation 126 of VAT regulations 1995 may be claimed by exporting the goods under CPC 22 00 000 and entering the reimported goods to CPC 40 00 065.

Goods that are re-imported into the UK without them having been altered whilst outside the EU, other than for say any necessary running repairs that did not increase their value, can be re-imported without payment of import

---

[12] www.gov.uk/government/publications/notice-266-rejected-imports-repayment-or-remission-of-duty-and-vat/

VAT using the Returned Goods Relief – see section **3.4**. Full details are in Notice 236.[13]

4.21.8 Processing Under Customs Control

Details of Processing Under Customs Control are provided in section **3.2**. Under PCC import VAT is suspended until the goods are processed and declared to free circulation when the import VAT is paid, based on the value of the processed products, not the value at importation. Import VAT will be due on the customs value of the goods declared plus the amount of customs duty payable. Any import VAT paid may be reclaimed as input tax in the usual way subject to the normal domestic VAT rules.

VAT only PCC

Under PCC the value of the goods released to free circulation is broadly the import value plus processing costs. Given the increase in value there would be no benefit in VAT only PCC since the processed goods would be subject to the same rate of VAT as if the processed products had been imported. Consequently, HMRC will refuse applications to use PCC for VAT-only purposes.

However, goods may be imported to PCC and supplied to another Member State under the Onward Supply rules. Any customs duty is paid in the UK, but the payment of import VAT is relieved using CPC 42 91 000 and the consignee in the country of receipt then accounts for the import VAT.

4.21.9 Inward Processing Relief

Details of Inward Processing Relief are set out in section **3.1**. Under IPR import VAT is payable at diversion to free circulation. It is based on the value of the diverted goods, inclusive of duty, at first entry to IP in the EU and the rate to be applied is that of the Member State of diversion at the date of diversion. No account can be taken of changes in the value of goods following their transfer from other IP declarants, as this will have been accounted for under the normal VAT supply rules.

Where an authorisation holder is diverting a single item or several items with the same duty rate bought from another Member State, In Notice 702/9 section 8.2 HMRC explain that the import VAT due can be calculated as follows:

Duty rate	**= 10%**
Duty suspended at first entry to IP in the EU (as shown on Form INF1)	= £400
Value for duty is £400 x 10	= £4,000
Total	= £4,400
VAT is £4400 x 20%	= £ <u>880</u>

Compensatory interest charges are not included in the value for VAT purposes.

---

[13] www.gov.uk/government/publications/notice-236-returned-goods-relief/

VALUATION DECLARATIONS AND STATEMENTS

Where several items with different duty rates are diverted the authorisation holder must ask the EU supplier to confirm the value for VAT of the diverted goods at import to their country.

Suspension goods diverted on their sale to a taxable person in another Member State may be eligible for relief from import VAT under the Onward Supply Relief provisions – see section **3.6**. If the goods originally intended for process and re-export are diverted to free circulation in the UK, payment of customs duty and compensatory interest is achieved by using CPC 42 51 000.

The authorisation holder making the diversion should produce an INF1 form which has already been endorsed by the Customs authority in the first Member State. If the authorisation holder does not have an endorsed INF1, the importer should send one to the first Member State to obtain details of the amounts due.

A taxable person in the UK who holds goods under IP Suspension may claim Onward Supply Relief providing the goods are:
- eligible for zero rating under Section 30 (8), of the VAT Act 1994;
- the goods so imported are the subject to that supply under Regulation 123 of the VAT Regulations 1995; and
- the goods are removed to another Member States within one month of the date of importation.

This results in the import VAT not being paid in any EU Member State, but VAT on the supply/acquisition is accounted for by the purchaser in the EU country of Arrival.

VAT only IP
'VAT only' inward processing may be authorised for goods upon which there is no duty liability. This can arise where either:
- the rate of import duty is nil by way of the tariff rate or preferential rate being applied; or
- the goods are imported from a country that is inside the Customs Territories of the EU but not within the VAT territories – see section **1.6.2**. Import VAT will become due if the goods are diverted to free circulation (including end use).

Interestingly, the applicant is not required to be registered for VAT to qualify for this relief. Further details can be found in Notice *221 Inward Processing Relief*.[14]

4.21.10 External and Internal Transit
Transit arrangements are described in section **2.10**. Any goods placed under external transit have the customs duty and import VAT suspended. Import

---

[14] www.gov.uk/government/publications/notice-221-inward-processing-relief/

VAT and customs duty will only become due if the goods are subsequently removed to free circulation in the UK.

Goods placed under internal transit may have the import VAT suspended in particular circumstances (e.g. the 'T2F' procedure for movements to/from special territories). Any goods imported from outside the EU that are not subject to a positive duty rate may be placed under external transit for import VAT purposes only. Goods imported from a country that is inside the Customs territory of the EU (see section **1.4.2**) must be imported under internal transit for import VAT purposes (Internal T2F procedure).

All the normal procedures for discharging transit apply.

4.22 Valuation rules for trade statistics

If *ad valorem* customs duty is chargeable as a percentage of the value of the imported goods, then the value for statistical purposes will be the same as the value calculated for customs purposes under any of Methods 1 to 6.

If *ad valorem* customs duty isn't chargeable on the goods, then the value to declare for trade statistics purposes will be based on the price paid or payable to the seller. However, a number of adjustments must be made. The following items should be added to the price paid or payable when calculating the value for trade statistics:

- freight;
- insurance;
- all other costs, charges and expenses connected with the sale and delivery of the goods to the port or place of importation in the UK; and
- selling commission.

Conversely, all of the following costs must be excluded:

- buying commission;
- selling commission incurred within the UK;
- cost of transport within the UK; and
- duty or tax chargeable in the UK.

If the goods have been imported free of charge or there has been no sale, the value for trade statistics purposes is to be calculated under any of Methods 1 to 6, but the items listed in this section, if they are not already included, must be added and excluded respectively.

If the goods have been processed or repaired outside the UK then the importer must include the cost of the process or repair and the value of the goods when exported. Exchange rate conversions are necessary where the import is invoiced in foreign currency.

Full details of the value for trade statistics purposes are set out in the Tariff, Volume I, Part 14, paragraph 2.7 (for imports) and paragraph 3.1 (for exports).

VALUATION DECLARATIONS AND STATEMENTS

5 Import duty and import VAT reliefs

A range of goods can be imported into the EU free of import duty and import VAT. HMRC has issued guidance in applicable Notices all of which are available on their website in the Library section.[1] In summary, the following goods are eligible (in alphabetical order):

- Aircraft ground and security equipment – Notice 198;
- Animals for scientific research – Notice 365;
- Antiques – Notice 362;
- Blood grouping, tissue typing and therapeutic substances – Notice 369;
- Capital goods – Notice 343;
- Chemical and biological substances for research – Notice 366;
- Commercial samples of "negligible value" – Notice 367;
- Decorations and awards – Notice 364;
- Donated medical equipment – Notice 341;
- Duty Free Allowances – Notice 1;
- Electricity and natural gas;
- Fuel, animal fodder and feeding stuffs, and packing for use during transportation;
- Gold;
- Goods for disabled persons – Notice 371;
- Goods for use by a charity – Notice 317;
- Goods for test – Notice 374;
- Inherited goods – Notice 368;
- Miscellaneous documents and other related articles – Notice 342;
- Museum and gallery exhibits – Notice 361;
- Sailing "pleasurecraft" to the EU – Notice 8;
- Scientific instruments – Notice 340;
- International science projects – Notice 340;
- Private gifts (postal packages) – Notice 143;
- Returned goods – Notice 236;
- Visiting forces (NATO) – Notice 431;
- Visitors to the UK – Notice 3;
- Visual and auditory materials – Notice 373; and
- Zero-rated articles, including printed matter.

5.1 Aircraft ground and security equipment

By concession (see HMRC Notice 48: *Extra Statutory Concessions ESC 2.7*) no import VAT or import duty is chargeable on the importation of the following ground and security equipment for aircraft by an airline of another contracting state of the Convention on International Civil Aviation ("Chicago Convention"):

---

[1] www.hmrc.gsi.gov.uk/library

- all repair, maintenance and servicing equipment; material for airframes, engines and instruments; specialised aircraft repair kits; starter batteries and carts; maintenance platforms and steps; test equipment for aircraft, aircraft engines and aircraft instruments; aircraft engine heaters and coolers; ground radio equipment;
- passenger-handling equipment: passenger-loading steps; specialised passenger-weighing devices; specialised catering equipment;
- cargo-loading equipment: vehicles for moving or loading baggage, cargo, equipment and supplies; specialised cargo-loading devices; specialised cargo-weighing devices;
- component parts for incorporation into ground equipment including the items listed above;
- security equipment: weapon-detecting devices; explosives-detecting devices; intrusion detecting devices; and
- component parts for incorporation into security equipment.

Claims for relief under this concession should be addressed to the HMRC EPU where the goods are to be cleared.

5.2 Animals for scientific research – Notice 365

Both "public" and "private" establishments can claim the relief. These bodies are defined as follows:

A public establishment is a body mainly involved in education or scientific research, which can include a division of a public establishment, examples being:
- universities, university medical schools, polytechnics and similar establishments;
- National Health Service and teaching hospitals, including medical schools with research laboratories;
- mobile health laboratories;
- research laboratories of government departments; and
- laboratories or research councils and similar bodies.

A private establishment is a body again mainly involved in education or scientific research and which has applied for, and received from the Home Office, a letter confirming the designation of the establishment under the terms of the Animals (Scientific Procedures) Act 1986.

For import duty purposes the term "animal" is not restricted to mammals and vertebrates and any animal described in the Tariff, chapters 1 or 3 or under heading 30 02 which has been bred or specially prepared for scientific research to be carried out by an eligible user may be imported free of duty (Notice 365 paragraph 2.1). However, for VAT purposes, in order to obtain VAT relief, the animals must be supplied free of charge. The animals must only be used for scientific research purposes and not lent, sold or transferred to any other body or person without first notifying HMRC.

To import animals free of Customs import duty and import VAT, the private establishment must apply for a letter from the Home Office confirming it is an establishment designated under the terms of the Animals (Scientific Procedures) Act 1986. A public establishment does not need such pre-authorisation.

Full details are in Notice 365.[1]

5.3 Antiques – Notice 362

For import duty purposes, antiques of an age exceeding 100 years which are classified under heading 97.06 of the Combined Nomenclature of the EU may be imported free of import duty.

For import VAT purposes antiques which are older than 100 years which are not a work of art or any collection or collector's piece that is of zoological, botanical, mineralogical, anatomical, historical, archaeological, paleontological, ethnographic, numismatic or philatelic interest, are eligible for a reduced valuation on importation under VAT Act 1994 section 21(4) and section 21(5)(b). This results in only the following categories of antiques being eligible:

- antiques of an age exceeding 100 years including items of numismatic interest provided they are not part of any collection or a collector's piece; and
- postage and revenue stamps of an age exceeding 100 years provided they are not part of any collection or a collector's piece.

Full details of how to calculate the reduced value are contained in VAT Notice 702: *imports* (see section **5.3.5.1**).[2]

5.4 Blood grouping, tissue typing and therapeutic substances – Notice 369

The relief covers all of the following items:
- therapeutic substances of human origin, which means human blood and its derivatives (whole human blood, dried human plasma, human albumin and fixed solutions of human plasmic protein, human immunoglobulin and human fibrinogen);
- blood-grouping reagents, which means all reagents whether of human, animal, plant or other origin used for blood-type grouping and for the detection of blood incompatibilities;
- tissue-typing reagents, which means all reagents whether of human, animal, plant or other origin used for the determination of human tissue types; and

---

[1] www.gov.uk/government/publications/notice-365-importing-animals-for-scientific-research-free-of-duty-and-vat/

[2] www.gov.uk/government/publications/vat-notice-702-imports/

- the special packaging essential for the transport of the above goods and also any solvents and accessories needed for their use which may be included in the consignments.

All of the following bodies can obtain the relief:
1) A public institution or laboratory such as:
   - a Strategic Health Authority (England), A Special Health Authority, NHS Trusts (England), Primary Care Trusts (England), Health Boards in Scotland, Health and Social Service Boards (Northern Ireland), Special Health Authorities in Scotland and Ministry of Defence Hospitals;
   - public health laboratories, research laboratories of Government Departments, research laboratories of research councils and similar bodies, all blood transfusion service establishments and the National Institute for Biological Standards and Control; and
   - all schools of pharmacy, medical schools, medical schools for Scottish Universities, Medical Research Council and Registered Charities.
2) A private establishment approved by the Department of Health (DoH) to receive such goods free of duty and VAT.

It is the importer's responsibility to keep control of the goods and use them only for non-commercial medical or scientific purposes.

Details on the relief are provided in Notice 369.[3]

5.5 Capital goods– Notice 343

Capital goods and other equipment include office and shop equipment or machinery and other tools of trade; means of transport used for the purposes of production or for providing a service; computer and other technical equipment needed to run the business; and for an agricultural business, any livestock belonging to it.

Relief is unavailable on the following classes of goods and businesses:
- means of transport which are not used for the purposes of production or for providing a service;
- supplies of any kind intended for human consumption or for animal feed;
- fuel and stocks of raw materials or finished or semi-finished products, including horticultural products for sale, such as plants, shrubs and seeds; and
- livestock belonging to dealers.

The relief conditions are very restrictive with only the following classes of businesses eligible to claim relief, i.e. those which:

---

[3] www.gov.uk/government/publications/notice-369-importing-blood-grouping-tissue-typing-and-therapeutic-substances-duty-and-vat-free/

- have completely ceased their activities outside the EU Customs Union, or in the Special Territories, or in countries having a Customs Union with the EU; and
- are moving to the UK to carry on a similar activity here; and
- if merging with a UK business, will produce or provide new products or services.

For the relief, "business" is defined as an independent economic unit of production or of the service industry, including limited companies, and independent economic units of companies; self-employed people (such as artists, poets, actors and journalists) and non-profit making organisations (such as charities or philanthropic bodies).

To be eligible, the goods must:
- have belonged to and been used by your business for at least 12 months before the transfer of activities to the UK;
- be used for the same purpose in the UK;
- be appropriate to the nature and size of your business; and
- be imported from their previous location within 12 months of the date your business ceased activities there.

HMRC can waive the first and last conditions in special cases depending on the circumstances. They cite the case, for example, of political upheaval in the country where the importer's business was previously located, which prevented at least 12 months use or import within 12 months of its cessation.

For import VAT purposes, in addition to satisfying the conditions for Customs import duty relief, the business must be concerned exclusively with making taxable supplies and either have, or expect to have a taxable turnover exceeding the UK VAT registration limits (currently £83,000).[4]

Full details can be found in Notice 343.[5]

5.6 Chemical and biological substances for research – Notice 366

The following bodies can obtain the relief:
1) A public establishment mainly involved in education or scientific research (this can include a division of a public establishment). Examples are:
    - universities, university medical schools, schools of pharmacy/chemistry, polytechnics and similar educational establishments;
    - National Health Service and teaching hospitals, including medical schools and research laboratories; and

---

[4] See www/hmrc.gsi.gov.uk/library for updates to the VAT registration thresholds.
[5] www.gov.uk/government/publications/notice-343-importing-capital-goods-free-of-duty-and-vat/

- research laboratories of Government Departments, research councils and similar bodies.
2) A private establishment mainly involved in education or scientific research and approved by the HMRC "National Import Reliefs Unit" (NIRU) to receive eligible goods free of Customs import duty and import VAT.

Relief is only available where the goods are to be used for non-commercial educational or scientific research and imported by or on behalf of an eligible body. Some of the eligible goods may already be subject to a 'nil' rate of import duty in the Tariff. Most are, however, liable to VAT at the full rate of 20%. Normally, relief should be claimed at the time of import but HMRC may accept a belated claim and repay the appropriate charges subject to certain conditions.

The importer must retain adequate evidence of the destruction or disposal of the goods such as commercial records clearly identifying the goods, and when they were last possessed or used.

If the importer wishes to examine, analyse or test the goods, rather than undertake research on them or with them, they may be able to claim the alternative relief under "Importing goods for test free of duty and VAT" explained in Notice 374 – see section **5.18** below. If the goods to be used in research are not listed, the importer can apply to HMRC for the Commission to consider the addition of further substances to the list set out in Section 4 of Notice 366, but only where the Commission is satisfied the goods are not produced in the EU, and by nature are mainly or exclusively suited for research purposes.

5.7 Commercial samples – Notice 372

Commercial Samples Relief is intended for importations made for trade promotion purposes only so it is not available for personal property or for use by any private individuals. HMRC define a 'commercial sample' as an imported item that can only be used in the UK as a demonstration sample of goods in soliciting orders for the types of goods they represent from potential customers of that product.

The samples should already be prepared and presented in an acceptable manner before importation to identify then as having negligible value and are imported solely with the intention to obtain future orders for the type of goods that they represent.

Relief is not available on goods that are:
- imported without the intention of obtaining further orders;
- not presented as samples at import, but intended for subsequently making into samples, for example, unaltered rolls of fabric import to be cut up and made into swatch books, which can be used other than as samples;

- small quantities of goods which are often described or labelled as 'samples' by the sender because of the amounts involved, or, if HMRC suspect that the goods have been deliberately misdescribed as such – these are not to be considered as 'commercial samples' and should not be declared to this relief;
- goods not presented as commercial samples at import but intended for subsequently making into samples (for example, unaltered rolls of fabric you import to cut up and make into swatch books);
- any excise goods, such as alcohol or tobacco products;
- goods which can also be used other than just as commercial samples;
- goods using the Low Value Bulking Import procedures cannot be considered as commercial samples; and
- 'give-away' goods intended as trade promotion items for immediate 'on-the-spot' use or consumption, destruction or distribution free of charge to the public at an official trade fair, exhibition or similar event where there is public access and/or participation, and where the amount of 'give-away' goods befits the level of participation of the importing participant at that event – such goods may qualify for the alternative relief explained in the Tariff, Volume 3 under Customs Procedure Code (CPC) 40 00 C32 or 49 00 C32, as appropriate.

Before importing the goods as commercial samples the importer and the supplier must identify those goods by the following methods.

Method A
Tearing, altering, perforating, slashing or defacing the items; and/or

Method B
Using permanent indelible marking or permanent labelling to clearly mark the item as a 'commercial sample'.

In addition to Methods A and B HMRC may also insist that any or all of the following methods are used as well.

Method C
Limiting the quantities of items within the consignment and/or for items like garments and footwear also limit the range of available sizes/dimensions of those items included within the consignment.

Method D
Limiting the frequency or occasions on when the importation of those consignments are made during a 12 month period.

Method E
Using an acceptable method of presentation that restricts the handling of the goods so that they can only be used to demonstrate them as proper commercial samples.

HMRC expects that the importer will ensure the goods meet either or both of Method A and/or Method B above, depending on the type of goods involved. Only if this pre-importation preparation is done correctly can the goods be accepted as proper commercial samples in which case HMRC will allow any relief on those imported goods. HMRC may also ask that one, some or all of the three additional methods – C, D and/or E – are also used depending on the commodity code of the intended commercial sample.

HMRC reserve the right to state that some commodities can't be prepared prior to import adequately enough, no matter what method is used from the above list, to then properly qualify as 'negligible value'. In those situations, those commodities will not be eligible for Commercial Samples Relief. 'Negligible' value isn't defined in the law. Emphasis is on the proper preparation and presentation of the imported goods so that they can only be used as demonstration items to solicit further orders of that particular product. Only where HMRC is satisfied that the goods can only be used as commercial samples, will they allow this relief to be applied.

Full details on how to enter the goods is set out in Notice 372.[6]

5.8 Decorations and awards – Notice 364

Only "entitled persons" can claim the relief. An entitled person is a person who has received a decoration or award in a third country/territory or is a person who is to present a decoration or award to an entitled person in the EU Customs Union.

Entitled persons need to prove to HMRC that they are able to qualify for the relief. This depends on the circumstances in which the decoration or award is made. HMRC will normally accept any certificate or press publicity material relating to the decoration or award, or a letter or statement from the donor or organiser of the event. To support the application to use this relief, if the importer is named personally and identified on this evidence, this will greatly enhance the possibility of successful approval. However, HMRC reserve the right to contact the donors or organisers to fully confirm all the evidence provided is genuine and legitimate.

The relief covers:
- decorations conferred by governments or Heads of State of third countries on people who normally reside in the EU Customs Union (for duty relief) or in the EU (for VAT relief);
- awards, trophies, cups, medals and similar articles of an essentially symbolic nature awarded free of charge as tributes or in recognition of activities in any field or for merit at a particular event, such as an international competition, or as an award for an act of courage or

---

[6]www.gov.uk/government/publications/notice-372-importing-commercial-samples-free-of-duty-and-vat/

dedication to persons who normally reside in the EU Customs Union (for import duty relief) or in the EU (for VAT relief). These can be awarded either in third countries/territories and imported by the recipient, or awarded by authorities or persons established in third countries/territories and imported for presentation in the EU Customs Union (for import duty relief) or in the EU (for VAT relief); or
- awards, cups, medals, trophies and souvenirs of a symbolic nature and limited value imported for distribution free of charge at business conferences or similar international events to persons normally resident in third countries/territories.

An entitled person's place of residence is where they spend at least 185 days in a period of 12 months because of their "personal ties" and occupational ties, if any. However, if the person's personal ties are in one country and their occupational ties are in another, HMRC will treat them as resident in the country of their personal ties if their stay in the country of occupational ties is in order to carry out a task of definite duration or they return regularly to the country of their personal ties.

There is an extensive list of ineligible goods, these being:
- watches, cameras, cars;
- long service awards made to employees by employers or colleagues;
- prizes won in unimportant competitions such as deck games and card games;
- articles bought with prize money;
- gifts or prizes given instead of payment;
- cases where the donor appears to be motivated largely by commercial considerations;
- any consumables such as alcoholic drinks, tobacco products, foods; and
- souvenirs distributed which are not in keeping with the nature of the event.

Details can be found in Notice 364.[7]

5.9 Donated medical equipment – Notice 341

Relief is available to health authorities, hospital departments and medical research institutions. The relief covers:
- instruments and apparatus intended for medical research, establishing medical diagnosis or carrying out medical treatment;
- spare parts, components and accessories specifically for eligible instruments and apparatus; and
- tools to be used for maintaining, checking, calibrating or repairing eligible instruments and apparatus.

---

[7] www.gov.uk/government/publications/notice-364-importing-decorations-and-awards-free-of-duty-and-vat/

IMPORT DUTY AND IMPORT VAT RELIEFS

To obtain relief, the goods imported must be donated by a charitable or philanthropic organisation, donated by a private individual or purchased with funds provided by a charitable or philanthropic organisation or with voluntary contributions. In the case of donated equipment, the donation must not involve any commercial intent on the part of the donor and the donor must not be connected with the manufacturer of the equipment.

The importer must retain control of and responsibility for all goods granted duty relief, and can only use them for medical treatment, diagnosis or research. They may only be loaned, hired out or transferred to another eligible establishment approved under this procedure and provided HMRC have been notified at the National Import Reliefs Unit (NIRU) first. Their address is

National Import Reliefs Unit
HM Revenue and Customs
Abbey House
Head Street
Enniskillen
County Fermanagh
Northern Ireland
BT74 7JL

Telephone: 02866 344 557
Fax: 0286 344 571
Email: niru@hmrc.gov.uk

If disposed in any other way the duty must be declared.

Even if not eligible for duty relief, VAT relief can be claimed where the goods are medical, scientific, computer, video, sterilizing, laboratory or refrigeration equipment; intended for use in medical or veterinary research, training, diagnosis or treatment; and purchased with charitable or voluntary contributions. The VAT relief also extends to charitable institutions providing rescue or first aid services and charitable institutions providing care, medical or surgical treatment for disabled people.

The importer must complete the appropriate declaration from VAT Notice 701/6 *Charity funded equipment for medical, veterinary etc. uses*[8] and present it to HMRC when importing the goods. HMRC may accept a belated claim for relief subject to certain conditions and importers should contact the HMRC National Advice Service for details.

Details of the relief are provided in Notice 341.[9]

---

[8] www.gov.uk/government/publications/vat-notice-7016-charity-funded-equipment-for-medical-veterinary-etc-uses
[9] www.gov.uk/government/publications/notice-341-importing-donated-medical-equipment-free-of-duty-and-vat/

5.10 Duty and VAT-free allowances

All travellers either arriving in the UK or returning to the UK from, say, a holiday abroad, are allowed to import a certain amount of duty/tax free goods for their personal use, known as an 'allowance'. If this allowance is exceeded, the person may have to pay duty and/or tax. To qualify for the tax/duty free allowances all of the following conditions must also be met:
- the goods must be transported personally;
- the goods must be for the person's own use or as a gift. "Gifts" that are paid for by the recipient, including any reimbursement of any expenses) are not gifts and duty and/or tax must be paid on arrival in the UK.

HMRC has published two tables for the allowances depending upon whether the person has arrived from another Member State or from outside the EU.

5.10.1 Arrivals from EU Member States

Although there are no limits to the alcohol and tobacco passengers can bring in from EU countries, HMRC are more likely to ask questions where more than the amounts below are carried:

Type of goods	Amount
Cigarettes	800
Cigars	200
Cigarillos	400
Tobacco	1kg
Beer	110 litres
Wine	90 litres
Spirits	10 litres
Fortified wine (e.g. sherry, port)	20 litres

5.10.2 Imports from outside the EU

If the allowances are exceeded, the person must make a declaration to HMRC when entering the UK from a third country/territory. This is also the case where the goods are for commercial use or if the person has more than 10,000 euros (or its equivalent) in cash. Import duty, excise duty (if the goods are tobacco products and alcoholic substances) and import VAT will all be due on the amount of the goods in excess of the allowances. In all instances Customs import duty is waived if the amount of the duty payable is less than £9.

For other goods brought into the UK by travellers, Customs import duty only applies on goods above £270 or £340 (whichever is appropriate) in value. Over this allowance and up to £630 duty is applied at a flat rate of 2.5%. For goods valued over £630, the duty and duties rate charged depends on the type of goods. The personal allowances at February 2016 are:

IMPORT DUTY AND IMPORT VAT RELIEFS

Product	Allowance
Alcohol	beer – 16 litres wine (not sparkling) – 4 litres Additionally passengers can bring in either: spirits and other liquors over 22% alcohol – 1 litre fortified wine (e.g. port, sherry), sparkling wine and alcoholic drinks up to 22% alcohol – 2 litres This last allowance can be split for example the passenger could bring 1 litre of fortified wine and half a litre of spirits (both half of their personal allowance).
Tobacco	One of the following products: 200 cigarettes; 100 cigarillos; 50 cigars; or 250g of tobacco or A combination of these allowances, for example, 100 cigarettes and 25 cigars. (both half of their personal allowance).
Other goods including perfume and souvenirs	Goods worth up to £390, unless arriving by private plane or private boat when the limit is £270. If any single item worth more than the allowance is imported, duty and/or tax must be paid on the full item value, not just the value above the allowance. Individual allowances cannot be grouped together to import an item worth more than the limit.

5.11 Food and plants

The importation of food and plants is strictly controlled. Some animal products may also be banned, although travellers may import a small quantity of some products from certain countries – see HMRC's leaflet *Bringing food products into the UK*.[10]

Most fruits, vegetables, seeds and bulbs are also subject to weight or quantity restrictions. Some plants and plant products (including potatoes) and loose soil may not be brought into the UK unless the relevant official licence has been obtained – see HMRC's leaflet *Bringing fruit, vegetable and plant products into the UK*.[11]

5.12 Gold

Importations and acquisitions of gold and gold coins, other than investment gold are chargeable with VAT at the standard rate. However, importations and acquisitions of gold by central banks are subject to special treatment. The importation of investment gold from a third country/territory and the importation of Gold (including gold coins) by a Central Bank from a third

---

[10] www.gov.uk/government/publications/bringing-food-products-into-the-uk
[11] www.gov.uk/government/ bringing-fruit-vegetable-and-plant-products-into-the-uk

IMPORT DUTY AND IMPORT VAT RELIEFS

country/territory is exempt from VAT. Code 40 00 73 is to be shown as the Customs Procedure Code (CPC) on the SAD/C88.

5.13 Goods for disabled persons – Notice 371

Relief is available to any organisation principally concerned with the education of or the assistance to disabled people, which the HMRC National Import Reliefs Unit (NIRU) has approved to receive the goods duty-free. A disabled person or their 'nominated carer' (meaning a person known to the disabled person, such as a parent, guardian, spouse or partner, or family member who acts as the disabled person's carer to also act upon their behalf) importing eligible goods for their own use can also import the goods free of duty and import VAT.

HMRC recommend that the nominated carer obtains a letter of support confirming this, from a medical professional, such as the disabled person's General Practitioner (GP) or hospital consultant, and to ensure that a copy of that letter is sent to NIRU (address at **Appendix B**)

Eligible goods include:
- any goods specially designed to be of educational, scientific or cultural help to people who are blind or partially sighted;
- any goods specially designed to give educational, employment or social help to people with physical or mental disabilities; and
- spare parts, components, tools and accessories specifically or recognisably intended for such goods.

In respect of people who are blind or partially sighted, all of the following articles are relieved:
- Braille paper;
- white canes;
- typewriters adapted for use by people who are blind or partially sighted;
- equipment for the mechanical production of Braille and recorded material;
- television enlargers for people who are blind or partially sighted;
- electronic orientator and obstacle detector appliances;
- teaching aids and apparatus specifically designed for use by people who are blind or partially sighted;
- Braille watches with cases not made of precious metals;
- 'CD' players, record players and cassette players specially designed or adapted for people who are blind or partially sighted;
- talking books, magnetic tapes and cassettes for the production of Braille and talking books;
- electronic reading machines;
- table games and accessories specially adapted or designed for people who are blind or partially sighted;
- all other articles specially designed to be of educational, scientific or cultural help to people who are blind or partially sighted; and

- spare parts, components, tools and accessories specially or recognisably intended for any of the above goods.

For disabled persons all of the following types of equipment are covered:
- purpose-made items and equipment, specifically designed for the sole use of the disabled person, to assist them in their ability to carry out everyday activities;
- purpose-made items and equipment, specifically designed for the sole use of the disabled person, to assist them in everyday mobility, but not to be used for standard generic wheelchairs and mobility light vehicles, or for motor vehicles or other methods of transport that have not already been specifically adapted for the sole use of the disabled person;
- other specifically designed items and equipment for the sole use of the disabled person, to assist them in vocational pursuits;
- teaching aids and apparatus specifically designed for use by people who are disabled;
- table games and accessories specially adapted or designed for people who are disabled;
- all other articles specially designed to be of educational, scientific or cultural help to people who are disabled; and
- spare parts, components, tools and accessories specially or recognisably intended for any of the above goods.

Non-specialised goods imported for subsequent adaptation to make them suitable for use by disabled people are excluded from relief. Any specialised adaptation must have been made before the goods are imported into the EU. Certain goods, such as printed matter designed for blind or partially sighted people, are free of import duty under the Tariff so importers need only follow the procedures in Notice 371 if they wish to claim relief on goods liable to a positive rate of duty.

Equipment which has been designed solely for use by disabled people and imported by either the disabled person, for their domestic or personal use or by charities for making available to disabled people for their domestic or personal use are zero-rated for VAT purposes. The following Notices explain the guidelines on such equipment: Notice 701/7 *VAT Reliefs for disabled people*.[12] Charities and other organisations should see Notice 701/1 *Charities*[13] for further information.

Where goods are not zero-rated, relief from VAT is available for goods which are:
- specially designed for the education, employment or social advancement of people who are blind or have a physical or mental disability; and

---

[12] www.gov.uk/government/publications/vat-notice-7017-vat-reliefs-for-disabled-people
[13] www.gov.uk/government/publications/vat-notice-7011-charities

- are imported by an HMRC NIRU-approved organisation principally engaged in the education of, or the provision of assistance to, people who are blind or have a physical or mental disability; and
- donated to the organisation with no commercial intent on the part of the donor.

There are limitations as to the use of the goods on which relief is claimed. These are:
- the goods imported must be for the disabled person's own use. If the disabled person intends to dispose of the goods at a later date, Customs import duty, but not import VAT, may be payable depending on the circumstances and affected persons should seek advice from the HMRC National Advice Service before doing so;
- an organisation can only use the goods to provide educational, scientific or cultural help to disabled people. The organisation must keep control and responsibility of the goods on which relief has been granted; and
- the organisation may lend, hire out or transfer the goods on a non-profit making basis to disabled people without payment of duty and VAT. It can also lend, hire out or transfer the goods to another organisation approved under this procedure, as long as NIRU is notified before this is done.

For goods imported by post, the importer should ask the sender to write clearly on the package and its accompanying Customs declaration (CN22 or CN23) *"Goods for disabled people: relief claimed"*.

Normally, relief is to be claimed at the time of import. However, if the importer fails to do this HMRC may accept a belated claim and repay the appropriate charges subject to certain conditions – see HMRC Notice 199: *Imported goods: Customs procedures and Customs debt*.[14]

5.14 Electricity and natural gas

With effect from 1 January 2005, import VAT has not been payable on the importation of gas through the natural gas distribution network or electricity.

5.15 Fuel, animal fodder and feeding stuffs, and packing for use during transportation

Fuels, animal fodder and animal feeding stuffs and packing associated with the transportation of goods is relieved of import VAT. This follows the UK liability for the supply of such articles.

5.15.1 Fuel and lubricants

The relief covers fuel that is contained in the "standard tanks" of a motor road vehicle or of a 'special container' used exclusively by such a vehicle or such special container. The law defines a 'special container' as any container fitted

---

[14]www.gov.uk/government/publications/notice-199-imported-goods-customs-procedures-and-customs-debt/

with specially designed apparatus for refrigeration, oxygenation, thermal insulation and other systems. Additionally, quantities of road fuel, not exceeding 10 litres per vehicle which are contained in portable tanks carried by a motor road vehicle, for its exclusive use are also relieved.

The relief is restricted, however, to a vehicle that is not classified as a "Special Purpose Vehicle" or which, by its construction and equipment, is designed for and capable of transporting goods or more than nine persons, including the driver. Lubricants contained in a motor road vehicle, for use exclusively by such vehicle and necessary for its normal operation during the journey, also benefit from the relief.

5.15.2 Fodder and feeding stuffs
To enable animals to be transported "humanely" the transport will usually be packed with appropriate litter, fodder and feeding stuffs. In such case, these goods for the animal's benefit are relieved of import VAT.

5.15.3 Packings
The relief also extends to disposable packings for the stowage and protection (including heat protection) of goods during their transportation to the UK, but only where the cost is included in the price paid for the goods transported.

5.16 Goods imported for onward dispatch to another Member State – Notice 702/7
Where goods have been imported into the UK, but are to be dispatched to another Member State under the "intra-EU" rules, they are relieved from import VAT. The goods must be dispatched to a "taxable person" in another Member State and the goods must be removed from the UK within one month of the date of importation, i.e. the date the goods enter free circulation, but HMRC may approve a longer period. The importer may be required to pay security to HMRC until satisfying HMRC that the goods have in fact been removed from the UK. See section **3.5** for more details.

5.17 Goods for use by a charity – Notice 317
HMRC has given general approval to import relevant goods free of import duty and import VAT to the following charitable and philanthropic organisations:
- those registered by the Charities Commission or the Office of the Scottish Charities Regulator;
- state organisations which are devoted to welfare; and
- the following, as long as they are non-profit making and their objective is the welfare of the needy:
  o hospitals;
  o youth organisations;
  o clubs, homes and hostels for the aged;
  o orphanages and children's homes;

IMPORT DUTY AND IMPORT VAT RELIEFS

- o organisations set up for the relief of distress caused by particular disasters in the EU Customs Union; or
- o organisations concerned with the relief of distress generally (such as the British Red Cross Society or the Salvation Army).

The relief covers:
- basic necessities for needy people;
- goods to be used or sold at charity events for the benefit of needy people;
- equipment and office materials to help run your organisation for the benefit of needy people; and
- goods to help deal with disasters in the EU Customs Union.

There are a number of goods that are restricted such as:
- alcoholic products (including alcohol-based perfume);
- tobacco and tobacco products;
- coffee and tea;
- motor vehicles other than ambulances;
- items associated solely with worship such as statues and pulpits; and
- any goods whose importation would give rise to abuse or major distortion of competition.

"Needy people" are those requiring any of the basic necessities being goods designed specifically to meet the immediate needs of people and which will be distributed free of charge to such needy people in the EU Customs Union or overseas. They include:
- food;
- medicines;
- clothing;
- blankets;
- orthopaedic equipment; and
- crutches.

Relief from import duty is allowed whether or not the charity has purchased the goods, but import VAT relief is only available where the basic necessities were obtained free of charge, i.e. donated.

The goods imported can be used at or sold at an "occasional" charity event, provided there are no more than four events a year. The charity must have received the goods free of charge from a person or organisation established outside the EU Customs Union and without any commercial intent on the part of the donor.

The relief also extends to machines, tools and equipment of the service industry, office materials, fixtures and fittings, provided they are received free of charge from a person or organisation established outside the EU Customs Union, without any commercial intent on the part of the donor and solely to

IMPORT DUTY AND IMPORT VAT RELIEFS

help run the charity and help it fulfil its charitable and philanthropic aims for the benefit of needy people.

The goods may be lent, hired out or transferred to another approved organisation or charity without the payment of import duty and import VAT, provided HMRC are informed of this intention before doing so. A failure to do this will render the organisation or charity liable to pay the duty and VAT if the goods are disposed of.

Full details of the relief are set out in Notice 317.[15]

5.18 Goods for test – Notice 374[16]

Import duty and/or import VAT relief is available on goods imported for testing to find out their composition, quality or other characteristics for information, or for industrial or commercial research.

Additionally, excise duty is relieved on goods imported to test machines for making/packing tobacco products. However, relief is denied on goods consumed by a person in the course of testing petrol or petrol substitutes and heavy oil for use as fuel for a road vehicle.

HMRC will not allow this relief if the testing is, or is part of, a sales promotion or publicity exercise. Goods imported for such purposes may, however, qualify for the alternative relief explained in Notice 372: *Importing commercial samples free of duty and VAT* – see section **5.7**.

Normally, the importer must completely use up or destroy the goods in the course of the testing. When the testing has come to its end the HMRC NIRU must be informed with the importer providing the following information:
- the place of importation or the postal depot;
- the number and date of the customs entry or postal docket;
- the quantity, value and description of the goods and date of receipt;
- full details of the tests, including the address(es) where the testing took place and where records are available for inspection;
- the date on which testing was completed; and
- details of any materials remaining and any proposals for their disposal.

'Materials remaining' includes goods not actually used, goods not completely consumed in the test and goods resulting from the test, including any waste and scrap. For any materials remaining after test the importer may:
- pay duty and VAT on them at the rates applying on the date of completion of the test;
- destroy them, free of duty and VAT, with HMRC's permission; or

---

[15] www.gov.uk/government/publications/notice-317-imports-by-charities-free-of-duty-and-vat

[16] www.gov.uk/government/publications/notice-374-importing-goods-for-test-free-of-duty-and-vat

- convert them into waste or scrap, with HMRC's permission, and pay any duty and VAT which may be due on the residue.

HMRC may also allow the re-export of any goods that remain on hand after the testing is complete. The importer will need to explain to the HMRC NIRU why the goods cannot be destroyed or converted into waste or scrap and have to be exported. If any Customs import duty or import VAT has to be repaid to HMRC, they will advise the importer of the procedure to be followed and will provide the necessary form.

Importers of any specified tobacco products (currently cigarettes and hand-rolling tobacco), which are intended for consumption in the UK, must ensure that the products bear a fiscal mark. It is an offence to possess, transport, display, sell, offer for sale or otherwise deal in tobacco products that should do so, but do not bear a fiscal mark. HMRC provide guidance on the fiscal mark requirements in Notice 476: *Tobacco products duty*.[17] The sale of tobacco products is also subject to health-labelling requirements and maximum tar content.

If the goods are to be transferred elsewhere, the conditions for relief must continue to be met and all the procedures in Notice 476 followed. However, excise goods may not be transferred outside of the UK. The HMRC NIRU must be provided with at least 48 hours prior written notice of to whom and where the goods are to be transferred. As there are special procedures for transferring goods to another country in the EU Customs Union, HMRC advise that importers contact the National Advice Service.

5.19 Goods related to war graves

The law allows a range of goods imported from a third country/territory in respect of war graves and cemeteries to be relieved of import duty and import VAT. The relief covers goods used by an approved organisation in the construction, upkeep or ornamentation of cemeteries, tombs and memorials in the UK, which commemorate war victims of other countries.

Additionally, coffins containing human remains and urns containing human ashes, together with accompanying flowers, wreaths or other ornamental objects are also relieved. They must be imported without any commercial intent by a person resident in a third country/territory for use at a funeral or to decorate a grave.

5.20 Inherited goods – Notice 368

A beneficiary of a person who has died can import goods left to them free of import duty and import VAT. The beneficiary must be an EU resident or a non-profit making company established in the EU. A person is treated as an EU resident if they stay in the EU for at least 185 days in any 12-month period because of either their personal ties or occupational ties, if any. If the person

---

[17] www.gov.uk/government/publications/excise-notice-476-tobacco-products-duty/

has personal ties in the EU and occupational ties in a different country, they may be treated as resident in the EU if:
- their stay in the country of occupational ties is in order to carry out a task of definite duration; or
- they regularly return to the EU.

The relief covers any goods included in the estate of the deceased that are intended for the beneficiary's personal use or for meeting his/her household needs. Examples are:
- jewellery, stamp collections, bicycles and private motor vehicles, caravans, trailers, pleasure craft and private aircraft;
- household furnishings;
- family pets and saddle animals; and
- portable items (such as a doctor's bag, musicians' instruments, photographers' cameras and equipment) used by the deceased in their trade or profession.

Relief is not available for a range of products such as:
- alcoholic drinks, tobacco and tobacco products;
- stocks of raw materials and finished or semi-finished products;
- tools of trade other than the portable items as explained below;
- commercial vehicles;
- livestock and stocks of agricultural products which are more than what are required to meet a family's normal needs;
- goods bought from the executor of the estate; and
- goods bought or received as a gift from the person who legally inherited them.

The relief also extends to articles inherited from a person who was a resident of the EU, but the property was located outside the EU at the time of their death. Additionally, if the deceased person was resident outside the EU at the time of their death, but the goods were already in the EU under the Temporary Admission (TA) regime, the relief granted under TA can remain.

In most cases, the goods cannot be imported free of duty and import VAT before the person bequeathing the goods has died, although they are part of the benefactor's will. The only time relief can be claimed is if:
- the goods were bequeathed to the current owner in the will of a deceased person;
- the will of that deceased person also stipulates that on the death of the current owner, the goods are to pass to the person importing;
- the importer can prove that the current owner has renounced ownership or been judged too ill or infirm to manage their own affairs; and
- the importer can provide a certificate or document given under the laws of the country concerned, stating that they are entitled to take the property absolutely under the terms of the will of the deceased person.

Ideally, the goods should be imported within two years from the date the estate is finally settled. If this is not possible the importer will need to contact HMRC to provide a detailed explanation of why this was the case. HMRC will then consider whether to make any special and exceptional allowances, depending on the circumstances and information provided.

If the goods are disposed of the person importing them will need to retain adequate evidence. This should show when they were imported along with copies of the original evidence that allowed HMRC to grant this relief, and also to ensure details to show when they left the importer's possession and/or were last used. All records of disposal must be kept for a minimum of four years.

Full details of the relief are provided in Notice 368.[18]

5.21 Miscellaneous documents and other related articles – Notice 342[19]

Relief covers miscellaneous documents and related articles which are either articles of an educational, scientific or cultural nature, or of a more general nature. Only relief from import duty is available on the former, whereas both import duty and import VAT relief is available on articles of a more general nature. If any of these goods are to be imported on a temporary basis relief might be available under the Temporary Admissions regime – see Notice 200: *Temporary Admission*.[20]

There is no relief from excise duty under these procedures, but alternative reliefs may be available, for example, any goods imported for examination, analysis or test, might qualify for relief under Notice 374: *Importing goods for test free of duty and VAT*.

The relief covers items such as:
- children's books of an educational, scientific or cultural nature;
- printed matter for the blind or partially sighted;
- tourist information literature;
- advertising material;
- objects to be submitted as evidence in courts; and
- trademarks, patterns or designs.

The relief is only available where the goods qualify for stipulated uses, these being provided in detail, with the relevant Tariff headings, in sections 4 and 5 of Notice 342. Section 4 details those goods were only duty can be relieved,

---

[18]www.gov.uk/government/publications/notice-368-importing-inherited-goods-free-of-duty-and-vat/
[19]www.gov.uk/government/publications/notice-342-importing-miscellaneous-documents-and-other-related-articles-free-of-duty-and-vat/
[20]www.gov.uk/government/publications/notice-200-temporary-admission

whereas section 5 details the goods of a more general nature where both import duty and import VAT can be relieved.

Also, in some cases, HMRC apply specific limits. For example, in the case of a consignment of advertising material comprising several copies of the same document, HMRC only allow relief if the total gross weight does not exceed one kilogram. For tourist information literature, HMRC only allow relief if the documents do not contain more than 25% of non-related commercial advertisements, i.e. unconnected with the main purpose of the publication.

For goods imported in a traveller's accompanied baggage, the traveller must declare them to HMRC at the Customs "Red Channel" or "Red Point" upon arrival in the UK. If eligible goods are imported as freight, relief can only be claimed by the importer completing a SAD/C88. Either the importer can do this themselves or they can ask an import agent to do this on their behalf.

Where the goods are to be imported by post, the importer should ask the sender before despatch of the goods to write clearly on the package and its accompanying Customs declaration (Form CN22 or Form CN23):

For goods in section 4 of Notice 342: *"Duty relief claimed."*

For goods in section 5 of Notice 342: *"Other miscellaneous goods – duty and VAT relief claimed."*

Normally, relief should be claimed at the time of import, but HMRC may accept a belated claim for relief subject to certain conditions and importers are asked to contact the National Advice Service for details.

5.22 Museum and gallery exhibits – Notice 361

Relief is available for exhibits for museums and galleries that are permanently imported from outside the EU Customs Union free of import duty and import VAT. Exhibits imported on a permanent basis from the "Special Territories" or countries having a Customs Union with the EU can be imported free of VAT. If exhibits are imported on a temporary basis before re-export, relief is available under the Temporary Admission regime – see Notice 200: *Temporary Admission.*[21]

Import duty relief is available where:
- the HMRC National Import Reliefs Unit (NIRU) has approved the importer's establishment;
- the exhibits are of a scientific, educational or cultural nature and not for sale;
- the exhibits are dispatched directly on import to the importer's approved establishment;
- the items concerned are used exclusively as exhibits under the importer's control; and
- full records are kept of the exhibits.

---

[21] www.gov.uk/government/publications/notice-200-temporary-admission

To obtain the import VAT relief, as well as all of the above conditions being met, the exhibits must have been donated free of charge. HMRC state in Notice 361 that they will relax this condition when the exhibits are bought from a private person or they are supplied to the importer for a purpose other than in the course or furtherance of any business, usually meaning for private purposes or for exhibit for example where entry to the museum etc. to view them is free of charge.

Some goods, including works of art, may already be subject to a nil rate of duty. However, most are liable to VAT, either at the standard rate or in the case of certain works of art at the reduced rate - see VAT Notice 702: *imports*.[22] The procedures laid out in Notice 361 only need to be followed where the importer wishes to claim relief on goods liable to a positive rate of import duty, and/or wishes to claim relief from import VAT.

The exhibits may be lent, hired out or transferred to another approved establishment without payment of duty and VAT provided the NIRU is notified before this intention is fulfilled. Customs import duty and import VAT must be repaid where the exhibits are disposed of in any other way.

5.23 Sailing "pleasure craft" to the EU – Notice 8

HMRC and the UK Border Agency (UKBA) are responsible for the management of fiscal, regulatory and enforcement activities at frontier locations. HMRC has overall responsibility for policy and procedures relating to the inward/outward pleasure craft reporting function. The UKBA has responsibility for implementing HMRC policies and procedures at the frontier and for the prevention of smuggling of dutiable or prohibited/restricted goods. The UKBA also has responsibility for immigration matters.

Jointly, HMRC and the UKBA also have a responsibility to other Member States of the European Union to control the frontier between the EU and countries that are not full members. The UKBA will still need to carry out checks on persons on board pleasure craft. Even so, only a small proportion of those who are on an intra-Community voyage will be asked to confirm that their last port of call was another place in the EU.

The Customs and Excise Management Act 1979 gives UKBA officers the necessary powers to stop, board and search a vessel and to ask questions. This applies whether the vessel sailed from a port within the EU or from a country outside the EU.

Some EU and other European countries, but not the UK, are partner to the Schengen Agreement under which border controls on persons between Schengen members have been abolished. Consequently, travellers from the UK to a Schengen country or those leaving for the UK from one may find that they are subject to additional checks when overseas because of the Schengen

---

[22]www.gov.uk/government/publications/vat-notice-702-imports/

commitment to reinforcing frontiers between Schengen members and countries which are not party to the Agreement. However, the UK's law and practices do not differentiate in any way between Schengen members and non-members.

As at April 2011, the Schengen members with coastlines, which were actually operating the Convention, were Belgium, Denmark, Finland, Germany, Iceland, Italy, the Netherlands, Norway, Portugal, Spain, Sweden, France Greece, Estonia, Lithuania, Latvia, Malta, Poland and Slovenia.

Pleasurecraft arriving from another EU Member State do not need to fly the 'Q' flag, but do if arriving from outside the EU where it can readily be seen as soon as entering the 12 mile limit for UK waters. The crew must not take down the flag until they have finished reporting to HMRC and any failure to comply could result in a penalty.

If the vessel carries any goods for industrial or commercial purposes it becomes a commercial vessel and is no longer a pleasure craft. Notice 69 *Report and Clearance by Ships Masters* explains the customs requirements for commercial vessels.[23]

When the pleasurecraft has arrived direct from a third country/territory, including the Channel Islands, HMRC are to be contacted by calling the National Yachtline on 0845 723 1110 to inform them if any of the following apply:
- VAT has not been paid on the vessel;
- goods in excess of the travellers' allowance are on board;
- goods which are to be treated as duty free stores are on board;
- there are any prohibited or restricted goods;
- there is any "notifiable illness" on board;
- there are any people on board who need immigration clearance; or
- there have been repairs or modifications, other than running repairs, which were carried out since the vessel last left the EU.

The declaration made to HMRC on arrival from a third country/territory must include all of the following:
- any animals or birds;
- any prohibited and restricted goods (including certain foods);
- any duty-free stores;
- the craft itself, if it is liable to VAT;
- any goods which, as a visitor, are intended to be left behind upon departure from the UK or another EU Member State;
- any tobacco goods, alcoholic drinks, perfumes and toilet water in excess of the duty-free allowances; and

---

[23] www.gov.uk/government/publications/notice-69-report-and-clearance-by-ships-masters/

- if a returning resident of the UK or another Member State, any other goods acquired on the voyage, where the total value of these goods exceeds £270. This allowance includes any equipment which may have been bought and fitted to the craft outside the EU.

All pleasurecraft that are less than 12 metres long are potentially liable to import duty when imported from a third country/territory, and all vessels 'designed or adapted for recreation or pleasure use' are liable to import VAT. If the craft is being temporarily imported from a third country/territory, it may qualify for relief from these charges under the Temporary Admission regime.

If the craft is being permanently imported on the transfer of the owner's permanent residence in a third country/territory, it may qualify for the change of residence relief – see **5.23.1**. A "VAT paid" craft previously exported from the EU may also qualify for relief on its return if it:
- is re-imported within three years of its export from the EU;
- is re-imported by the person who exported it from the EU; and
- it has had no more than running repairs outside the EU that did not increase its value.

Where the craft is being imported as a personal belonging of a person who is relocating their normal home to an EU country, import duty and import VAT may be relieved.

5.23.1 Change of Residence relief

Where a person is moving their normal home from a non-EU country to an EU country, including the UK, they may import a vessel free of customs duty and import VAT providing that they:
- have lived outside the EU for a continuous period of at least 12 months;
- have possessed and used the vessel outside the EU for at least six months prior to importation;
- did not get the vessel under a duty/tax free scheme (see below);
- declare the vessel to an officer;
- will keep the vessel in the EU for private use; and
- do not sell, lend, hire out or otherwise dispose of the vessel in the EU within 12 months of importation unless the importer must notify the Personal Transport Unit first, on Telephone: 01304 664 171, and duty and VAT is paid on disposal.

However, if the vessel was purchased under a duty/tax free scheme in the vessel's country of origin or departure, relief from customs duty and import VAT will only apply if at the time of purchase the owner was:
- a diplomat;
- a member of an officially recognised international organisation;
- a member of NATO or UK forces, or the civilian staff accompanying them, or the spouse of such a member; or

IMPORT DUTY AND IMPORT VAT RELIEFS

- able to prove that duty and tax has subsequently been paid and has not been, nor will be, refunded.

If the owner does not arrive with the vessel personally, it will not normally be released until they do arrive. However, it may be released for storage under certain conditions.

To declare a vessel, and to claim any relief from duty and VAT that may apply on transfer of residence, the owner should complete form C104A (Vessels) and should be ready to produce to HMRC the vessel and all evidence of use and possession outside the EU such as registration papers and berthing fees. The rules regarding a person's 'normal home' are complex so in cases of doubt the owner should contact the VAT, Excise and Customs telephone helpline on: 0300 200 3700.

Where a non-EU vessel is temporarily imported and a claim for relief under Temporary Admission has been made (see **5.23.3**) and then it is decided to move the normal home to the UK, the owner may still be able to apply for Transfer of Residence relief subject to the conditions above.

5.23.2 Use within EU waters

If the vessel is used within EU waters VAT is due on the vessel's value at the time of import unless, say, TA relief is allowed. VAT is payable on pleasurecraft bought in the EU and which are expected to remain in the EU.

EU residents should only use a vessel in the Community if it is VAT paid or 'deemed' VAT paid. Documentary evidence supporting this should be carried at all times as the owner or 'skipper' may be asked by customs officials to provide evidence of the vessel's VAT status, either in the UK or in other Member States. Documentary evidence might include:

- an original invoice or receipt;
- evidence that VAT was paid at importation; or
- invoices for materials used in the construction of a 'Home-Built' vessel.

A registration document on its own does not prove the VAT status of the vessel, as there is no link in the UK between the registry of the vessel and the payment of VAT.

Certain vessels that were in use as private pleasure craft prior to 1 January 1985 and were in the EU on 31 December 1992, may be deemed VAT paid under the Single Market transitional arrangements. As Austria, Finland and Sweden joined the EU later, the relevant dates for vessels in these countries are 'in use' before 1 January 1987 and moored in EU on 31 December 1994.

5.23.3 Pleasurecraft Temporarily Admitted (TA)

EU law allows pleasure craft that are kept in a third country/territory to be temporarily admitted into the EU free of import duty and VAT, subject to certain conditions. The conditions vary according to whether the craft has

IMPORT DUTY AND IMPORT VAT RELIEFS

been imported to the EU for private or for commercial purposes and requires that it be registered outside the EU in the name of a person established in a third country/territory or, if not registered outside, is owned by a person established in a third country/territory. Alternatively, the craft can be temporarily registered in the EU with a view to re-exportation in the name of a person established in a third country/territory.

Full details of the TA requirements are provided in section 5 of Notice 8.[24]

5.24 Scientific instruments – Notice 340

Relief is available to bodies that are mainly involved in education or scientific research, which extends to divisions of any public establishment, provided that all such research is undertaken on a non-commercial basis. Examples are:
- universities, polytechnics and similar educational establishments;
- National Health Service and teaching hospitals, including medical schools and research laboratories;
- public health laboratories; and
- research laboratories of Government Departments, research councils and similar bodies.

The relief covers:
- scientific instruments and apparatus;
- spare parts, components and accessories specifically for scientific instruments and apparatus which have been granted relief; and
- tools to be used for maintaining, checking, calibrating or repairing eligible instruments and apparatus.

Relief from import VAT is more limited, it being restricted to goods imported for use in medical or veterinary research, training, diagnosis or treatment. Such goods are zero-rated for VAT – VAT Notice 701/6: *Charity funded equipment for medical, research, veterinary etc. uses*[25] provides full details about zero-rating along with the conditions and procedures.

The establishment importing the goods must keep control of and be responsible for the goods on which relief has been granted. The goods may be lent, hired out or transferred to another approved establishment, as long as the HMRC NIRU is notified before this intention is fulfilled. Import duty and import VAT must be repaid where the exhibits are disposed of in any other way.

5.25 International science projects

Relief is also available for goods imported into the EU for international scientific research programmes. The conditions are that the equipment:

---

[24] www.gov.uk/government/publications/notice-8-sailing-your-pleasure-craft-to-and-from-the-uk/
[25] www.gov.uk/government/publications/vat-notice-7016-charity-funded-equipment-for-medical-veterinary-etc-uses

IMPORT DUTY AND IMPORT VAT RELIEFS

- is imported by or on behalf of a scientific research establishment based outside the EU Customs Union;
- is intended for use by, or with the agreement of, the members or representatives of the establishment based outside the EU Customs Union in accordance with scientific co-operation agreements;
- is to carry out international scientific research programmes in approved establishments based in the EU Customs Union; and
- remains the property of an organisation or person based outside the EU Customs Union.

For goods destined for the UK, the head of the scientific research establishment based outside the EU Customs Union, or their authorised representative, must apply to the HMRC NIRU for approval to import the goods free of duty. The HMRC NIRU then has to forward the application to the Commission for consideration.

Where the goods are to be imported by post, the importer should ask the sender, before dispatch of the goods, to write clearly on the package and its accompanying Customs declaration (Form CN22 or Form CN23): *Scientific Instruments – relief claimed.*

Normally, relief should be claimed at the time of import, but HMRC may accept a belated claim for relief subject to certain conditions. Importers are asked to contact the National Advice Service for details.

Details of how to claim the relief are provided in Notice 340.[26]

5.26 Private gifts (postal packages) – Notice 143

Notice 143 describes the customs and VAT procedures for the import and export of goods by post through Royal Mail or Parcelforce Worldwide. It also applies to gifts received through the post. The arrangements set out in Notice 143 do not apply when a full import declaration SAD/C88 is required. The SAD/C88 must be used for all the following imports:

- goods with a value exceeding £2,000 declared to home use and free circulation;
- goods for which relief from customs duty and import VAT is being claimed, for example, inward processing relief, outward processing relief, temporary importation; and
- certain exports including all goods for export with a value exceeding £2,000.

Information on the procedures to be used for such imports and exports are provided in Notice 144: *Trade imports by post: how to complete customs documents.*[27]

---

[26]www.gov.uk/government/publications/notice-340-importing-scientific-instruments-free-of-duty-and-vat/

5.26.1 Procedures

Under international postal agreements the sender must complete a Customs declaration (Form CN22 or Form CN23) which in most cases should be affixed to the package. The declaration includes a description of the goods, the value and whether they are gifts or commercial items. Any Post Office abroad should be able to give advice to the sender. Because the importer is legally responsible for the information on the declaration, it is important to ensure, wherever possible, that the sender makes a complete and accurate declaration. If no declaration is made, or the information is inaccurate, the package may be delayed while HMRC make further enquiries, or in some cases the package and its contents may be seized.

Most goods arriving in the UK/EU from third countries/territories are liable to any or all of import duty, excise duty and import VAT and must be paid whether the goods are purchased or received as a gift. Taxes are also due where the goods are new or used (including antiques) and are for the importer's private use or are for re-sale.

5.26.2 De minimis limits

The limits for these imports, above which taxes must be paid are:
- commercial consignments of £15 or less are free from import duty and import VAT, for example, goods purchased over the internet with an intrinsic value not exceeding £15 will not be charged any duty or VAT, but this does not include excisable goods such as alcohol, tobacco products, perfume or toilet waters;
- a gift with a value of £34 or less will be free from customs import duty and import VAT, but this does not include alcohol, tobacco, perfumes and toilet waters;
- import duty becomes payable if the value of the goods is over £135, but duty is waived if the amount of duty calculated is less than £7.

The monetary threshold fell to £15 from £18 for goods imported on or after 1 November 2011. Also, from 1 April 2012, the low-value relief was withdrawn for mail order goods imported into the UK from the Channel Islands under a distance selling arrangement.

To qualify as a gift:
- the Customs declaration must be completed correctly;
- the gift must be sent from a private person outside the EU to a private person(s) in the UK;
- there is no commercial or trade element and the gift has not been paid for either directly or indirectly; and

---

[27] www.gov.uk/government/publications/notice-144-trade-imports-by-post-how-to-complete-customs-documents/

IMPORT DUTY AND IMPORT VAT RELIEFS

- the gift is of an occasional nature only, for example, for a birthday or anniversary.

Goods purchased from a third country/territory to give as a gift to a relative or friend, whether or not addressed to that person, is treated as a 'commercial consignment' for which the import VAT relief threshold is £15.

Gifts of alcohol and tobacco products below £34 qualify for relief from import duties and import VAT, subject to the following limits:

Tobacco products	Quantity
Cigarettes; **or**	50
Cigarillos (cigars with a maximum weight each of 3 grammes); **or**	25
Cigars	10
Smoking tobacco	50 grammes
Alcohol and alcoholic beverages	
distilled beverages and spirits of an alcoholic strength exceeding 22 per cent by volume; undenatured ethyl alcohol of 80 per cent by volume and over; **or**	1 litre
distilled beverages and spirits, and aperitifs with a wine or alcohol base, tafia, saké or similar beverages of an alcoholic strength of 22 per cent by volume or less; sparkling wines and fortified wines; **or**	1 litre
still wines	2 litres

If gifts of alcohol and tobacco are sent in excess of the quantities shown in the above table, relief from import duty will only apply up to the limits shown above, and the consignment will not benefit from any relief of import VAT. *Excise duty is payable on all alcohol and tobacco products regardless of whether they are a gift.*

Neither import duty nor excise duty is chargeable on perfumes and toilet waters. However, import VAT is chargeable if more than 50gms of perfume or 0.25 litres of toilet water are imported or where they are more than £34.

Where a single package contains gifts that are clearly intended for several people, for example, members of the same family, the £34 VAT relief applies to each individual person, provided the goods are:
- individually wrapped;
- specifically addressed to them;
- declared separately on the Customs declaration; and
- within the allowances specified.

If more than one individual package is addressed to a particular person the value of the goods will be aggregated and if the total value exceeds £34, import VAT will be charged and if the value exceeds £135 import duty may also be due.

If a package contains a number of different types of goods intended for more than one person, and these are separately described and given a value on the

IMPORT DUTY AND IMPORT VAT RELIEFS

Customs declaration, the waiver of import duty will apply to each item. For import VAT purposes, any number of items will be granted relief provided the aggregate value is less than the import VAT threshold, currently £34. However, the value of an item cannot be divided so, for example, if a package contains five items each with a value of £8, only four items will be entitled to relief with charges payable on the fifth item.

When one item is sent to two people and its value exceeds £34, it is not possible to aggregate each person's gift relief, and the value of an individual item itself cannot be divided; for example one item with a value of £50 sent to two individuals cannot benefit from the gift relief.

An illustration of this is shown below:

Goods sent as gifts	Relief given
One item valued at £34 or below	Free of Customs Duty and import VAT.
One item valued at £34	Import VAT is chargeable on the full value.
Five of the same items valued at £8 each	Four items are relieved of import VAT leaving import VAT chargeable on the remaining one item.
Five different items valued at £120 each	Import VAT is chargeable on the full value.
One item valued at £300	Customs Duty is charged (but will not be collected if the amount of duty is less than £7). Import VAT is chargeable on the full value.

The UK Border Agency (UKBA) examine all postal packages arriving in the UK from outside the EU for prohibited or restricted goods such as drugs, indecent or obscene material, weapons, endangered species and counterfeit goods, and also to confirm that the description and value stated on the declaration is correct.

HMRC also check the Customs declaration to determine if import duty, excise duty and import VAT is chargeable. Examination might also be required when the sender has not completed the declaration correctly and in such cases the opening, repacking and resealing of the package is carried out by Royal Mail staff under HMRC's instruction.

5.26.3 Charges

Import charges are calculated by the UK Border Agency at the postal depots where the packages are received. Customs Duty becomes payable if the goods are over £135 in value but is waived if the amount, when calculated is less than £7. The amount of Customs Duty charged will depend on the type of goods imported and the value stated on the customs declaration CN22/CN23 (converted to £sterling using the rates of exchange for the month of importation as shown on the HMRC website).

IMPORT DUTY AND IMPORT VAT RELIEFS

The percentage varies depending on the type of goods and their country of origin. Duty is charged on:
- the price paid for the goods, plus
- any local sales taxes, plus
- postage, packing and insurance.

However, the cost of postage is excluded from the calculation for Customs Duty on gifts except where the sender has used the Express Mail Service (EMS) as opposed to a standard mail service. Where the value of gifts is below £630 per consignment, a flat rate of duty of 2.5% will be applied, but only if it is to the importer's advantage.

Excise Duty is charged on alcohol and tobacco products and is additional to Customs Duty. The Excise Duty on alcohol products such as wines and spirits depends on the alcohol content and volume. In the case of wine and cider it depends on whether they are sparkling or still. Duty on cigarettes is based on a percentage of the recommended retail selling price plus a flat rate amount per 1,000 cigarettes. On other tobacco products, for example, cigars or hand rolling tobacco, Excise Duty is charged at a flat rate per kilogram.

Import VAT is charged at the same rate that applies to similar goods sold in the UK and applies to commercial goods over £15 in value, and on gifts that are over £34 in value. However, commercial consignments sent to the UK from the Channel Islands do not benefit from any relief of import VAT. The value of the goods for import VAT is based on the:
- basic value of goods, plus
- postage, packing and insurance, plus
- any import (Customs or Excise) duties charged.

As with Customs Duty, the cost of postage is excluded from the calculation for VAT on gifts except where the sender has used the Express Mail Service (EMS) as opposed to a standard mail service.

Used goods are still liable to the same duty and VAT charges as if they were new. However, this may vary depending on their age and condition.

HMRC has special arrangements that allow some overseas traders to charge, collect and pay over to HMRC the import VAT for goods purchased on the internet that would normally be chargeable at the time the goods are imported. These arrangements operate under "Memoranda of Understanding" (MoU) signed with certain overseas Customs and postal authorities. The countries that have an MoU with HMRC are the Channel Islands, Hong Kong, Singapore and New Zealand. Overseas traders wanting to use this procedure must be authorised to do so by their authorities.

Once authorised, foreign businesses are issued with a unique authorisation number, which they must show on the Customs declaration or packaging. Also they will include the statement 'Import VAT Prepaid'.

Where these arrangements are used the importer will not be charged a Royal Mail handling fee when the package is received. A VAT-registered business purchasing goods for use in their business should keep the outer wrapper and invoice from the supplier to support their claim to input tax.

5.26.4 Regular importers

Persons who regularly declare bulk low-value imports to several consignees may apply to HMRC to bulk the imports. This is the 'Low-Value Bulking Imports' (LVBI) concession and prior authorisation from HMRC is required from the National Import Reliefs Unit (NIRU) for an application form (see **Appendix B** for address).

LVBI allows a single import entry declaration to be made, which must have a manifest attached that identifies the individual items and their final delivery address details in that consignment, with sufficient detail for customs control purposes. Import declarations for low-value goods must be entered to HMRC on Form SAD/C88 (or electronic equivalent) using the correct Customs Procedure Code (CPC) for the imported goods.

The LVBI concession must not be used with another simplified import procedure, e.g. it must not be used with Customs Freight Simplified Procedures (CFSP) – see section **2.11.6**. Also, the LVBI concession may not be used for imports of low-value commercial goods.

5.26.5 Packages received from other Member States

Although there is no import duty and import VAT on the goods when they are supplied within the EU, the UKBA carry out selective checks to ensure that no prohibited goods such as drugs, indecent or obscene material, weapons etc. are received in the UK from other EU countries.

However, because goods from the 'Special Territories', that is, countries who are not included in the fiscal territory of the EU, are subject to excise duty and import VAT, they are processed in the same way as goods imported from third countries/territories. The EU and Turkey established a Customs Union on 1 January 1996 and many goods from Turkey no longer attract import duty, but excise duty and import VAT still apply.

5.26.6 Receiving Alcohol and tobacco from other Member States

The receipt of alcohol and tobacco by post on a commercial basis is known as 'Distance Selling', with the goods being liable to both excise duty and import VAT. The sender should have made prior arrangements to account for these taxes no later than the date of dispatch from the dispatching Member State. It is in the purchaser's own interests to ensure these arrangements have been completed; otherwise the goods may be liable to forfeiture. HMRC provide guidance about this in Notice 203A: *Registered Consignors.*[28]

Goods received for the purchaser's own personal use, for example, a gift from another person, or that they have posted to themselves from another Member State, will be liable to excise duty, but not import VAT. The UK excise duty must be secured before the goods are posted or transported, using the 'Distance Selling' procedure. All enquiries about the duty liability of goods received should be directed to the National Excise Helpline on 0300 200 3700.

Gifts of alcohol and tobacco dispatched from the Special Territories are free of import duty, but they are liable to excise duty and import VAT.

5.27 Returned Goods Relief (RGR) – Notice 236

See section **3.4**. The full conditions required to be satisfied to claim RGR for Customs import duty are provided in section 5 of Notice 236 and those for RGR import VAT are in section 6.

5.27.1 Import duty relief

In addition to the conditions set out in section 5 of Notice 236, importers must comply with the following requirements in order to claim import duty RGR on re-imported goods that were previously held either under Inward Processing Relief (IPR) or end-use relief.

IPR goods
RGR can be reclaimed on the re-importation of non-free circulation goods (or goods incorporating non-free circulation components) which were previously relieved from import duty under IPR arrangements, provided that the importer:
- pays the amount of duty originally relieved under IPR;
- meets all other relevant RGR conditions in the checklist at section 5; and
- declares the goods to Customs Procedure Code (CPC) 40 00 58.

Where goods have been imported more than once under IPR, the sum to be paid for RGR purposes is the amount which would have been due had the goods been diverted to free circulation after completion of the last IPR transaction. Full details of the amount previously relieved under IPR must be provided on Form C1314, which is to accompany the SAD/C88.

End-use goods
RGR can be reclaimed on re-imported goods which were previously imported under end-use relief, as long as all the relevant conditions in the checklist at section 5 are met. If the goods are re-imported to end-use again, relief from paying a reduced rate of import duty under end-use can also be claimed under RGR.

---

[28] www.gov.uk/government/publications/excise-notice-203a-registered-consignees/

IMPORT DUTY AND IMPORT VAT RELIEFS

RGR is not limited to goods moving solely between the UK and third countries/territories and it can also be claimed on "triangulation" (*not to be confused with Triangulation for 'intra-EU' removals* – see section **9.12**) goods. Triangulation is the exportation of goods from one Customs Union country to a third country/territory, followed by their re-importation into another Customs Union country, for example, France to America and then back to the UK. Import duty and Common Agricultural Policy (CAP) RGR can be claimed on the re-importation of such goods.

Intra-EC transactions

Import duty and CAP RGR cannot be reclaimed for movements of goods solely between Member States. If Community goods are received from another Member State via a "European Free Trade Area" (EFTA) country, under the "Community/common transit" (CT) procedures, there is no need to claim RGR. The CT procedures may also apply if Community goods are received from another EU Member State via a non-Community territory (other than EFTA) under a single transport document.[29]

5.27.2 Import VAT

The conditions for claiming import VAT RGR are set out in the checklist at section 6 of Notice 236. As a "taxable person" (in the UK meaning a legal or natural person who is or is required to be VAT registered), RGR avoids the need for the person to have to pay and reclaim VAT repeatedly, for example, for goods taken outside the EU on approval and brought back unsold, or tools and equipment which are returned after use outside the EU.

However, an alternative to claiming VAT RGR is to pay or defer the VAT due on re-importation and, subject to the normal rules, deduct it as input tax on the business' next VAT return. HMRC will issue the C79 VAT certificate or VAT copy of the SAD/C88 in such cases. Most goods are liable to VAT at the standard rate, but certain works of art, antiques and collectors' items are entitled to an effective VAT rate of 5% – see VAT Notice 702: *imports*.

For VAT purposes, goods returned to the UK from the Special Territories and countries which have Customs unions with the EU are treated as imported goods. That is because these areas are outside the VAT fiscal territory of the EU – see section **1.6.1**. To claim VAT RGR on such goods, the importer must declare them on the SAD/C88 and use Customs Procedure Code CPC 49 23 F01; the importer can also claim a waiver of the three-year time limit using the former CPC.

Taxable persons may also claim import and/or excise duty RGR when the goods are simultaneously released for free circulation without payment of VAT for zero-rated onward supply to another Member State using CPC 63 23

---

[29] www.gov.uk/guidance/transit-and-other-suspensive-regimes provides full details of the CT arrangements

IMPORT DUTY AND IMPORT VAT RELIEFS

F01 to claim RGR in these circumstances – see VAT Notice 702/7: *Import VAT relief for goods supplied onwards to another country in the EU*.[30]

VAT RGR does not apply to goods returned from elsewhere in the fiscal territory of the EU. Goods sent to or received from another Member State are neither imports nor exports for fiscal purposes. The VAT rules on "Acquisition" apply to goods returned to a UK business from within the EU for the purposes of the business. A non-taxable person need pay no further VAT on goods returned to them from another Member State, provided they had acquired the goods VAT-paid.

5.28 Visiting forces – Notice 431

Goods and services can be supplied free of VAT, indirect taxes and import duty to the following forces and organisations, provided the conditions described Notice 431 are fulfilled:

- NATO visiting forces in the UK, specifically those from Albania, Belgium, Bulgaria, Canada, Croatia, Czech Republic, Denmark, Estonia, France, Germany, Greece, Hungary, Iceland, Italy, Latvia, Lithuania, Luxembourg, Netherlands, Norway, Poland, Portugal, Romania, Slovakia, Slovenia, Spain, Turkey and United States of America (USA);
- the NATO International Military Headquarters at Northwood and Innsworth; and
- the American Battle Monuments Commission in respect of supplies of goods and services for the maintenance of the US military cemeteries at Brookwood and Madingley.

A UK VAT-registered business can supply goods and services to visiting forces free of VAT, import duty, excise duty, landfill tax and climate change levy, provided the conditions described in Notice 431 are fulfilled. Relief is also available from Common Agricultural Product levies (see Notice 800: *CAP Exports*) and Air Passenger Duty (see Notice 550: *Air Passenger Duty*).

Goods which have been sold free of tax or duty to a UK-based visiting force or a member of their personnel may not be sold on, given or otherwise disposed of to a person who does not enjoy the same privileges, without payment to HMRC of the taxes and duties which have been relieved.

5.28.1 Supplies to US visiting forces

Most goods or services supplied to US visiting forces can be supplied free of VAT, and certain goods free of import duty, provided at least one of the following applies:

- the supplier has a written contract or purchase order from an authorised US visiting forces contracting officer;
- payment is made with a Government Purchase Card (GPC);

---

[30] www.gov.uk/government/publications/vat-notice-7027-import-vat-relief-for-goods-supplied-onward-to-another-country-in-the-ec

IMPORT DUTY AND IMPORT VAT RELIEFS

- payment is made with a Procurement (PRO) card;
- payment is made with a Non-Appropriated Fund (NAF) card;
- goods are being supplied from a Customs or excise warehouse; or
- the goods have been imported and processed under the Inward Processing Relief (IPR) regime – see Notice 221: *Inward Processing Relief*.[31]

This includes:
- goods and services supplied to shops on US NATO bases in the UK (operated by the Army and Air Force Exchange Service (AAFES));
- resale outlets run by Morale Welfare and Recreation and Lodging;
- hotel accommodation provided to members of US NATO visiting forces; and
- road fuel used to transport US NATO forces' goods, personnel or school children in the UK under a contract with the US NATO visiting force.

US visiting forces may be supplied with tax and duty-free goods from a Customs or excise warehouse for their official use. Where goods have been imported and processed under the IPR regime the supplier can supply them to US forces free of import duty.

Goods that have been entered to Customs warehousing may be removed from the warehouse for supply to US forces free of import duty and import VAT. The visiting force removing the goods from the warehouse must declare the removal on a SAD/C88, using Customs Procedure Code (CPC) 40 71 007 with box 8 showing the name and EORI number of the NATO visiting force.

5.28.2 Supplies to NATO International Military Headquarters (IMHQ)

Goods or services can be supplied free of VAT to a NATO IMHQ, provided the supplier has an official contract or purchase order from the IMHQ authority. The contract or purchase order must be:
- with a specific and named NATO IMHQ;
- approved by an authorised signatory of the IMHQ; and
- signed by the authorised signatory of the IMHQ. This must not be a rubber stamp or photocopy, and any faxed order must be confirmed in writing.

The contract or purchase order must also include the following statement:

"I hereby certify that the goods and services listed are being purchased for official use by the North Atlantic Treaty Organisation and should be supplied free of VAT in accordance with the agreement with HM Customs and Excise Reference PRIV 59/16."

Where a supplier receives a contract or purchase order containing these elements, they may treat the supply as being zero-rated for VAT purposes. The supplier should obtain an official receipt on completion of the supply and

---

[31] www.gov.uk/government/publications/notice-221-inward-processing-relief

retain this with the contract or purchase order in their VAT records as supporting evidence for the zero-rated supply.

5.28.3 Motor vehicles

A motor vehicle can be supplied VAT-free to any NATO visiting force in the UK for its official use or to a member of any NATO visiting force for their personal use or for the use of their family. Each individual is allowed to own only one motor vehicle free of VAT at any one time, plus a second if his or her spouse is present in the UK. No relief is available to anyone who is a UK national, or anyone who is permanently resident in the UK.

The customer must demonstrate entitlement to receive a tax-free vehicle. If the vehicle is for the official use of US NATO visiting force, they must follow the procedures described in paragraphs 3.2, 3.3 and 3.4 of Notice 431. In all other cases, the customer must provide a properly completed and authorised Form C&E 941 if the supply is from a Customs warehouse, or Form C&E 941A in other cases. Upon receipt of the completed, signed, form the supplier may treat the supply as being zero-rated for VAT.

5.28.4 American cemeteries

Goods or services supplied to the American Military Cemetery and Memorial at Madingley, Cambridge and Brookwood, Surrey can be free of VAT provided they're solely used for the maintenance of those cemeteries. In order to zero rate the supply the supplier must have an official written order or contract from the American Battle Monuments Commission in Paris, or from the American Military Cemetery and Memorial in Cambridge, signed by an official of one of these organisations.

The order or contract must certify that the goods and/or services are supplied for the maintenance of US military cemeteries in the UK. When the supply is complete, the supplier must obtain and keep in their VAT records an official receipt, or a stamped certificate, to show that the goods or services have been received in accordance with the terms of the contract or order. The supply can then be zero-rated.

5.29 Visitors to the UK – Notice 3

Notice 3 explains how a private individual can import their personal belongings and a private motor vehicle into the UK from a third country/territory free of import duty and import VAT.[32]

There are a number of reliefs in addition to the "Personal allowances" available to all travellers – see section **5.10** above. "Temporary Admission" (TA) relief for personal effects or a private motor vehicle may be available if the individual's normal home is outside the EU – see section **3.8**.

---

[32]www.gov.uk/government/publications/notice-3-bringing-your-belongings-pets-and-private-motor-vehicles-to-uk-from-outside-the-eu/

5.29.1 Personal effects

TA relief can be claimed for personal effects reasonably required for a journey such as clothing, toiletries, personal jewellery and other articles clearly of a personal nature, including pets. Relief is available for a stay in the EU up to a maximum of 24 months. Relief is also available for sporting firearms and ammunition but the individual will need to hold a Full TA authorisation, which can be obtained from HMRC by completing and submitting Form C&E 1331 at least one month before the intended date of importation.

Further education students coming to stay in the EU to study on a full-time basis do not need to use the TA procedures for clothing and household linen or items to be used in their studies, for example calculators and PCs, and household effects for furnishing their accommodation.

For personal belongings under €10,000 in value (except pets and firearms) the traveller can go through the Green 'nothing to declare' Channel. For belongings that exceed this value, on import the traveller needs to apply for Simplified TA authorisation by making a declaration on SAD/ C88 quoting CPC 53 00 D04 (or CPC 53 00 003 where VAT only is due) and providing security.

5.29.2 Private motor vehicles

TA relief is available on a motor vehicle temporarily admitted for private use (including any accompanying spare parts, accessories and equipment) if:
- it is registered outside the EU or, if not registered, belongs to the individual or someone else who has their normal home outside the EU;
- it is not sold, lent or hired, or otherwise disposed of in the EU; and
- it is re-exported from the EU within six months.

However, a motor vehicle that belongs to a student or someone fulfilling an assignment of a specific duration, for example a work contract, in the UK can remain in the EU for the period of their studies or until the end of that assignment. If the student or other entitled person wishes or needs to extend their stay in the UK, the period allowed under TA relief can, in exceptional circumstances, be extended within reasonable limits. They should write to the National Import Reliefs Unit (NIRU) to explain why an extension is needed.

Additionally, there is relief for an EU resident where they import a vehicle from a third country/territory for later export as an emigrant. Import duty and import VAT are relieved provided the vehicle is exported within three months of its arrival in the EU and if requested by HMRC, the person can provide evidence of their emigration status.

5.29.3 Pet animals

Pet cats, dogs (including guide and assistance dogs) and ferrets must meet certain conditions to be able to enter or re-enter the UK without quarantine from listed countries.

IMPORT DUTY AND IMPORT VAT RELIEFS

They must have:
- a microchip;
- been vaccinated against rabies (at a minimum age of 12 weeks);
- an EU pet passport or official third country veterinary certificate;
- tapeworm treatment (for dogs only);
- an authorised carrier and approved routes; and

wait three calendar months from date of blood sample was taken before travelling, the vet must supply a copy of the test results and it must show that the vaccination was successful. Pet rabbits and rodents from countries outside the EU must spend four months in quarantine and have a rabies import licence and must enter into the UK at a Border Inspection Post (BIP). Visitors should consult HMRC's guidance notes about bringing animals from unlisted non-EU countries.[33]

Except all of the following countries, which are "listed", all other countries are "unlisted" and special procedures must be followed.

Listed countries:
Antigua and Barbuda, Argentina, Aruba, Ascension Island, Australia, Bahrain, Barbados, Belarus, Bermuda, BES Islands (Bonair, Saint Eustatius and Saba), Bosnia-Herzegovina, British Virgin Islands, Canada, Cayman Islands, Chile, Curaçao, Falkland Islands, Fiji, French Polynesia, Hong Kong, Japan, Malaysia, Mauritius, Mexico, Montserrat, New Caledonia, New Zealand, Russian Federation, Saint Maarten, Singapore, St Helena, St Kitts and Nevis, St Lucia, St Pierre and Miquelon, St Vincent and The Grenadines, Taiwan, The former Yugoslav Republic of Macedonia, Trinidad and Tobago, United Arab Emirates, USA (includes American Samoa, Guam, Northern Mariana Islands, Puerto Rico and the US virgin Islands), Vanuatu, Wallis and Futuna.

5.29.4 Guide dogs and assistance dogs

Guide dogs and other assistance dogs are allowed to travel in the aircraft cabin with their owners. Owners must check that the airline has an agreement with the Animal and Plant Health Agency (APHA) to carry assistance dogs or they may experience delays when arriving in the UK. The Guide Dogs Association website has more advice about assistance dogs travelling.[34]

When the pet arrives in the UK, the pet checker will scan the animal's microchip and check the accompanying documents. If these are not in order or the animal has not been properly prepared for travel it will be put into quarantine or sent back to the country it travelled from and the owner will be liable for the cost for this.

---

[33] www.gov.uk/take-pet-abroad/listed-and-unlisted-countries to ensure they can bring the animal into the UK
[34] see www.guidedogs.org.uk/

5.29.5 Transfer of residence

Persons who are either moving to the EU or are returning to the EU after living abroad, for example secondees, can bring in their belongings or motor vehicle free of import duty and import VAT so long as they:
- are moving their normal home to the EU;
- have lived outside the EU for a continuous period of at least 12 months;
- have possessed and used them for at least six months outside the EU before they are imported;
- did not get them under a duty/tax free scheme;
- declare them to HMRC;
- will keep them for their personal use; and
- do not sell, lend, hire out or otherwise dispose of them in the EU within 12 months of importation, unless first notifying HMRC and paying Customs import duty and import VAT on disposal.

Eligible goods are household effects and personal property and for the owner's own use. It does not extend to items held under trusts, corporations, companies, associations, groups or organisations.

They include clothing, furniture, portable tools of trade, pets and other household and personal effects, but not alcoholic drinks or tobacco products. Relief is only available on those items where they are carried personally and they are within the duty-free allowances.

The owner should provide HMRC with any official documentation and papers held, that will help show the owners have used and possessed these items for their own personal family use, for example:
- any purchase invoices, dated delivery notes, repair or maintenance bills, guarantees or warranties;
- any foreign registration or licensing papers;
- any police certificate of registration; and
- any insurance policy documents, especially household contents lists of the items in their previous residence.

If the change of residence first involves a move to the UK before the permanent move to another EU country the person must seek permission from that country's Customs Authority before moving there. In this case there are two options available:
- before importing the household effects and personal property into the EU, the person or their shipping agent should apply direct for the Relief to the Customs Authority in charge of where the person plans to live; or
- after shipping the consignment of household effects and personal property into the UK as the first 'point-of-arrival', an application for the relief should be made direct to the customs authority responsible for where they intend to move home to, during which time their goods are either stored

IMPORT DUTY AND IMPORT VAT RELIEFS

pending the decision on granting the relief, or the goods can be moved under transit procedures.

The belongings or a vehicle can arrive in the UK before the person arrives. In this case they must arrive no more than six months before moving or returning to the UK, unless occupational commitments have forced the earlier transfer in which case HMRC will allow an appropriate extension. However, HMRC may call for security for the duty and tax. HMRC will discharge the security when a person arrives and can prove that they qualify for the relief. Additionally, the belongings or a vehicle can arrive in the UK after the person arrives but they should normally arrive no more than 12 months after the date of moving or returning to the UK.

HMRC Customs Information Paper No 56 explaining these rules in detail.[35]

5.29.6 Items bought under "Duty and tax-free" regimes

Duty and tax relief is only available on items that were originally bought in a duty and tax-free regime when they were purchased by diplomats, members of an officially recognised international organisation or a member of NATO or the UK forces, including the civilian staff accompanying them or the spouse of one of these. Alternatively, relief will be granted where the purchaser can prove that duty and tax have since been paid and have not been, nor will be, refunded.

5.29.7 Personal possessions and motor vehicles retuning to the EU

The international transfer of jobs and lifestyles often means that individuals return to the EU after a period spent abroad. The return of personal possessions and a motor vehicle can be relieved of import duty and import VAT as follows:

Import duty
- if the possessions, or any components, were previously imported into the EU, that any import duty was paid and not refunded when they were exported from the EU;
- they have had no alteration outside the EU other than necessary running repairs; and they are brought back to the EU within three years.

VAT
- they were taken outside the EU by the individual or on their behalf;
- any VAT or equivalent turnover tax had been paid on them in the EU and not refunded when they were taken outside the EU;
- they were not purchased free of VAT or equivalent turnover tax in the EU under any personal export schemes; or

---

[35] www.gov.uk/government/publications/customs-information-paper-56-2014-entitlement-to-relief

- they have had no alteration outside the EU other than necessary running repairs and they are brought back to the EU within three years.

For both Customs import duty and import VAT purposes, HMRC will waive the three-year time limit where the other conditions are met, and they are satisfied that the possessions or motor vehicle were previously located in the EU and are not being imported in the course of the individual's or any other person's business.

Where the EU has agreed a Preferential Trade Agreement with another country the importer may be able to claim a preferential (reduced or nil) rate of Customs Duty at import if:
- they are covered by the provisions of that agreement;
- they satisfy the relevant origin conditions; and
- proof of preferential origin (a valid preference certificate or where applicable, a declaration on an invoice or other commercial document) is produced to HMRC if required.

However, the importer will still have to pay import VAT.

5.29.8 "Marriage relief"

The relief applies to persons who are newly married or who are shortly to marry and are coming to live in the EU. The wedding outfits of the bride and groom and their other household effects can be imported free of import duty and import VAT, provided that the following criteria are met:
1) the individual(s) have had their normal home outside the EU for a continuous period of at least 12 months;
2) they are moving their normal home to the EU on marriage;
3) they declare them to HMRC together with proof of the marriage; and
4) they do not sell, lend, hire or otherwise dispose of the possessions in the EU within 12 months of importation, unless first notifying HMRC and paying import duty and import VAT on their disposal.

HMRC state in Notice 3 that they will normally waive the first condition if the individual could not meet this due to circumstances beyond their control. The relief can be claimed no matter how long the goods have been owned and whether the actual wedding takes place in or outside the EU. The relief is also still claimable where either partner already lives in the EU before the wedding or only one partner is moving their normal home to the EU because their spouse already lives there.

There are some exceptions to the relief, these being motor vehicles and their trailers, caravans, mobile homes, pleasure boats, aircraft and alcoholic drinks and tobacco products.

Relief also covers wedding gifts for the bride and groom provided the following conditions are met:
- the gifts are intended personally for the bride and groom;

IMPORT DUTY AND IMPORT VAT RELIEFS

- they are of a kind normally given on marriage;
- they are given by persons who normally live outside the EU; and
- they are declared to HMRC on arrival together with proof of the marriage.

Again, the relief does not apply to alcoholic drinks and tobacco products and there is a maximum allowance of £800 per wedding gift, but there is no monetary limit for wedding gifts brought to the EU as part of an individual's personal belongings.

The goods must arrive between two months before the wedding and four months after the wedding and they will be free of import duty and import VAT as long as the proof of the wedding is provided to HMRC. However, where the goods arrive before the wedding, HMRC will ask for security of the import duty and import VAT, which will be repaid upon satisfactory proof of the wedding being provided to them later. If the individual is unable to meet the conditions for relief for any possessions or a private motor car, then import duty and import VAT will be due on the relevant items.

HMRC will ask to see a copy of the marriage certificate or marriage license or similar proof as officially authorised evidence.

5.30 Visual and auditory materials – Notice 373[36]

Provided they are of an educational, scientific or cultural nature, relief is available on the following goods:
- films and film strips;
- newsreels/video tapes of current news value, but limited to two copies for copying purposes, and archival film material for use with newsreels/video tapes;
- microcards or other information storage media required in computerised information and documentation services;
- recordings;
- wall charts, patterns, models and mock-ups designed solely for demonstration and education purposes; and
- materials for programmed instruction, holograms for laser projection and multi-media kits.

Some, but not all, of these goods may already be subject to a 'nil' rate of import duty. Most are, however, liable to import VAT at the standard rate. The procedures laid out in Notice 373 only need to be followed where the importer wishes to claim relief on goods liable to a positive rate of duty, and/or wishes to claim relief from import VAT. However, VAT relief is only available where the goods have been produced by the United Nations (UN) or one of its specialised agencies.

---

[36] www.gov.uk/government/publications/notice-373-importing-visual-and-auditory-materials-free-of-duty-and-vat/

For non-UN produced goods, the relief can only be obtained by educational, scientific or cultural establishments approved by the National Import Reliefs Unit (NIRU). Approval from NIRU is not required for goods produced by the UN or its agencies. There are no restrictions on the use or disposal of UN produced goods. However, goods produced by non-UN bodies can only be lent, hired out or transferred to another approved establishment without payment of duty where the NIRU has given its permission before the intention is fulfilled. If non-UN produced goods are disposed of in any other way, import duty and import VAT must be repaid to HMRC. Details of how to apply for authorisation to dispose of goods or to repay any import duty and import VAT should be obtained from the HMRC National Advice Service.

5.31 Zero-rated articles including printed matter

VAT Act 1994, Schedule 8 sets out a range of goods and services that are zero-rated in the UK. Not all items falling within Schedule 8 can be zero-rated on import. This includes:

- the construction of buildings and materials (group 5);
- gold (group 10);
- drugs, medicines and aids for handicapped persons (group 12, items 1 and 1A); and
- drugs, medicines and aids for handicapped persons (group 12 items 2-20) which are neither imported by a handicapped person for domestic or personal use, nor imported by a charity for making them available to handicapped persons (by sale or otherwise) for domestic or personal use.

There is a wide range of printed matter that is zero-rated on import. Notice 342 sections 4 and 5 provide full details of this matter, also reproduced below:

Description	Tariff heading
Goods of an educational, scientific or cultural nature relieved from Customs import duty:	
1. microfilms of books, children's picture books and drawing or colouring books, school exercise books (workbooks), crossword-puzzle books, newspapers and periodicals, printed documents or reports of a non-commercial character, and of loose illustrations, printed pages and reproduction proofs for the production of books.	3705 20 00
2. reproduction films for the production of books, but excluding those for magazines, periodicals etc.	3705 10 00 & 3705 90 00
3. children's picture, drawing or colouring books.	4903 00 00
4. maps, charts and diagrams of interest in scientific fields such as geology, zoology, botany, mineralogy, palaeontology, archaeology, ethnology, meteorology, climatology and geophysics.	4905 99 00
5. architectural, industrial or engineering plans and designs, and reproductions thereof.	4906 00 00
6. catalogues of books and publications, being books and	4911 10 90

publications offered for sale by publishers or booksellers established outside the territory of the European Communities.	
7. catalogues of films, recording or other visual and auditory materials of an educational, scientific or cultural character.	4911 10 90
8. posters for the promotion of tourism and tourist publications, brochures, guidebooks, timetables, pamphlets and like publications; whether or not illustrated, including those published by private concerns, designed to encourage the public to travel outside the territory of the European Communities, including microcopies of such articles*.	4911 10 90
9. bibliographical information material for distribution free of charge*.	4911 10 90
10. loose illustrations, printed pages and reproduction proofs to be used for the production of books, including microcopies of such articles*.	4911 99 00
11. microcopies of books, children's picture books and drawing or colouring books, school exercise books (workbooks), crossword-puzzle books, newspapers and periodicals and of documents or reports of a non-commercial character*.	4911 99 00
12. publications designed to encourage the public to study outside the territory of the European Communities, including microcopies of such publications*.	4911 99 00
13. meteorological and geophysical diagrams.	4911 99 00
14. maps and charts in relief, of interest in scientific fields such as geology, zoology, botany, mineralogy, palaeontology, archaeology, ethnology, meteorology, climatology and geophysics.	9023 00 80
15. other printed matter, including printed pictures and photographs, in relief for the blind and partially sighted.	4911(various)
* the exemption does not however apply to articles in which the advertising matter covers more than 25% of the surface. In the case of publications and posters for the promotion of tourism this percentage applies only to non-related commercial publicity.	
Other goods relieved from Customs import duty and import VAT:	
1. Documents sent free of charge to the public services of member states.	Chapters 48 and 49 and any other relevant headings
2. Publications of foreign governments and publications of official international bodies intended for distribution without charge.	
3. Ballot papers for elections organised by bodies set up in third countries.	
4. Specimen signatures and printed circulars concerning signatures sent as part of customary exchanges of information between public services or banking establishments.	
5. Official printed matter sent to the central banks of the member states.	
6. Reports, statements, notes, prospectuses, application forms and other documents (including valid issued share and bond	

	certificates) drawn up by companies registered in a third country and sent to the bearers or subscribers of securities issued by such companies. Note-share and bond certificates which require registration by the fiscal agent before becoming valid are not eligible for relief.	
7.	Files, archives, printed forms and other documents to be used in international meetings, conferences or congresses, and reports on such gatherings.	Chapters 48 and 49 and any other relevant headings
8.	Plans, technical drawings, traced designs, descriptions and other similar documents imported with a view to obtaining or fulfilling orders in third countries or to participating in a competition held in the customs territory of the Community.	
9.	Documents to be used in examinations held in the customs territory of the Community by institutions set up in third countries.	
10.	Printed forms to be used as official documents in the international movement of vehicles or goods, within the framework of international conventions.	
11.	Printed forms, labels, tickets and similar documents sent by transport undertakings or by undertakings of the hotel industry in a third country to travel agencies set up in the customs territory of the Community. (Travel agencies include airlines, railway undertakings, ferry operators and similar organisations).	
12.	Printed forms and tickets, bills of lading, way-bills and other commercial or office documents which have been used.	
13.	Official printed forms from third country or international authorities, and printed matter conforming to international standards sent for distribution by third country associations to corresponding associations located in the customs territory of the Community.	
14.	Tax and similar stamps proving payment of charges in third countries.	49.07 and any other relevant headings
15.	Photographs, slides and stereotype mats for photographs, whether or not captioned, sent to press agencies or newspaper or magazine publishers.	37.05, 49.11 or 84.42 50 and any other relevant headings
16.	Recorded media (e.g. microfilms, punched cards, punched paper tape and sound recordings etc) used for the transmission of information sent free of charge to the addressee, in so far as duty free admission does not give rise to abuse or to major distortions of competition.	All relevant headings
17.	Objects to be submitted as evidence or for like purposes to the courts or other official agencies of the member states.	All headings
18.	Printed advertising material including catalogues, price lists,	49.11

	directions for use or brochures, relating to goods for sale or hire, transport, commercial insurance or banking services offered by a person carrying on a business outside the EU whose name is clearly displayed thereon, provided that each document or, in the case of a consignment comprising several copies of the same document, the total gross weight, does not exceed one kilogram. Bulked consignments from one sender to a single recipient are not eligible for relief.	
19.	Articles for advertising purposes (other than covered by (18) above), of no intrinsic commercial value, sent free of charge by suppliers to their customers, which apart from their advertising function, are not capable of being used otherwise.	All relevant headings
20.	Trademark, patterns or designs and their supporting documents, as well as applications for patents for invention or the like, to be submitted to the competent bodies to deal with protection of copyrights or the protection of industrial or commercial patent rights.	All relevant headings
21.	Documents sent to be distributed free of charge for the purpose of encouraging persons to visit foreign countries, in particular to attend cultural, tourist, sporting, religious, trade or professional meetings or events, including foreign hotel lists, and yearbooks published by or on behalf of official tourist agencies and timetables for foreign transport services, provided the documents do not contain more than 25% of private advertising (excluding advertising for Community firms).	49.10 and 49.11 and any other relevant headings

6 Accounting for import duty and import VAT

6.1 Determining the VAT amount due

The import duty (including import VAT) is the "Customs debt" and is due to the Commission (not the UK); in the UK it is collected by HMRC on the Commission's behalf. A detailed description on Customs debt is provided in section **2.12**.

Unless the goods are placed under Excise warehousing or one of the Customs arrangements listed in Notice 702/9: *Import Customs Procedures*[1] and, as explained in section 3, the payment of the import VAT due must normally be made either at the time of importation, or be deferred together with any duty due, provided the importer or their agent are approved to use the deferment scheme – see section **6.5** below.

Unless the goods are relieved of VAT, for example children's clothes (zero-rated) or certain healthcare products (reduced-rated), they are liable to import VAT at the standard-rate. Some products could also be exempt from VAT so it is essential that at the time of completing the SAD/C88 that the VAT liability of the relevant goods is confirmed.

Most importantly, if goods are being imported or re-imported under one of the various reliefs set out in section 3 it is vital that the correct entry is made to avoid import duty and import VAT being charged.

As an alternative to deferring the payment of all the import charges on an entry to either the importer's or the agent's deferment account, payment of the VAT may be deferred to the importer's account and all other charges to the agent's. Volume 3 of the HMRC Tariff explains how to do this. Further information can also be found in Notice 101: *Deferring Duty, VAT and other charges*.[2] and **6.5** below.

The import entry must be presented at the HMRC National Clearance Hub. If the consignment is covered by a single commodity code for Customs purposes, but includes goods liable to VAT at both the standard and zero rate (such as clothing for adults and children), the importer or agent must complete a separate item on the entry for the goods liable to each rate of VAT. Special rules apply to the completion of the tax lines in the calculation of taxes box (box 47) depending on whether the entry is presented at a manual or Customs computerised location.

When the precise amount of import duty and import VAT due cannot be assessed at the time the declaration is presented, release of the goods can

---

[1] www.gov.uk/government/publications/vat-notice-7029-vat-import-customs-procedures/
[2] www.gov.uk/government/publications/notice-101-deferring-duty-vat-and-other-charges/

usually be allowed on payment of a deposit or the provision of security to cover the amount of duty considered to be in dispute.

A VAT-registered importer may pay the import VAT outright, based on the value for VAT that includes the highest potential duty amount. An import VAT certificate (form C79) will be issued and the importer can claim repayment of the import VAT on their VAT return under the normal rules. Alternatively, the importer may provide security for the disputed amount of VAT.

However, this might not be an advantage since if this method is selected a C79 will not be issued until after the duty amount has been adjusted. The adjustment may not take place until some weeks after the deposit has been made, depending on how long it takes to produce the necessary evidence. Therefore, input tax recovery may be delayed accordingly. Importers who are not VAT-registered must secure the amount of VAT in dispute.

6.2 Amendments to Declarations and of the sums due to HMRC

Where an amendment of the import declaration is made after the goods have been released out of official charge and this results in *less* import VAT being payable than was originally declared and paid, the importer can reclaim the higher amount of tax as input tax in the normal way. However, the importer could choose to deal with it in the following way:

Non VAT-registered and non-fully taxable traders can claim overpaid customs duties and import VAT using form C285 *Application for repayment/remission*.[3]

VAT-registered traders can use form C285 to claim repayment of overpaid customs duties, but must claim the equivalent of any overpaid import VAT as input tax on their VAT return subject to the normal VAT rules.

Where the overpayment of customs duty or import VAT is made via a deferment account (see **6.5** below) the importer may (regardless of their VAT status) apply to have their deferment account adjusted to reflect the correct amount of duty or import VAT. The request for a current month adjustment must be made on form C285 and sent to the National Duty Repayment Centre (NDRC) at:

HMRC
National Duty Repayment Centre
Priory Court
St John's Road
Dover CT17 9SH

Telephone: 03000 582687

---

[3] public-online.hmrc.gov.uk/lc/content/xfaforms/profiles/forms.html?contentRoot= repository:///Applications/Customs_A/1.0/C285&template=C285.xdp

ACCOUNTING FOR IMPORT DUTY AND IMPORT VAT

Fax: 03000 583027
Email: NDRC Enquiries ndrcenquiries@hmrc.gsi.gov.uk

Where amendment of a declaration results in *more* import VAT being payable, the importer must submit the additional payment, and a completed form C18 to the HMRC National Clearance Hub (NCH) office at:

C18 Team
NCH
HMRC
Ralli Quays
3 Stanley Street
Salford M60 9HL

The additional payment will appear on the import VAT certificate (form C79).

In a UK VAT group registration, although the "Representative Member" is the nominated VAT registrant on behalf of all the constituent members, the Customs debtor is the member stated on the SAD/C88. However, all VAT group members are jointly and severally liable for the VAT debts of a fellow group member that arises during their period of membership, so if the Customs debt is, in fact, import VAT then each extant group member will be liable to HMRC for these debts.

6.3 Postal Imports
There are two sets of rules for imports received by post, based on the value of the consignment.

Imports below £2,000
Where the importer is registered for VAT and they are importing goods in the course of their business Royal Mail/Parcelforce request the payment of VAT when the package is delivered. The importer must keep the charge label postal wrapper and any Customs declaration (that is, form CN22 or form CN23) that was attached to the package to support any claim to input tax.

Imports above £2,000
For postal imports with a value greater than £2,000 a declaration on the SAD/C88 must be lodged and this will be sent to the importer for completion. The SAD/C88 should be returned to HMRC with an invoice and/or other acceptable evidence of the value of the goods. Import VAT and any other charges due at importation must be paid before the goods can be released to the importer but this may be done by use of the deferment account if the importer is approved.

Following payment HMRC will send to the importer a copy of the declaration to support any claim to input tax deduction. Further information regarding postal imports is provided in Notices 143: *A guide for international post users* and 144: *Trade imports by post: how to complete Customs documents.*

The VAT can be claimed under the Postponed Accounting System as explained in section **6.6.1**.

The importer may account for the VAT in Box 1 ("Output tax") of the VAT return for the period covering the importation. A corresponding amount can be entered in Box 4 ("Input tax") in the same VAT return and HMRC will not issue a C79. The evidence to support the claim to import VAT is the invoice from the supplier. HMRC can, however, require an importer to give security for the VAT at issue.

Importers must ensure that their UK VAT number is clearly identified on the postal package to avoid being charged import VAT, as a cash refund will not be credited to the importer if any errors are made. The charge label, postal wrapper and any Form CN22 or Form CN23 must be retained as evidence to support the importer's claim to input tax.

6.4 Unregistered importers

Importers who are not registered for VAT must declare goods on importation and pay or defer the import VAT in the same way as anyone who is registered for VAT. However, as they are not entitled to reclaim the import VAT paid as input tax, they will not receive an import VAT certificate (C79). Unregistered importers *can* still claim import VAT paid on goods when VAT was *overpaid at importation*. They should make a written request on form C285 as explained in section **6.2** above.

Claims for remission of the import VAT can also be made where the goods are not what were ordered or are otherwise not in accordance with contract. The procedure for making the claim is set out in Notice 266: *Rejected imports: repayment or remission of duty and VAT* as explained in section **3.7**.[4]

6.5 Duty Deferment

Under duty deferment the import duty and import VAT due to be paid at the time the import entry is lodged can be paid a later date. Deferment can be arranged by an importer themselves, the owner of goods in a warehouse, or an import agent (including warehousekeepers) who enter the goods for importers or owners, provided they hold a Deferment Approval Number (a DAN) and which identifies their duty deferment account.

By holding an approved DAN importers, owners or agents can delay paying the charges for an average of 30 days so they do not have to pay immediately each time they want to clear goods. Simply by inserting the DAN on import entry documentation a month's charges can be settled with a single payment using the convenience of direct debit. Deferment also enables HMRC to normally clear the goods more quickly because they do not have to handle payments for each transaction. HMRC do not charge for the deferment

---

[4] www.gov.uk/government/publications/notice-266-rejected-imports-repayment-or-remission-of-duty-and-vat/

ACCOUNTING FOR IMPORT DUTY AND IMPORT VAT

account but the importer or agent must provide a guarantee as a form of security in order to be approved.

All of the charges listed below can be deferred:

Name of charge	Circumstances
Import Value Added Tax (VAT)	Where payable on imported goods at the time of import or on removal from HMRC warehouses or from a free zone
Customs duties	
Excise duties (including tobacco products duty)	
Levies imposed under the Common Agricultural Policy (CAP) of the EC	
Positive Monetary Compensatory Amounts under the CAP	
Anti-Dumping or Countervailing Duties imposed by the EC	
Compensatory interest on IPR goods diverted to free circulation	
Temporary Import interest on TI goods diverted to free circulation	
Interest charges on Customs debts	
Excise duty VAT	Where payable on the following home-produced or home manufactured goods on removal from excise warehouse: a. spirits and liqueurs (including perfumes and composite goods containing excisable spirit) b. wine and made-wine fortified or rendered sparkling in the warehouse c. cider and perry, d. beer; and e. other alcoholic beverages; and Where payable on hydrocarbon oils on removal from warehouse
Tobacco products duty	Where payable on tobacco products on removal from registered tobacco premises
C 18 Post Clearance Demands	Where Customs charges have been under declared and additional charges are due

The charges are deferred during one calendar month (the accounting period) and must be paid as a total sum on the 15th day of the next month and if the 15th day is not a working day, on the next working day after it. This means that

ACCOUNTING FOR IMPORT DUTY AND IMPORT VAT

charges can be deferred for between two and six weeks giving an average of 30 days credit.

The deferment position is slightly different for excise duty where the accounting period runs from the 15th of a month to the 14th of the next month. Payment must be made on the 29th of the latter month (or 28 February in non-leap years). If the 29 (or 28 February in non-leap years) is not a working day, on the working day before that.

The holder of the DAN must pay the amount owing per deferment period by the BACS system of Direct Debit. HMRC arrange for the total amount deferred in the accounting period to be debited automatically on the appointed payment day. Currently whilst the UK is operating outside of the European Single Currency it is not possible to make BACS Direct Debit payments in Euro.

If the BACS payment fails the deferment account holder must settle the amount owing immediately. Deferred debts which are not paid as they fall due may result in the duty deferment facility being stopped or even withdrawn. This could affect other customs facilities that are dependent upon duty deferment. Deferred Customs debts may also be subject to interest charges.

Import agents can be exposed in this position because, where the agent is acting in their own name but on behalf of an importer, they are jointly and severally liable for any customs debt that may arise.

6.5.1 Security

Under EC law all customs debts incurred when goods are cleared must be secured if they are not being paid at that time. As such, the granting of duty deferment facilities depends on the provision of adequate security. HMRC can, under the same legal provisions, also select the appropriate form of security for its Duty Deferment Scheme.

HMRC require security in the form of a guarantee from a bank, insurance company or building society only. Guarantees provide the most effective, practical and flexible way of securing duty deferment charges. Additionally the bank, insurance company or building society must have HMRC's approval to act as a guarantor. Most banks, insurance companies and building societies have this approval, but in cases of doubt the applicant should contact the HMRC Central Deferment Office (CDO) at:

HM Revenue and Customs
Banking Operations
Central Deferment Office
6th Floor North West
Alexander House
21 Victoria Avenue

Southend-on-Sea
Essex SS99 1AA

Telephone: 01702 36 7425/7429/7431/7450[5]
Fax: 01702 366091

No other form of security, or guarantor, is acceptable.

The guarantee must be applied for using Form C1201, which has been specifically worded, in agreement with the relevant financial authorities, to cover the Duty Deferment Scheme only. By applying for deferment the importer and their guarantor agree to its conditions and clauses within.

The guarantor agrees to cover each and every sum deferred up to an overall maximum amount in any calendar month. This amount is the deferment limit for the month and must be enough to cover all deferrable liabilities for any calendar month period. Security must be provided to cover fully all customs and excise duties deferred. However, import VAT may not need to be fully secured where Simplified Import VAT Accounting (SIVA) is approved – see below.

6.5.2 Simplified Import VAT Accounting (SIVA)

SIVA is a scheme that was introduced on 1 December 2003 and is an integral part of the Blueprint for International Trade, the main objective of which is to increase voluntary compliance whilst facilitating legitimate trade. The implementation of this reduced security scheme marks a step towards achieving this goal – see section **2.4**.

SIVA aims to provide compliance cost savings for legitimate businesses and should contribute to UK importers, whatever their size, improving their competitiveness. This is because SIVA eases the financial impact on importers by reducing the level of financial security required to guarantee the payment of Import VAT through the Duty Deferment System.

Importers must be authorised to operate SIVA. This may mean that where the only charges going through a deferment account are import VAT, no guarantee is required at all. Customs and excise duties must still be fully secured. Once approved for SIVA, importers will be able to calculate the level of deferment guarantee that may be required before making contact with the guarantor and submission of the duty deferment application.

Traders applying for a deferment account can also apply for SIVA, subject to the qualifying criteria set out below. The SIVA application Form SIVA 1 can be downloaded from the HMRC website at www.hmrc.gov.uk where further detailed SIVA information can also be found. The SIVA application forms should be completed and returned to:

---

[5]CDO phone enquiry lines are open Monday-Friday, 9am-12.30pm and 1.30pm-4.30pm

ACCOUNTING FOR IMPORT DUTY AND IMPORT VAT

SIVA Approvals Team
HM Revenue and Customs
Ruby House
8 Ruby Place
Aberdeen AB10 1ZP

A set of forms consists of:
- C1200 Application for Approval of Deferment Arrangements
- C1201 Guarantee for Payment of Sums Due to the Commissioners of HMRC   C1202 Duty Deferment – instruction to your bank or building society to pay by Direct Debit
- C1207N Standing authority for agent/freight forwarder to request deferment of duty payment against Importer's DAN.

To obtain SIVA approval businesses must:
- have a duty deferment agreement with HMRC;
- have been registered for VAT for at least three years; and
- have a good history of VAT compliance.

Importantly, they must not:
- owe any money to HMRC;
- have been charged with a serious offence by HMRC;
- have defaulted on payments more than once in the last 12 months;
- have any default surcharges in the last months; and
- have transferred the business as a going concern in the last three years unless the transfer happened because of a change in legal status, such as becoming a limited company.

Businesses that do not already have a duty deferment facility should apply for SIVA first. HMRC will not approve SIVA where the applicant has any of the following difficulties:
- administration;
- liquidation;
- insolvency;
- receivership; or
- other financial difficulties.

Once approved for SIVA the deferment account will have two limits:
(a) a deferment account limit which must be sufficient to cover all deferred charges; and
(b) a deferment guarantee level which must be backed up by a deferment guarantee and sufficient to cover all deferred customs and excise duties.

Full details of SIVA are provided by HMRC in Notice 101.[6]

---

[6] www.gov.uk/government/publications/notice-101-deferring-duty-vat-and-other-charges/

6.6 Recovery of import VAT

The definition of "input tax" is contained in VAT Act 1994 section 24(c)(1) which includes *"VAT paid or payable by him on the importation of any goods from a place outside the Member States"*, provided that the goods or services are used or are to be used for the purpose of any business carried on or to be carried on by, in this case, the importer.

VAT Act 1994 section 26 (1) then adds that

> The amount of input tax for which a taxable person is entitled to credit at the end of any period shall be so much of the input tax for the period (that is input tax on supplies, acquisitions and importations in the period) as is allowable by or under regulations as being attributable to supplies within subsection (2) below.

Subsection (2) lists the types of transactions that the taxable person (the importer) must make in order to recover the input tax. Subsections (3) to (5) provide further rules on how much input tax and in what circumstances any apportionment or adjustment must be made.

Where a taxable person either imports goods which belong wholly or partly to someone else, and/or after importation are to be used wholly or partly for non-business purposes, then the tax due on importation is not available for credit as input tax; however, a separate claim may be made to recover the VAT amount paid. This would apply, for example, where a registered marine repair trader imports a privately-owned yacht for repair and subsequent delivery to its owner in the UK. Traders may make a separate claim for repayment which will be allowed to the extent that a double charge to tax would otherwise arise, e.g. where the importer is part-owner of the goods and subsequently sells all or part of his interest in them by way of supply made in the course or furtherance of business.

For importers that are importing the goods for the purposes of their business, the normal evidence of the import VAT paid is the monthly certificate, known as form C79. HMRC send the C79s to the VAT/EORI registered person whose VAT registration number is shown in box 8 of the SAD/C88. Importers must ensure that they quote the correct EORI number on the SAD/C88, since any mistakes could result in the VAT paid not appearing on their own C79, or indeed, the import VAT that properly belongs to another importer could be shown on their C79.

If an importer discovers that import VAT belonging to a different importer has been credited to their C79, the VAT shown must not be reclaimed as input tax as it is not incurred in furthering the importer's own business. If the importer or the agent that made the import declaration later corrects the error, a negative amount will appear on the next C79. If the VAT shown has been reclaimed incorrectly, the importer must show the negative amount as a credit on the VAT deductible side of their VAT account in order to reduce the amount of input tax they can properly claim in that period.

ACCOUNTING FOR IMPORT DUTY AND IMPORT VAT

If an importer considers that any amount of import VAT paid or deferred is missing from a C79 this could be because the relevant item reflects an import that is not recorded in C79s, the business is newly registered and the EORI registration has not been applied for or is not completed, or the item could have an import VAT accounting date within the month that falls into the next period.

If none of these explanations apply, it could be the case that the importer or their agent has misquoted the EORI number on the SAD/C88. In this case, the importer should contact the centralised processing unit dealing with post-clearance non-revenue amendments at HMRC. Their address is:

Custom House
Post Clearance Amendments
Ralli Quays
3 Stanley Street
Salford M60 9HL

Telephone: 03000 588453
Fax: 03000 588462
Email: nchcie@hmrc.gsi.gov.uk

The C79 is issued in connection with most import procedures, and also post importation corrections and removals from a Customs warehouse. Some types of importation however, do not appear on the C79 and alternative evidence of import VAT having been paid is required.

The following entries and VAT amounts appear on the C79 (see Notice 702 section 8.15):

Import procedure	Previous evidence for input tax deduction
A: Air/sea imports	
The SAD (C88) Manually processed	SAD (C88) – authenticated copy 8
Trader input/computer processed	Weekly VAT certificate issued by Customs computer report TW-AH or TW-BH
Input/computer processed	Weekly VAT certificate issued by Customs computer report TW-AH or TW-BH
B: Post entry correction	**Form C18**
C: Removals from warehouse	
Customs warehouse	Form C259 – authenticated copy 4
Excise or Customs warehouse	Duty payment Form W5, W6 or W20 or Duty deferment Form W5D, W6D or W20D
Hydrocarbon oils	Duty payment W50 Duty deferment VAT 908

The following entries and VAT amounts do not appear on the C79 (see Notice 702 section 8.16). HMRC will accept these documents as proof that import VAT has been paid and can be reclaimed as input tax.

ACCOUNTING FOR IMPORT DUTY AND IMPORT VAT

Import procedure	Previous evidence for input tax deduction
A: Air/sea imports	
Bulked entries - Single Administrative Document (SAD)	Customs authenticated invoices
Registered consignees	Customs authenticated invoices
SAD (simplified)	PE33 (not authenticated by Customs)
Transit Shed Register (TSR) – imports not exceeding £600 (non-DTI)	Customs authenticated commercial invoice (or local variations of procedure) certified by Customs. The concession allowing use of copies of agents' disbursement invoices in certain circumstances will continue.
B: Postal imports	
Exceeding £2000 – SAD	SAD - authenticated copy 8
Not exceeding £2000 (Customs declaration Form CN22/CN23)	No input tax evidence is issued. "Postponed Accounting" can be used by VAT-registered person (see section **12.1** below). Importers produce commercial evidence of importation when required. When postponed accounting is not used, satisfactory evidence of tax payment.

Additionally, a VAT invoice issued by a freight forwarder or import agent that has paid and/or deferred the import VAT on the importer's behalf can be used as evidence to support the recovery of the import VAT.

C79s cover all imports declared in each calendar month and should be received by the business on or about the 24th day of the month following the month of import, for example, an October certificate covering transactions with accounting dates in October, will be issued on or about 24 November. The C79s are posted to the address recorded on the main VAT register, which means that for a VAT group registration, a single certificate is issued to the representative member's address showing all imports made by the individual members.

The original certificate or Customs issued replacement is the prime evidence for claiming input tax deduction. However, the business may copy and distribute certificates as required for internal accounting purposes. HMRC will also allow a self-accounting branch to use a photocopy of the certificate as an accounting document for the purpose of input tax deduction, provided the original is made available for inspection if requested by the control officer.

The date that counts for input tax recovery is the accounting entry representing each import, not the date when the certificate is issued, so, for example, if the VAT return period ends on 31 October, the input tax for that period, subject to the normal rules, is all entries dated within the October certificate which is not issued until 12 November. Negative amounts may

ACCOUNTING FOR IMPORT DUTY AND IMPORT VAT

appear on the certificate which means these are either repayments of import VAT or corrections of errors.

Where importers have "non-standard tax periods" and the issue date of the 12th of the month causes difficulties, they can consider applying to HMRC for permission to estimate input tax.

HMRC keep for a period of six years, microfiche copies of all monthly certificates issued. If an importer loses or mislays a C79, they can obtain replacements from HMRC at:

HM Revenue & Customs
VAT Central Unit, Microfilm Section
8th Floor, Alexander House
Victoria Avenue
Southend-on-Sea
SS99 1AU

New businesses that are required to be registered for VAT, or changes effected in the VAT status of a business, for example where a company joins or leaves a VAT group, must first obtain an EORI number completing parts A and C of the Form C220, EORI application, before they can receive import VAT Certificates. It is vital therefore that prompt applications are made whenever the business changes its VAT status.

6.6.1 "Postponed Accounting System" (PAS) for imports by post – VAT recovery

As explained in section **6.3** large numbers of smaller value consignments arrive in the UK by post. HMRC has retained the PAS methodology of clearing the goods and allowing importers to account for, and recover, import VAT on the business' VAT returns. HMRC provides full guidance regarding postal imports in Notice 143: *A guide for international post users*[7] and Notice 144: *Trade imports by post: how to complete Customs documents.*[8]

Where goods not exceeding £2,000 in value are imported by a taxable person by post (other than by Datapost), VAT chargeable on importation may be accounted for under the Postponed Accounting System, i.e. by the business making equal and opposite entries on the output tax (box 1) and input tax side (box 4) of its VAT account.

The overseas supplier must quote the consignee's VAT registration number and show the nature, quantity and value of the goods on the Customs' declaration accompanying the package.

---

[7] www.gov.uk/government/publications/notice-143-a-guide-for-international-post-users/

[8] www.gov.uk/government/publications/notice-144-trade-imports-by-post-how-to-complete-customs-documents/

The equal and opposite entries on the VAT return mean that a fully taxable business is able to reclaim the same amount of VAT as that accounted for to HMRC in the output tax entry. However, where the business is unable to reclaim all of its input tax, because for example it is partially exempt, there will be a cost because not all of the output tax can be reclaimed in box 4 as input tax.

6.6.2 Merchandise In Baggage (MIB) – Evidence of VAT paid

Section **2.12.7** explains the rules concerning the importation of MIB. Where MIB goods are imported by a VAT-registered trader that is able to reclaim it as input tax they can do so under the normal rules. Evidence of VAT payment will be provided either at importation or, for regular importers, on their monthly statement of VAT on imports (form C79).

6.7 Goods imported into the UK by a third country/territory supplier

Goods imported from a third country may involve a chain of supplies. For example:

A may supply the goods to B;

B then supplies them to C; and

C in turn supplies them to D.

At some stage the goods are imported into the UK and so the place of each supply will depend on who acted as the importer. HMRC provide the following explanation in their Imports Guidance Manual at VATPOSG3600 of the VAT treatment for such supplies:

If it were **A** – all three of the supplies take place in the UK.

If it were **B** – the first supply (**A** to **B**) is outside the UK, with the subsequent supplies (**B** to **C** and **C** to **D**) taking place in the UK.

If it were **C** – the first two supplies (**A** to **B** and **B** to **C**) are outside the UK and only the last supply (**C** to **D**) takes place in the UK.

If it were **D** – all three supplies are outside the UK.

Where, or to whom, the goods are delivered in the UK following importation does not affect the position.

Confusion sometimes arises in cases where delivery of the goods does not follow, say, the invoices generated by the supply chain. In the above example, taking C as the importer, it may be that the goods move directly from A to C. Also the documentation relating to the supply from B to C may be delayed until after importation.

But all this is immaterial. The crucial point is that the goods are imported into the UK and C is the importer. The supply from B to C is therefore outside the scope of UK VAT irrespective of where the goods were at the time of supply.

ACCOUNTING FOR IMPORT DUTY AND IMPORT VAT

6.7.1 UK agents

A third country/territory supplier that is not supplying the goods at or above the UK VAT registration threshold, and whom is not registered for UK VAT, can arrange for a UK-resident agent who is registered for UK VAT, to import and supply the goods on the supplier's behalf. In this way the third country/territory supplier can avoid the need to be registered for VAT in the UK. The third country/territory supplier and the appointed UK agent must agree that the UK agent will issue full "tax invoices" for the supplies of the goods within the UK.

The supply of services by the UK agent to the third country/territory supplier may be subject to VAT or may be relieved of UK VAT depending upon the place of belonging rules – see HMRC Notice 741A: *Place of supply of services.*[9]

Where a UK agent agrees to act on behalf of a third country/territory supplier, the agent will be treated as importing and supplying the goods as the principal. Therefore, the agent must make any necessary Customs entries as the importer and pay or defer any Customs import duty and import VAT and take delivery of the goods. The agent can reclaim the import VAT as input tax, subject to the normal rules, but must treat the transactions as a supply by them and charge and account for VAT on the onward sale to the supplier's "customer", acting as a principal in the normal way.

Alternatively, a third country/territory supplier may not wish to appoint a UK agent and would prefer to register for UK VAT when the value of supplies exceeds the extant UK VAT threshold (currently £83,000). Details about the UK VAT registration threshold and the liability to be registered for UK VAT are provided by HMRC in Notice 700/1: *Should I be registered for VAT?*[10]

If a third country/territory supplier makes taxable supplies in the UK, but has no business establishment in the UK, they may choose one of three options:
- appointing a tax representative to deal with their UK tax affairs;
- appointing an agent to deal with their UK tax affairs; or
- dealing with their VAT obligations themselves.

HMRC provide guidance on these options in Notice 700/1.

---

[9] www.gov.uk/government/publications/vat-notice-741a-place-of-supply-of-services/
[10] www.gov.uk/government/publications/vat-notice-7001-should-i-be-registered-for-vat/

7 Remission of import duty and import VAT

7.1 Goods "not in accordance with contract"
Where goods that have been imported prove to be "not in accordance with contract", repayment or remission of customs import duty and import VAT is available, where:
- they have been rejected because at the time of declaring them to a customs procedure involving payment of charges, such as release for free circulation, they:
    o are defective;
    o do not comply with the terms of the contract under which they were imported; or
    o were damaged before being cleared;
- the goods are those declared to HMRC;
- any use of the goods was solely to establish that they were defective or did not comply with the contract; and
- they have not been sold after the importer found them to be defective or did not comply with the contract.

No customs import duty is due on any goods shown to have been short-shipped or lost in transit before release from Customs charge into free circulation. If the importer can prove to HMRC that damage occurred before the goods were released from Customs charge into free circulation, they can ask for the customs value to be amended.

Claims must be made within 12 months of the date the customs charges became due, for example, when declared for free circulation and for an amount exceeding 10 euros. If only part of an article is defective, and all the other conditions for remission are met, the difference between the duty charged on the complete article as imported and the duty which would have been charged on that article had it been imported separately without the defective part, can be reclaimed. The reclaim is to be based on the rate of duty applying at the time of the original customs declaration involving duty payment.

The goods must be disposed of in one of the following ways:
- by exporting them outside the customs territory of the EU;
- by destroying them; or
- by placing them in a customs warehouse.

HMRC then treat the goods as non-Community goods, and you can subsequently declare them to free circulation or another customs procedure, or re-export them.

Claims can also be made for goods that have been imported into another Member State provided all the conditions set out in HMRC Notice 266: *Rejected*

REMISSION OF IMPORT DUTY AND IMPORT VAT

imports: repayment or remission of duty and VAT are satisfied.[1] –Adjustments need to be made for goods that are also subject to the CAP Regulations. If import duty and/or CAP charges were paid on goods imported from a third Country/territory and a claim for remission of duty is allowed as per Notice 262, the goods are considered to have been removed from free circulation. Accordingly, the importer cannot then claim any CAP export refund on the goods.

7.1.1 Goods "not in accordance with contract" – Import VAT

As explained in section **3.7.2** a fully-taxable VAT-registered person i.e. a person or business that is able to recover all of the VAT it incurs ("input tax"), subject to the normal disallowances, importing goods for business purposes should normally deduct the import VAT by obtaining form C79 (the Import VAT Certificate). However, as an alternative, the importer may use the procedures set out in Notice 266 to claim a direct repayment of import VAT, and surrender the VAT certificate relating to the goods. When the importer claims a direct repayment, they must make a signed declaration on Form C&E 1179 that they have not, and will not, make a corresponding claim for input tax deduction on a VAT return. If the claim for remission is for a part consignment, HMRC will issue an amended copy of the VAT Certificate after having made the repayment.

An importer who is not registered for VAT or a partially exempt VAT-registered importer may use the procedures set out in Notice 266 to claim a direct repayment of tax.[2]

Finally, a wholly-exempt person i.e. a person or business that is unable to recover any of the VAT it incurs because it makes supplies that are wholly exempt from VAT, or a VAT-registered person that is importing the goods for a purpose other than for the course of their business, should also follow the procedures in Notice 266 to reclaim VAT as well as any other charges.

7.1.2 Goods "not in accordance with contract" – excise duty

Excise duty may also be reclaimed, provided the goods:
- were imported in pursuance of a contract of sale;
- were not in accordance with the contract because they were of the wrong description, quality or condition or were damaged in transit;
- have not been used more than was necessary to discover that they were defective or did not comply with the contract of sale;
- have not been offered for sale after they were found to be defective or not in accordance with contract; and

---

[1] see www.gov.uk/government/publications/notice-266-rejected-imports-repayment-or-remission-of-duty-and-vat/
[2] Ibid

- are, with the consent of the seller and under HMRC's control, either returned by the consignee to the seller abroad, or destroyed at the expense of the consignee.

HMRC will not repay excise duty on goods that have been:
- imported on approval, "sale or return" or similar conditions;
- received in excess of the number ordered;
- received after an agreed delivery date;
- remain unsold;
- subject to licensing when a licence is not issued;
- imported by or on behalf of a company that has gone into liquidation or receivership, and not covered by these conditions; or
- imported because a mistaken order was made.

If these conditions are not met, the importer may still be eligible to reclaim excise duty 'drawback' under the alternative arrangements described in Notice 207: *Excise duty: Drawback*.

7.2 Goods imported in "special situations" – import duty and import VAT

Import duty and import VAT can also be remitted in what HMRC describe in Notice 266 as "special situations" – see section **3.7.3**. HMRC provide these as examples only. If an importer believes their situation justifies repayment or remission of import duty and import VAT, HMRC will examine the merits of the importer's case.

7.3 Offences

The importer or any person held liable with the importer (see **2.12.1**) commits an offence if they make any "breach" of, or failure to comply with:
- any provision of the relevant Community Regulations, namely, Council Regulation (EEC) 2913/92 and Council Regulation (EEC) 2454/93;
- any requirement or condition imposed by HMRC under the Regulations;
- any undertaking that they give to HMRC; or
- the requirement for presentation, Summary Declaration or Customs entry of goods, or for the assignment of goods to some Customs-approved treatment or use.

Two main customs penalties operate under civil law:
- Customs Civil Penalties (CCPs) may be imposed when businesses have contravened customs rules and regulations that relate to customs duty, community export duty, community import duty, import VAT or duties of a preferential tariff country – CCPs may also be imposed for contraventions of customs rules and regulations in regard to exports; and
- Customs Civil Evasion Penalties (CCEPs) may be imposed when it can be established that a business has dishonestly evaded the payment of an import duty, an export duty or import VAT.

For some irregularities a direct CCP may be considered appropriate. These are issued for serious errors or where HMRC has given clear written advice which has been ignored. Each case is looked at on its own merit and most cases would not result in a direct penalty being issued. HMRC may reduce penalties where they are satisfied there are mitigating circumstances.

HMRC encourages traders to comply with regulations. Issuing warnings is part of HMRC procedure to support traders without having to issue financial penalties. HMRC may issue warning letters or in certain circumstances financial penalties to traders for the first contravention of customs rules and regulations. HMRC will consider all the facts of the case and then select the most appropriate course of action.

HMRC can detain or seize goods and the containers or vehicles carrying them when the correct duty and or import VAT has been evaded or when they have been used to carry or are packed with goods that are prohibited or restricted. HMRC will treat the importation of restricted goods without the correct documentation and the importation of prohibited or counterfeit goods as criminal offences.

7.3.1 Customs Civil Penalties (CCP)

Customs Civil Penalties (CCP) are designed to encourage compliance with legal obligations, and may be imposed when a business has contravened statutory requirements relating to various types of customs duties and procedures.

A CCP may be imposed when a trader has contravened customs rules/regulations relating to various types of customs duty, import VAT and exports. Schedules containing details of the relevant rules and descriptions of who is liable as well as the maximum penalty amounts that may be imposed for a contravention are available in Notice 301,[3] for schedules of the relevant rules, export penalties and how HMRC calculates and notifies customs civil penalties for contraventions of legal requirements.

HMRC levy penalties based on the seriousness of the offences. Penalties start at £250, which will usually be the first penalty, becoming progressively larger until the maximum is reached. The normal progression will be £250, £500, £1,000, with additional steps of £2,000 and £2,500 for the higher maximum. However, HMRC will ultimately determine the monetary amount of the penalty based on the individual circumstances of the case.

Where HMRC discover several serious errors during an audit they will penalise each error separately, but at the same rate. However, multiple minor contraventions for precisely the same mistake will be treated as a single error,

---

[3] www.gov.uk/government/publications/excise-notice-301-civil-penalties-for-contraventions-of-customs-law/

but HMRC may increase the normal penalty where a contravention is particularly serious.

For example, where the amount of Customs Duty or non-recoverable VAT under-declared exceeds £50,000 HMRC may charge at a rate two steps higher than indicated above, for example, £1,000 as a first penalty. Conversely, where an under-declaration exceeds £100,000 HMRC may charge the maximum penalty irrespective of whether it is a first or subsequent penalty.

7.3.2 Customs Civil Evasion Penalties (CCEP)

There are different penalties that HMRC officers can issue for fraudulent paperwork or evading duty. HMRC will not normally prosecute in the criminal courts where a person has been invited to co-operate with their investigation, but they reserve the right to do so.

CCEPs for breaches of EU and UK customs law were introduced in the Finance Act 2003. They are levied where HMRC has reasonable grounds to believe that customs duties or import VAT has been evaded or sought to be evaded. Business may face a CCEP if HMRC are satisfied that duty and/or import VAT has been evaded and dishonest conduct can be established. The duties and relevant taxes covered by CCEPs include UK customs duty, EU customs duty, import VAT and customs duties in the agricultural sector.

A CCEP may be imposed by HMRC when they are satisfied that a business has evaded the payment of a relevant tax and duty or if any repayment rebate, drawback, relief, exemption or allowance to which they are not entitled has been claimed. Additionally, HMRC may still seize the goods but they will be returned when the penalty is paid.

CCEPs are based on a percentage of the duty evaded or where the importer sought to evade it. The penalty is equal to the duty dishonestly evaded or sought to be evaded. HMRC can reduce penalties to recognise the help traders provide in establishing how the evasion arose and in quantifying the duty amount involved.

Although traders don't have to co-operate with an HMRC investigation, the level of their penalty may be reduced further if they do. If they choose to co-operate, they must:
- attend interviews;
- supply information promptly;
- admit early the extent of the arrears and how they arose;
- answer questions honestly and accurately;
- give relevant facts to establish the true liability; and
- co-operate until the investigation ends.

HMRC will consider how much the trader's co-operation has saved its officers in time and resources when determining by how much to reduce the penalty.

REMISSION OF IMPORT DUTY AND IMPORT VAT

HMRC also take into account how forthcoming a trader has been about unpaid or late levies, or any other information required.

8 Exports

8.1 Background

It is important to recognise the distinction between an "export" from the EU and an intra-EU "Dispatch" (see section 0) because there are fundamental differences in the evidential requirements to support VAT zero-rating. Commentary on intra-EU Dispatches is given in **Chapter 9** of this book. The main HMRC guidance on Exports is published in Notice 703.[1]

The capacity for a UK business to develop export markets has never been greater with the opening up of international trade links, and the UK Government committed to driving growth. This is achieved by both UK Trade and Investment (UKTI)[2] and the Department for Business, Innovation and Skills (BIS)[3] providing dedicated resources to exporters. UKTI[4] helps UK-based companies succeed in the global economy by providing business opportunities and expert trade advice and support and BIS can help smooth the way for UK businesses when undertaking business abroad.

UKTI offers expertise and contacts through its extensive network of specialists in the UK, and in British embassies and other diplomatic offices around the world. It provides UK companies with the tools they require to be competitive globally and its services include:

- an export 'health-check' to assess the business' trade development needs and help with developing an export strategy and plan of action;
- access to an experienced "International Trade Adviser" who can provide support as the business grows internationally;
- specialist help with tackling cultural and language issues when communicating with overseas customers and partners;
- advice on how to go about market research and the possibility of a grant towards approved market research projects;
- ongoing support to help the business continue to develop overseas trade and investigate dealing with more sophisticated markets; and
- advice on a range of international trade help that is available from UKTI and partnering organisations.

Certain types of goods need an export licence to be legally exported, for example, dual-use goods such as nuclear, chemical or communications goods, radioactive sources and military items such as firearms and ammunition. In some cases (the majority of dual-use goods), the controls only apply to exports

---

[1] www.gov.uk/government/publications/vat-notice-703-export-of-goods-from-the-uk
[2] see www.ukti.gov.uk/export.html
[3] see www.bis.gov.uk/EUMarketAccessUnit
[4] www.uktradeinvest.gov.uk

EXPORTS

outside the EU, but in the case of military goods, an export licence is required for all destinations.[5]

Also, Certificates of Free Sale are required by many overseas countries for the importation of various consumer products such as food, cosmetics and medicines. Their purpose is to prove that the goods are sold in the domestic market and, therefore, comply with national standards. The exporter is asked to complete an application form and provide documentary evidence with regard to contents of the product and availability in the domestic market. Requests for information should be sent to **cfs.enquiries@bis.gsi.gov.uk**.

For the UK alone, total trade exports for 2015 were £305.2 billion and total trade imports were £411.9 billion meaning the UK was a net importer for 2015 of £106.7 billion, something that the UK Treasury is always looking to address by encouraging the export of UK manufactured goods.

At the time of writing, the debate on whether the UK should remain a Member State of the EU is in full swing; the decision to stay or leave will have a direct and major impact on these trade statistics since many commentators are predicting a catastrophic impact on the UK economy if the 'Brexit' campaigners succeed in persuading the UK electorate that leaving the EU is in the UK's best interests.

From a purely VAT perspective, every export of goods to a third country/territory and every removal of goods from the UK to another Member State qualifies for VAT zero-rating, provided all the commercial and fiscal documentation confirms this status. Therefore, annually, VAT of £610 million (at the standard-rate of 20%) is potentially relieved (but not all goods would be zero-rated 'domestically' such as children's clothing).

However, supposing that only 10% of the annual sum reported as being exported is either diverted to the UK market or is not supported by acceptable evidence, VAT of £61 million per annum would be permanently lost to the UK Treasury. The additional problem of "Missing Trader Intra-Community" or "MTIC" VAT fraud where such items as mobile phones and computer chips are transacted in "Carousels" cross-border, exacerbates this problem. Even though MTIC fraud is still conducted across the EU on an enormous scale it pales into insignificance when compared to Excise "Diversion fraud" being where excise duty is lost because of erroneous supply chains and evasion. The Commission has stated that Diversion fraud is the greatest threat to the EU's whole budgets and is struggling to combat it. In the UK a new Regulation to help combat alcohol fraud is being introduced by requiring any wholesaler of alcoholic goods to be registered as an approved trader. Whether this will plug any holes will remain to be tested.

---

[5] see www.businesslink.gov.uk/exportcontrol

According to the case *Federation of Technological Industries v Customs and Excise Commissioners* ([2004] EWCA Civ 1020) decided in 2002-3, the estimated cumulative cost of such frauds to the UK alone at that time was between £1.65 and £2.64 billion per year. However, the Commission estimates that MTIC fraud costs European taxpayers up to £240 billion a year, which is estimated as twice the European Union's annual budget. MTIC fraud has mutated and now can incorporate all high value goods such as designer goods, health products, jewellery etc. and extends to trading in such 'products' as carbon emissions. Therefore, in view of these figures and the cost to the UK Treasury, HMRC and the Commission see this area as a main risk and control it vigorously.

8.2 Types of export

There are two types of exports, "Direct" and "Indirect". For VAT purposes, a direct export is where the goods are removed under the control of or on behalf of the supplier, whereas an indirect export is where the goods are removed under the control of or on behalf of someone other than the supplier. However, the definitions of direct and indirect exports differ for import duty purposes and a direct export is simply where the goods leave the EU without travelling via another Member State, whereas an indirect export is where the goods leave the EU via another Member State. Indirect exports are controlled using the EU wide "Export Control System" (ECS).

Both methods of export create their own issues, particularly in the production of evidence to support the zero-rating that is acceptable to HMRC. Often exporting businesses can produce the necessary evidence of export, but not within the statutory deadlines. This failure can result in HMRC assessing for VAT because the proof of export was not obtained in time – see section **8.17**.

8.2.1 Direct exports and VAT

For a direct export of goods, the physical removal can be by any of the following means:
- in personal baggage;
- in the customer's transport;
- in the supplier's transport;
- by rail, postal service, or courier;
- by a shipping line, transport company, airline; and
- by pipeline.

Zero-rating of a direct export is only achieved when all of the following conditions are met:
- the goods must be physically removed from the EU within the stipulated time limits;
- all appropriate HMRC and commercial documents must be obtained within the stipulated time limits;
- all supplementary evidence of the transaction must be retained such as orders, invoices, faxes, letters of credit etc.; and

EXPORTS

- all legal notices directed by HMRC in VAT Notice 703: *export of goods from the UK* (which has the force of law) are met.

To be zero-rated, the goods must not be delivered to any address in the UK or other Member State, even if on an intermediate leg of an international transport delivery (unless they are being exported under a "groupage" arrangement – see section **8.14.1**), and must not be collected by the customer or any one acting on their behalf, even where it is claimed they are for subsequent export.

8.2.2 Indirect exports and VAT

For an indirect export of goods, the physical removal can be by any of the following means:
- in personal baggage;
- in the customer's transport;
- by courier; and
- by a shipping line, transport company or airline.

Zero-rating of an indirect export is only achieved when all of the following conditions are met:
- the customer is an "overseas person" that does not have any business establishment in the UK from which "taxable supplies" are made;
- Before 1 October 2013 was not registered for VAT in the UK;
- the customer is not "resident" in the UK;
- the customer obtains proof of export and delivers this to the supplier;
- the customer ensures that the goods are physically removed from the EU within the stipulated time limits; and
- all legal notices directed by HMRC in VAT Notice 703: *export of goods from the UK* are met.

Suppliers should be prepared to take a deposit or seek other surety from the customer or their agent for the amount of VAT that will be due on the value of the invoiced supply, should the acceptable evidence of export from the EU not be produced to them within the stipulated time limits, or at all. If the goods are found in the UK after the time that they were destined for export, HMRC may seize them as well as assessing for the VAT not declared on their sale and assessing for any penalty, which commences at up to 30% of the tax avoided. Interest is also due on the amount of VAT assessed and lost to the Treasury between the last day on which they should have been exported and the date any assessment is finally paid to HMRC. Further, unless HMRC has given its approval to the customer, the goods must not be used in the EU between the time they leave the supplier's premises and their subsequent export. Again, HMRC can seize the goods where this requirement is not met.

The inability of the supplier to categorically prove that the goods sold to a customer "over-the-counter" and for export in the customer's accompanied baggage was tested in both the VAT Tribunal and the Court of Appeal in the case of *Henry Moss of London Ltd. v Commissioners of Customs and Excise*. In this case the customers had claimed that the goods were for export, and they had handed the customers a Form C273 as required by Notice 703 (October 1975 version), but the Appellant had not received the forms back from the customers, duly stamped by HMRC at a point of export from the EU, with confirmation of export.

In the Court of Appeal Lord Justice Denning observed that:

> the Commissioners were entitled to impose very strict conditions for being satisfied. Unless there were strict conditions, VAT could be evaded very easily". Accordingly, "it was necessary for the Commissioners to devise machinery to prevent people from getting out of paying VAT... the machinery is just about as good as could be devised to stop evasion.

Lord Justice Templeman also observed that the trader:

> could bring pressure to bear on the customer by requiring payment by the customer of the whole or part of the appropriate VAT as a deposit until the certificate (Form C273) is produced.

8.2.3 Agents

A supplier (or for indirect exports a customer) can appoint a freight forwarder, shipping company, airline or other person to handle the export transactions and produce the necessary declarations to Customs on their behalf. The agent must then take reasonable steps to ensure that the goods are as described by the exporter; that the customs formalities are complied with and that the goods are exported within the time limits. Because zero-rating for exports from the EU is based entirely on the physical delivery of the goods and on the evidence that is obtained and retained to prove the physical delivery, it is vital that agents keep records of each export transaction and supply the evidence of export to the exporter. Additionally, this evidence must also be obtained within the stipulated time limits.

8.3 Customs procedures relating to exports of goods

The export of goods is obviously a major risk area to the UK Treasury and the evidential requirements are strict. Therefore, a customs declaration is required for all goods exported. The procedures relating to the export of goods from the EU are detailed in Notice 275: *Customs Export Procedures*.[6]

Exporting businesses must remember that as part of their anti-smuggling responsibilities and to prevent avoidance or abuse all goods are liable to check and physical examination by HMRC. This will be advised through CHIEF, with HMRC referring to examinations as 'Route 2' checks, and many examinations are conducted by the UK Border Agency on HMRC's behalf.

---

[6]www.gov.uk/government/publications/notice-275-customs-export-procedures/notice-275-customs-export-procedures#introduction

EXPORTS

Notification of the arrival of the goods at the required location for Customs control is referred to as 'presentation of the goods to Customs'.

EU safety and security legislation sets minimum time limits for the presentation of goods to Customs to allow risk assessment to take place:
- for 'deep sea' containerised cargo, at least 24 hours before the goods are loaded;
- for 'short sea' containerised cargo, at least two hours before leaving the port;
- for air traffic, at least 30 minutes before departure from an airport;
- for rail and inland waters traffic, at least two hours before departure;
- for road traffic, at least one hour before departure; and
- for supplies for ships and aircraft at least 15 minutes before departure

These are the minimum legal deadlines that were agreed for both import and exports after consultation with various trade bodies. Commercial practicalities may necessitate the presentation to take place earlier. An electronic 'Arrival' message is sent to CHIEF by a person authorised to hold a CHIEF 'Loader' role. Following submission of the 'Arrival' message, the Export Declaration will be validated, legally accepted and risk-assessed by HMRC.

Details of the CHIEF system are set out in section **2.11.5**.

8.3.1 National Export System (NES)

Businesses involved in international trade (for example, the export or import process) are required to apply for an Economic Operator Registration and Identification (EORI) number – see section **2.4**.

To control the export of goods in a 'real-time' environment, HMRC has developed the "National Export System" (NES) which is an electronic, CHIEF-based, system – see section **2.11.5**. To manage and control exports from the EU (directly from the UK or indirectly via another Member State), HMRC require Export Declarations for all of the following reasons:
- to meet legal obligations on the movement of goods from the EU;
- to meet EU safety and security requirements for risk assessment purposes;
- to ensure that export licensing requirements are met;
- to provide accurate details for the Overseas Trade Statistics;
- to prevent the unauthorised return of duty free or VAT zero-rated goods into the home market;
- to provide customs information and confirm export for VAT and Excise purposes; and
- to enable checks to be carried out on goods subject to specific Customs or CAP controls.

Overseas Trade Statistics provide important information about the UK's export trade with third countries and are a vital tool in affording the UK Government with economic indicators – see Background in section **8.1**. The economic importance of trade statistics means that the UK's export processes incorporate validation of export information provided to CHIEF.

An Export Declaration must be made when:
(a) goods are being exported, either directly or indirectly, to a third country (including European Free Trade Association countries) for example, any non-EU country;
(b) goods are sent to one of the 'special territories' of the Community;
(c) CAP goods are exported to those entitled destinations listed in Regulation (EEC No 612/09) Article 33, which states:
For the purposes of this Regulation, the following shall be treated as exports from the Customs Territory of the Community:
(a) supplies within the Community for victualling to:
   i. seagoing vessels (able to stay as sea when wind is in excess of 8 (gale force) on the Beaufort scale); and
   ii. aircraft serving on international routes, including intra-Community
(b) supplies to international organisations established in the Community
(c) supplies to armed forces stationed in the territory of a member state but not serving under its command

Export Declarations must be submitted electronically to CHIEF and both the exporter and their representative can do so. Data is entered into the CHIEF computer system where it validates and processes the four stages of an export:
- electronic submission of Export Declarations prior to the shipment of the goods;
- electronic 'Presentation' of the goods to Customs (in the UK this is the 'Arrival' message into CHIEF);
- electronic 'Customs Clearance' granting Permission to Progress (P2P); and
- electronic 'Departure' message which puts the export into a final state on CHIEF.

All declarations must be submitted into the CHIEF System as 'not Arrived' where format and technical validations will take place. The Export Declaration must be electronically submitted using one of the approved NES routes being:
1. Indirect link to CHIEF through a Community Systems Provider (CSP) using the exporter's own software or that provided by an independent software company; or
2. Direct communication links to CHIEF through the Government Gateway.

In rare and exceptional circumstances a paper Export Declaration (C88/ESS) may be submitted to NES for input by HMRC staff (Customs Input Entry (CIE)). CIE declarations must be submitted to the National Clearance Hub (NCH) at Salford:

HM Revenue and Customs
National Clearance Hub
Ralli Quays 3 Stanley St
Salford M60 9LA

EXPORTS

Fax: 0800 496 0699
Email: NCHCIE@hmrc.gsi.gov.uk and NCHLAP@hmrc.gsi.gov.uk

8.4 Community Transit and the New Computerised Transit System (NCTS)

Community Transit (CT) allows goods that are not in free circulation in the EU i.e. non-Community goods, to move between two points within the EU free of import duties and other charges. It may also be used for the movement of Community goods which, between their point of departure and point of destination in the EU, have to pass through the territory of a third country/territory. An extension of the CT procedure is the "Common Transit" procedure which allows movements between the EU and EFTA countries and between the EFTA countries themselves, to be controlled and similarly relieved of duty and taxes.

NCTS is a European-wide electronic system, and it provides better management and control of Community/Common Transit movements. Each country's own NCTS processing system is connected, through a central domain in Brussels, to all of the Member States' systems. NCTS is a completely separate system from CHIEF, not inter-connected in any way, so separate declarations for transit are required.

8.5 The Transport International Routiers (TIR) procedure

The TIR carnet allows goods in road vehicles or containers sealed by a Customs authority to cross one or more countries en-route to their third country/territory destination with the minimum of Customs interference (the CT procedures must be used for transit movements that are wholly within the EU). Requirements to provide export declarations are unaffected by the TIR provisions.

8.6 Admission Temporarie – Temporary Admission (ATA) Carnet

ATA carnets may be used to simplify customs clearance of goods being temporarily exported. They replace normal customs declarations both at export and re-import and also replace normal customs documents and security requirements in many countries worldwide into which the goods are being temporarily imported.

However, a simplified declaration 'C21' may be required to be entered to CHIEF at 'inventory-linked' ports or airports to clear the inventory system. Goods covered by ATA carnets are subject to normal export prohibitions and restrictions and licensing rules. However, the carnets may not be used for goods that are:
- exported for processing or repair;
- exported by post; and
- not in free circulation before export from the UK.

Certain Chambers of Commerce issue ATA carnets in the UK subject to receiving guarantees or deposits; the main is:

London Chamber of Commerce and Industry
33 Queen Street
London EC4R 1AP
Phone: 020 7248 4444

HMRC has issued detailed guidance on ATA carnets in Notice 104: *ATA Carnets*[7]

8.6.1 Types of Export Declarations
There are four types of Export Declarations:
- a Full Export Declaration;
- a Simplified Export Procedure;
- an Exit Summary Declaration and
- a C21-Customs Clearance Request.

8.6.1.1 *Full Export Declaration*
Under the Full Export Declaration, the exporter or their agent completes a full pre-shipment entry which should include information on the following:
- the goods;
- the people consignor/consignee/declarant, including EORI numbers;
- safety and security data;
- the means of transport; and
- any documentation requirements.

Key data elements on an Export Declaration include the Customs Procedure Code (CPC) and the Declaration (and/or Master) Unique Consignment Reference number (DUCR or MUCR).

8.6.1.2 *Simplified Declaration Procedure (SDP)*
SDP can only be used by an authorised business or its agent. The SDP allows authorised businesses and agents to declare goods for export by submitting a simplified, electronic, pre-shipment entry to CHIEF. Specific criteria must be met to obtain authorisation. Most exporters or their agents using simplified procedures submit a full Export Declaration to CHIEF, but they may request authorisation to use the simplified two-part Export Declaration, made up of the following:
(a) part one is a "Pre-Shipment Advice" (PSA) containing brief details input to CHIEF before the export is shipped; and
(b) part two is a "Supplementary Declaration" (SD) submitted post-shipment containing all the details that would have been contained in a Full Export Declaration. The SD must be submitted within 14 days of the actual export of the goods.

---

[7] www.gov.uk/government/publications/notice-104-ata-and-cpd-carnets/

EXPORTS

This two-part Export Declaration may be used in conjunction with "Local Clearance Procedure" (LCP) for inland locations such as the exporter's own premises or another authorised place such as a freight forwarder and/or Supplementary Declaration Procedure for frontier locations such as UK ports and airports.

Most goods are eligible for Simplified Declaration Procedures. Exceptions are prohibited goods, which must never be exported, restricted goods i.e. those for which export licences are required and goods covered by certain other customs procedures. It is possible, however, to export licensable goods from approved inland premises by submitting a full Export Declaration before shipment.

8.6.1.3 Export Summary Declarations

Export Summary Declarations were introduced with the implementation of the EU-wide Export Control System. An Exit Summary Declarations (EXS) is necessary for consignments which are not covered by an Export Declaration which includes safety and security data or not covered by an inbound Entry Summary Declaration (ENS) under the Import Control System (ICS) – see section **2.8.1**.

In the UK the CHIEF Export Declaration includes all of the safety and security fields of an EXS. This is referred to as the 'Combined' fiscal and safety and security declaration. In most cases, because outgoing UK Exports will have already met ECS safety and security requirements there will be no need to submit an EXS at the Office of Exit in another Member State.

However, there are three principal instances when an EXS will be required:

(1) third country status goods (or former EU goods now 'not in free circulation') being trans-shipped in the UK either where the goods have been in Temporary Storage for more than 14 calendar days or where the exporting carrier is not aware of the content of the ICS ENS under which the goods would have entered the EU (or where the ENS data has changed significantly since entry);
(2) UK export goods going to another Member State, but being physically trans-shipped in a third country, (e.g., from the UK port of Felixstowe, unloaded in the Egyptian port of Alexandria for loading to a new vessel bound for Limassol in Cyprus) - these goods will need an EXS on the way out of the UK and an ENS on the way back into Cyprus; and
(3) for shipper owned empty containers, where a carrier is being paid to move someone else's container rather than repositioning their own.

As there may either be no UK exporter or the exporter will not be aware that there is an EXS requirement, responsibility for lodging the EXS declaration will usually be with the carrier.

In the UK the EXS needs to be 'Arrived' and 'Departed' in the same way as any other Export Declaration using a DUCR.

8.6.1.4 *Form C21- Customs Clearance Request*

A Form C21 is used to secure electronic release (from CHIEF or air(port) inventory systems. The Customs Procedure Code and related notes will indicate which fields require completion. For exports, a C21 may be used at both inventory and non-inventory linked locations.

A C21 may be required to release goods from an air(port) inventory system when no Export Declaration on CHIEF is required, for example:

- goods with an "Export Accompanying Document" (eAD) where the goods were declared for export in another member state but will exit the EU from the UK;
- goods under cover of an "Admission Temporaire" (ATA) carnet, where the goods are travelling as freight rather than in passengers' baggage and the freight needs to be cleared on CHIEF (the carnet still needs to be presented to Customs and stamped, but the C21 using CPC 10 00 041 releases the goods on CHIEF; and
- if the exporter is authorised to use SASP and are advised to use a C21 with a specific CPC.

Where the C21 cross references to another document the reference should be identified on the C21 in boxes 40 and 44.

8.6.2 Merchandise In Baggage (MIB)

Merchandise In Baggage refers to commercial or business goods taken to a country outside the EU in the passenger's hand luggage. MIB includes goods acquired for a company, goods for sale, spare parts and trade samples, etc. whether or not they are permanently imported/exported, temporarily imported/exported, in transit or liable to customs charges.

A declaration on form C88/ESS is only required when the MIB goods are for export to a country outside the EU or to one of the 'special territories' and must be completed in the Member State where the export movement starts.

In the UK the person carrying the MIB must declare the goods to Customs. Therefore they must arrive well before the scheduled departure time and present the goods to the export officer at the (air)port of departure together with the completed customs export declaration and any other required documentation such as an export licence.

Where the goods are exported in baggage or in a private motor vehicle, the traveller must include 'MIB' in box 44 of the export SAD/C88 and arrive well before the scheduled departure time, presenting the goods and copy 2 and copy 3 (marked 'for VAT purposes only') of the SAD/C88 to the MIB officer at the UK place of export from the EU. Copy 3 will be handed back to the traveller as evidence of export.

EXPORTS

Where the customer collects the goods from the supplier's premises and arranges transportation in baggage or in a private motor vehicle the supplier must give the customer a completed SAD/C88 with the supplier's name and VAT number shown in box 2. This will make sure that the customer does not include these supplies on a single SAD/C88 covering goods purchased from a number of UK suppliers. If they did this, they would be unable to provide an original officially certified copy 3 for the supplier's records.

Again, the customer must arrive well before their scheduled departure time and present copy 2 and copy 3 (marked 'for VAT purposes only') of the SAD/C88 with the goods, to the MIB officer at the UK place of export from the EU. The MIB officer will certify the reverse of copy 3 to show that goods have been shipped and hand it back to the customer. The customer should send the copy 3 back to the supplier as evidence of export for retention in their VAT record.

Where either the traveller or the overseas customer leaves the EU via another Member State copy 3 of the SAD/C88 will be certified by Customs at the place they leave the EU. This must be retained as proof of export.

Full details of the MIB procedures with details on completion of the SAD/C88 are provided by HMRC in Notice 6: *Merchadise in Baggage*.[8]

Full details of the export data process via CHIEF are set out in Notice 275: *Customs export procedures*.[9]

8.7 Excise goods

As explained in the Background in section **8.1**, because of the widespread fraud in excisable goods, businesses must be authorised by HMRC to deal in duty-suspended goods. Full details of being approved are provided by HMRC in Notice 196.[10]

The main Regulations relating to excise goods are the "The Warehousekeepers and Owners of Warehoused Goods Regulations" (WOWGR) and a summary of the main duty points is provided in paragraph 5.10 of Notice 196. All businesses wishing to trade in excise duty suspended goods must be approved as a "Registered Consignor" before doing so.

A Registered Consignor is a natural or legal person approved by HMRC who, in the course of their business and under the conditions set by HMRC, dispatches excise goods under excise duty suspension arrangements to persons authorised to receive duty-suspended goods upon their release to free

---

[8] www.gov.uk/government/publications/notice-6-merchandise-in-baggage/
[9] www.gov.uk/government/publications/notice-275-customs-export-procedures/notice-275-customs-export-procedures#the-nes
[10] www.gov.uk/government/publications/excise-notice-196-excise-goods-registration-and-approval-of-warehousekeepers-warehouse-premises-owners-of-goods-and-registered-consignors/

circulation. Excise goods are considered to be in free circulation after the completion of all the import declaration formalities associated with the appropriate Customs Procedure Code (CPC). For movements from the port, airport or a customs suspensive regime, a CPC code within the 07 or 68 series must be used. However, at the time of writing, HMRC is reviewing all the CPC codes within the 07 and 68 series in respect of how the import VAT is to be declared. Therefore, until the outcome of this review is announced businesses must continue to follow the present requirements of the CPC codes.

8.7.1 Excise Movement Control System (EMCS)

EMCS is an EU-wide electronic system for recording and validating movements of duty-suspended excise goods within the EU. Authorised warehousekeepers and registered consignors moving duty-suspended excise goods must register and enrol for EMCS. The Registered Consignor of the duty-suspended excise goods must complete and submit a message known as an eAD using EMCS before a movement of excise goods can take place.

Once the detail entered on the eAD has been validated, EMCS will generate a unique "Administrative Reference Code" (ARC) for that particular movement. The ARC is required to travel with the goods and must be made available for presentation when requested by the relevant authorities during the course of the movement. This means the consignor must provide the person accompanying the goods, for example, the driver of the vehicle during the course of the movement, with a printed version of the validated eAD or any other commercial document on which the unique ARC is clearly stated.

Generally, EMCS must be used for the following movements of excise goods in duty suspension:

- intra-UK movements of alcohol and tobacco where the goods are moving between tax warehouses within the UK;
- intra-EU movements of all excise goods where they are moving between approved persons or premises in different Member States;
- movements to the place where the excise goods will leave the territory of the EU, either as a direct export from the UK or an indirect export via another Member State; and
- movements by registered consignors from the place where the excise goods are released to free circulation.

Details of the EMCS process are provided by HMRC in section 2 of Notice 197.[11]

---

[11] www.gov.uk/government/publications/excise-notice-197-receipt-into-and-removal-from-an-excise-warehouse-of-excise-goods/excise-notice-197-receipt-into-and-removal-from-an-excise-warehouse-of-excise-goods#warehousing-for-export-wfe.

8.7.2 Warehousing For Export (WHE)

Warehousing for export is the warehousing of excise goods (excluding alcoholic liquors chargeable with excise duty) that are already released for consumption (UK duty paid), for removal to a destination outside the UK. This means that WHE arrangements cannot be used for alcohol such as wine, beer or spirits. The owner of the goods, subject to eligibility, may be able to claim a refund of the excise duty under the excise duty drawback scheme.

Goods may be removed from an excise warehouse for:
- home use on payment of duty (sometimes referred to as 'released for consumption');
- dispatch under duty suspension to other approved UK warehouses, including those on the Isle of Man;
- dispatch under duty suspension to approved persons or premises in other EU Member States;
- export to non-EU countries in duty suspension; and
- entitled miscellaneous removals.

All duty-suspended movements from an excise warehouse or the place of release to free circulation must be covered by financial security which is a guarantee provided by an approved guarantor who undertakes to pay money to HMRC if an irregularity occurs, or is deemed to occur, during a movement of excise goods in duty suspension. Only companies approved by HMRC may act as guarantors, but most banks and insurance companies have this approval.

The movement security is based on the average amount of duty suspended on one week's movements calculated by reference to all movements in the previous twelve months, allowing for seasonal variations with a minimum security of £20,000.

Excise duty payments may be paid monthly where the business is approved under deferment arrangements. Additionally, businesses may be eligible for authorisation under the "Excise Payment Security System" (EPSS) to make deferred payments of excise duty without providing a guarantee (for removals from warehouse only).

8.8 European Community export preferences

A number of countries, including Chile, Israel, Mexico, South Africa and those within EFTA give preferential treatment to certain goods 'originating' in the EU, which means that customers in such countries pay a reduced or nil rate of customs duty on importing the EU-exported goods – see Notice: 827 *European Union Preferences – export procedures* for details.[12]

---

[12] www.gov.uk/government/publications/notice-827-european-union-preferences-export-procedures/

However, the rules for determining EU preferential 'origin' are very specific as, for example, goods manufactured in the EU do not necessarily 'originate' here for the purpose of EU Preference, neither do they automatically acquire EU origin simply because EU duty was paid on them or because they were purchased from a UK or other EU source. HMRC has issued Notice 828: *Tariff preferences – rules of origin for various countries* to assist with this complex area.[13]

Both Notices give information about the origin rules that must be met for goods to qualify for preferential tariff treatment. The Department of Business, Innovation and Skills should be contacted if the actual duty rates that will apply in the country of import are required. Their address is:

The Department of Business, Innovation and Skills
Overseas Trade Division
1 Victoria Street
London SW1H 0ET

8.9 Proof of export

For VAT zero-rating purposes, the exporting business must produce either official or commercial evidence of the physical export of the goods from the EU, with equal weight put on both. However, each type must be supported by supplementary evidence to show that a transaction has actually taken place which relates to the goods that were physically exported. If, in HMRC's view, the evidence produced to support the export is deemed to be unsatisfactory, VAT zero-rating will not be allowed and the supplier of the goods will be liable to account for the VAT due, treating the "consideration" as VAT-inclusive.

8.9.1 Official evidence

Official evidence is produced by HMRC, for example "Goods Departed Messages" (GDM) or a screen print from CHIEF showing the appropriate status codes (generated by NES).

For direct exports, where the Office of Exit field on the Export Declaration (box 29) has not been completed, reports printed from CHIEF archive system (MSS) will show a final CHIEF status of ICS60. This indicates that the goods left the UK and the EU and will help support claims for VAT zero-rating by providing official evidence of export.

For Indirect exports where the Office of Exit field (box 29) has been completed, the evidence that the goods have exited the EU comes from the closure of the ECS message which is passed to CHIEF. The confirmed closure of an ECS closure message for an Indirect export is forwarded to CHIEF and changes the status on CHIEF to ICS62. This status can be viewed on CHIEF and can help

---

[13] www.gov.uk/government/publications/notice-828-tariff-preferences-rules-of-origin-for-various-countries/

the VAT team establish that Indirect exports have properly exited the EU and are entitled to VAT zero-rating.

Sometimes, when goods have arrived at the air(port) but for some reason a departure message is not input, CHIEF will issue an "Assumed Departure Message" within a specified timescale. However, this message is not accepted as evidence for VAT zero-rating. Alternative commercial transport evidence as described in **8.9.2** below must be produced.

8.9.2 Commercial evidence

Commercial evidence usually describes the physical movement of the goods and includes, for example:
- authenticated sea-waybills;
- authenticated air-waybills;
- "PIM/PIEX" International consignment notes;
- master air-waybills or bills of lading;
- Certificates of Shipment containing the full details of the consignment and how it left the EU; or
- "International Consignment Note/Lettre de Voiture International" (CMR) fully completed by the consignor, the haulier and the receiving consignee, or "Freight Transport Association" (FTA) own account transport documents fully completed and signed by the receiving customer.

The CMR provides evidence of the identity of the contracting parties when goods are transferred by road. It is in three parts and is completed and signed by the sender of the goods, the carrier and the person receiving the goods. Where the overseas customer arranges for the goods to be collected ex-works the CMR alone is not conclusive evidence that the goods in question have left the EU but, where the CMR is used as part of the evidence, it is important that the information is complete and all the details legible.

For exports by airfreight the supplier must obtain and keep an authenticated master or house air-waybill endorsed with the flight prefix and number, and the date and place of departure. For exports by sea, exporters must keep one of the copies of the shipped bill of lading or sea-waybill (certifying actual shipment) or, where a shipping company does not issue these, a certificate of shipment given by a responsible official of that company.

For Merchandise In Baggage see section **8.6.2** above.

Photocopy certificates of shipment are not normally acceptable as evidence of export, nor are photocopy bills of lading, sea-waybills or air-waybills (unless authenticated by the shipping or airline).

8.9.3 Supplementary evidence

Supplementary evidence consists of the customer's order, the sales contract, inter-company correspondence, a copy of the export sales invoice, the advice note, consignment note and packing list, insurance and freight charges documentation, evidence of payment, and/or evidence of the receipt of the goods abroad.

8.9.4 Tertiary legislation – HMRC Notices having the "force of law"

VAT Notice 703: *export of goods from the UK* section 6.5 makes it clear that the evidence produced must clearly identify **all** of the following:
- the supplier;
- the consignor (where different from the supplier);
- the customer;
- the goods;
- an accurate value;
- the export destination; and
- the mode of transport and route of the export movement.

Vague descriptions of goods, quantities or values are not acceptable. For instance, 'various electrical goods' must not be used when the correct description is '2000 mobile phones (Make ABC and Model Number XYZ2000)'. An accurate value, for example, £50,000 must be shown and not excluded or replaced by a lower or higher amount.

The proof of export must be kept for six years and be readily available to any visiting HMRC Officer to substantiate the zero-rating of all exports. **If the exporter does not hold the correct export evidence, within the appropriate time limits, the goods supplied become subject to VAT at the appropriate UK VAT rate.** HMRC will assess for VAT on goods that they agree have physically been exported if the evidence is not obtained within the stipulated time limits, charging interest and potentially a penalty (that starts at up to 30% of the tax in "error"), even if the evidence is subsequently produced, but after the time limits. If any of the required evidence is lost or mislaid duplicate evidence of export may be obtained, but it must be clearly marked "DUPLICATE EVIDENCE OF EXPORT" and be authenticated and dated by an official of the issuing company.

8.9.5 Goods supplied "Ex-Works" (EXW)

A supply of goods where the customer arranges for their collection at the supplier's premises ("EXW") bears considerable risk for the supplier in that they may not obtain satisfactory proof of export within the time limits, or at all, to support the zero-rating. Before zero-rating the supply and releasing the goods to the customer, the supplier must confirm what evidence of export is to be provided to it.

If the evidence of export does not show that the goods have left the EU within the appropriate time limits, or is found, upon examination, to be unsatisfactory then the supplier will become liable for payment of the VAT. Therefore suppliers should consider whether to include the requirement for the buyer to provide export evidence as part of the sales contract and/or

EXPORTS

secure by, for example, taking a deposit from the customer equal to the amount of VAT potentially liable to HMRC, if the evidence is not provided in time. The deposit can be refunded when the supplier obtains evidence that proves the goods were exported.

For such supplies, copies of transport documents alone will not be sufficient. Accordingly, the information held must also identify the date and route of the movement and the mode of transport involved. It should also include all of the following:

- a written order from the customer which shows their name and address, and the address where the goods are to be delivered;
- a copy sales invoice showing the invoice number, customer's name and a description of the goods;
- the delivery address for the goods;
- the date of departure of goods from the supplier's premises and from the EU;
- the name and address of the haulier collecting the goods;
- the registration number of the vehicle collecting the goods and the name and signature of the driver;
- the place at which the goods are to be taken out of the EU by an alternative haulier or vehicle, and the name and address of that haulier, its registration number and a signature for the goods;
- the route chosen, for example, the Channel Tunnel or port of exit;
- copies of travel tickets; and
- the name of the ferry or shipping company and the date of sailing or airway number and airport.

The information held should also include (if applicable) the trailer number, full container number and the name and address for consolidation, groupage or processing. All of the above information should be obtained at the time the goods leave the EU and can be obtained from the customer, the haulier, the freight forwarder.

8.10 Evidence of export under New Computerised Transit System

The NCTS is in use in all Member states of the EU and the Common Transit countries. Its use is mandatory for businesses wishing to move goods under the CT procedure.

When goods are entered as a Transit declaration into the NCTS an electronic message is sent to the Customs office of departure. When accepted the system allocates a movement reference number, which is a unique registration number, given to identify the movement. The "Anticipated Arrival Record" message is sent by the office of departure to the destination Customs office.

Goods moving under the transit procedure must be accompanied by a "Transit Accompanying Document" (TAD) for presentation at destination or in case the goods are diverted or there are any incidents during transit. The TAD can be printed out at the Customs office of departure or, if the IT system printing can accommodate barcodes, at the exporter's own premises. TADs are authenticated by the system and do not need to be stamped by Customs. When the goods arrive at the destination country, it is important that the TAD is presented to Customs at the office of destination, so that they can inform the NCTS that the goods have arrived.

Authorised consignors are approved to:
- declare goods to CT without presenting them at the office of departure;
- print the TAD and, where applicable, the list of items at the consignor's premises;
- remove goods under Customs control directly from their authorised location – this could be the authorised consignor's own premises or an approved customs facility such as a warehouse, a Designated Export Place, Enhanced Remote Transit Shed (ERTS) or other temporary storage facility; and
- have automatic 'timed-out' release of goods, provided that no control decision is taken by the office of departure – depending upon the conditions of authorisation, 'time-out' may be outside the normal opening hours of the office of destination.

Authorised consignees are approved to:
- receive the goods and documentation direct to their own premises, or another authorised location, for example a port/airport or other approved place such as a Customs warehouse, ERTS or other temporary storage facility, without the requirement to present the goods and TAD to Customs at the office of destination;
- send their arrival notification message to the relevant office electronically; and
- receive automatic 'timed-out' permission to unload the goods, provided that the goods are not subject to further controls or inspections by the office of destination – depending upon the conditions of authorisation, 'time-out' may be outside of the normal opening hours of the office of departure.

Where goods have been entered to NCTS, official evidence of export will be confirmation that the CT procedure has been discharged. The exporter or agent can obtain this confirmation from NCTS by entering the unique Movement Reference Number. (When NCTS is used the Goods Departed Message (GDM) generated by NES is not accepted as evidence for VAT zero-rating because in these circumstances the GDM only confirms that the goods have left the UK, not that the goods have left the EU).

8.11 Goods exported via another Member State

If the goods to be exported have first travelled to another Member State, for example, as part of a groupage arrangement, the supplier must obtain evidence that the goods have finally left the EU. Normal commercial evidence is required as well as the Customs Authority's official evidence. This is normally the "Export Administrative Document" (EAD) accompanying the SAD/C88 or NES-equivalent form authorised at the point of exit from the EU.

Given that the goods to be exported may be in transit within the EU for some time, the exporter must be fastidious in obtaining the satisfactory proof of export within the time limits as they are statutorily fixed. The normal procedure at the point of exit from the EU is for the authorising Customs Authority to certify the accompanying export document ("attestation") and will return it to the consignor. Under NES the exporter is able to produce a certified EAD from their computer system. The EAD contains a unique "Movement Reference Number" (MRN) declaration number allocated by CHIEF in the bottom left hand corner in the section marked 'Office of export control'. HMRC have agreed the format of the EAD with all other Member States – see **8.10** above.

8.12 Ports or airports without access to NES

Where no computerised system is in place at the port or airport of exit, the exporter or agent can arrange with HMRC to manually enter a departure message when the goods are exported. HMRC should be asked for a printed copy of the "DEVD option 2 screen" showing the ICS code '60' to use as official proof of export. This, together with the supporting commercial evidence, will be accepted as evidence for zero-rating.

8.13 Goods exported to the Channel Islands

Although the Channel Islands are part of the Customs Territory of the EU they do not form part of its fiscal territory. Therefore, under the VAT Regulations 1995 (SI 1995/2518) exports to the Channel Islands have to comply with the Community Customs Code and its Implementing Provisions and a Customs declaration is required for goods exported to the Channel Islands.

Excise goods or goods subject to Customs controls (for example restricted goods) being exported to the Channel Islands will always require a SAD/C88 declaration which is normally made by using the National Export System – see section 8.3.1. In the case of goods not subject to Customs or Excise controls one of the following declaration procedures may be used:
- a bulk NES declaration by the shipping line supported by individual *"Consignment Note and Customs Declarations"* (CNCD); or
- individual NES declarations by exporters.

At UK south coast ferry ports a combined CNCD with a supporting itemised schedule of goods exported may be used in place of the SAD/C88 and sea

EXPORTS

waybill for manifested freight. A CNCD may be on an approved standard commercial document or a partly completed SAD/C88.

Therefore, evidence of export for goods sent to the Channel Islands is made up of the following (as appropriate):
- official proof of export produced by NES – see section **8.9.1**;
- goods shipped by air – an authenticated master air-waybill or house air-waybill – see section **8.9.2**;
- goods carried as Merchandise in Baggage – a Customs certified copy 3 of the SAD/C88) – see section **8.6.2**;
- goods shipped through a freight forwarder – a certificate of shipment issued by the freight forwarder or an authenticated copy of the CNCD;
- goods shipped through a fast parcel or courier service – evidence as per section **8.14.2.2** below; or
- goods shipped directly by the south coast ferry companies – an authenticated copy of the CNCD as described above.

8.14 Particular types of export – proof required

As well as the fundamental sources and types of evidence set out in section **8.9** above, particular types of exports require additional evidence. These are described in the sections below.

8.14.1 "Groupage"

"Groupage" or "consolidation cargo" is the term applied to an aggregated load of goods being exported and the freight forwarder is usually shown as the consignor in the shipping documents. The freight forwarder must keep copies of the original bill of lading, sea-waybill or air-waybill, and all consignments in the load must be shown on the container or vehicle manifest. The individual exporter will be issued with a certificate of shipment by the freight forwarder, often supported by an authenticated photocopy of the original bill of lading, a sea-waybill or a house air-waybill. The certificate of shipment must be an original and authenticated by an official of the issuing company unless it is computer produced, on a once-only basis, as a by-product of the issuing company's accounting system.

The certificate of shipment can be in any format, but must be an original and will usually contain the following information:
- the name and address of the issuing company;
- a unique reference number or issuer's file reference;
- the name of the exporter (and VAT number, if known);
- the place, port or airport of loading;
- the place, port or airport of shipment;
- the name of the export vessel or the aircraft, flight prefix and number;
- the date of sailing or flight;
- the customer's name;
- the destination of the goods;

EXPORTS

- a full description of the goods exported (including quantity, weight and value);
- the number of packages;
- the exporter's invoice number and date, if known;
- the bill of lading or air-waybill number (if applicable); and
- the identifying number of the vehicle, container or railway wagon.

8.14.2 Goods exported by post

Goods exported by post may be zero-rated if they are direct exports and the supplier holds the necessary evidence of posting to an address outside the EU. The evidence to support zero-rating varies according to the type of package/parcel, as follows:

8.14.2.1 Letter post or airmail

The goods must be presented to the Post Office with a fully completed certificate of posting form. This can be Form C&E 132 used for single or multiple packages or Form P326 used for single packages only. Alternatively, exporters can use a Certificate of Posting for International Mail, or a Royal Mail Collection Manifest, available from a Royal Mail sales advisor, for use by customers using their Business Collections Service, where the Royal Mail collection driver will sign the certificate as having received the parcel.

8.14.2.2 Parcels

Parcelforce Worldwide (www.parcelforce.com) operates a range of international parcel services. The customs declaration may either be a paper an online version of the 'Despatch Pack'. A fully completed Customs declaration is required for every parcel (even if multiple item consignments are being sent) as every parcel may be inspected by Customs on an individual basis. Each Despatch Pack must contain a full and clear description of all the items within the parcel including quantity, weight, and value of the goods.

Where the parcel is collected by Parcelforce at the exporter's premises the collection driver will provide a despatch pack for completion if one has not already been completed, and will sign the receipt copy. For an online version the collection driver will sign the online receipt or manifest.

Where the parcel is taken to a Post Office the completed receipt copy from the despatch pack will be handed back, together with a printed proof of shipment from the Post Office 'Smartpost' system. This will show the overseas delivery address, date of despatch and unique consignment number (which will match the unique consignment number on despatch pack customer receipt). The exporter must keep both the proof of shipment and the customer receipt as proof of postage.

In addition to the individual parcel declarations described above, account customers of Parcelforce Worldwide who export on a regular basis have two additional potential sources of information listing multiple export parcels, these being the "Worldwide Despatch Manager" (WDM), where online users can print a manifest, which lists all despatched parcels or a Statement of Account. All of the individual parcel declarations, plus either the manifest or the statement of account listing each export will provide proof of export for VAT purposes.

8.14.3 Courier and fast parcel services

Courier and fast parcel operators specialise in the shipment of small consignments to overseas destinations within guaranteed times. Couriers will either use a documentary system based upon the Despatch Pack system (as per **8.14.2.2** above) or other commercial documents such as invoices which routinely bear details of the unique air-waybill numbers for each shipment. In addition, many express companies are able to offer a "track and trace" service via their websites where the movement of consignments can be traced through to the final destination. This information can be printed and can also be used to confirm that the goods have left the EU.

Other couriers use a type of Despatch Pack which contains accounting data, a Customs export declaration and receipt copies of a house air-waybill or consignment note. A Despatch Pack must be completed for each overseas address and consignee and the driver collecting the parcels will endorse the receipt copy and return it to the consignor. This, plus the statement of account issued by the express operator, listing each export shipment, will provide commercial proof of export.

If more than one courier is required to transport the parcel, say, across long distances and is unaware of which one completed the Customs declaration, then the exporter must rely on commercial evidence of export, usually fully-completed transport documents. If the overseas customer is arranging for the goods to be exported by courier the supplier should ascertain what proof of export will be provided to enable VAT zero-rating.

8.14.4 Exports by rail

The export of a parcel by rail is usually accompanied by a consignment note such as a five-part "PIM/PIEX" and, together with copy 4 of the "International Consignment Note" plus the railway statement of account, is acceptable evidence of export and receipt for the goods.

The export of cargo in bulk is accompanied by the five-part "Convention International des Marchandises par Chemin de Fer" (CIM) consignment note which contains the "Uniform Rules concerning the contract for International Carriage of goods by rail". The exporter can use the copy of the consignment note, endorsed with a railway stamp, as the evidence of export.

8.14.5 Exports by auctioneers

Because auctioneers can act in a number of ways it is important to determine before the goods are sold whether the auctioneer is acting in its own name or

EXPORTS

as an agent. Information on the role of auctioneers is set out in Notice 700: *The VAT Guide*,[14] and Notice 718/2 *The VAT Auctioneers' Scheme*.[15]

8.14.5.1 *Auctioneer acting in the exporter's name*

Where the goods are sold through an auctioneer who is not acting in their own name and they export the goods the supplier may zero-rate their supply provided a certificate of export is obtained from the auctioneer. The certificate in the following form must be provided to the supplier within three months of the date of the auction. The auctioneer must hold valid evidence of export for the goods.

Air or sea freight
Example of a Certificate of export for goods sold at auction and exported direct by the auctioneer as air or sea freight

I, ……………………………………………….(full name of signatory) certify that the article(s) detailed below and sold as Lot No(s)…………………………………….at auction by me on ………………………………………………..(date of sale) has/have* been exported from the EU on the undermentioned vessel/aircraft*:

Description of article(s) LOT No Value £'s

Name of export vessel, or aircraft flight prefix and number

Port or airport of loading……………………………………

Date of sailing or departure………………………………….

Destination……………………………

Bill of lading or air-waybill number (where appropriate)………………………………

Identifying number of container or railway wagon(if used)……………………………………………………………

………………………………………………….(Signature of auctioneer)

Date……………………………………

*Delete as necessary

---

[14] www.gov.uk/government/publications/vat-notice-700-the-vat-guide
[15] www.gov.uk/government/publications/vat-notice-7182-the-vat-auctioneers-scheme/

Parcel post or fast courier service
Example of a Certificate of export for goods sold at auction and exported direct by the auctioneer by parcel post or courier service

I, ...(full name of signatory) certify that the article(s) detailed below and sold as Lot No(s)...at auction by me on ....(date of sale) has/have* been exported from the EC by post/courier service*:

Description of article(s) LOT No Value £'s

Place of posting...

Method of posting (parcel/letter and so on)......................................

Date of posting..

Destination...

Certificate(s) of posting numbers held by me..

....(Signature of auctioneer)

Date..

*Delete as necessary

8.15 Time limits for exporting the goods and for obtaining proof of export

The time limits in which the goods must be exported, by either a direct or indirect means, are set out in Notice 703 section 3.[16]

In all cases, the time limit begins at the time of supply (see section **8.16**) and the goods must be finally exported from the EU. Stipulated time limits also apply to goods that are involved in processing or incorporation into other goods prior to export, irrespective of the country where the processing or assembly etc. takes place, but this limit is extended to six months. The supplies must not be zero-rated where the goods have not been exported within these time limits. The Notice 703 table is reproduced below:

---

[16] www.gov.uk/government/publications/vat-notice-703-export-of-goods-from-the-uk/vat-notice-703-export-of-goods-from-the-uk#conditions-and-time-limits-for-zero-rating - and they have the force of law

EXPORTS

Type of export	Time limit for exporting the goods	Time limit for obtaining proof of export
Direct (under the control of the supplier) and indirect (ex-works) exports	3 months	3 months
Supplies of goods involved in groupage or consolidation prior to export	3 months	3 months
Exports through auctioneers	3 months	3 months
Goods delivered to the Foreign & Commonwealth Office (FCO) for export through diplomatic channels	3 months	3 months
Goods ordered by a responsible person of an installation situated outside UK territorial waters	3 months	3 months
Goods ordered by the Ministry of Defence (MOD) and other Government departments provided they are directly exported	3 months	3 months
Goods to be delivered to overseas authorities provided they are ordered through their embassies, High Commissions or UK purchasing agents	3 months	3 months
Supplies of goods involved in processing or incorporation prior to export	6 months	6 months
Thoroughbred racehorses (subject to conditions to be found in Notice 700/57 Administrative Agreements entered into with trade bodies). This notice also sets the conditions for extending the time limits to 12 months (see section **8.9.4**)	6 months	6 months

8.16 "Time of supply" and "tax point" for exports

Although the export of goods is zero-rated, subject to the requisite evidence and time limits being met, the supply is still a "taxable supply" for VAT purposes, the zero-rate being a positive rate of tax. The time of supply and therefore the tax point is important because it crystallises the date from which the relevant three and six months' time limits for exporting the goods commence.

The time of supply and therefore the tax point is either the date when:
- the goods are physically sent to the customer by the supplier, or are "made available" by the supplier for the customer to collect them, or the customer collects them and removes them from the control of the supplier; or
- the receipt of part or all of the payment for the goods is obtained from the customer.

However, for some exports there is no tax point because there hasn't been a supply for VAT purposes. These are where:

- the supplier transfers its own goods from their UK business to a branch outside the EU – see **8.17.1**;
- the supplier delivers or transports goods to a place in a third country/territory where they are to be installed on behalf of a customer under a "supply and install" contract, the place of supply being where the installation takes place – see **8.17.3**;
- goods are delivered or transported to a third country/territory for a temporary period, for example for an exhibition or conference etc. – see **8.17.4**; and
- the goods are delivered under a "sale or return" contract where the goods remain the property of the seller until the customer chooses to purchase them (a supply will only take place at that point) – see **8.17.5**.

The supplier is still required to account to HMRC for the disposal of the goods. So he must obtain proof of export to ensure they are not assessed on the deemed disposal of the goods in the UK or other EU Member State. The supplier must also declare the re-importation of the goods to HMRC on their landing in the UK.

8.17 Particular types of exports

In addition to the general rules set out above, there are some specific rules that relate to particular types of exports and to particular customers in third countries/territories. Each type of delivery can only be zero-rated for VAT purposes where the strict rules are satisfied. The particular exports referred to are:

- goods delivered to a non-UK branch of the same legal entity – **8.17.1**;
- goods lost or stolen in transit – **8.17.2**;
- goods for "supply and install" contracts – **8.17.3**;
- goods for exhibition or processing abroad – **8.17.4**;
- goods supplied on "sale or return" terms – **8.17.5**;
- supplies to "overseas persons" – **8.17.6**;
- racehorses – **8.17.7**;
- supplies to the Ministry of Defence etc. – **8.17.9**;
- certain supplies in connection with the management of defence projects – **8.17.10**;
- supplies to Government departments (excluding the Foreign and Commonwealth office) – **8.17.11**;
- supplies to regimental shops – **8.17.12**;
- goods exported after process or incorporation into other goods – **8.17.13**;
- goods exported following several chain transactions – **8.17.14**;
- exports by members of VAT groups – **8.17.15**;
- exports of freight containers – **8.17.16**;
- stores for ships and aircraft – **8.17.17**;
- supplies delivered to shipping companies and airlines – **8.17.18**;
- stores for sale on-board ships etc. – **8.17.19**;

EXPORTS

- stores for Her Majesty's ships – **8.17.20**;
- British Forces Post Office (BFPO) – **8.17.21**;
- exports of goods to oil rigs, gas rigs and "continental shelf" installations – **8.17.22**;
- tools for the manufacture of goods for export – **8.17.23**;
- goods exported by a charity – **8.17.24**;
- supplies to persons departing from the EU under the "Retail Export Scheme " – **8.17.25**;
- exports of motor vehicles – **8.17.26**;
- the "Personal Export Scheme for motor vehicles – **8.17.27**;
- "sailaway boats" – **8.17.28**;
- marine fuel – **8.17.29**;
- Hydrocarbon oils – **8.17.30**;
- supplies at "Duty and Tax-Free" shops – **8.17.31**; and
- computer software – **8.17.32**.

8.17.1 Goods delivered to a non-UK branch of the same legal entity

Although the transfer of goods from a UK business to a branch outside the EU is not a supply for VAT purposes, the businesses in the UK is required to keep proof of export as evidence of the transfer.

Additionally, the UK business must declare to HMRC any goods returned to the UK. The UK business is able to reclaim any related input tax subject to the normal rules, but the value of the transferred goods is not included in the VAT returns (Box 1 and Box 6).

In their Exports VAT Manual at VEVEXP 80310 and VEXP80320 HMRC provide examples of direct and indirect exports to a non-EU branch, as follows:

Direct transfer
In this example
- a UK company has a non-EU permanently established branch. The parties are part of the same legal entity; and
- a UK supplier delivers the goods to the non-EU permanently established branch and sends the invoice to the UK associated company (or invoices the non-EU branch).

The supply may be zero-rated under section 30(6) VAT Act 1994, provided the conditions in Notice 703 are met, because the UK supplier is responsible for the physical export of the goods. This applies equally where the transaction is invoiced to the UK company where the invoice is sent to the non-EU branch.

EXPORTS

Indirect transfer
In this example
- a UK company has a non-EU permanently established branch. The parties are part of the same legal entity; and
- a UK supplier sells goods for export to the non-EU permanently established branch and sends the invoice to the UK associated company (or invoices the non-EU branch); and
- the UK supplier delivers the goods to a freight forwarder employed by the customer (or the freight forwarder collects the goods from the UK supplier); and
- the freight forwarder exports the goods to the non-EU permanently established branch.

The supply cannot be zero-rated because:
- the non-EU branch is part of the UK company;
- therefore, the supply is made to a taxable person with a business establishment in the UK, with a subsequent transfer of own goods to the non-EU associated company; and
- the conditions set out in regulation 129 of the VAT Regulations 1995 cannot therefore be met.

This applies equally where the transaction is invoiced to the UK company or where the invoice is sent to the non-EU branch – see section **8.17.6**.

8.17.2 Goods that are lost, stolen or destroyed before leaving the UK

Whether any UK VAT is due on the goods depends upon the circumstances of the loss or destruction as follows:
1) if they are lost etc. before a supply has taken place then no VAT is due;
2) where the goods were supplied as a direct export no VAT is due provided the supplier can demonstrate the loss, theft or destruction by reference to accounting records, police enquiries, insurance claims etc.; and
3) where the goods were supplied as an indirect export HMRC will call for VAT if the goods have been delivered in the UK to the overseas person or his representative.

8.17.3 Goods for "supply and install" contracts

There is no UK supply where goods are exported to a third country/territory which are to be installed there by the supplier for his customer as the supply is treated as taking place in the country where the goods are installed. However, the supplier must still hold valid proof of export to demonstrate to HMRC how the goods were disposed of and must also declare any goods returned to the UK. The goods also need to be declared to HMRC upon their return to the UK. Any related input tax can be deducted (subject to the normal rules) but the value of any transferred goods should not be included in Box 6 of the VAT return.

8.17.4 The temporary export of goods for exhibition or processing

There is no UK supply where goods are exported to a third country/territory for the purposes of being exhibited there or processed into other goods. However, the supplier must still hold valid proof of export to demonstrate to HMRC how the goods were disposed of and must also declare any goods returned to the UK. The goods also need to be declared to HMRC upon their return to the UK. Any related input tax can be deducted (subject to the normal rules) but the value of any transferred goods should not be included in Box 6 of the VAT return.

8.17.5 Goods supplied on "sale or return" terms

There is no UK supply where goods are exported to a third country/territory under supply or return terms where the goods remain the property of the supplier until adopted by the purchaser. However, the supplier must still hold valid proof of export to demonstrate to HMRC how the goods were disposed of and must also declare any goods returned to the UK. Any related input tax can be deducted (subject to the normal rules) but the value of any transferred goods should not be included in Box 6 of the VAT return.

8.17.6 Supplies to "overseas persons"

Where HMRC are satisfied that goods intended for export have been supplied to an 'overseas person' who is not a taxable person, the supply is zero-rated. An 'Overseas person' is a person not resident in the UK, a trader who has no business establishment in the UK from which taxable supplies are made, or an overseas authority (i.e. any country other than the UK or any part or place in such a country or the government of any such country, part or place). This includes goods ordered through embassies, High Commissions and purchasing agents of foreign governments in the UK.

Supplies to overseas persons are indirect exports and must meet the normal conditions for the zero-rating of such supplies. Supplies of goods to overseas authorities which are ordered through their Embassies, High Commissions or purchasing agents in the UK, can be zero-rated provided:

- the suppler keeps a separate record of each transaction including evidence that the supply has been made to an overseas authority, for example the order for the goods, sales invoice made out to the overseas authority, evidence of payment from the overseas authority etc.;
- the goods are exported and proof of export is obtained within three months; and
- the goods are not used between the time of leaving the supplier's premises and the time of export, either for their normal purpose or for display, exhibition or copying.

EXPORTS

8.17.7 Racehorses (Notice 700/57/14)[17]

Where a racehorse is supplied to an overseas person, but is to remain in the UK for breaking, conditioning, training or covering before export, the British Horseracing Board and the Thoroughbred Breeders Association have agreed a Memorandum of Understanding with HMRC that the vendor can ask HMRC to extend the time limit for the removal of the racehorse from the UK from six months to twelve months from the date of purchase. However, the horse must not be raced in the UK before export and the relief cannot be transferred to another overseas person.

8.17.8 Supplies to the Ministry of Defence and overseas military establishments

The Ministry of Defence is registered for VAT in the UK and all supplies to them, or to any military establishment in the UK on their behalf, is liable to UK VAT at the appropriate rate. However, a direct export of goods to an overseas military or similar installation may be zero-rated provided the supplier complies with the normal evidence of export rules etc.

8.17.9 Certain supplies in connection with the management of defence projects

Supplies in connection with International Collaboration (Defence) Arrangements (ICDAs) are zero-rated under a Memorandum of Understanding (MoU) agreed by world Governments. An "International Collaboration Arrangement" is any arrangement made between the UK government and the government of one or more other countries (or any government-sponsored international body, e.g. NATO) for collaboration in a joint project of research, development or production. The arrangement must specifically provide for participating governments to relieve the cost of the project from taxation.

The MoU contains a mutual tax waiver clause unequivocally committing all participating governments to ensure that their national taxes do not bear on the project or, failing that, to bear them themselves. There is no specific reference to International Collaboration Defence Projects (ICDPs) in EC law. However, the UK's authority to zero-rate supplies in connection with these projects is derived from EC Sixth Directive Article 28 paragraph 2(a) and EC Second Directive Article 17 (which allows zero-rates in force on 31 December 1975 to be retained). ICDPs are eligible for zero-rating by virtue of Item 2 of Group 13, Schedule 8 of the VAT Act 1994.

---

[17] www.gov.uk/government/publications/vat-notice-70057-administrative-agreements-entered-into-with-trade-bodies/vat-notice-70057-administrative-agreements-entered-into-with-trade-bodies#agreement-with-the-thoroughbred-breeders-association-about-arrangements-under-which-racehorse-owners-may-register-for-vat-and-the-procedures-that-must-be-followed-march-1993

8.17.10 Supplies to Government Departments other than the Foreign and Commonwealth office (FCO)

The supply of goods to Government Departments can only be zero-rated if the goods constitute a direct export to a destination outside the EU and the supplier complies with the conditions set out in Notice 703. A certificate of receipt for the goods is obtained from the FCO within three months of the time of supply of the goods. See VAT Notice 703, para 12.1. Goods destined for export but delivered to Government Departments in the UK, even if ordered for, or by, overseas persons cannot be zero-rated.

8.17.11 Supplies to regimental shops

Special conditions exist to allow the zero-rating of supplies of goods where the regiment (or an equivalent military unit) is about to be posted to a location outside the EU. Suppliers can zero-rate the supply of goods (except new and second-hand motor vehicles) to regimental shops provided:

- each written order received from the President of the Regimental Institute (PRI) states that the regiment is about to take up an overseas posting and that the goods ordered will be exported from the EU;
- the goods are delivered to the PRI ready packed for shipment no more than 48 hours before the Regiment is due to depart for the overseas posting the goods are exported outside the EU; and
- the supplier retains a certificate of receipt signed by the PRI which clearly identifies the goods, gives full shipment details and states the date on which they were exported from the EU.

The PRI will keep a full record of such transactions for reference purposes for a period of not less than six years.

8.17.12 Goods exported after process or incorporation into other goods

In cases where the goods are delivered to a third person in the UK who is also making a taxable supply of goods or services to that overseas person, the supplier can zero-rate the supply provided that all of the following conditions are met:

- the goods are only being delivered and not supplied to the third person in the UK;
- no use is being made of the goods other than for processing or incorporation into other goods for export;
- the goods are exported from the EU and evidence of export within the specified time limits is obtained and the business records show:
    i. the name and address of the overseas person the invoice number and date;
    ii. the description, quantity and value of the goods;
    iii. the name and address of the third person in the UK to whom the goods were delivered;

iv. the date by which the goods must be exported and proof of export obtained; and
v. the date of actual exportation.

The business records must be able to show to HMRC's satisfaction that the goods supplied have been processed or incorporated into the goods exported. Where such supplies are made, an extension to the normal time limits for exporting the goods and obtaining satisfactory evidence of export is allowed for up to six months – see section **8.15**.

In cases where the third person is not in the UK, but is in another Member State the same conditions will generally apply to allow the supplier to zero-rate the supply. However, the supplier should establish the full facts behind the particular supply in question before assuming that zero-rating is appropriate. If the supplier intends to make such a supply and is unsure as to whether it may be zero-rated, HMRC advise that the supplier should contact the National Advice Service.

If the supplier does not meet all of the above conditions then the supply cannot be zero-rated as an export and VAT must be accounted for. Consequently, it is essential that the supplier establishes at the time of supply what type of export documentation the third party will send to support the zero-rating of the UK supply.

8.17.13 Goods exported following several chain transactions

Where goods are exported following a series of UK supplies only the final supply to a third country/territory may be zero-rated. HMRC provides the following example in Notice 703 para 4.1:

- company 'A', based outside the EU, orders goods from Company 'B' that is UK based; and
- company 'B' purchases the goods from Company 'C', that is also UK based, but does not take delivery of the goods; because
- company 'C', at the request of Company 'B', sends the goods direct to Company 'A'.

Here there are two separate transactions which should be treated as follows:

- the supply of the goods from company 'C' to company 'B' is a supply in the UK and must be invoiced at the appropriate rate of UK VAT; whereas
- the supply of goods from company 'B' to company 'A' is zero-rated as an export subject to the relevant conditions being met.

8.17.14 Exports by members of VAT groups

All supplies of goods by any member of a VAT group are treated as being supplied by the "Representative Member". Any supply of goods between members of the group is disregarded for VAT until the point at which a supply is made to a customer outside the VAT group. Where a member exports those goods then the necessary proof of export must be obtained to allow the Representative Member to account for the transaction in the group

VAT return. If the subsidiary member in question failed to obtain the requisite proof of export then the Representative Member on behalf of all the members, that have joint and several liability for the tax declarations of the group (whilst they are members of it), would be liable for the VAT.

8.17.15 Freight containers – see Notice 703/1

Freight containers, whether new or second-hand, are treated as goods for the purposes of VAT. The export of containers is zero-rated subject to the normal rules and zero-rating extends to the goods carried in them. HMRC has issued Notice 703/1: *Supply of freight containers for export or removal from the UK*[18] to explain their VAT treatment.

A container is defined as "an article of transport equipment (lift-van, moveable tank or other similar structure):
- fully or partially enclosed to constitute a compartment intended for containing goods;
- of a permanent character and accordingly strong enough to be suitable for repeated use;
- specially designed to facilitate the carriage of goods, by one or more means of transport, without intermediate reloading;
- designed for ready handling, particularly when being transferred from one mode of transport to another;
- designed to be easy to fill and to empty; and
- having an internal volume of one cubic metre or more.

The term container includes:
- the accessories and equipment of the container, appropriate for the type concerned, provided that such accessories and equipment are carried with the container;
- air transport containers whatever their internal volume; and
- 'flats' or 'Lancashire flats' (bases with or without head and tail boards, which are designed to carry goods and have the floor area of a 20 ft or 40 ft container) although not strictly covered by this definition HMRC treat them in the same way.

The term 'container' shall not include:
- vehicles, accessories or spare parts of vehicles;
- packaging; or
- pallets, road vehicles and trailers including those with fixed tanks.

Supplies of freight containers for direct export may be zero-rated provided the conditions set out in Notice 703 are met.

---

[18] www.gov.uk/government/publications/vat-notice-7031-supply-of-freight-containers-for-export-or-removal-from-the-uk/

HMRC explain in paragraph 3.2 of Notice 703/1 (which has the force of law) that to zero-rate the sale of a freight container in an indirect export, the supplier must obtain a written undertaking from the customer that the container will be exported from the EU and will not be used within the EU except for:
- a single domestic journey before export of the container, on which inland freight may be carried between two points within the UK. This is allowable only if the route brings the container reasonably directly from the point of supply to the place where it is to be loaded with export cargo or exported; and
- international movements of goods, which may include a journey within the UK for the purpose of loading or unloading the goods.

Of particular note, however, is that unlike other deliveries as explained in section **8.17.13** a chain of supplies can be zero-rated where the above conditions are satisfied.

8.17.16 Ships and aircraft stores
"Stores" are goods and provisions for use in a ship or aircraft and include fuel, goods for running repairs or maintenance, for example lubricants, spare and replacement parts, goods for general use on board by the crew, and goods for retail sale to passengers carried on the voyage or flight, but who use the stores only on board. However, there is no stores relief available for goods used on road vehicles, e.g. coaches or for Channel Tunnel trains.

Although goods for general use on board ships or aircraft departing for an eventual destination outside the UK qualify as stores, goods ordered by individual crew members for their own private use do not. These individuals may be entitled to relief from VAT under the terms of the Retail Export Scheme (RES) – see **8.17.24**.

Stores used for the fuelling and provisioning of vessels and aircraft can only be zero-rated where they are for use on a voyage or flight with a 'non-private' purpose and with an eventual destination outside the UK and they are shipped from the UK within three months of the supply. However, Extra Statutory Concession 9.2 covers supplies of marine fuel to vessels for voyages in home waters (see section **8.17.28** below). Additionally, all of the following conditions must be satisfied for the relevant supplies to be zero-rated:
- when placing the order the person to whom the goods are to be supplied declares in writing that the goods are for use as stores on a voyage or flight which is to be made for a non-private purpose; and
- the supplier obtains and holds a written order or confirmation given by the master, commander, owner or duly authorised agent of the ship or aircraft. This must include a declaration that the goods are solely for use as stores on a named ship or aircraft that is entitled to receive duty free stores for the voyage in question, i.e. to an eventual destination outside the UK.

Aircraft making through international flights are eligible to receive VAT free stores even if the aircraft makes one or more stops in the UK in the course of such a flight; and
- the supplier sends the goods:
  (a) direct to the ship or aircraft; or
  (b) through freight forwarders for consolidation and delivery direct to the ship or aircraft; or
  (c) addressed and delivered to the master of a named vessel c/o the shipping line or agent;

and
- the supplier obtains and holds a receipt confirming delivery of the goods on board the ship or aircraft, signed by the master, commander or other responsible officer of the ship or aircraft. Applications from individual airlines requesting permission for the certificate to be signed by a responsible official of the airline (usually the Duty Engineer) may be allowed subject to approval by HMRC and on condition that:
  (a) the signatory is in a position to issue the certificate based on personal knowledge of the flight details; and
  (b) the airline maintains adequate documentation to enable HMRC staff to verify their entitlement to relief; and
  (c) where the supplies are made to an eligible vessel or aircraft direct from a bonded warehouse not operated or owned by the supplier, the supplier holds a certificate of export as described in paragraph 7.10 of Notice 703: *export of goods from the UK*. The advice note issued by the warehousekeeper normally serves this purpose.

If suppliers fail to meet the conditions governing the supply of stores, they must not zero-rate the supply and must account for VAT as appropriate. If they subsequently obtain the necessary statements and receipts or certificates, they may adjust their records and zero-rate the supply.

In cases where there are intermediate suppliers before the eventual supply to the ship or aircraft, the intermediaries must account for VAT at the appropriate rate as a UK supply. If goods are supplied to a shore-side storage tank they may not be zero-rated unless the customer is the final exporter of the goods and the supplier holds the necessary evidence.

8.17.17 Stores delivered direct to shipping companies and airlines

VAT-registered shipping lines or airline operators can choose to have all their supplies, including goods for shipment as stores on their ships or aircraft, delivered to their premises. Because the supplies are delivered to a UK-landed depot VAT is chargeable at the appropriate rate. However, the shipping or airline company can deduct input tax subject to the normal rules and the subsequent transfer of the goods from their premises to the ship or aircraft for use as stores is not a supply for VAT purposes.

Where an airline makes only international non-private flights, a blanket declaration of entitlement may be accepted instead of individual ones for each flight. This blanket declaration, signed by a responsible employee of the company, must state that all of the goods supplied to them are solely for use as stores, on non-private foreign-bound flights – that is, to a destination outside the UK. The company must also undertake that should they operate domestic flights at a later date, they will inform their supplier before receiving further stores.

8.17.18 Stores for sale on-board ships etc.

The arrangements described in **8.17.17** also apply to goods supplied for sale in ships' shops even though there may be no taxable supply at the time of shipment, for example the transfer of a supplier's own goods under 'sale or return' terms. Where goods have been shipped on a foreign-going ship or aircraft, any later sale of the goods will be a supply outside the UK and there will be no further VAT liability unless they are re-landed in the UK. However, it should be noted that VAT is chargeable on goods sold on board a vessel on a coastwise journey or on an aircraft on an internal UK flight.

Where stores are supplied and subsequently re-landed in the UK they are treated as imports and care needs to be taken with accounting for any import VAT that might be due – see **Chapter 2** *ad seq* above.

8.17.19 Supplies of mess and canteen stores for HM ships

Notice 703 para 10.7 states that supplies of goods for use as mess and canteen stores on HM ships which are about to leave for a foreign port or a voyage outside UK territorial waters of more than fifteen days duration are zero-rated. However, the goods must be ordered for the general use on board by members of the ship's company, and the Commanding Officer must certify each order as follows:

> HMS................ is deploying from the United Kingdom for service abroad on..................(date) calling at a foreign port or on a voyage outside territorial waters of more than fifteen days' duration and these stores are for use by members of the crew during the deployment.

The supplier must deliver the goods direct to the ship for loading on board, obtain a receipt for them on board and keep it to support their claim for zero-rating.

The supply of duty-free goods on sale or return terms to messes in HM ships cannot be zero-rated when they are delivered to the ship as there is no taxable supply at that time. The taxable supply occurs only when:
- the goods are adopted, that is when the customer pays for the goods or otherwise indicates his wish to keep them; or
- at the end of twelve months or any shorter period that has been agreed for the goods to be bought or returned.

EXPORTS

The supplier is responsible for ensuring that they are informed by the messes when the goods were adopted. If adoption occurs when the vessel is in UK territorial waters the supply is taxable, but if adoption takes place outside UK territorial waters there is no supply for VAT purposes. VAT is chargeable at the appropriate rate on sales of goods in canteens and shops on board HM ships in UK ports or on coastwise voyages. If the ship is outside UK territorial waters at the time of sale the supply is outside the scope of VAT. However, VAT is due if the goods are re-landed in the UK.

Where there is no supply at the time of delivery on board, VAT is chargeable at the appropriate rate on sales of goods in canteens and shops on board HM Ships in UK ports or on coastwise voyages. If the ship is outside UK territorial waters any sale of goods is outside the scope of VAT and is taxable only if the goods are re-landed in the UK.

8.17.20 Exports by British Forces Post Office (BFPO)

Supplies made via the British Forces Post Office (BFPO service to members of the British forces that are based outside the EU) are zero-rated if the supplier has a written order from the member of the forces confirming that they are based outside the EU, sufficient information confirming that the BFPO number is outside the VAT territory of the EU, and evidence of delivery to the BFPO depot in the UK.

8.17.21 Exports of goods to oil rigs, gas rigs and "continental shelf" installations

The definition of continental shelf installations includes oil rigs, drilling units, accommodation platforms and similar oil or gas exploration / exploitation structures, drill ships, tankers, jack-up rigs, semi-submersible rigs and "Floating Production Storage and Offloading" (FPSO) vessels which are often stationed at fixed locations. The legislation differentiates the following types of "export":

1. Exports to installations outside EU territorial waters:
   - Goods supplied and exported by you to an installation not owned by the exporter can be zero-rated as a direct export provided that the goods are physically exported and valid proof of export is obtained within three months of the time of supply.
   - Goods that are sent to an installation owned by the supplier or to replenish their own stocks on an installation they do not own are not supplies for VAT purposes since these movements are treated as the transfer of their own goods. HMRC, however, still require that the supplier holds valid proof of the movement to demonstrate how the goods were disposed of.
2. Goods supplied for sale on installations which are situated outside UK territorial waters:

- UK territorial waters consist of the waters within 12 nautical miles of the coastlines of England, Scotland, Wales and Northern Ireland and supplies to installations in these locations are zero-rated provided:
    (a) the supplier obtains a written order for the goods from a responsible person on the installation to which the goods are to be sent;
    (b) the goods are supplied either direct to the installation or through an agent for consolidation followed by direct delivery to the installation, and
    (c) the supplier obtains a receipt for the goods, signed by a responsible person on the installation, within three months of the time of supply.

8.17.22 Machine tools used in the UK to manufacture goods for export (see Notice 701/22)

"Machine tools" are goods that are used in the manufacture of other goods, for example, jigs, patterns, templates, dies, moulds, punches and similar tools. A manufacturer may be able to zero-rate the supply of a machine tool where it has been used to manufacture goods that are exported to a third country/territory, or are dispatched to another Member State (see **Chapter 9**) and the conditions for zero-rating are met.

HMRC explain in Notice 701/22[19] that all of the following conditions must be met for the manufacture of the tool to be zero-rated:

- the machine tool is supplied to an "overseas authority", an "overseas body" or an "overseas trader";
- the supplier obtains a signed statement (or other similar definite evidence) from their customer that they are neither registered nor required to be registered for VAT in the UK and they are not an authority, body or trader in another Member State;
- the machine tool is used for manufacturing goods that are exported from the UK to a third country/territory; and
- the supplier obtains commercial documentary evidence that the goods have been exported.

An "overseas authority" means any country other than the UK or any part of, or place, in a country or the government of any such country, part or place. An overseas body means a body established outside the UK and an overseas trader means a person who carries on a business and has his principal place of business outside the UK.

---

[19] www.gov.uk/government/publications/vat-notice-70122-tools-for-manufacture-of-goods-for-export/vat-notice-70122-tools-for-manufacture-of-goods-for-export#zero-rating-machine-tools-used-to-manufacture-goods-for-export-or-removal-to-an-eu-country

8.17.23 Goods exported by a charity

Charities in receipt of grants or donations to be able to fulfil their "core" objectives and responsibilities are making, for VAT purposes, "non-business" supplies. The VAT incurred by the charity in furtherance of these activities is irrecoverable. Where a charity makes supplies that for VAT purposes are classed as "business" activities, the income becomes VATable (unless it is exempt under the exempt Schedules) and the VAT incurred on such activities is reclaimable. Business activities can be the sale of goods such as Christmas cards, tee-shirts and merchandise advertising the charity or the provision of services such as receiving sponsorship income.

Where a charity exports goods to a third country/territory, HMRC allows the charity to treat the exports as a "business" supply and this enables the charity to reclaim VAT on the purchase of the exported goods. It could also enable the charity to recover a proportion of its overhead VAT. As a dispensation charities are relieved of the burden to obtain proof of export under VATA 1994, Sch 8 Grp 15, item 3, but it is prudent for charities that export goods to retain such commercial evidence that will also act as satisfactory proof of export and delivery to the third country/territory.

8.17.24 Supplies to persons departing from the EU under the "Retail Export Scheme" ("tax-free shopping")

The VAT Retail Export Scheme allows overseas visitors to the UK to claim a VAT refund on most goods that they buy and export from the EU. HMRC has issued guidance to retailers and travellers in Notice 704: *VAT Retail Exports*[20] and Notice 704/1: *Tax free shopping in the UK*[21] (there are also Spanish, Arabic and Japanese language versions).

An "overseas visitor" is defined as:
- a traveller (including a member of the crew of a ship or aircraft) who is not established in the EU and whose normal 'domicile' or 'habitual place of residence' is outside the EU; **and**
- who intends to leave the UK for a final destination outside the EU, with the goods, by the last day of the third month following that in which the goods were purchased for example, goods purchased on 3 February would have to be exported by 31 May; **and**
- the goods are exported from the EU, the purchaser having produced them, their receipts and the VAT refund document to the Customs Authority at the point of departure from the EU.

---

[20] www.gov.uk/government/publications/vat-notice-704-vat-retail-exports/
[21] www.gov.uk/government/publications/vat-notice-7041-tax-free-shopping-in-the-uk/

A person's "domicile" or "habitual residence" is the place entered as such on their valid passport, identity card or other acceptable document, such as a driving licence.

Overseas visitors entering the UK as students or migrant workers are only entitled to purchase goods under the scheme during the last four months of their stay in the UK. Such visitors will have been issued with a pre-entry visa from the UK and in the case of work periods of six months or more a separate work permit document is issued in the UK. The visa is contained in the overseas person's passport and shows the start and end date for the study or work period authorised. Retailers should ask to see the visa or work permit before selling goods under the scheme.

EU residents may also qualify to use the scheme if they intend to leave the EU permanently for a minimum period of twelve months. To qualify under this provision the person must:

- intend to leave the UK with the goods by the last day of the third month following that in which the goods were purchased for an immediate destination outside the EU; **and**
- remain outside the EU for a period of at least 12 months; **and**
- export the goods having produced them, their receipts and the VAT refund document to the Customs Authority at the point of departure from the EU.

Typically, the acceptable evidence of an entitled EU resident's use of the scheme would be an overseas work permit, approved visa application, or residency permit etc.

All of the following types of goods are excluded from the scheme:

- new and second-hand motor vehicles for personal export (see section **8.17.26** below);
- boats sold to visitors who intend to sail them to a destination outside the EU (see section **8.17.27** below);
- goods over £600 (excluding VAT) in value exported for business purposes;
- goods that will be exported as freight or unaccompanied baggage;
- goods requiring an export licence, with the exception of antiques;
- unmounted gemstones;
- bullion (over 125g, 2.75 troy ounces or 10 Tolas);
- goods for consumption in the EU – no certification of export will be given for used consumable items, for example, perfume which is wholly or partly consumed in the EU;
- goods purchased by mail order including those purchased over the Internet; and
- zero-rated goods such as books and children's clothing.

Also, goods sold to entitled persons by mail order or over the Internet will fall within the export rules set out in Notice 703 as "normal exports". However, a

EXPORTS

mail order company or an Internet retailer with a retail outlet can use the scheme for goods sold from that outlet provided they comply with all the conditions set out in Notice 704.

The scheme also cannot be used for services supplied to customers such as hotel accommodation, meals and car hire. This applies even where services are sold with the goods, for example labour costs for fitting spare parts to a motor vehicle. Where a vehicle brought into the UK for the use of the overseas visitor requires repairs, the sale of the spare parts only and not the cost of fitting can be included in the scheme.

If any goods bought under the scheme in the EU are to be consumed or remain in the EU the purchaser must clearly delete those items from any VAT refund document for certification by the Customs Authority when finally leaving the EU. The VAT refund document must show only those items which are being exported.

Tax-free goods can be bought from any retailer operating the scheme. At the time of purchase the retailer will request proof that the customer is eligible to use the Scheme, for example a passport. The customer will then be asked to complete and sign some simple details on a refund form which can be Form VAT 407 (or a shop or refund company's own version of it) or a VAT Retail Export Scheme sales invoice. However, the customer must complete one of these forms as till receipts alone are not acceptable. The form should be completed at the time of purchase in the presence of the retailer. Retailers are entitled to ask for a deposit to cover the amount of VAT otherwise due in the sale of the goods to safeguard them against non-return of a certified copy of the Form VAT 407.

Where a retailer chooses to use their own version of the refund form they may use an officially approved invoice, which must comply with the UK's full particulars for a VAT invoice.

For a "simplified" invoice, i.e. where the total consideration for a supply (including VAT) is less than £250, the following information must be included in it:
- the retailer's name, address and VAT registration number;
- the time of supply;
- a description sufficient to identify the goods supplied;
- the total amount payable including VAT; and
- for each rate of VAT chargeable, the gross amount payable including VAT and the VAT rate applicable.

For a full VAT invoice i.e. for sales exceeding £250 (including VAT) the following information must be included in it:
- the retailer's name, address and VAT registration number;
- an identifying number;

EXPORTS

- the date of issue;
- the time of supply (tax point - only needs to be shown if different from the date of issue);
- the customer's name (or trading name) and address (where an approved invoice is used for the scheme the usual address will be the customer's place of residence outside the EU);
- a description identifying the goods (or services) supplied;
- the total amount payable, excluding VAT;
- the rate of any cash discount offered;
- the unit price; and
- the total amount of VAT charged, shown in sterling.

For each description of goods (and services) the invoice must show the quantity of goods (or extent of the services), the rate of VAT and the amount payable, excluding VAT.

Alternatively, and provided the customer agrees, a retailer may issue a "modified" VAT invoice showing the VAT-inclusive amounts of each supply instead of the VAT exclusive values. However, in all other respects the modified invoice should show the details required for a full VAT invoice.

If the customer is leaving the EU directly, i.e. not travelling to any other Member State before finally leaving the EU, they must present the goods and the refund form to HMRC at the port or airport of departure ensuring that any items checked in as hold baggage are produced to HMRC before checking in baggage.

Alternatively, if the customer is leaving the EU by means of transit via another Member State then any goods carried as hand baggage must be produced to the Customs Authority in the last EU Country with the refund form before finally departing the EU. Any goods carried in the aircraft's hold must be produced to HMRC in the UK with the refund form before the baggage is checked in.

After certification by HMRC or the Customs Authority in another Member State, the customer can either post the form back to the retailer to arrange payment of the refund (or, post the form back to a commercial refund company acting on the customer's behalf), or hand the form to a refund booth to arrange immediate payment. Whichever method is used should have been agreed between the customer and the retailer at the time of purchase.

An agent acting on the customer's behalf will usually charge an administration fee which should be clearly annotated on the refund form. If the customer decides to leave goods bought under the Scheme in the EU, the VAT refund document must be amended before being presented for certification at the relevant departure point.

EXPORTS

Retailers are advised to treat any sale of standard-rated and lower-rated goods made under the scheme as liable to VAT until they have received the VAT refund documents appropriately certified by HMRC or another EU Customs Authority. They can then arrange to remit the VAT taken as deposit to the customer. Retailers must note that if the customer returns VAT refund documents which have not been certified by HMRC or another EU Customs Authority, the relevant supplies cannot be zero-rated and any liability to account for VAT rests with them.

Any sum deducted by the retailer to cover administrative or handling expenses, from say the VAT refunded, can also be zero-rated as it is consideration for the supply of the service of arranging an export of goods to a third country/territory.

8.17.24.1 *Non-EU Passengers on intra-EU cruises*

There are special arrangements for goods bought by non-EU persons enjoying cruises in the EU. Non-EU passengers on wholly intra-EU cruises may not have access to their luggage and purchases made under the VAT Retail Export Scheme from disembarkation until they arrive at their final non-EU destination. They cannot, therefore, produce their goods and VAT refund document to the Customs officer for stamping at their point of final departure from the EU. Therefore, for wholly intra-EU cruises which commence within the UK and where the final port of disembarkation is also within the UK, HMRC introduced a special arrangement on 1 July 2003.

Where individual purchases are less than £1,000 cruise operators may produce an omnibus bulk refund document for all eligible goods purchased on board by entitled individual passengers. The omnibus refund document must accompany the individual passenger's luggage to the airport of departure. If satisfied the Customs officer will stamp the bulk refund form and return it to the cruise operator. However, the cruise operator must account for VAT on any goods on the bulk refund form not exported from the EU within the prescribed limits.

Where individual purchases are in excess of £1,000 the normal VAT 407 form or equivalent must be completed and the passenger must produce the goods and the form for stamping to the Customs officer at the point of final departure from the EU.

8.17.25 Exports of motor vehicles

The supply of a new or used motor vehicle, can be zero-rated in the following circumstances:
- as a direct export provided that it is not used or delivered in the EU before it is exported;
- as an indirect export provided that it is not subsequently used except for the trip to the place of departure from the EU; or

- where it is sold to a private individual under the terms of the "Personal Export Scheme".

8.17.26 The "Personal Export Scheme" for motor vehicles

The Personal Export Scheme allows motor vehicles that are to be used temporarily in the UK before export to a third country/territory to be purchased free of VAT. Subject to some restrictions the vehicle may also be used for a limited period in other Member States before being finally exported to a destination outside the EU. New or used motor vehicles, motorcycles or motor caravans are eligible, but pedal cycles or trailer caravans are excluded from the scheme.

Only the following persons may purchase vehicles fee of VAT:
1. Overseas visitors meaning persons that have not been in the EU for more than either:
   - 365 days in the two years before the date when applying to use the Scheme; **or**
   - 1095 days in the six years before the date when applying to use the Scheme; **and**
   - who intend to leave and remain outside the EU with the motor vehicle for a period of at least six months.
2. Entitled EU residents meaning persons that have been in the EU for more than:
   - 365 days in the two years before the date when applying to use the Scheme; **or**
   - 1095 days in the six years before the date when applying to use the Scheme; **and**
   - who intend to leave and remain outside the EU with the motor vehicle for a period of at least six months.

An overseas visitor may take delivery of the vehicle and use it in the UK during the last 12 months of their stay in the EU whereas an entitled EU resident may only take delivery of the vehicle and use it in the UK during the last six months before finally leaving the EU. If the purchaser is unable to export the vehicle because it has been stolen or involved in an accident and written-off, the VAT amount not paid at the time of purchase will become due.

Entitled persons may make temporary visits with the vehicle to another Member State without facing formal HMRC enquiries on returning to the UK, but only if the vehicle is returned to the UK before the due date for exportation and the purchaser still intends to finally depart with the vehicle from the EU by that date. If, whilst visiting another Member State, the purchaser decides to remain with the vehicle in that country, they need to notify the Customs Authority there and pay VAT and any other local taxes due.

However, purchasers are advised not to make a temporary visit to a third country/territory prior to the final date for export shown on the Form VAT

EXPORTS

410, as when the vehicle is re-imported into either the UK or another Member State, the VAT amount not paid at the time of purchase will become due. Upon re-importation into the EU, the purchaser must declare the vehicle to the Customs Authority at the place of re-importation producing either the vehicle registration document (VX302) for new vehicles or the Form VAT 410 for used vehicles.

A vehicle that has been exported from the EU will be subject to import VAT upon re-importation unless it can be relieved (see Notice 3: *Bringing your personal belongings and motor vehicle to the UK from outside the EU* and section **5.29.7** above). If, however, the vehicle is re-imported six months or more after the date for export shown in the registration document (VX302), or in the case of used vehicles the date on the VAT 410 form, or it can be shown that the owner and the vehicle have remained outside the EU for at least six consecutive months, the VAT payable will be based on the value of the vehicle at the time of re-importation. In all other cases, the VAT that was not paid when the vehicle was bought will become due.

Full details about the Personal Export Scheme are set out in Notice 707.[22]

8.17.27 Sailaway boats

HMRC's Notice 703/2[23] explains the scheme in detail.

The scheme allows an "entitled person" to buy a boat for export from the EU without paying VAT. A 'sailaway' boat is defined as one which is to be delivered to the buyer or their authorised skipper within the EU and exported under its own power to a destination outside the VAT Territory of the EU. The scheme can only be used for the private purchase of a boat that is only to be used for private (non-commercial) purposes.

An entitled person is an overseas visitor who intends to export the boat under its own power to a third country/territory within six months of the date of delivery.

Before 1 January 2012 UK residents who intended to export the boat to a destination outside the EU could also use the scheme, but they are no longer eligible. The date of delivery is normally the date that the boat leaves the manufacturer or supplier. However, UK residents may be able to purchase a boat VAT-free provided that the seller arranges the direct export of the boat to a destination outside the EU.

The scheme cannot be used for boats exported on a trailer, or for exporting parts or accessories, but these may be zero-rated under the Personal Export Scheme (see section **8.17.26** above). It also cannot be used for boats that are to

---

[22] www.gov.uk/government/publications/vat-notice-707-vat-personal-export-scheme/
[23] www.gov.uk/government/publications/vat-notice-7032-sailaway-boats-supplied-for-export-outside-the-eu/

be operated commercially, for example fishing trawlers or for tourist sightseeing trips. However, these vessels can still be zero-rated if they are exported as normal freight and the acceptable evidence of export is obtained within the stipulated time limits. Finally, the scheme excludes new vessels to be removed to any other Member States or second-hand boats to all Member States except Cyprus.

Exports of boats under the "direct exports" legislation are excluded from this scheme but if the boat is not to be used in the EU before it is exported, the supplier can arrange for the boat to be delivered direct to a destination outside the EU free of VAT.

Before supplying a boat under the scheme the boatyard must ensure that the buyer is entitled to use the scheme and they intend to export the boat from the EU within the permitted time limits and provide them with a copy of Notice 703/2 and an application form VAT 436. The boatyard should ensure the form VAT 436 is fully completed by them and the buyer, the boatyard submitting Part 2 of the form to the Personal Transport Unit (PTU) at least two weeks before the boat is delivered to the buyer.

All notifications should be serially numbered in the top right hand corner and submitted to the PTU at the following address:

HM Revenue & Customs
Personal Transport Unit (PTU)
Priory Court
St John's Road
Dover CT17 9SH

Phone: 01304 664171
Fax: 01304 664179

At the time of sale the boatyard must ensure that the buyer knows that they cannot dispose or attempt to dispose of the boat in the EU by hire, pledge as security, sale, gift or any other means. The boatyard must also keep a separate record of the sale and agree with the buyer how any refund of the deposited VAT will be repaid. The sales invoice must clearly show that the supply of the boat was made under the Sailaway boat scheme.

The sale of the boat cannot be zero-rated until the boatyard receives proof from the buyer that the boat has been removed from the EU. If the boatyard does not obtain and hold evidence to show that the boat was exported within the stipulated time limits, VAT must be accounted for. If a deposit of the VAT due has been taken, then it should be brought to account, or alternatively, if a deposit has not been taken, VAT is to be accounted for on the taxable proportion of the invoiced amount of consideration received.

EXPORTS

The uses of the forms vary according to whether a boat departs to a third country/territory directly from the UK or via another Member State. The forms needed are:

1. Form VAT 436 Notification of VAT-free purchase of a Sailaway boat and buyer's declaration.
   - Original copy 1 – copy for certification by a HMRC officer
   - Copy 2 – HMRC copy
   - Copy 3 – buyer's copy
   - Copy 4 – seller's copy.
2. Form SAD/C88 – copies 1 to 3
   - Copy 1 – Community transit copy where applicable (seller to take a copy for their own records)
   - Copy 2 – for HMRC
   - Copy 3 – for certification when the boat finally leaves the EC.
3. Form C1331 Notice of intended departure – to advise departure from the UK.

Suppliers must keep a separate record of all boats sold under the scheme.

If a boat that was supplied tax free at purchase is brought back to the EU it must be declared to the Customs Authority in the Member State of importation. The seller should ensure that the buyer is fully aware of the need to make an import declaration. Import VAT will be payable unless some other relief is available, for example Temporary Admission (TA) relief – see section **5.23.3**.

8.17.28 Supplies of "marine fuel"
Under Extra Statutory Concession 9.2 (see Notice 48: *Extra Statutory Concessions)*[24] commercial vessels engaged on voyages within UK territorial waters or within the limits of a UK port may receive certain types of marine fuel free of VAT providing all the conditions set out in VAT Notice 703: *exports and removals of goods from the UK* concerning proof that the ship is departing from the UK and evidence of removal is obtained. However, this relief extends only to those supplies of fuel which were zero-rated prior to 1 July 1990 under the Value Added Tax Act 1983 Schedule 5 Group 7 item 4 which essentially is "rebated gas oil." that cannot be used in road vehicles. Therefore, it does not apply to petrol, DERV or lubricating oils.

8.17.29 Hydrocarbon oils
Hydrocarbon oils are subject to UK excise duty and are normally held in warehouses approved by HMRC until the time of delivery. Sales of such hydrocarbon oils within these warehouses prior to delivery are disregarded for VAT purposes. Hydrocarbon oils may be delivered by pipeline or Road Tanker Wagons (RTWs) to the end-user. All such pipelines and RTWs must be

---

[24]www.gov.uk/government/publications/vat-notice-48-extra-statutory-concessions/

approved by HMRC if they are to be used to convey products that have not been declared as available for "free circulation" (if any import duty or import VAT is due on the goods at import) or excise duty has not been paid on them at that point in time. The export of such products must also be verified by official and commercial evidence (see section **8.9** above) to be produced within the stipulated time limits (see section **8.15**).

8.17.30 Supplies at "Duty and Tax-Free" shops

Supplies from duty/tax-free shops to passengers travelling to third countries/territories would not normally be entitled to zero-rating since they do not meet the conditions for direct or indirect exports. However, by concession (see Notice 48: *Extra Statutory Concessions,* para 9.1)[25], the supplier may be regarded as the exporter provided the goods are exported directly to a territory outside the EU. Duty/tax free shops must be authorised by HMRC to act as such and they are normally placed within "airside" or "portside" areas of controlled airports and ferry terminals. The retailer must be satisfied that the passenger is departing from the UK on a scheduled flight or ferry by examining the passenger's boarding card, ticket and/or passport.

8.17.31 Computer software

The export of standard or "normalised" computer software packages are regarded as supplies of goods, which may be zero-rated on export from the EU, subject to the normal proof of export and time limits etc. However, supplies of specific items of software tailored to the individual requirements of a company and software that is transmitted by telephone or other data network are generally regarded as supplies of services and are therefore subject to the legislation concerning the international supply of services (HMRC has issued Notice 741A: *Place of supply of services* to offer guidance in this matter)[26]

8.18 Trade Associations and contact details

Exporters and business wishing to export goods can obtain further guidance about the commercial aspects of specific exports from freight forwarders, shipping companies or airlines at the appropriate ports or airports.

The UKTI and the Department for Business Industry and Skills[27] to will be able to provide advice on export markets and exporting in general.

The UK Chambers of Commerce also has a wealth of information for businesses trading internationally.[28]

---

[25] www.gov.uk/government/publications/vat-notice-48-extra-statutory-concessions/vat-notice-48-extra-statutory-concessions#international-field
[26] www.gov.uk/government/publications/vat-notice-741a-place-of-supply-of-services/
[27] www.gov.uk/government/organisations/department-for-business-innovation-skills
[28] www.britishchambers.org.uk/business/international-trade/

9 Intra-EU Transactions

9.1 Background

The advent of the "Single Market" in 1993 introduced the concept of intra-EU trading with the dispensing of all Customs formalities for the movement of goods between Member States. With the absence of routine fiscal controls under the Single Market the risk of diversion of goods either into the UK or free circulation within the EU increases, with the subsequent potential loss of VAT either in the UK or in another Member State. EC mutual assistance agreements require each Member State to ensure that goods within free movement in the EU are properly documented.

Whilst not entirely related to intra-EU trading, the "VAT Gap", meaning the difference between the VAT considered by tax authorities and the European Commission to be accountable on countries' gross domestic product and the amount of VAT actually collected, is still at a staggeringly high level. At the time of writing the VAT Gap in the UK, using 2013 figures, was considered to be £10.9 billion whilst that for the whole EU for 2013 was estimated as £119 billion. A large part of this shortfall is through Missing Trader Intra-Community or 'MTIC' fraud, also known colloquially as "Carousel fraud" and from "diversion fraud" chiefly of excise-free goods being diverted from legitimate supply chains to the black market economy.

However, there is a marked incidence of VAT not being brought to account simply because the rigid compliance conditions for a VAT-free movement of goods across EU borders are not understood and are not therefore applied. The most basic example of this is where the supplier in the Member State of Dispatch uses the purchaser's EU VAT number to zero-rate the sale and record the movement on their EC Sales List quoting the purchaser's own VAT number, but the purchaser either doesn't recognise that they should account for Acquisition VAT on the Arrival of the goods in their own (or any other) Member State or, indeed, apply it correctly.

For cross-border transactions between fully VATable businesses, the purchaser's failure to account for Acquisition VAT does not lead to an actual loss of tax in the purchaser's Member State because the Acquisition VAT can be reclaimed as "input tax". But it might be pertinent for the purchaser's Member State to include the loss of Acquisition VAT in its national "VAT Gap" statistics since it has simply not been brought to account although input tax is reclaimable.

It might also be attractive to the supplier's Member State to record the "loss" of VAT that could have been charged because the correct application of cross-border transactions has not occurred and in the absence of Acquisition VAT being brought to account by the purchaser, output VAT was in fact deemed chargeable. But without foretelling that all of this might take place it is impossible for the supplier's Member State to know in advance that the purchaser will not account for Acquisition VAT.

Every Member State uses the businesses' EC Sales Lists and VAT returns to compile trade statistics for all transactions into and out of their own Member State and therefore there can be both real and perceived inaccuracies that feed into the statistics compiling the VAT Gap. It is open to debate whether there is a duplication of statistics counted between Member States' recording the under-collection of VAT from cross-border trade and therefore the size of the quoted figures should be viewed with a degree of scepticism.

However, for cross-border transactions where the purchaser is partially exempt the failure to account for Acquisition VAT results in an actual revenue loss to the purchaser's Member State as the purchaser is unable to reclaim all of the Acquisition VAT as input tax. Wholly exempt or unregistered purchasers are unable to supply a VAT number to the supplier so most suppliers will automatically charge VAT.

Therefore, although the stated aim of the Single Market is to facilitate the free movement of goods across EU borders it does not necessarily result in the fiscally-free movement of those goods and in many instances either too much or too little VAT is collected, or none at all.

9.2   Introduction to cross-border movements

The movements of goods between Member States are no longer referred to as exports and imports and import duty and import VAT are no longer levied on them. These terms have been replaced by "Dispatches" for the removal of goods from the place of departure of the goods and "Arrivals" or "Acquisitions" for the place of arrival of those goods. VAT is due on the Arrival in the country of Arrival and is known as "Acquisition Tax". The rules have led to the need for customers who take title to goods in the place of their Arrival (or Dispatch) to be VAT-registered there, often resulting in multiple VAT registrations across Member States. Because there can be removals irrespective of the goods being sold, for example the transfer of a legal entity's own goods to create a "consignment" stock in another Member State, businesses can find that they must also be registered in other Member States just to manage the VAT position.

Because of the relaxation of Customs controls in respect of the actual physical delivery of the goods, Member States' tax authorities rely upon the business' VAT accounts and commercial records to manage and collect VAT. The Member States have agreed, through the Commission, to police these movements, using the "Mutual Assistance" regulations and agreements to collect unpaid VAT.

Different VAT treatment pertains to supplies to business customers ("B2B") and to private or "non-business" customers ("B2C"). Not all seemingly B2B transactions can be treated as such because the customer, although being a commercial organisation, is not viewed, for VAT purposes, as being "in business" or is VAT-registered (a pre-requisite in the UK legislation, but not in the EC Directive) resulting in UK VAT being due on the goods. Examples of this are charities and quasi-government bodies. For a B2B intra-EU supply, the means of collecting VAT largely depends on whether the recipient of the supply is registered for VAT in the Member State of Arrival, whereas the place of supply and therefore the Member State in which VAT is due on a B2C supply largely remains in the supplier's Member State (although there are, of course, significant variations).

All businesses conducting trade with other Member States must declare the totals of their Dispatches and Arrivals on their VAT returns. Businesses whose intra-EU trade exceeds a legally set threshold have to complete additional statistical information called "Statistical Supplementary Declarations" ("SSDs") or "Intrastat" returns or "Recapitulative Statements". There are SSDs for Arrivals from other Member States and Dispatches to other Member States. Statistics for the UK's (and other EU Member States) Balance of Payments returns are compiled from the SSDs and information supplied on the VAT returns. Additionally, businesses that supply goods intra-EU also need to complete "EC Sales Lists" ("ESLs") to record the actual values of sales to other EU VAT-registered businesses on a line-by-line basis, but only where the calendar quarterly limits are exceeded.

In addition to the "normal" intra-EU transfer of goods rules, there are a range of special situations, these being:
- transfers of an entity's own goods – section **9.8**;
- temporary movements of goods – section **9.9**;
- installed or assembled goods – section **9.10**;
- intra-EU processing, repair etc. – section **9.11**;
- "triangulation" – section **9.12**;
- supplies to diplomatic missions, consulates, international organisations and NATO visiting forces – section **9.13**;
- "call-off" stocks – section **9.14**;
- consignment stocks – section **9.15**;
- excise goods – section **9.16**;
- goods supplied on sale or return, or similar terms – section **9.17**;
- goods sold on intra-EU transport – section **9.18**;
- samples – section **9.19**; and
- goods sent for testing – section **9.20**.

9.3 Dispatches

A Dispatch is the removal of goods from one Member State to another usually by or under the control of the supplier, but can be by or under the control of the purchaser (see section **9.3.3.1**). The UK uses the term "zero-rating" rather than "exemption" used in EC law to avoid confusion with the use of exemption elsewhere in UK law. The UK VAT law relating to the zero-rating of removals of goods for VAT purposes is Value Added Tax Act 1994 sections 30(8), 30(10) and Regulation 134 of the Value Added Tax Regulations 1995.

A supply of goods that are situated in the UK to a customer in another Member State can only be zero-rated where:

- the supplier obtains and records on their VAT sales invoice the customer's EU VAT registration number, including the two-letter country prefix code; **and**
- the goods are sent or transported out of the UK to a destination in another EU Member State; **and**
- valid commercial evidence is retained to prove that the goods have physically been removed from the UK within the stipulated time limits (see section **9.3.2**).

The removal cannot be zero-rated by the UK supplier if they are sold to a UK VAT-registered customer even if the goods are subsequently removed to another Member State. However, the supply can be zero-rated if that customer is also registered for VAT in another Member State, they provide their EU VAT registration number to the supplier who can quote it on their sales invoice and the goods are physically removed to another Member State.

The removal also cannot be zero-rated if the supplier delivers to, or allows the goods to be collected by, a UK customer at a UK address, or allows the goods to be used in the UK in the period between their supply and their removal, except where specifically authorised to do so.

The Commission has made available a database of all Member States' VAT numbers under the "VIES" programme.[1] In addition to the VIES system, HMRC expects suppliers to undertake a check of the customer's stated VAT number(s) under their normal due diligence procedures.

Europa also provides the names and addresses for valid UK VAT registration numbers. Additionally, UK suppliers can identify themselves by entering their own UK VAT registration number which will enable them to print out a validation record of the date and time that the enquiry was made and confirmed. If it subsequently turns out that the customer's number was invalid, for example, the tax authorities' database was not up to date, the supplier will be able to rely on the validation record as one element to demonstrate their "good faith" as a compliant business and, in the UK, to justify why they shouldn't be held jointly and severally liable for any VAT fraud and revenue losses which might occur. HMRC also recommends that suppliers regularly check their customers' EU VAT registration number(s) to ensure that the details are still valid and the number(s) have not been deregistered. Finally, businesses can also contact the VAT Helpline on 0300

---

[1] ec.europa.eu/taxation_customs/taxation/vat/traders/vat_number/index_en.htm

200 3700 to validate VAT registration numbers and verify that the names and addresses are correct.

If a valid EU VAT registration number cannot be obtained and quoted on the supplier's sales invoice VAT must be charged and brought to account in the supplier's VAT return. Similarly, if the goods are not removed or the supplier has doubts that the goods will not be physically removed from the UK within the time limits, they should charge and account for VAT on the value of the supply; they may consider taking a deposit from the customer for the amount shown as VAT as security.

The supplier should carry out normal due diligence procedures such as bank and trade credit-worthiness references to check the status of the customer before commencing to trade with them. HMRC strongly recommend that the supplier obtains confirmation of their EU VAT registration number in writing and should retain this on file because one of the conditions for zero-rating the supply is that a valid EU VAT number is held for every customer.

The following table provides details of the formats of VAT numbers issued by other Member States:

Member State	Country Code	Number format	Number of characters
Austria (1)	AT	U12345678	9
Belgium (2)	BE	0123456789	10
Bulgaria	BG	012345678 or 0123456789	9 or 10
Croatia	HR	12345678901	11
Republic of Cyprus (3)	CY	12345678X	9
Czech Republic (4)	CZ	12345678; or 123456789; or 1234567890	8, 9 or 10
Denmark	DK	12345678	8
Estonia	EE	123456789	9
Finland	FI	12345678	8
France (5)	FR	12345678901; or X1234567890; or X123456789; or XX123456789	11
Germany (6)	DE	123456789	9
Greece	EL	012345678	9
Hungary	HU	12345678	8
Ireland (7)	IE	1234567X; or 1X23456X; or 1234567XX	8 Second character can also be '+' or '*' 9
Italy	IT	12345678901	11
Latvia	LV	12345678901	11

Lithuania	LT	123456789; or 123456789012	9 or 12
Luxembourg	LU	12345678	8
Malta	MT	12345678	8
Netherlands (8)	NL	123456789B01	12
Poland	PL	1234567890	10
Portugal	PT	123456789	9
Romania	RO	01234567890	2 to 10 digits
Slovakia (Slovak Rep)	SK	1234567890	10
Slovenia	SI	12345678	8
Spain (9)	ES	X12345678; or 12345678X; or X1234567X	9
Sweden	SE	123456789001	12
United Kingdom	UK	123 4567 89	9

Notes:
1. First character is always U.
2. Nine digits prior to 1 April 2005. Prefix any 9 digit numbers with "0".
3. Last character must be a letter.
4. Where 11, 12 or 13 numbers are quoted – delete the first 3 as these are a tax code.
5. May include alpha character(s), either first, second or first & second. All alpha characters except I and O are valid. Must be the 11 alpha numeric TVA number, not the 14 digit SERIT number.
6. Must be the nine character Umsatzsteuer Identifikationsnummer (ust - Id Nr) not the 10 character Umsatzsteuer nummer.
7. Includes one or two alpha characters – either last, or second & last.
8. The tenth digit is always B. Three digit suffix will always be in the range B01 to B99
9. Includes one or two alpha characters – first or last, or first & last.

9.3.1 Goods removed after process or incorporation

If, before removal to the customer in another Member State, the goods are delivered to a third person who is, for example, processing or incorporating the goods for the customer, their supply can be zero-rated provided:
- the supplier obtains and shows on their VAT sales invoice the customer's EU VAT registration number, including the two-letter country prefix code; **and**
- the goods are only being delivered and not supplied to the third person in the UK; **and**
- no use is made of the goods other than for processing or incorporation into other goods for removal; **and**
- valid commercial evidence is retained to prove that the goods have physically been removed from the UK within the stipulated time limits (see section **9.3.3**).

The supplier's records must also show all of the following details:
- the name, address and VAT number of the customer in the EU;
- the invoice number and date;
- the description, quantity and value of the goods;
- the name and address of the third person in the UK to whom the goods were delivered;
- the date by which the goods must be removed;
- proof of removal obtained from the person responsible for transporting the goods out of the UK; and
- the date the goods were actually removed from the UK.

The accounting records must also be able to show that the goods supplied have been processed or incorporated into the goods removed from the UK. These rules also apply where the third person is not in the UK, but in another Member State.

9.3.2 Time limits for removing the goods
In all cases the time limits for removing the goods from the UK to another Member State and obtaining valid evidence of removal will begin from the "time of supply". These are three months, including supplies of goods involved in groupage or consolidation prior to removal, (see section **9.3.3.2**) or six months for supplies of goods involved in processing or incorporation prior to removal (see section **9.3.1** above). The time of supply is the earlier of when the supplier receives payment for the goods supplied or the date the goods are removed or are "made available" to the customer for collection and removal by them.

9.3.3 Evidence of removal
Unlike with an export of goods to a third country/territory, there are usually no "official" Customs documents for a removal of goods to another Member State. There are exceptions to this, for example, in respect of goods imported for onward removal to another Member State where the original documents may be produced as evidence of their removal (see section **5.16**).

Normal commercial evidence acceptable to HMRC includes:
- the customer's order (including their name, VAT number and delivery address for the goods);
- inter-company correspondence;
- a copy sales invoice (including a description of the goods, an invoice number and the customer's EU VAT number etc.);
- an advice note;
- the packing list;
- commercial transport document(s) from the carrier responsible for removing the goods from the UK, for example an International Consignment Note (CMR) fully completed by the consignor, the haulier and signed by the receiving consignee;

- details of insurance or freight charges;
- bank statements as evidence of payment;
- a receipted copy of the consignment note as evidence of receipt of the goods abroad; and
- any other documents relevant to the removal of the goods in question which would normally be obtained in the course of the intra-EU business.

Photocopy certificates of shipment or other transport documents are not normally acceptable as evidence of removal unless authenticated with an original stamp and dated by an authorised official of the issuing office. However, whatever documents are used as proof of removal must clearly identify the supplier, the consignor (if different from the supplier), the customer, the goods, an accurate value, the mode of transport and route of movement of the goods, and the EU destination. HMRC insist (see Notice 725: *Single Market* para 5.2) that if the evidence is found to be unsatisfactory the supplier could become liable for the VAT due so vague descriptions of goods, quantities or values are not acceptable. In para 5.2 HMRC provides the following example of a vague description versus an accurate description:

> Vague descriptions of goods, quantities or values are not acceptable. For instance, 'various electrical goods' must not be used when the correct description is '2000 mobile phones (Make ABC and Model Number XYZ2000)'. An accurate value, for example, £50,000 must be shown and not excluded or replaced by a lower or higher amount.

In Notice 725 HMRC place particular attention on goods crossing the Northern Ireland – Republic of Ireland land boundary as it would be fairly easy to move goods given the remote countryside and that there are limited 'land boundary' frontier controls. Depending on the circumstances of the removal, HMRC recommend that the supplier obtains the types of evidence set out in Table D in section **9.22** to meet the conditions for zero-rating.

In respect of motor vehicles that the customer collects in Northern Ireland and removes to Ireland, it may be difficult to obtain satisfactory evidence of their removal from the UK. In these circumstances, HMRC state that a copy of the vehicle registration document issued by the authorities in the Republic of Ireland is obtained as this will normally provide satisfactory evidence of removal if supported by the other evidence described in this section.

In such circumstances the supplier might actually deliver the goods to the customer. HMRC recommend that the supplier retains proof of the travel arrangements such as tickets to demonstrate that an intra-EU journey took place. Table C at section **9.22** provides further details.

9.3.3.1 *"Indirect" removals*

An indirect removal is one where the customer or someone on their behalf arranges for the physical removal of the goods instead of the supplier. If the EU customer is arranging removal of the goods it can be difficult for the supplier to obtain adequate proof of removal as the carrier is contracted to the customer, so the supplier should consider taking a deposit equivalent to the amount of VAT that would have to accounted for if the customer did not provide satisfactory evidence of the removal.

An indirect removal demands enhanced checks and evidence; copies of transport documents alone will not be sufficient and the information must identify the date and the route of the movement of goods and the mode of transport involved. It should include all or most of the following items:
- a written order from the customer which shows their name, address and EU VAT number and the address where the goods are to be delivered;
- a copy sales invoice showing the customer's name, EU VAT number, a description of the goods and an invoice number;
- the date of the departure of the goods from the UK premises and from the UK place of exit;
- the name and address of the haulier collecting the goods;
- the registration number of the vehicle collecting the goods and the name and signature of the driver and, where the goods are to be taken out of the UK by a different haulier or vehicle, the name and address of that haulier, that vehicle registration number and a signature for the goods;
- the route taken, for example, the Channel Tunnel or the port of exit;
- copies of the travel tickets;
- the name of the ferry or shipping company and the date of sailing or the airway number and airport;
- the trailer number (if applicable);
- the full container number (if applicable); and the name and address for consolidation, groupage, or processing (if applicable).

The proof of removal must be retained for six years and made readily available so that any VAT assurance officer is able to substantiate the zero-rating of all removals.

9.3.3.2 Groupage and consolidation

The freight forwarder must keep copies of the original bill of lading, sea-waybill or air-waybill, and all consignments in the load must be shown on the container or vehicle manifest. The supplier will be issued with a Certificate of Shipment by the freight forwarder, often supported by an authenticated photocopy of the original bill of lading, a sea-waybill or a house air-waybill. Where such consignments are being removed, the forwarder may be shown as the consignor in the shipping documents.

Certificate of Shipment

Where goods are removed as part of a groupage arrangement or are consolidated with other businesses' goods, "Certificates of Shipment" are usually produced by packers and consolidators involved in road, rail and sea groupage consignments; these agents usually only receive a single

authenticated transport document from the carrier. Although the Certificate of Shipment can be in any format, it must be an original and will usually contain the following information:
- the name and address of the issuing company;
- a unique reference number or issuer's file reference;
- the name of the supplier of the goods (and VAT number if known);
- the place, port or airport of loading;
- the place, port or airport of shipment;
- the name of the ship or the aircraft flight prefix and number;
- the date of sailing or flight;
- the customer's name;
- the destination of the goods;
- a full description of the goods removed to another Member State (including quantity, weight and value);
- the number of packages;
- the supplier's invoice number and date if known;
- the bill of lading or air-waybill number (if applicable); and
- the identifying number of the vehicle, container or railway wagon.

9.3.3.3 Removals by post

Goods posted to the customer in another Member State may be zero-rated if the supplier holds the necessary evidence of posting. The forms listed below, together with the Parcelforce Worldwide statement of account or parcel manifest listing each parcel or multi-parcel, are acceptable evidence of removal:
- for letter post or airmail: a fully completed certificate of posting presented with the goods, and stamped by the Post Office; and
- for parcels: a Parcelforce specific barcoded label, a copy of the Parcelforce Worldwide conditions of carriage, and a printed receipt.

An individual barcode label must be affixed to every parcel. If the parcel is to be collected from the business' premises the collecting driver will sign the printed receipt. If the parcel is taken to a Post Office, the counter clerk will provide a printed proof of shipment from the Post Office "SmartPost" system. This will show the overseas delivery address, date of dispatch and unique consignment number and should be retained as proof of shipment. Suppliers that are account customers of Parcelforce Worldwide are also able to use the "Worldwide Dispatch Manager" (online users can print a manifest which lists all dispatched parcels) or a "Statement of Account".

9.3.3.4 Fast courier services and parcels

Most courier and fast parcel operators do not issue separate Certificates of Shipment. Instead they use the invoice for moving the goods from the UK, which bears details of the unique air-waybill numbers for each shipment. Additionally, many express companies offer a 'track and trace' service via their websites where the movement of goods can be traced through to the final destination. This information can be printed and also be used to confirm removal from the UK.

Some companies still use the "Despatch Pack", which contains accounting data, a Customs export declaration and receipt copies of the relevant airwaybill or consignment note and which are issued to customers to complete for each removal from the UK. Unlike with exports an export declaration does not need to be completed for goods being sent to another EU Member State, but a Despatch Pack must be completed for each overseas address and consignee. The driver collecting the parcels will endorse the receipt copy and return it to the consignor. This, plus the statement of account listing each removal, provides evidence of removal from the UK.

Due to the complexities of the movement of goods within the courier/fast parcel environment, often more than one company is involved in the handling and ultimate removal of the goods. The supplier may not be certain as to which courier/fast parcel company has removed the goods and if there is any doubt about this the supplier needs to establish what proof of removal they will receive from the company to whom they give the goods.

For an indirect removal, i.e. where the EU customer arranges for the goods to be removed by courier, the supplier needs to ascertain what proof of removal the customer will provide to them to enable zero-rating. The supplier should consider taking a deposit equivalent to the amount of VAT that would have to be accounted for if the satisfactory evidence of the removal were not produced, repaying this on production of certified commercial documents.

9.3.4 Goods not removed

Irrespective of who removes the goods, either the supplier or a customer, the goods can only be zero-rated when all the conditions are satisfied. If the goods have either not been removed or satisfactory evidence of their removal is not obtained (and kept) within three months (or six months for goods involved in processing or incorporation before removal) and the goods would be subject to VAT in the UK, VAT is to be accounted for on the invoiced amount or consideration received. For a VAT rate of 20% the VAT element is 1/6 (7/47 when VAT was 17.5% (before 4 January 2011)).

If the goods are subsequently removed from the UK and/or the supplier later obtains evidence showing that the goods were removed, the supply may be zero-rated and the VAT adjusted in the accounting period in which the evidence is obtained. However, this is not permitted where the goods have been used in the UK before their removal, unless this was specifically authorised by HMRC.

9.3.5 Invoicing

The supplier must normally issue a VAT invoice within 30 days of making the supply where the following applies:

- standard-rated goods or services have been supplied to a registered person in the UK;
- goods or services, other than exempt supplies, have been supplied to a person in another Member State;
- goods or services have been supplied to a non-taxable person such as a public body, a charity or an unregistered business in another Member State;
- distance sales of goods, for example mail order contact lenses, have been supplied to unregistered persons in other Member States; and
- a new means of transport, including motor vehicles, boats or planes, has been supplied to persons in other Member States.

A VAT invoice should also be issued by the supplier within 30 days of having received a payment on account from a customer in another Member State.

For a supply made to a person in another Member State, in addition to the 'normal' data fields, the invoice must show all of the following details:
- the letters 'GB' (the 'country identifier' for the UK) as a prefix to the VAT registration number; and
- the VAT registration number, if any, of the customer in the other Member State, including the country identifier as a prefix; and
- in the case of a new means of transport, a description which identifies it as such; and
- a reference to indicate that the supply is a zero-rated intra-EU supply of goods.

Details about VAT invoicing can be found in Notice 700: *The VAT Guide*.[2]

9.4 "B2C" supplies and "Distance Selling"

Distance selling is the term applied to a sale by a supplier in Member State "A" to a customer in Member State "B" that is not registered or liable to be registered for VAT and the supplier delivers the goods to the customer. Colloquially these movements are called "B2C" and the customers are known as "non-taxable persons". Such persons will include private individuals, public bodies, charities and businesses which are not VAT-registered because their turnover is below the registration threshold or whose activities are entirely exempt. The most common examples of distance sales are goods supplied by mail order or goods ordered over the internet.

The basic position is that the supplier charges and accounts for VAT at the rate applicable to the goods in their own Member State until such time as the annual value of sales to all customers in each Member State exceeds the *de minimis* threshold for the relevant Member State, at which point the supplier is

---

[2] www.gov.uk/government/publications/vat-notice-700-the-vat-guide/vat-notice-700-the-vat-guide#vat-invoices-general-rules

required to become VAT-registered in that Member State. Member States can apply one of two permitted thresholds, based on calendar years.

Alternatively, the supplier may choose to register before reaching the threshold(s) in the Member State (s) where the customer receives the goods to take advantage of lower VAT rates and therefore reduce the VAT due on the Distance Sales. Suppliers should conduct a cost/benefit analysis of the VAT saved against the costs of registration and fiscal representation, which most Member States require for securing the VAT. However, suppliers of excise goods, for example, alcoholic drinks, perfumes etc. to customers in other Member States under distance selling arrangements, are required to register and account for VAT in that Member State, irrespective of the value involved.

Once the supplier has taken up the option to account for VAT in another Member State, they no longer charge UK VAT on these sales. They are normally required to remain registered in that Member State for at least two calendar years from the date of the first supply following registration there. Following this period, if the annual value of these supplies remains below the registration threshold they can choose to cancel their option to register there and must notify HMRC of their decision. They will then revert to charging UK VAT on these sales. This option may become preferable where the Member State concerned increases, or the UK decreases, the rate of VAT due on the relevant goods.

In the UK, as in a number of other EU Member States, the facility exists for closely controlled groups of companies to be VAT-registered in a "VAT Group" and account for VAT as a single VAT registration. Although each VAT group member is, and remains, a legal entity in its own right, it is treated as a single taxable person in the UK. Group members must therefore individually monitor the value of their own distance sales to each Member State. Where the value of sales in a calendar year exceeds a Member State's distance selling threshold, that group member will be liable to register for VAT there in its own right. Group members also still have the ability to register in other Member States whilst their annual value of distance sales remains below the Member State's threshold.

The Distance Selling thresholds are detailed in the Commission's website.[3]

Where the supplier is trading above the UK Intrastat threshold they must report their distance sales to all non-taxable persons on the Intrastat Supplementary Declaration, even when the distance sales from the UK are below the distance selling threshold in the Member State of Arrival – see **9.21.3**.

---

[3] ec.europa.eu/taxation_customs/resources/documents/taxation/vat/traders/vat_community/vat_in_ec_annexi.pdf

INTRA-EU TRANSACTIONS

9.4.1 Goods removed to the UK under distance selling

Businesses in other Member States that make distance sales to the UK above the UK threshold are liable to be registered for VAT in the UK. They must then charge and account for UK VAT on their distance sales. However, any supplies involving goods subject to excise duty are not subject to the threshold and the supplier must register for VAT as soon as they make a supply of these goods. Suppliers in other Member States can also register early in the UK for their distance sales as explained in section **9.4** above. Details of how to register for UK VAT are provided by HMRC in Notice 700/1: *Should I be registered for VAT?*[4]

9.5 "New Means of Transport"

In the EU most goods are charged with VAT in the country in which they are purchased. However, for a new motor vehicle ("Motorised Land Vehicle"), boat or aircraft, VAT will be due in the Member State of destination where it falls within the definition of 'New Means of Transport' (NMT) and it is sold to a customer who intends to take it to another Member State within two months of purchase. A motorised land vehicle is defined below.

A 'means of transport' is any of the following when intended for the transport of passengers or goods:
- a ship or boat more than 7.5 metres long (about 24.6 feet);
- an aircraft with a take-off weight of more than 1550 kilograms (about 3,417 lb); or
- a motorised land vehicle, which:
  - has an engine with a displacement or cylinder capacity of more than 48 cubic centimetres; or
  - is constructed or adapted to be electrically propelled using more than 7.2 kilowatts (about 9.65 horsepower).

There are additional criteria that must be met before a NMT qualifies to be zero-rated as "new", which in turn rely on the phrase "first entered into service". Either of the conditions can be met for the particular NMT to qualify.

Boats and aircraft
- it must be less than three months before the boat or aircraft was first entered into service; or
- boats must have travelled for less than one hundred hours and aircraft must have travelled for less than forty hours before being first entered into service.

"Motorised land vehicles"
- it must be less than six months before it was first entered into service; or

---

[4] www.gov.uk/government/publications/vat-notice-7001-should-i-be-registered-for-vat/

- it must have travelled under its own power for less than six thousand kilometres before being first entered into service.

"First entered into service"
For boats or aircraft "first entered into service" means the **earlier** of:
- the date it was delivered from its manufacturer to its first purchaser or owner; or
- the date it was first made available to its first purchaser or owner; or
- the date it was first taken into use for demonstration purposes, by the manufacturer.

For motorised land vehicles "first entered into service" means the **earlier** of:
- the date it was first registered for road use in the Member State of manufacture, or
- the date when it was first liable to be registered for road use there.

For motorised land vehicles which are removed from the Member State of supply *without being registered for the road*, it is the earlier of:
- the date it was made available to the first purchaser; or
- the date it was taken into use for demonstration purposes by its manufacturer or sole concessionaire.

9.5.1 Removing an NMT from the UK – private persons

The removal of an NMT from the UK will only be zero-rated where the following conditions are met:
- the means of transport must be 'new';
- the owner or their authorised chauffeur, pilot or skipper must personally take delivery of the new means of transport in the UK;
- it must be removed from the UK to the Member State of destination within two months of the date of supply; and
- a declaration on a Form VAT 411 must be made, the owner stating their intention to remove the NMT from the UK and pay any VAT due in the Member State of arrival.

If the NMT is being purchased under a finance agreement, it is the finance company that is buying the NMT from the supplier (car dealer etc.) and the finance company sells the NMT to the "owner". In this case the finance house is to be shown as the supplier of the NMT and the dealer must send the second copy of Form VAT 411 to the finance house for their retention.

The NMT cannot be used on UK roads unless it has been licensed and registered, and is properly insured. If the purchaser fails or is unable to remove an NMT from the UK within the two-month period allowed, they are required to notify HMRC and pay the VAT due. A failure to do so may render the NMT liable to forfeiture, which may be "restored" to the owner on payment of a penalty, in addition to payment of the VAT.

INTRA-EU TRANSACTIONS

When a motorised land vehicle is finally removed from the UK, the Driver and Vehicle Licensing Agency (DVLA) require the tear-off portion of the Form VX302 to be completed and collected by HMRC at the point of departure to be returned to the DVLA. In the case of a temporary removal to another Member State, say for a holiday, the Form VX302 is not to be completed as this will cause problems on its return to the UK, as the licence is cancelled.

9.5.1.1   Selling an NMT before removal – refunds of VAT

"Non-taxable" persons such as unregistered businesses and private persons may purchase an NMT for resale. Such persons may be entitled to a refund of the VAT paid to the supplier of the NMT where they are selling the NMT to another person who intends to remove the NMT to another Member State within two months of the date of supply and they can demonstrate that they have paid VAT on the NMT by producing an invoice etc.

To claim a refund the re-seller should write to HMRC's Personal Transport Unit ("PTU") at least 14 days (but no more than one month) before they expect to sell the NMT. HMRC will advise the re-seller if they wish to examine the NMT before it is sold, to confirm its eligibility for refund. See **Appendix B** for the PTU address.

9.5.2   Removing an NMT from the UK – UK VAT-registered supplier

The rules concerning the removal of an NMT from the UK to another Member State vary according to whether the customer is VAT-registered in the Member State of Arrival or is a private or unregistered customer.

9.5.2.1   Customer VAT-registered

All of the following conditions must be met to zero-rate the supply:
- the customer's VAT registration number (with the two-digit country code prefix) must be shown on the VAT invoice, **and**
- the NMT must be dispatched or transported to another Member State within two months of the date of issue of the VAT the invoice for the supply, **and**
- the supplier must hold valid commercial documentary evidence, which confirms that the NMT has been removed from the UK.

An ESL should be completed when the value of supplies made in the calendar quarter are exceeded.

Where the purchaser buying the NMT in the UK for removal to another Member State is registered for VAT in another EU Member State (it can be a third Member State), the UK supplier may zero-rate the supply under the normal intra-EU dispatch rules. To benefit from zero-rating the NMT must be removed from the UK within two months of the time of supply. The purchaser must account for any tax due on the Acquisition in the Member State of destination, under the laws of that State.

9.5.2.2 *Customer not VAT registered*

The removal of an NMT to a person who is not registered for VAT in the Member State of Arrival can still be zero-rated, the difference being that their unregistered status provides them with no possibility of reclaiming the Acquisition VAT that is due in their Member State (in some Member States Acquisition VAT on NMTs can be reclaimed where the NMT is being used for the purposes of the customer's business).

The supplier must meet all the conditions in order to zero-rate the removal to the customer who becomes liable for any VAT in their Member State. Again, the means of transport must qualify as 'new', must be removed from the UK to another Member State within two months of the date of supply, and both the supplier and the customer must make a joint declaration about the transaction on a Form VAT 411 which must be submitted to HMRC within 42 days of the end of the calendar quarter to which it relates; if not completed properly, UK VAT will be due on the supply.

9.6 Acquiring NMTs in the UK – unregistered persons

Often, due to the highly competitive trade in motor vehicles across the EU, UK residents will purchase new motor vehicles from suppliers based in other Member States. A private individual (or a business or legal entity which is not registrable for VAT in the UK) who purchases an NMT in another Member State to bring to the UK, must notify HMRC within 14 days of its arrival in the UK or its acquisition, whichever is the later. HMRC can issue a financial penalty for a failure to notify them within this period. Form VAT 415 should be used and sent to the PTU at Dover (see section **9.5.1.1** above for their address).

VAT is due at the time of acquisition which is the earlier of the 15th day of the month following the one in which the NMT was made available to, or taken away by, the customer (sometimes referred to as the date of removal), or the date of issue of the tax invoice. The VAT is calculated on the total amount paid for the NMT (excluding all trade-ins, part-exchanges or special discounts not freely available to the general public), including any extras fitted to it at the time it was supplied, plus any delivery or incidental charges made by the supplier.

For VAT purposes, amounts of money must always be expressed in sterling so if the invoice is in another currency, the PTU will convert it into sterling using the rate of exchange current at the time of Acquisition. The person acquiring the NMT in the UK must pay the Acquisition VAT on HMRC's demand within 30 days of the date on which it was issued. All movements of NMTs to the UK are liable to VAT, except where the NMT is a vehicle constructed or adapted for a disabled person.

9.6.1 NMTs relieved from Acquisition VAT

Certain persons are able to obtain an NMT in the UK from another Member State free of Acquisition VAT, these being diplomats, members of an officially recognised international organisation, or members of NATO or the civilian staff accompanying them, each of whom are returning from service in another Member State.

Members of the NATO forces or NATO civilian staff can claim relief from VAT at the end of their tour on permanent posting back to the UK. They must be in possession of Form BFG 414 if returning from Germany or Form BFC 414 from Cyprus, in order to register their vehicle in the UK.

These forms are available from (respectively):

Customs and Immigration
British Forces Liaison
Germany
BFPO40

or

SBA Customs
RAF Akrotiri
BFPO57

Members returning from any other Member State must provide HMRC with evidence to show that the host authority relieved the tax on the purchase of the NMT.

Diplomats can claim relief if they produce both evidence of their tax-free status from their head of mission and confirmation that the host Member State granted relief on the NMT.

If owners of a Means of Transport (which is not "new") make temporary visits to the UK bringing their vehicle with them, VAT is only due where relevant *de minimis* criteria are exceeded. To be exempt from Acquisition VAT, the owner must be "normally resident" in another Member State which means that they have spent at least 185 days in the last twelve months there because of their work and personal connections. If, however, they have no work connections or their work and personal connections are in different countries, then they will usually be considered to be resident in the country where their personal connections are.

If they change their plans and decide to stay in the UK keeping their NMT here, they do not need to notify HMRC of its removal unless either:
- it was supplied to them tax-free because of their special status in the Member State in which they were been living or working; and
- the supply took place within the six months prior to their arrival in the UK if it is a vehicle or three months if it is a boat or aircraft; and

- it was supplied to them tax-free for removal from the Member State of supply, and no EU taxes have been paid on it; and
- when it was brought into the UK it was not required to be registered for road use in the UK (because the traveller was intending to remain in the UK for less than six months in a 12 month period), but the traveller now intends to remain in the UK and will register and license the vehicle with the DVLA.

Where an EU person brings a means of transport to the UK that is not new on a permanent basis, UK VAT is not due where the person did not purchase it with the intention of acquiring it into the UK, it is no longer a 'New Means of Transport', and VAT has been paid on its purchase in the Member State of supply. However, regardless of whether it is new or otherwise HMRC must be advised of its Arrival through the Notification of Vehicle Arrivals (NOVA) system. The EU person will be unable to license and register the vehicle with the DVLA until HMRC have received notification of its arrival and confirmed that no VAT is due.

9.6.2 Acquiring NMTs in the UK – VAT-registered persons

Section **9.7** below explains the rules concerning the Acquisition of goods in a Member State by a VAT-registered purchaser. To enable the supplier to zero-rate the NMT in their Member State the purchaser needs to provide them with their UK VAT registration number. The purchaser should account for the Acquisition VAT due on the NMT on the VAT return covering its Arrival in the UK. If the NMT is a vehicle, it must be licensed and registered before it is used on public roads. The DVLA Local Office will ask the purchaser to complete a Form VAT 414 declaring the VAT-free status of the vehicle and the VAT registration number used to make the acquisition into the UK.

If the purchaser, for example a car dealer, is to on-supply the NMT in the UK they must still account for Acquisition tax on the vehicle. If it forms part of the dealer's "stock in trade", the dealer may recover input tax equal to the amount of Acquisition tax declared and must also charge output tax on the full value of the supply to their customer.

An intermediary who arranges the supply of an NMT for an unregistered person from a supplier in another Member State direct to that person, may, with that person's authorisation, notify the Acquisition of the NMT to the PTU. The customer, or acquirer if he is the principal, is responsible for the declaration made on their behalf and for the payment of the VAT, which is due. The intermediary may, however, make the payment on their behalf.

When trading as an intermediary the business must ensure that the customer is provided with the sales invoice from the supplier and the invoice clearly shows the name and address of the acquirer of the NMT and the amount they have paid to the supplier. The intermediary should also distinguish clearly between transactions in which they act as an intermediary, and the transactions in which they acquire and supply an NMT to the order of a person in the UK, in which case they are the Acquirer and must account for Acquisition tax.

Details of how to notify arrivals of NMTs in the UK are set out in VAT Information Sheet 06/13.[5]

9.7 Arrivals and Acquisitions

An Acquisition in the UK occurs where there is an intra-EU movement of goods to the UK, the goods are received here by a VAT-registered trader and the supplier is registered for VAT in the Member State of departure (Dispatch). Where these conditions are fulfilled, the recipient is required to account for VAT on the goods acquired in the UK, called "Acquisition VAT". Acquisition VAT must be accounted for on the VAT return covering the period in which the tax point occurs and the Acquirer may treat this as input tax on the same VAT return, subject to the normal rules, for example, production of a purchase invoice and evidence that the goods were physically delivered to them.

As with the Dispatch of goods by a UK business to a customer in another Member State (see section **9.3** above) to be able to zero-rate the supply the supplier must have the customer's valid UK (or other Member State) VAT registration numbers. It is essential, therefore, that UK businesses keep their Member State suppliers notified of all changes to their UK (and other Member State) VAT registration numbers so that the VIES validation can take place (see section **9.3** above). All members of UK VAT groups have the same VAT number, issued to the "Representative Member" so should be particularly careful to ensure that the Representative maintains up to date VAT registration details.

The "tax point" or time of acquisition is the earlier of the 15th day of the month following the one in which the goods were removed or the date the supplier issued their invoice. Acquisitions are liable to VAT at the same rate as domestic supplies of identical goods supplied in the UK so, for example, no Acquisition tax is due on the Acquisitions of goods which are currently zero-rated in the UK for example children's clothes and most foods (of a kind for human consumption). Whether any payment has been made for the goods removed is immaterial.

The VAT on an Acquisition is always due in the Member State where the goods are received. However, there is a "fallback" provision that applies where the VAT registration number quoted to the supplier to secure zero-rating has been issued in a different Member State to that of the Arrival. In that event, the Acquisition tax must be accounted for in the Member State of

---

[5] www.gov.uk/government/publications/vat-information-sheet-0613-notification-of-vehicle-arrivals/

registration, but the customer also remains liable to account for Acquisition VAT in the Member State of Arrival, which can create issues where both Member States claim that the Acquisition VAT ought to be declared in their country. For example, HMRC will assert that the Acquirer is liable to account for Acquisition tax in the UK unless it can be demonstrated that Acquisition VAT has already been accounted for in the Member State to which the goods were dispatched.

In real terms, this can create considerable issues for the purchaser because some Member States apply dispensations that either relieve the original supplier, the intermediate supplier or the end customer from accounting for Acquisition Tax or even paying VAT on certain transactions.

For example, there is presently a degree of uncertainty for businesses trading in alcoholic goods situated within excise warehouses in France. In a large number of Member States buying or selling alcoholic products within "tax warehouses" does not necessarily lead to a tax liability because both excise duty and VAT are suspended. In the UK, for instance, VAT Act 1994 s.18 allows excise goods to be placed in a tax warehouse free of excise duty and VAT.

Example: French rules (as at March 2016)
A supplier in Germany sends its own stock of duty-free excise goods 'cross-border' to a French warehouse. A UK intermediate supplier buys the stock within the warehouse and sells it whilst still warehoused to its own customers that are registered for VAT in France.

Under the principal rule, Acquisition VAT due in France is to be accounted for by the German supplier as the goods constitute the transfer of "Own goods" to France – see **9.9**. However, under a derogation from the principal rule, the German supplier is excused VAT registration in France where:
(a) it sells the goods within three months of them having arrived in the warehouse; and
(b) the UK supplier is registered for French VAT; and
(c) the UK supplier has a technical Acquisition tax liability in France.

However, the French VAT code exempts from Acquisition VAT the Arrival of the goods in France where the UK supplier supplies the goods to customers that are registered for VAT in France. In this case those customers account for the VAT that would be due by the UK supplier under the French domestic reverse charge (which is compulsory). So, where the derogation applies, although there is a technical Acquisition in France by the UK supplier, because it is exempted there is no loss of VAT to the French Tax Authority.

However, as a result of the differing treatment of own goods between France, and in this case Germany and the UK, there can be considerable confusion between all parties as to which of them should account for Acquisition VAT in France. Under the UK rules and the principal VAT Directive the UK supplier understands that the German supplier should register for VAT in France and account for the Acquisition

INTRA-EU TRANSACTIONS

VAT on the Arrival of its own goods in France. But the German supplier, with knowledge of the French derogation, is exempted from French VAT registration so it has no liability to account for Acquisition VAT in France. The result is that neither has registered for VAT in France and no Acquisition VAT has been accounted for.

However, the German supplier may have already quoted the UK supplier's UK VAT number on its German EC Sales List (because it is not required to register for French VAT), recording this as an intra-EU movement because it has a customer 'quoting' a foreign (UK) VAT number. Conversely, in the UK supplier's view, there has not been an intra-EU Dispatch and Arrival (because the goods have been purchased by it in the warehouse i.e. under its control they do not physically leave Germany to arrive in France), therefore it has no requirement to account for French (or UK) Acquisition VAT.

In this situation, the UK supplier has seemingly failed to account for Acquisition VAT anywhere and HMRC have been known to challenge this failure calling for UK Acquisition VAT to be accounted by the UK supplier under the fallback arrangements.

The sting in the tail however is that the Court of Justice of the European Union (CJEU) has ruled in a case called *Facet Holding BV (C-539/08)* that in such circumstances the Acquisition VAT demanded by HMRC cannot be reclaimed as input tax in the UK leaving the UK supplier severely exposed.

In the situation where the tax authority in the country of Arrival demands payment of Acquisition VAT there and UK Acquisition VAT has also been brought to account, UK businesses acquiring goods in such circumstances can obtain a refund from HMRC, but only where they have not claimed, or have been unable to claim, full input tax credit for that acquisition, i.e. they are partially exempt etc.

As can be seen in the above example, whilst the implementation of the Principal VAT Directive should apply uniformly across the EU Member States, where Member States have negotiated derogations for specific transactions, the businesses engaged in intra-EU trading can experience considerable issues and at worse considerable exposure to tax, interest and penalties.

9.7.1 Value of the Acquisition

The amount of tax due on an Acquisition is the tax value multiplied by the appropriate VAT rate. The "tax value" is, usually, what is paid or payable for the goods, also called the "consideration". The consideration is what the customer must pay to the supplier to obtain the goods, including all additional costs such as transport costs and deferred instalments if buying the goods, for example, on hire purchase terms etc. The value of the Acquisition for goods subject to excise duty or, in the case of EU accessionary states, import duty or agricultural levy, must include the duty and/or levies applicable to those goods.

The tax value of an Acquisition for various situations is as follows:

INTRA-EU TRANSACTIONS

- where the consideration is wholly in money, the amount paid or payable;
- where the consideration is non-monetary, for example, the supply is made in return for payment in goods or services, or is monetary and non-monetary, the monetary equivalent of the consideration calculated by reference to the price, excluding VAT, which would have to be paid if the consideration were monetary;
- where the consideration involves a discounted amount and the discounted amount is paid, the discounted amount;
- where the consideration includes the offer of a conditional discount which is dependent upon some future event, for example on condition that more goods are purchased from the supplier, or payment is made within a specified period of time, the full amount paid. Where the discount is subsequently earned, the tax value is reduced and the amount of tax accounted for can be adjusted (but this can only be done where the Acquirer has not claimed, or has been unable to claim, full input tax credit for that Acquisition);
- where there is no consideration, for example a transfer of an entity's own goods (see section **9.8**), or when goods are supplied without charge, in either case, what it would cost the Acquirer or the person transferring the goods to the Acquirer, to purchase the goods in question at the time of the Acquisition.

Where the value of the Acquisition is in a foreign currency, it should be converted to sterling using either the UK market selling rate at the time of the Acquisition or the "period rate of exchange" published by HMRC for customs purposes. Exceptionally, rates used for commercial purposes may be approved by HMRC, but only where they are based on the UK currency market and they can be objectively verified and can be adjusted to reflect market fluctuations. However, forward rates or methods deriving from forward rates are not acceptable.

9.8 Transfer of an entity's own goods to another Member State

One of the flaws of the Single Market is that all movements of goods intra-EU fall to be treated as "supplies". This covers, for example, the transfer within the same legal entity of goods removed from one Member State to another, say between branches of the same company, The supply may be zero-rated in the UK as per the conditions explained in section **9.3** above, but the entity will normally be liable to account for Acquisition VAT in the Member State of Arrival – but see the example given in section **9.7** where a Member State applies a derogation.

Therefore, the UK entity will probably need to be registered for VAT in the Member State of Arrival and to account for any VAT due in that Member State on a subsequent supply the goods there. The VAT number obtained in the Member State of Arrival will be used to support the zero-rating of the deemed supply in the UK. If the UK entity does not register for VAT in the Member State of Arrival it should treat the supply as a domestic supply in the UK and must account for UK VAT on the deemed transfer at the appropriate UK rate.

Where suppliers in other Member States are transferring their own goods to the UK, they are similarly required to determine if they are required to be VAT-registered in the UK to account for Acquisition VAT and to account for UK VAT on any onward supply of the goods.

However, where the supplier is selling products that are zero-rated in the UK such as foods these rules can create something of an absurd position because there is no UK Acquisition VAT for zero-rated goods.

Example – Dutch supplier of meat products sending goods to the UK for distribution (as at March 2016)
To be able to zero-rate in the Netherlands the transfer of the goods removed from the Netherlands to the UK, the Dutch supplier needs to have a UK VAT number and quote this on its Netherland's VAT invoices. Although the goods are zero-rated in the UK without the UK VAT number in the Netherlands it would have to account for VAT on the transfer.

In the UK, there is no Acquisition VAT because the products are zero-rated foods (see section **9.7**). Therefore, under UK legislation the Dutch supplier can be excepted from UK VAT registration where all of the supplies it makes in the UK are zero-rated.

Additionally, the supply of logistics and warehousing services supplied by the UK logistics company to the Dutch supplier are subject to the Reverse Charge in the Netherlands see **Chapter 12**) so there is little, if any, UK VAT incurred by the Dutch supplier, thereby ordinarily removing a need for it to be registered for VAT in the UK to reclaim UK VAT.

Consequently, the only reason that UK VAT registration is sought is to remove the deemed VAT charge on the transfer of the goods from the Netherlands to the UK.

9.9 Temporary movement of goods

Where goods are removed from one Member State to another in order to make a supply of services there or for temporary use there, the requirement to become VAT-registered in the Member State of Arrival and to account for Acquisition VAT can be dispensed with. However, if the intention to use the goods in this way changes, VAT registration in the Member State of Arrival might be required.

9.9.1 Supplies of services in the Member State of Arrival

Where the goods are being removed to another Member State to enable the supplier to fulfil a specific contract and the supplier both intends to return the goods to the Member State of Dispatch and they do not have a place of business in the Member State to which the goods are temporarily transferred, for example a branch or representative office, then the transfer can be ignored for these purposes. This can apply to tools and equipment to be used there, for example to repair or service machinery. It also applies to goods that are loaned or leased to somebody in another Member State.

9.9.2   Goods for temporary use in the Member State of Arrival

Goods that would be eligible for relief from Customs import duty within the Temporary Admission regime (see section **3.8** above) and which are to remain in the other Member State for no longer than two years, can be transferred without the need to register and account for Acquisition VAT in the Member State of Arrival as they are de-supplied for these purposes.

9.9.3   Changes in circumstances

For goods removed in the circumstances described in sections **9.9.1** and **9.9.2** where the conditions no longer pertain, for example, where the goods are disposed of locally rather than returned to the UK or they are to remain in the other Member State for more than two years, the original movement should be treated belatedly as a deemed supply and Acquisition.

9.9.4   Register of own movements

Although the transfer of an entity's own goods is not treated as supplies for VAT purposes, the entity making the transfer must still retain commercial evidence that the goods left the UK and have later returned. A register of temporary movements of goods must also be kept, recording all goods temporarily moved to and from the UK.

All of the following details must be recorded:
1. the date of removal for goods removed from the UK;
2. the date of arrival for goods removed from another Member State;
3. the date the goods are returned;
4. a description of the goods;
5. the reason for the movement, for example for processing or assembly; and
6. the consideration for the supply, if applicable.

9.10   Goods for installation or assembly in another Member State

Goods are often removed abroad by the contractor to be installed or assembled, e.g. plant and machinery for installation at the customer's factory. The supply is treated as taking place where the installation or assembly of the goods is carried out. Under the basic place of supply rules the contractor is liable to be registered for VAT in the Member State in which the installation or assembly takes place.

However, some Member States take up the Commission's option to operate a simplified procedure which permits the VAT-registered customer to account for the VAT due under the Reverse Charge (see **Chapter 12**) meaning that the supplier is not required to register in those circumstances. The movement of the goods involved between Member States as part of a supply of installed or assembled goods is not treated as a supply of own goods. Consequently, there is no Acquisition in the Member State of installation or assembly.

The UK operates the simplified procedure, so suppliers from other Member States who undertake supply and install contracts in the UK may be excepted from registering here. The supplier may only use the simplified procedure where the customer is registered for VAT in the UK, they are registered for VAT in another Member State, and they are not required to be registered in the UK for any other reason. The UK customer has no option other than to apply Acquisition VAT on the goods brought to the UK where the overseas supplier notifies them that they are using the simplified procedure.

Additionally, the overseas supplier must also issue the customer with a VAT invoice within 15 days of the date on which the supply would otherwise have taken place under normal UK time of supply rules for goods and inform HMRC of this decision by writing to them at the Non-Established Taxable Persons Unit (NETPU), whose address is:

HM Revenue & Customs
Ruby House
8 Ruby Place
Aberdeen AB10 1ZP

The notification must include their name, address and EU VAT registration number, the name, address and VAT registration number of their UK customer, and the date on which they began, or will begin, the installation or assembly of the goods. A separate notification must be made for each customer no later than the date of issue of the first invoice to the customer concerned. The notification to the UK customer to advise them that the supplier is using the simplified arrangements must be sent no later than the date the first invoice is issued to them.

9.11 Goods removed for process or repair

Provided the goods removed for process or repair are returned to the UK after the services have been completed there is no deemed supply of own goods. The business must record the movement of the goods in their Temporary Movements register (see section **9.9.4** above) and retain commercial evidence that the goods have been removed from the UK. The business must account for VAT on each of the supplies of services received as a "Reverse Charge" – see **Chapter 12** – and details of which are set out in HMRC Notice 741A: *Place of supply of services.*[6]

The Reverse Charge is a mechanism whereby recipients of services received from abroad (both other Member States and third countries/territories) account for VAT in the country of "import" as though they had been supplied within that country. It is a similar regime to the Single Market intra-EU

---

[6]www.gov.uk/government/publications/vat-notice-741a-place-of-supply-of-services/

transactions rules, but applies solely to services and has a VAT "anti-avoidance" motive to capture the input tax the customer cannot reclaim, but which must be accounted for as an output tax under the Reverse Charge. The Reverse Charge affects unregistered or partially exempt businesses such as banks, insurance companies etc. Where applicable the business must also complete an Arrival SSD (see HMRC's Notice 60: *Intrastat General Guide*).[7]

Where goods are sent to a supplier in the UK by a customer in another Member State there is no requirement for the supplier to account for VAT on the movement of the goods provided they are returned to the customer when the work has been completed. Similarly, provided the customer is registered for VAT elsewhere within the EU the supplier is not required to charge VAT on the supply of their services and the customer will account for this as a Reverse Charge.

In order for the Reverse Charge to apply and the removal to be disregarded, the goods must be returned to the Member State of Dispatch. If the goods are not returned, they become subject to the normal intra-EU supply and Acquisition rules and the owner of the goods may be liable to register for VAT in the Member State concerned.

9.11.1 Work performed on goods before being removed to another Member State

Sometimes, goods being purchased from another Member State are required to have work performed on them before they are removed to the customer's Member State. The work may be performed by more than one supplier and they may be located in different Member States. In such cases the customer must account for Acquisition VAT on the supply of the goods and account for VAT on each of the supplies of "imported" services received as a Reverse Charge. Where applicable the customer must also complete an Intrastat Arrival SSD.

Where a customer in another Member State purchases goods from a UK supplier but the goods require to be processed or assembled before being dispatched, the supplier of the unfinished goods can continue to treat the supply as a Dispatch from the UK (see section **9.3**) provided all of the relevant conditions are satisfied. The onus to obtain proof of removal from the UK still rests with the supplier of the unfinished goods and they need to ensure that the customer provides them with evidence of their removal once the processing etc. has been completed. Any failure to obtain proof of removal will render the supply being liable to UK VAT. The UK suppliers of processing or assembly work can treat their supplies of services as zero-rated where they obtain the customer's EU VAT number and can also prove that the goods left the UK.

---

[7] www.gov.uk/government/publications/notice-60-intrastat-general-guide/

9.12 "Triangulation" and "Chain Transactions"

Triangulation is the term used to describe a chain of intra-EU supplies of goods involving three parties. Instead of the goods physically passing from one to the other in sequence of order, they are delivered directly from the first to the last party in the chain. A diagrammatical example is shown below:

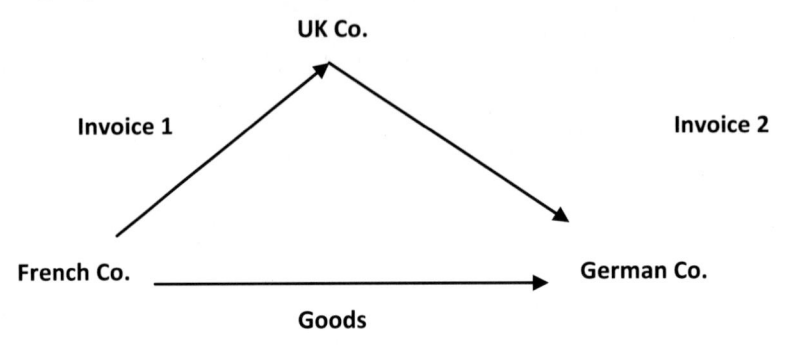

```
                    UK Co.
                   ▲      ╲
      Invoice 1   ╱        ╲   Invoice 2
                 ╱          ▼
    French Co. ──────────────→ German Co.
                    Goods
```

Here a UK company receives an order from a customer in Germany. To fulfil the order the UK supplier in turn orders goods from their own supplier in France. The goods are delivered from France to Germany. Any business might become involved in triangulation as either the first supplier of the goods (the French company in this example), the intermediate supplier (the UK company in this example), or the final customer (the German company in this example).

In the example, the supplies made are as follows:
- the French company can zero-rate the supply to the UK company subject to the conditions described in section **9.3** above; and
- the UK company is treated as acquiring and supplying those goods in Germany and is liable to register for VAT there unless the simplified procedure described in section **9.12.1** below is used.

Without any dispensations or modifications to the "normal" intra-EU position, the first supplier in any triangular transaction can zero-rate their supply of the goods subject to the removal conditions being met, but the intermediate supplier may be liable to register for VAT in the Member State to which the goods are delivered and account for VAT on the Acquisition and on their onward supply in that Member State, whilst the ultimate customer not need to do anything as they are receiving a domestic supply.

9.12.1 Simplified procedure

The simplified procedure removes the requirement for the intermediate supplier (the UK company in the above example) to be registered for Acquisition VAT in the Member State of the Arrival of the goods (Germany as above) and to account for VAT on the onward supply of the goods. The intermediate supplier can use the simplified procedure if they:
- are already registered for VAT within the EU;

- are not registered, or otherwise required to be registered, in the Member State to which the goods are delivered; and
- their customer is registered for VAT in the Member State of Arrival.

A UK intermediate supplier making supplies of goods to a customer in another Member State must perform all of the following accounting steps to enjoy the simplification procedure and avoid having to register in the Member State of Arrival of the goods:

- use their UK VAT registration number to allow the EU supplier to zero-rate the supply of goods in the Member State from which the goods were Dispatched;
- issue a VAT invoice to their customer containing all the details normally required for intra-EU supplies;
- include the supply on their UK EC Sales List quoting the VAT number of their customer in the Member State of destination of the goods;
- enter the total value of triangular supplies to each EU customer in that quarter on their EC Sales List on a single line separately from any other intra-EU supplies to that customer;
- identify their triangular transactions by inserting the figure "2" in the indicator box (the notes on the reverse of the EC Sales List give further details); and
- omit details of triangular transactions on their UK VAT return and Dispatch SSD.

Similarly, an intermediate supplier in another Member State making supplies to a customer in the UK can avoid having to register for VAT in the UK by using the simplified procedure. To do so they must do all of the following:

- issue a VAT invoice to the UK customer containing all the details required by the Member State in which they are VAT-registered;
- issue that invoice within 15 days of the date on which the supply would otherwise have taken place under normal UK tax point rules for supplies of goods;
- write to the Non-Established Taxable Persons Unit at HMRC (see section **9.10** above) including the following information:
    - their name, address and EU VAT registration number used, or to be used, to obtain zero-rating of the initial supply of the goods;
    - the name, address and VAT registration number of their UK customer (a separate notification must be made for each customer no later than the date of issue of the first invoice to the customer concerned); and
    - the date the goods were first delivered, or are intended to be delivered, to the UK customer under this arrangement.
- send a copy of the notification to their UK customer no later than the date the first invoice is issued to their customer to advise them that they are using the simplified arrangements and so the UK customer is required to account for the Acquisition VAT.

On receipt of the copy of the supplier's notification to HMRC, the UK customer must account for Acquisition VAT on the goods supplied to them under the simplified procedure and submit Arrival SSDs for the goods supplied.

If the intermediate supplier is not established in the EU or is not registered for VAT anywhere in the EU, then the VAT treatment changes such that the first supplier will be making a domestic supply because they don't have an EU VAT number to quote on their sales invoice. However, in acquiring/supplying the goods involved, the intermediate supplier may be required to register in either the Member State of Dispatch or Arrival.

Where the movement of the goods is to a third country/territory, triangulation is not an issue. The supplier may, regardless of the location of the other parties, treat the supply as an export, subject to the rules set out in **Chapter 8**.

9.12.2 Non-EU goods

The triangulation simplification arrangements do not apply where the movement of goods is from a place outside the EU. Therefore, it may be necessary for the first supplier or the intermediary supplier to register for VAT in the Member State where the supply takes place, depending on who imports the goods.

9.12.3 "Chain transactions"

Where there are more than three countries or more than three businesses involved in the transactions, they are generally referred to as "chain transactions". Each chain will have its unique supply matrices into which the VAT reporting must fit. Wherever possible, the simplification procedure is to be pursued and registration for the intermediate traders avoided. Often, the VAT reporting will follow the "Incoterms" and which business is responsible for arranging the freight logistics. Businesses should seek expert assistance where such transactions take place. An explanation of Incoterms is provided in **Appendix A**.

9.13 Supplies to diplomats, "international organisations" etc.

Under international agreements, some people and bodies working in the international arena and hosted by other Member States may make purchases free of VAT. The host government determines what bodies and persons qualify and may impose limitations. Relief is only available to an "international organisation" which means an organisation established by a treaty between sovereign governments so excludes other collaborative arrangements between non-governmental bodies such as limited companies or charities. Bodies such as the European Union, the United Nations and its various subsidiary organisations, and the North Atlantic Treaty Organisation (NATO) are included. A 'NATO visiting force' means an armed force contingent that belongs to a NATO Member State, is stationed in a Member State, and does not belong to the state in which it is stationed.

Goods supplied to these bodies can be zero-rated when the supplier obtains a Certificate of Entitlement, and the goods are for the official use of an embassy, a high commission, a consulate, an international organisation, a NATO visiting force, a British armed force contingent based in Cyprus; or for the personal use of a member of staff of one of these bodies.

The goods must be removed to an official address of the embassy, high commission, consulate, international organisation or force in another Member State or in one of the Sovereign Base Areas in Cyprus and may be consigned to the Post Office or to a courier or fast parcel service, including the British Forces Post Office (BFPO). If the goods are intended for a British embassy or high commission in another Member State, the goods may be consigned to the Foreign and Commonwealth Office for delivery through diplomatic channels.

The supplier must obtain and keep proof of the removal of the goods from the UK to the customer's address in the host country, but proof of posting is sufficient for these purposes. If the supply is for a contingent of British forces in Cyprus or its staff, or for a NATO visiting force in Germany or its staff, the order must be placed by an Official Procurement Agency for the force, such as the NAAFI or a regimental purchasing officer.

Certain services also qualify to be zero-rated provided the strict criteria are met. The supplier must similarly obtain a certificate of entitlement and the order for the services must be placed by an official of the organisation who is based in an office of the force or international organisation in a Member State other than the UK.

A supply of services to British forces in another Member State must in also satisfy the following conditions:
- the service must consist of training, software development, a supply of staff, or goods forwarding;
- for training, the trainees must all be members of a British contingent based in a Member State other than the UK, or members of British forces Cyprus;
- for software development, the software must be for the use of the force, and not for use in the UK;
- for a supply of staff, the staff must work exclusively for the force in the visiting force's host country or in a Sovereign Base Area in Cyprus; and
- if the service is goods forwarding, the goods must all be forwarded to or from the force's premises in the other Member State or in a Sovereign Base Area in Cyprus.

A "Certificate of Entitlement" is a certificate bearing the original signature of the head or acting head of the embassy, high commission, consulate, visiting force contingent or international organisation, with evidence of the qualifying status of the signatory, or can be any other form of certificate specified by their host government. Exceptionally in the case of a supply for the British force in Cyprus or its members, or for a visiting force in Germany or its members, the

supplier must obtain and keep a certificate from the person placing the order uniquely identifying the supply for which relief is claimed, and claiming entitlement as follows:
- for British forces in Cyprus – under Article 14(1)(g) of EC Council Directive 77/388/EEC; or
- for a visiting force in Germany – under Article 15(10) of EC Council Directive 77/388/EEC.

9.14 "Call-off" stocks

Call-off stocks are goods transferred by the supplier between Member States, to be held for an individual customer in the Member State of Arrival pending "call-off" for use by the customer as they need them with title and ownership of the goods remaining with the supplier. The rules concerning call off stocks only apply where the goods are destined for a single identified customer either for consumption within their business, for example as part of a manufacturing process, or to make onward supplies to their own customers. Movements of goods to maintain the supplier's own stocks in another Member State, or where they are available for call-off by more than one customer, are to be dealt with as consignment stocks (see section **9.15** below).

Where goods are removed from the UK to be held as call-off stock in another Member State the normal intra-EU rules apply so that the supply is treated as taking place in the UK and may be zero-rated subject to the conditions described in section **9.3** above. Where a UK business receives goods to be held in the UK as call-off stock by a supplier in another Member State the normal intra-EU rules apply and the supplier should account for Acquisition tax as explained in section **9.7** above.

9.15 "Consignment" stocks

Consignment stocks are goods that a supplier removes to another Member State to fulfil future supplies they intend to make in that country. The important feature is that the removal of the goods occurs before a customer has been found for them and can include goods not meeting the conditions necessary for the VAT treatment as call-off stocks (see section **9.14** above). Consignment stocks are treated as a transfer of own goods for VAT accounting and reporting purposes and the VAT treatment is as set out in section **9.8**.

9.16 Excise goods

Goods subject to excise duty can be removed between Member States free of duty (duty suspension) where the traders concerned are approved to do so. With effect from 1 April 2010, the "Registered Excise Dealers and Shippers" ("REDS") arrangements were replaced by an entirely new scheme to which HMRC Public Notice 203A refers, termed "Registered Consignees", in accordance with Council Directive 2008/118/EC. REDS were traders who had been approved and registered by HMRC to receive excise goods from other Member States and to account for the duty on duty-suspended excise goods.

INTRA-EU TRANSACTIONS

For VAT purposes the removal between VAT-registered suppliers and customers follows the normal intra-EU Dispatch and Arrival rules set out above.

REDS were not authorised to hold or dispatch goods under duty suspension, but were required to account for duty owed immediately, on monthly returns on a duty deferment basis, normally at the point when the excise goods were received by them or by the importer on whose behalf they were acting. Conversely, Registered Consignees are authorised by HMRC to receive and account for duty on duty-suspended excise goods received from other Member States, but who may not hold or dispatch duty-suspended goods. They may only receive duty-suspended goods from Tax Warehouses or Registered Consignors in other Member States, which exclude UK warehouse-keepers. To be approved by HMRC as a Registered Consignor, the applicant must be able to:

- demonstrate a business need supported by a viable business plan;
- be registered for VAT;
- have no unspent convictions or adverse compliance history with HMRC; and
- hold a duty deferment account, for which a security is required.

Additionally, the "Excise Movement and Control System" ("EMCS") was introduced on 1 April 2010 for recording and validating all movements of duty-suspended excise goods within the EU, replacing the system whereby a paper "Accompanying Administrative Document" ("AAD") accompanied all goods. All excisable goods must travel with an approved validation document to prove their status, the intended destination of the goods and to prevent fraud. From 1 April 2010 an electronic record (an "e-AD") must be raised on the EMCS and is automatically transmitted to the destination Tax Warehouse. There must also be a financial guarantee to cover all excise duty liabilities during the movement.

For supplies where UK excise duty has already been paid the goods should travel with a "Simplified Administrative Accompanying Document" (SAAD). The customer must also provide evidence that the excise duty has been paid in the Member State of destination or secured to the satisfaction of the VAT authorities there, before the supplier dispatches the goods.

For supplies to persons or businesses that are not registered for VAT, the supply can be zero-rated provided the goods are not for the person's private use, they are removed or dispatched from the UK to a destination in another Member State by or on behalf of the customer, and a validated e-AD is held. If these conditions are not met, the customer is liable for the excise duty and VAT and if duty-suspended goods go missing in transit then the person who supplied the movement guarantee will be liable for the duty, along with any person who may be jointly and severally liable.

INTRA-EU TRANSACTIONS

The dispatch of excise goods to persons in another Member State who are to consume them for private purposes are covered by the distance selling rules (see section **9.4** above). Additionally, the supplier must pay the excise duty due on the goods in the Member State of Arrival at the time the goods are delivered so they may have to register there for excise duty purposes. In the UK, persons receiving goods under the distance selling arrangements, must appoint a duty representative to account for UK excise duty, before the goods are dispatched.

Where goods are removed from a tax warehouse in the UK to a destination outside the UK, the supplier does not have to pay the VAT normally due on such removal. Here, either the person making the final supply in warehouse or the person removing the goods can zero-rate the supply provided the conditions set out in **Table M** below are met. The supplier must ensure that the zero rating conditions are established before the goods are delivered to avoid any doubt as to where responsibility to account for VAT rests.

Details of the EU-wide EMCS (export controls system) are set out in section **8.7.1**.

9.17 Goods removed under "sale or return" arrangements

Where goods are removed to another Member State under sale or return terms, they are treated for VAT purposes as not being supplied until they are adopted by the customer, which occurs when the customer indicates that they are going to keep the goods.

The supplier should treat the removal of sale or return goods as a transfer of own goods (see section **9.8**) which means that the supplier has a deemed Acquisition of the goods in the Member State of Arrival. Further, when the goods are sold from that Member State, a supply of those goods occurs in that country and the supplier may need to register there to account for any VAT due on the Acquisition and supply of the goods. The same rules apply to the removal of sale or return goods by suppliers in other Member States removing the goods to the UK and they also need to be registered for VAT in the UK to record the Acquisition Tax and account for any VAT due on their subsequent sale.

9.18 Goods sold on "intra-EU transport"

Goods which are supplied on board a ship, aircraft or train in the course of 'community transport' are treated as supplied at the 'point of departure'. Therefore, French VAT is due for goods sold on board a cross-channel ferry leaving France for the UK and UK VAT for a journey from the UK to France. Pricing will need to take account of the different VAT rates that apply in France and the UK to ensure profits are maintained for the same goods sold in all journeys. For services provided on board intra-EU transport see **11.2.12**.

9.19 Samples

The removal of goods that qualify as samples are disregarded for intra-EU Dispatch and Acquisition purposes. To qualify as a sample the relevant goods must satisfy the following criteria (see HMRC Notice 700: *VAT General Guide* section 8.8).[8]

9.19.1 General

The general conditions are that the owner:
- makes no charge for the samples; and
- supplies them for genuine business purposes as an illustrative or typical example of their product.

9.19.2 Samples given to the general public via an intermediary

These primarily involve samples supplied by a manufacturer to a retailer for distribution as samples to the retailer's customers for quality approval or marketing purposes etc. The sample is not viewed as being supplied for VAT purposes where:
- neither the supplier, nor the intermediary charge for them;
- they are supplied for genuine business purposes and they are to be given as an illustrative or typical example of the product;
- the final customer receives only one example of each product;
- the samples remain the supplier's property until they are given to the final customer; and
- any samples which are not used are returned to the supplier or are destroyed.

The supplier and the person receiving the samples should keep records of all goods received for these purposes and the results of any research performed on them to prove they have not been diverted to other uses or sold.

9.20 Goods sent for testing

The removal of goods sent to, or received from, another Member State for testing are disregarded provided that ownership remains unchanged and the goods are either returned to the Member State of departure or are destroyed. The supplier and the person undertaking the testing should keep records of all goods received for these purposes and the results of the tests performed on them to prove they have not been diverted to other uses or sold.

9.21 Record-keeping requirements

The absence of frontier controls has resulted in an absence of HMRC-produced statistics that assists the Government and financial institutions etc. in compiling statistics of trade, which of course is a fundamental economic measurement. Therefore, businesses that either dispatch goods to other Member States or acquire goods from other Member States, or do both, are

---

[8] www.gov.uk/government/publications/vat-notice-700-the-vat-guide/vat-notice-700-the-vat-guide#output-tax-particular-situations

INTRA-EU TRANSACTIONS

required to produce these vital statistics for the Government. Unsurprisingly, HMRC will levy penalties on businesses that fail repeatedly to either complete the necessary declarations, or for not taking this responsibility seriously enough and making mistakes in the data provided.

Therefore, in addition to completing the VAT return, businesses may have to complete the following declarations:

- an "EC Sales List" ("ESL") which lists goods that have been dispatched to VAT-registered businesses in other Member States;
- a "Services" ESL recording services supplied to customers in other Member States that are subject to the reverse charge procedure in the customer's Member State – see **Chapter 12**; and
- an (Intrastat) "Supplementary Statistical Declaration" ("SSD"), which is completed for supplies of goods by larger businesses.

9.21.1 VAT returns

All businesses registered for UK VAT must complete two boxes on their VAT returns showing the total value of goods dispatched to other Member States and the total value of goods acquired from other Member States. Additionally, those businesses with a value of trade in goods with other Member States above the Intrastat threshold for either Acquisitions or Dispatches must complete SSDs each month. See **Table S** at section **9.22** for the details required on VAT returns.

The VAT due on an Acquisition should be declared on the VAT return for the period in which the tax becomes due, i.e. the period when the time of Acquisition (tax point) occurs (see section **9.7**). The business may also treat this tax as input tax on the same VAT return, subject to the normal rules for claiming input tax.

Although there is no VAT due on the dispatch of the goods to a customer in another Member State, the value of the goods removed should be included in Box 8 of the VAT return that covers the tax point of the movement (see section **9.3**).

In addition to the normal VAT records VAT-registered businesses engaged in intra-EU trade must also keep all of the following records:

For Acquisitions:
- VAT invoices issued by suppliers in other Member States;
- documents relating to goods acquired by from other Member States;
- copies of Arrival SSDs, if applicable.

For Dispatches:
- VAT invoices issued to customers in other Member States;
- documents relating to goods despatched to other Member States;
- copies of completed EC Sales Lists; and
- copies of Dispatch SSDs, if applicable.

9.21.2 EC Sales Lists (ESLs)

All businesses registered for VAT have to submit ESLs to HMRC for their EU supplies of goods and/or services subject to the Reverse Charge in their customer's Member State – see **Chapter 12**. The information provided on the ESL is used in the UK and by other Member States to ensure that VAT has been correctly accounted for.

ESLs are only to be completed for supplies to businesses in other Member States that are VAT-registered and can provide the supplier with a valid VAT registration number. If a supply is made to a business which is not registered for VAT in their Member State, because say, it is below the VAT registration threshold, but which has provided evidence that it is in business (for place of supply purposes – see section **11.2.3**) these supplies are to be excluded from the ESL. This is because the absence of a VAT registration number would cause the ESL to be rejected by HMRC's computer. Also, because ESLs are only required for taxable supplies where the recipient is liable to account for VAT under the Reverse Charge provisions, supplies that are zero-rated in the customer's Member State are excluded as there is no Reverse Charge requirement. UK suppliers should therefore ascertain as best as possible if the relevant goods or services are subject to VAT in the customer's country; rather than being termed "zero-rated" as in the UK; the equivalent term in most Member States is "exempt with credit". If, subsequently, it becomes clear that a supply categorised and reported as taxable is in fact exempt, or vice versa, the business must submit a VAT 101B ESL Correction sheet.

However, in some cases the receipt of the supply by the customer in their own Member State could result in the customer being required to register for VAT in respect of the value of Arrivals in their Member State. If this occurs and the customer subsequently provides the supplier with a VAT registration number for them, an amendment should be made to the ESL using form VAT 101B "ESL Correction sheet".

ESLs must be completed for the following categories of removals:
- the supply of goods to a business registered for VAT in another Member State;
- the transfer of the entity's own goods (see section **9.8**);
- for intermediaries in triangular transactions between VAT-registered traders in other Member States (see section **9.12**);
- where a business makes supplies of services subject to the Reverse Charge in the customer's Member State (see section **11.2.3** and **Chapter 12**);
- for goods that would be zero-rated if supplied within the UK; and
- for goods supplied free of charge, the value being the cost of the goods to the business.

The following types of removals are not to be included on the ESL:
- samples, provided the conditions described in section **9.19** above are met;

INTRA-EU TRANSACTIONS

- supplies of goods under the Distance Selling arrangements (see section **9.4**); and
- the temporary movement of own goods, unless the conditions relating to the transfer change (see section **9.9**).

ESLs can be submitted in paper format on Form 101 or electronically using:
- an online form;
- an upload facility for large data (CSV or XML) files;
- UN-EDIFACT (to use this method an e-mail should be sent to ecu@hmrc.gsi.gov.uk to register); or
- by visiting the Electronic Data Capture Services section of the HMRC website for the Trade Specification – see www.hmrc.gov.uk/edifact

The benefits of submitting data electronically include:
- a user friendly system;
- front-end validation of data (i.e. identification of errors on screen);
- a facility to view past Internet submissions;
- a secure system using 'SSL' encryption technology; and
- time-stamped acknowledgement of data submitted.

There are distinct benefits to submitting ESLs electronically such as reducing:
- paperwork;
- manual entry delays;
- time spent on correcting errors; and
- administration costs.

The frequency of the submission of ESLs depends upon a number of factors, chiefly whether the supply of goods or services, and for goods only, the quarterly value (excluding VAT) of those supplies has exceeded the threshold; there is no requirement to submit nil ESLs. If the business makes supplies of services only, the business is required to submit an ESL for each calendar quarter ending 31 March, 30 June, 30 September and 31 December, but it may choose to submit monthly ESLs if these are preferred.

However, if the business makes supplies of goods, and the value of those supplies has not exceeded £35,000 (excl. VAT) in the current, or four previous quarters, it will be required to submit an ESL for each calendar quarter ending 31 March, 30 June, 30 September, and 31 December, but again may choose to submit monthly ESLs.

If the business makes supplies of goods and services, but the value of the supplies of goods is above the quarterly threshold (currently £35,000) it is required to submit monthly ESLs for goods, but has the choice to either:
- report both goods and services in each month, (using indicator '3' to identify supplies of services), or
- report only goods in months 1 and 2, and in month 3 report goods for the month and services for the whole quarter (using indicator '3' to identify supplies of services).

If the business makes supplies of goods and services and is allowed to use the Annual Accounting Scheme making one VAT return annually, it can apply to the VAT Helpline (telephone number 0300 200 700) for approval to submit an annual ESL and agree the due date for submission. This is only permitted where:
- the total annual taxable turnover does not exceed £145,000; and
- the annual value of supplies made to other Member States is not more than £11,000; and
- the supplies made do not include New Means of Transport (boats, aircraft and motorised land vehicles (see section **9.4** for definitions)).

Permission to submit an annual ESL may also be given by HMRC where:
- the business has a low level of EU dispatches (as described above); and
- the total taxable turnover does not exceed the VAT registration threshold plus £25,500;
- the annual value of supplies made to other Member States is not more than £11,000; and
- the supplies do not include New Means of Transport (boats, aircraft and motorised land vehicles (see section **9.5** for definitions)).

In this case, where HMRC approve the application, the business will be allowed to complete a less detailed ESL, showing only the VAT registration numbers of the EU customers. Actual values are not required, but the business must enter a nominal value of £1 for each entry on the ESL.

For all frequencies of submissions of ESLs, and for goods and services, paper ESLs must be submitted to HMRC within 14 days of the end of the reporting period, and electronic ESLs must be submitted within 21 days of the end of the reporting period. The information that must be included on an ESL is set out in **Table T** at section **9.22**.

There are monetary penalties for failures to submit ESLs by the due dates, varying between £5, £10 or £15 per day for the period they are late. The rate levied depends on the number of times the business has previously been late in submitting ESLs and will remain liable to penalties without notice until 12 months have elapsed without further default.

If an ESL is submitted that contains a "material inaccuracy" which is not disclosed when discovered by the business, a penalty of £100 may be levied by HMRC. Material inaccuracies fall into three main categories:
- data is missing from the ESL;
- there are factually incorrect lines on the ESL; or
- an invalid VAT number is used.

However, the penalty may be waived if the business can satisfy HMRC that it has a "reasonable excuse" for the error. HMRC do not provide details of what, in their opinion, are reasonable excuses, but will not accept genuine mistakes, honesty and acting in good faith. The law provides specifically that it is not a reasonable excuse to rely on another person to perform any task on the business' behalf. HMRC add in Notice 725 at section 17.13 that misquoting a VAT number for the customer that does not conform to the published format for the customer's Member State, or using a VAT number which HMRC has said is invalid, will not be accepted as a reasonable excuse for the material inaccuracy. In such cases, the supplier may also be liable to account for the VAT on any supplies where they have not met the requirements for zero-rating.

Businesses are required to inform HMRC when they discover errors in the ESLs where they exceed £100, or an incorrect VAT registration number has been quoted, or the wrong transaction type indicator has been used.

Individual branches of a legal entity, individual companies within a group registration, or self-accounting branches of a group member have the option to submit one ESL for the business or to apply to the VAT Helpline (telephone 0300 200 3700) to submit individual ESLs. If this is approved, separate forms or electronic submissions can be used and HMRC will issue a three-digit identifier for each branch or company. However, where the total value of goods supplied from all the branches of a business is more than £70,000 (excluding VAT) in the current or previous four quarters, each branch will have to submit a monthly ESL.

9.21.3 "Intrastat"

In the UK all VAT registered businesses carrying out trade with other Member States must declare the total value of goods supplied to other Member States ("Dispatches") and the total value of goods acquired from other Member States ("Arrivals") by completing two boxes on their VAT returns. The deemed VAT due to HMRC on an Arrival is called Acquisition VAT – see section **9.7**. Those businesses over a legally set threshold are also required to provide more detailed information on "Statistical Supplementary Declarations" (SSDs). Intra-EU trade statistics are compiled from the SSD's and estimations made using the information on the VAT returns.

"Intrastat" is the name given to the system for collecting statistics on the trade in goods between Member States. Intrastat replaced Customs declarations as a source of trade statistics within the EU and the requirements are similar in all Member States. Supplies of services are excluded from Intrastat except where they are charges related to the contract to supply goods, for example freight and insurance.

These declarations are briefly explained below, however, full guidance is provided by HMRC in their Notice 60: *Intrastat*.[9] SSDs can also be made

---

[9] www.gov.uk/government/publications/notice-60-intrastat-general-guide/

electronically, and detailed guidance on this and updates on all Intrastat matters can also be obtained at www.uktradeinfo.com.[10]

The UK threshold for Arrivals at March 2016 is £1.5 million, whilst the UK threshold for Dispatches at March 2016 is only £250,000. However, businesses whose trade in either Arrivals or Dispatches exceeds the "Delivery Terms" threshold (at March 2016 £24 million) are required to provide additional delivery terms information on their SSDs. If a business exceeds the threshold for Arrivals, but not for Dispatches, delivery terms must be provided for Arrivals only and if the threshold for the Dispatches is exceeded, but not for Arrivals, delivery terms must be provided for Dispatches only.

Unlike the Arrivals and Dispatches thresholds, if a business exceeds the Delivery Terms' threshold during the calendar year, they do not have to start submitting delivery terms data until 1 January of the next calendar year and only then if the Arrivals and/or Dispatches remain above the new threshold set for the following year.

The Arrivals and Dispatches thresholds apply on a calendar year basis, and once exceeded, SSDs must continue to be submitted until the end of the calendar year. Further, if only one of the two thresholds is exceeded, the business need only complete SSDs for the movements exceeded.

Penalties can be incurred when SSDs are persistently late, missing, inaccurate or where only part of a month's EU trade is declared. However, HMRC view penalties as a last resort and can provide help on the completion of the SSD's for businesses experiencing difficulties. The penalty regime is a criminal one and could result in proceedings in a Magistrates Court. This could lead to a maximum fine of £2,500 being imposed for each offence. However, there may be the opportunity to 'compound' any proceedings which involves the offer of an administrative fine in lieu of any Court proceedings. If this happens a fine of a minimum of £250 would be applied for each offence, (each declaration is considered one offence).

SSDs can be submitted via the internet or by Electronic Data Interchange (EDI). Internet submission is available to all Intrastat businesses including branches of companies submitting data independently of their head office and agents submitting on behalf of Intrastat businesses. The secure system is accessed by username and password via either the HMRC or uktradeinfo websites, and there are two methods of completion:
- by keying data directly onto an online form; or
- by an offline option using a CSV (Comma Separated Variable) file, preparing a CSV file is easy or you can use the HMRC pre-prepared Excel spreadsheet (Generator Tool).

---

[10] www.uktradeinfo.com/Intrastat/Pages/Intrastat.aspx

INTRA-EU TRANSACTIONS

Both methods are submitted via the HMRC system. Validation checks are carried out on all mandatory fields during completion or submission and any errors found are identified for correction.

Wherever possible, Intrastat requirements align with VAT requirements. For example, the value to be declared for Intrastat is normally the invoice or contract price (exclusive of VAT), as used for VAT purposes. This allows the integration of Intrastat records with normal business VAT records, thus minimising the overall burden on a business.

Goods which have moved between the UK and another EU Member State by way of trade. This includes goods:
- bought and sold;
- transferred within the same legal entity;
- sent for or returned after processing;
- supplied as part of a contract for services;
- to be installed or used in construction;
- supplied free of charge;
- on long term hire, loan or operational lease; and
- lost or destroyed.

Some movements are excluded from SSDs these being:
- movements not by way of trade (for example personal goods such as travel luggage or items involved in moving house, ballast etc.);
- goods in transit including goods which are in transit through the UK. This applies even when there are stops or temporary storage, provided that these are for transport reasons;
- certain purely temporary movements where the goods are to be returned to the original EU country within two years and there is to be no change of ownership;
- monetary gold;
- means of payment which are legal tender and securities, including means which are payments for services such as postage, taxes, user fees;
- goods moving between the UK and its territorial enclaves (for example embassies, armed forces bases) in another Member State or moving within the UK to an enclave of another Member State;
- goods used as carriers of customised information, including software;
- software downloaded from the internet;
- commercial samples and advertising material provided free of charge;
- goods sent for or returned after repair; and means of transport travelling in the course of their work, including spacecraft launchers at the time of launching;
- means of transport travelling in the course of their work, including spacecraft launchers at the time of launching;
- newspapers and periodicals supplied under direct subscription; and

- the supply of machine tools that remain in the UK and are used to manufacture goods that are dispatched to the EU.

The value of the goods declared on the SSD must be in sterling. The exchange rate used for VAT purposes is acceptable and may be the UK selling rate published in national newspapers, banks or the period rate published by HMRC, which is available at **www.uktradeinfo.com** or **www.hmrc.gov.uk** or from the National Advice Service on telephone 0300 200 3700. Speculative exchange rates such at that on the date of settling a supplier's invoice or forward rates or rates derived from forward rates are not acceptable.

Sometimes, because of the way in which certain goods are traded, it is difficult to establish the value of the goods at the time of making the SSD. HMRC can authorise the use of a 'best estimate' of the value and the SSD can be amended when the true value becomes known. However, HMRC will not allow a "best estimate" to be used because of any delay caused by processing and reconciliation of invoices within the business' organisation.

Detailed methods of establishing a value can be found in Chapter 3 of the Community Customs Code (Council Regulation (EEC) No 2913/92), which in turn can be found in the Official Journal (L series) no. 302 for 1992. This is available online at **eur-lex.europa.eu** by clicking on *'Official Journal'*, scrolling down and clicking on 'Other Years' and entering the date (1992), the series (L) and the number of the OJ as search criteria. Valuation methods for import duty are also set out in Chapter 4 of the Code and application can be made to HMRC to use these values.

9.21.3.1 Completion of the SSDs

HMRC Notice 60 section 6 provides comprehensive instructions on how to complete the SSDs.

Notice 60 section 7 provides advice on reconciling VAT declarations with the corresponding SSDs. Whilst it is a basic principle of Intrastat that the VAT return figures should be used as control totals, providing a check that SSDs are complete and accurate, there are times when the two declarations will not agree, because of the different reporting requirements of the two systems. HMRC state that they may query differences between the two sets of figures and visiting officers will ask businesses to explain any differences. Notice 60, section 7 provides examples of how differences can arise and steps businesses can take to minimise the errors.

HMRC will perform periodic visits to assure themselves that systems used to complete SSDs are robust and to check the accuracy of the SSDs. The visit will normally be made to the business' premises, but, may, exceptionally be made to an agent's premises where this is considered appropriate. In line with VAT requirements, businesses required to submit SSDs must preserve all records relating to Intrastat for at least six years, including all data stored electronically. A business wishing to computerise part or all of its Intrastat records must obtain HMRC's permission before doing so.

Sections 9 to 21 of Notice 60 explain in great detail all of the reporting requirements (data fields etc.) that are needed to complete accurate SSDs and should be referred to at all stages of the reporting cycle.

Businesses can obtain information on all aspects of the Intrastat system from HMRC **at www.uktradeinfo.com**, by telephoning **01702 367485**, or by emailing **uktradeinfo@hmrc.gsi.gov.uk**.

9.22 Tables of VAT liabilities for Intra-EU movements

Table A   Equivalent of Value Added Tax (VAT) in other Member States

Member State	VAT Equivalent
Austria	Mehrwertsteuer (Mwst) Umsatzsteuer (Umst)
Belgium	Belasting over de Toegevoegde Waarde (BTW)
	Taxe sur la Valeur Ajoutée (TVA)
Bulgaria	Данък Добавена Стойност (Д Д С)
Cyprus	Φόρος Προστιθέμενης Αξίας (ΦΠΑ)
Croatia	PDV Id. Broj (PDV-1D)
Czech Republic	Daň z přidané hodnoty (DPH)
Denmark	Omsaetningafgift
Estonia	Käibemaks
Finland	Arvonlisavero (ALV)
France	Taxe sur la Valeur Ajoutée (TVA)
Germany	Mehrwertsteuer (Mwst)
	Umsatzsteuer (Umst)
Greece	Arithmos Forologikou Mitroou (FPA)
Hungary	Általános Forgalmi Adó (ÁFA)
Ireland	Value Added Tax
Italy	Imposta sul valore Aggiunto (IVA)
Latvia	Pievienotãs vértîbas nodoklis
Lithuania	Pridetines vertes mokestis (PVM)
Luxembourg	Taxe sur la Valeur Ajoutée (TVA)
Malta	Value Added Tax
Netherlands	Omzetbelasting (OB)
	Belasting over de Toegevoegde Waarde (BTW)
Poland	Podatek od towarów I uslug
Portugal	Imposto sobre o Valor Acrescentado (IVA)
Romania	Tăxa pe valoarea adăugată
Slovakia	Daň z přidanej hodnoty (DPH)
Slovenia	Davek na dodano vrednost (DDV)
Spain	Impuesto sobre el Valor Anadidio (IVA)
Sweden	Mervardeskatt (MOMS)

Table B   Reporting requirements for intra-EU movements

Type of movement	VAT Return	EC Sales List	Supplementary Declaration
Dispatches			
Goods supplied to VAT-registered customers in other Member States where zero-rating conditions are met.(1)	boxes 6 and 8 – value of supply.	Yes – customer's VAT number and value of supply.	Yes – as a dispatch (value of supply).
Goods supplied to customers in other Member States where zero-rating conditions are not met.(2)	box 1 – output tax*	No	Yes – as a dispatch. See also section 9.4 regarding distance sales and Notice 60 Intrastat General Guide.
Arrivals			
Acquisitions of goods from VAT-registered suppliers in other EU Member States	box 2 – acquisition VAT for goods positive-rated in UK. box 4 – input tax subject to normal rules boxes 7 and 9 – value of acquisition.	No	Yes – as an arrival (value of supply). Customer must provide their EU supplier with their VAT number for supplier to quote on the sales invoice.

*see also requirements for evidence and time limits in section **9.3**

Notes
(1) Supply may be zero-rated
(2) UK VAT charged at appropriate rate. (But see section **9.4** about distance selling.)

INTRA-EU TRANSACTIONS

Table C   Lost, destroyed or stolen goods

Where goods have been lost, destroyed or stolen the supplier needs to determine whether any VAT liability exists.

Where goods are lost, destroyed or stolen and this occurs...	then...
in the UK before supply (e.g. whilst in storage awaiting delivery or collection),	if there has been no supply, no VAT is due.
while being transported in the UK by either the supplier or the customer	VAT is due **unless** evidence of loss, destruction or theft (e.g. an insurance claim or police investigation) is held
while being transported outside the UK by either the supplier or the customer	the goods may continue to be zero-rated **provided** valid proof of removal of the goods from the UK of the customer are held (The customer may still be liable to account for acquisition tax in its Member State. Also there may be additional VAT liabilities if the loss, destruction or theft occurs en-route through a Member State. In that event the supplier should check the position with the VAT authority in the Member State concerned.

Table D   Goods crossing the Irish land boundary

HMRC state that the supplier should obtain all of the following types of evidence as proof of removal.

If the goods are...	then commercial evidence should include...
removed by road by an independent carrier	a copy of the carrier's invoice or consignment note, supported by evidence that the goods have been delivered to a destination in the Republic of Ireland (e.g. a receipted copy of the consignment note).
removed by rail	the consignor's copy of the consignment note signed by the railway official accepting the goods for delivery to your customer.
removed in supplier's own transport	a copy of the delivery note showing the customer's name, address, EU VAT number and actual delivery address in the Republic of Ireland if different, and a signature of the customer, or their authorised representative, confirming receipt of the goods.
collected by the customer or their authorised representative	a written order completed by the customer, which shows their name, address, EU VAT number, the name of the authorised representative collecting the goods, the address in the Republic of Ireland where the goods are to be delivered, the vehicle registration number of the transport used, and a signature of the customer, or their authorised representative, confirming receipt of the goods.

INTRA-EU TRANSACTIONS

Table E   Postal Services and proof of export/removal

The following types of evidence to support the movement are available from the Royal Mail/Parcelforce

Method of posting	Evidence required
Letter post or airmail	A fully completed certificate of posting form presented with the goods, and stamped by the Post Office. Acceptable forms are: • Form C&E 132 for single or multiple packages taken to the Post Office. Blank forms may be obtained from the HMRC website - www.hmrc.gov.uk or by phoning the VAT Helpline on 0300 200 3700. • Form P326 available from the Post Office and used for single packages taken to the Post Office, or • a Certificate of Posting for International Mail Only, or a Royal Mail Collection Manifest, available from a Royal Mail sales advisor, for use by customers using their Business Collections Service, where the Royal Mail collection driver signs the certificate. • Information on Royal Mail international services is available at www.royalmail.com/
Parcels	Parcelforce Worldwide operates a range of international parcel services. If any of these are used they will provide: • a service specific barcoded label • a customs export declaration (for non-EU destinations only) • a copy of the Parcelforce Worldwide conditions of carriage, and • a printed receipt, which is the proof of shipment for all destinations. An individual barcode label must be affixed to every parcel. Customs export declarations are not required for goods being sent to another EU Member State. If the parcel is collected from the supplier's premises the collecting driver will sign the printed receipt. This is the proof of shipment for EU destinations. If the parcel is taken to a Post Office, the counter clerk will provide a printed proof of shipment from the Post Office SmartPost system. This will show the overseas delivery address, date of dispatch and unique consignment number. This is to be kept as printed proof of shipment. In addition to the individual parcel declarations described above, account customers of Parcelforce Worldwide have two further potential sources of information listing multiple parcel dispatches. These are: Worldwide Dispatch manager (WDM) – online users can print a manifest which lists all dispatched parcels, and a Statement of Account. All of the individual parcel declarations, plus either the manifest or the statement of account listing each dispatch will provide proof of removal for VAT purposes. Information on Parcelforce Worldwide International services is available at www.parcelforce.com/

INTRA-EU TRANSACTIONS

Table F   Establishing the tax value of an acquisition

Acquisition VAT is accountable on the sterling value of positive-rated goods that arrive in the UK from other Member States. The value of an acquisition needs to be established in order to quantify the Acquisition Tax and this is to be established as follows:

Where...	Then the tax value of your acquisition is...
the consideration is wholly in money,	the amount paid.
the consideration is non-monetary, for example the supply is made in return for payment in goods or services, or is monetary and non-monetary,	the monetary equivalent of the consideration calculated by reference to the price, excluding VAT, which would have to be paid if the consideration were monetary.
the consideration involves a discounted amount and the discounted amount is paid	based on the discounted amount.
the consideration includes the offer of a conditional discount which is dependent upon some future event, for example on condition that more goods are bought from the supplier, or payment is made within a specified period of time	based on the full amount paid. If the discount is earned later, the tax value is reduced and the amount of tax accounted for can be adjusted (but this should only be done where input tax has not been claimed, or full input tax credit for that acquisition is not allowable).
there is no consideration, for example a transfer of own goods (see section 9.8), or when goods are supplied without charge	in either case, what it would cost the acquirer, or the person transferring the goods, to purchase the goods in question at the time of the acquisition.

INTRA-EU TRANSACTIONS

Table G   Transfers of own goods to another Member State

Movements involving a business' own goods must be reported as follows:

Type of movement	VAT return	EC Sales List	Supplementary Declaration	Notes
Transfers from the UK to other Member States.	boxes 6 and 8 – value based on cost of goods	Yes – value based on cost of goods.	Yes – as a dispatch (value based on cost of goods).	A deemed supply in the UK. It may be zero-rated subject to the removal conditions
Transfers from other Member States to the UK.	box 2 - acquisition VAT for positive-rated goods in UK. box 4 – input tax subject to normal rules boxes 7 and 9 – value based on cost of goods.	No	Yes – as an arrival (value based on cost of goods).	There is an acquisition in the UK by the owner of the goods.

Table H   Goods removed for temporary use etc.

Movements involving goods sent for temporary use in another Member State must be reported as follows:

Type of movement	VAT Return	EC Sales List	Supplementary Declaration	Notes
Goods sent from the UK used in making a supply of services in another Member State that remain out of the UK for less than 2 years.	No	No	No	Requirement to keep a register of goods moved temporarily
Goods sent from the UK used in making a supply of services in another Member State that remain out of the UK for more than 2 years.	No	No	Yes – as a dispatch (value based on cost of goods).	Requirement to keep a register of goods moved temporarily
Temporary transfer of goods from UK which would be eligible for temporary importation relief if sent from outside EU that remain out of the UK for less than 2 years	No	No	No	Requirement to keep a register of goods moved temporarily

INTRA-EU TRANSACTIONS

Table I   Installed or assembled goods

Movements involving installed or assembled goods sent to another Member State must be reported as follows:

Type of movement	VAT Return	EC Sales List	Supplementary Declaration
Goods sent from UK for installation or assembly in another Member State.	box 6 – value of supply box 8 – value based on cost of goods at time of dispatch.	No	Yes – as a dispatch (value based on cost of goods if known, otherwise open market value).
Goods sent from another Member State for installation or assembly in UK where supplier registers for VAT in UK	box 1 - output tax. box 6 - value of supply.	No	Yes – as an arrival (value based on cost of goods if known, otherwise open market value).
Goods installed or assembled in the UK where supplier elects to use simplification procedure.(1)	box 2 - acquisition VAT. box 4 - input tax (subject to normal rules) boxes 7 and 9 - value of acquisition.	No	Yes – as an arrival (value based on cost of goods if known, otherwise open market value).

Notes
1. Customer is responsible for reporting requirements.

Table J   Goods sent for process or repair

Movements involving goods sent to another Member State for process or repair and return must be reported as follows:

Type of movement	VAT return	EC Sales List	Supplementary Declaration	Notes
Repaired goods				
Goods sent to another Member States for repair – owner's reporting requirements.	No	No	No	
Goods received back in the UK by owner after repair in another Member State – UK owner's reporting requirements.	box 1 – output tax* box 4 – input tax, subject to normal rules box 6 – value of repair services.	No	No	*Output tax accounted for on repair services as a reverse charge
Goods for repair received in the UK from other Member	No	No	No	

286   TRADING PLACES

States – UK repairer's reporting requirements.				
Repaired goods returned to customer in another Member State – UK repairer's reporting requirements	box 6 – value of repair service.	No	No	VAT on repair services accounted for by EU customer as a reverse charge
Processed goods				
Goods sent from UK for process in another Member State – UK owner's reporting requirements.	No	No	Yes – as a dispatch (value based on cost of goods).	
Goods returned to UK from EU processor – UK owner's reporting requirements(1)	box 1- output tax* box 4 – input tax subject to normal rules box 6 – value of the processing services.	No	Yes – as an arrival (value based on cost of goods and cost of process)	
Goods received for process in UK from EU customer – UK processor's reporting requirements.	No	No	Yes – as an arrival (value based on cost of goods if known, otherwise open market value).	
Goods returned after process in UK to EU customer - UK processor's reporting requirements (2).	box 6 –value of process.	No	Yes – as a dispatch (value based on cost of goods, if known, otherwise, open market value and cost of process).	

Notes
1. Output tax accounted for on processor's services as a reverse charge.
2. VAT on processing services accounted for by EU customer as a reverse charge.

INTRA-EU TRANSACTIONS

Table K   *Treatment of Supplies in Triangulation*

For supplies involving three parties, known as "triangulation", the VAT treatment within the EU is normally as follows:

If you are the...	you may...
first supplier	zero-rate the supply of the goods subject to the evidence of removal and time limit conditions
intermediate supplier	be liable to register for VAT in the Member State to which the goods are delivered and account for VAT on the acquisition and on your supply.
the final customer	not need to do anything as you are receiving a domestic supply (but see the simplified procedure described in section **9.12.1**)

Table L   *"Call-off" and "Consignment" stocks*

Movements involving goods sent to another Member State as call-off or consignment stocks must be reported as follows

Type of movement	VAT Return	EC Sales List	Supplementary Declaration	Notes
Call-off stocks				
Goods sent as call-off stocks from the UK to another Member State.	boxes 6 and 8 – value based on cost of goods.	Yes – value based on cost of goods.	Yes - as a dispatch, (value based on cost of goods).	The supply may be zero-rated.
Goods received in the UK as call-off stocks.	box 2 - acquisition VAT for positive-rated goods in UK. box 4 – input tax subject to normal rules. boxes 7 and 9 – value based on cost of goods.	No	Yes – as an arrival (value based on cost of goods).	There is an acquisition by the UK customer.
Consignment stocks	See Table G			

Table M   *Excise goods*

All excisable goods moving between Member States must travel with an accompanying document; there are two types of accompanying document:
- an Administrative Accompanying Document (AAD), and
- a Simplified Administrative Accompanying Document (SAAD)

Examples of the circumstances in which they are used are as follows:

INTRA-EU TRANSACTIONS

If the movement of goods is between warehouses and...	then...
they are moving under authorised duty suspension arrangements (for example an excise warehouse)	the consignor must complete an AAD. There must also be a financial guarantee to cover all excise duty liabilities during the movement. The consignee must complete a certificate of receipt for the goods on the reverse of Copy 3 of the AAD and return it to the consignor.
UK excise duty has already been paid	the goods should travel with SAAD. The customer must also provide evidence that the excise duty has been paid in the Member State of destination or secured to the satisfaction of the VAT authorities there, before the supplier dispatches the goods.

Table N   Excise goods being exported/removed from the UK

The following table provides an overview of the VAT implications when goods are removed to a place outside the UK:

Where goods are removed from warehouse to	the VAT treatment is
A country outside the EU	Any VAT which would be due on removal to UK home use is not payable. Supplies of goods removed from the UK may be zero-rated as exports subject to meeting the conditions in VAT Notice 703: *export of goods from the UK*. An EC Sales List (ESL) is not required
A VAT-registered customer in another Member State	A supply of goods to a customer who is VAT-registered in another EU country may be zero-rated where the goods are moving outside the warehousing system provided the conditions in Notice 725: *The Single Market* are met. An ESL and an entry in box 8 of the VAT return is required
A tax warehouse in another EU Member State	For UK VAT purposes, any supply of the goods may be disregarded provided they are removed directly to a registered tax warehouse in another EU country. An ESL, or an entry in Box 8 of the VAT return is not required

Table O   Goods sent on 'sale or return', 'on approval' or similar terms

These are goods which are not supplied until they are adopted by the customer. Adoption occurs when the customer indicates that they are going to keep the goods. Until then the customer has an unqualified right to return

INTRA-EU TRANSACTIONS

them at any time, unless there is an agreed time limit after which the goods are to be automatically treated as accepted.

Table O1 **Accounting for VAT**

Goods sent...	Then...
from the UK on sale or return, approval or similar terms to somebody in another Member State	They are treated as a transfer of own goods (see Table G). This means that: • there is an acquisition of the goods in the Member State to which the goods are sent • there is a supply of those goods in that Member State if, and when, the goods are eventually adopted by the customer, and • the supplier may need to register there to account for any VAT due on the acquisition and supply of the goods
to the UK from another Member State on sale or return, approval or similar terms	They are treated as a transfer of own goods (see Table G). This means that: • there is an acquisition of the goods in the UK • there is a supply of those goods in the UK if, and when, the goods are eventually adopted by the customer, and • the supplier will also be liable to register for VAT in the UK, to account for any VAT due on the acquisition and supply of the goods.

Table O2 **Reporting requirements**

Type of movement	VAT Return	EC Sales List	Supplementary Declaration	Notes
Goods sent from UK to another Member State.	boxes 6 and 8 – value based on cost of goods.	Yes – value based on cost of goods	Yes – as a dispatch (value based on cost of goods)	See Table G (transfers of own goods). This assumes the sender of goods is registered for VAT in the Member State of arrival.
Goods sent to UK from another Member State.	box 2 – acquisition VAT for positive-rated goods in UK. box 4 – input tax subject to normal rules. boxes 7 and 9 - value based on cost of goods	No	Yes as an arrival (value based on cost of goods).	There is an acquisition in the UK by the owner of the goods. This assumes the sender of goods is registered for VAT in the UK.

Table P   *Samples*

Movements of goods that qualify as samples are disregarded for intra-EU supply and acquisition purposes. Details of the conditions that must be met to treat something as a sample can be found in Notice 700: *The VAT Guide* at section 8. The reporting requirements are:

Type of movement	VAT Return	EC Sales List	Supplementary Declaration
Samples sent to, or received from, another Member State.	No	No	No (when the goods are supplied free of charge).

Table Q   *Goods sent for testing*

Goods sent to, or received from, another Member State for testing are disregarded from VAT reporting provided that ownership remains unchanged and the goods are either returned to the Member State of departure or are destroyed. The Reporting requirements are:

Type of movement	VAT Return	EC Sales List	Supplementary Declaration
Goods sent to, or received from, another Member States for testing.	No	No	No (unless it is known at time of dispatch that they will be tested to destruction – if so value based on cost of goods).

Table R   *Temporary movement registers – evidence required*

Where goods are sent to or received from another Member State on a temporary basis (where they are to be returned within a period of two years after their first removal or receipt) a register of these temporary movements must be kept. The following information is to be recorded.

Item	Information
1	For goods being sent out of the UK - the date the goods were removed.
2	For goods received from another Member State – the date the goods arrived.
3	The date the goods are returned.
4	A description of the goods
5	The reason for the movement (for example process work).
6	The consideration for the supply, if applicable.

INTRA-EU TRANSACTIONS

Table S *VAT returns for supplies and acquisitions of goods*

On the VAT Return (Form VAT 100) there are a number of boxes to gather information on the value of goods sold to, or bought from, other Member States and 2 boxes for VAT due on acquisitions. These are:

Box Number	Description
2	Total VAT due on EU acquisitions in the period.
4	Amount of VAT deductible on any business purchase including acquisitions of goods and related costs from other EU Member States (subject to the normal input tax rules).
6	Total value of all of the business sales including supplies to other EU Member States.
7	Total value of purchases including acquisitions from VAT-registered suppliers in other EU Member States.
8	Total value of supplies of goods and directly related costs (such as freight and insurance charges) to Member States in the period (excluding VAT). The value entered in box 8 should be the total of all intra-EU supplies of goods made in that reporting period (excluding VAT) and not just the value of payments received. (Figures entered in this box must also be included in the box 6 total.)
9	Total value of acquisitions and directly related costs (such as freight and insurance charges) from Member States in the period (excluding VAT). (Figures entered in this box must also be included in the box 7 total.)

Further information about Form VAT 100, can be found in Notice 700/12: *Filling in your VAT Return.*[11]

---

[11] www.gov.uk/government/publications/vat-notice-70012-filling-in-your-vat-return/

Table T   Information included in EC Sales Lists

All of the following information must be provided.

Information	Description
Country code	The 2 letter prefix which identifies the customer's country code as shown in section 9.3
Customer's VAT registration number	The VAT registration number of each customer in the other Member States. The table in section **9.3** shows the only acceptable format of EU VAT numbers. HMRC recommend that suppliers check customers' EU VAT registration numbers regularly using the Europa website – see section **9.3** and footnote
Total value of supplies in £s sterling	The total value for the appropriate period of: • goods and related services which have been supplied to each customer, leaving the indicator column blank (related services are services which form part of the price of the goods such as freight charges and insurance); • triangular transactions, entered on a separate line for each customer and using code '2' in the indicator column; and • supplies of services subject to the reverse charge in the customer's Member State, entered on a separate line for each customer and using code '3' in the indicator column. • supplies of services made to a business which is not registered for VAT in their Member State because, for example it is below the registration threshold, but which has provided evidence that it is in business (for place of supply purposes), should be excluded. The figure of £1 must be inserted in the value column for each entry where a simplified annual ESL is being submitted.

10 Recovery of VAT "Cross-Border"

10.1 Introduction

Despite the major step forward in VAT being brought to account in the Member State in which the transaction is deemed to take place (the "Destination System" – see **Chapter 1**) and the introduction of the "General Rule" for supplies of services made in a "B2B" context – see section **11.2.1** – businesses will inevitably incur VAT in other Member States when they do business in those countries, for example, on hotel accommodation etc.

The Member States have agreed principles of reclaims for businesses that are established in another Member State from that in which the VAT has been incurred and for non-EU businesses that have incurred VAT in the EU. In the UK, HMRC has provided detailed guidance on claims in VAT Notice 723A.[1] There are two schemes, one being for EU businesses that have incurred VAT in other Member States and one for non-EU businesses. These are explained in **10.2** onwards.

10.2 EU Scheme

The paper-based cross-border refund mechanism has been abandoned because it was both a cumbersome and lengthy process with claimants waiting inordinate periods to obtain a refund (and in some countries never receiving one). Following agreement between EU Finance Ministers, EU legislation to reform the system was adopted in February 2008, as part of the VAT package of legislation and the electronic system was adopted for all claims submitted on or after 1 January 2010.

Requests for refunds are dealt with by the Member State of Refund (MSR). The amount refundable is determined under the deduction rules of the MSR and the relevant repayment will be made directly by that Member State to the business. The system is an electronic one, with specified timescales and interest payable by the MSR if these are not met. Electronic claims will be completed and submitted via the competent authorities in the Member State in which the claimant is established (Member State of Establishment or MSE).

10.2.1 Eligibility criteria

To be eligible to make and receive a refund the applicant must be a taxable person established in a Member State other than the MSR, or their authorised agent. The applicant must meet all of the following conditions:
(a) The applicant must not be registered, liable or eligible to be registered in the MSR; and
(b) The applicant must have no fixed establishment, seat of economic activity, place of business or other residence there; and

---

[1] www.gov.uk/government/publications/vat-notice-723a-refunds-of-vat-in-the-european-community-for-ec-and-non-ec-businesses/

RECOVERY OF VAT "CROSS BORDER"

(c) During the refund period the applicant must not have supplied any goods or services in the MSR with the exception of:
 (i) transport services and services ancillary thereto; and
 (ii) supplies of goods or services where VAT is payable by the person to whom the supply is made.

The applicant completes an electronic claim within an ePortal and forwards this to its own MSE tax authority for checking before, if it is satisfactory, being forwarded to the MSR. Basic registration checks will be carried out by the MSE before the application is forwarded electronically to the MSR.

The MSE will not forward the application to the MSR where during the period of refund any of the following apply.
(a) The applicant is not a taxable person for VAT purposes.
(b) The applicant makes only exempt supplies.
(c) The applicant is covered by the exemption for small enterprises.
(d) The applicant is operating the flat-rate scheme for farmers.

If the MSE decides not to forward the application to the MSR it must notify the applicant of this decision.

10.2.2 Applications

A separate application must be completed for each Member State. Applications can be commenced and stored in an incomplete state on the ePortal system and may be recalled and finalised to be submitted at a later date.

The refund period must not be more than one calendar year or less than three calendar months unless the period covered represents the remainder of a calendar year, for example where interim applications have already been submitted earlier in the year, or if the applicant has recently become VAT registered. If the refund application relates to a period of less than a calendar year, but not less than three months the minimum amount claimable is EUR 400 or the equivalent in national currency. If the refund application relates to a period of a calendar year or the remainder of a calendar year the minimum amount claimable is EUR 50 or the equivalent in national currency.

Properly completed applications must be submitted to the MSE at the latest by 30 September of the calendar year following the refund year. Where an applicant deregisters for VAT during the refund year it should submit the application as soon as possible following the date of deregistration.

VAT that has been incurred on supplies of goods or services received in the reference years and invoiced with a tax point and goods imported into the MSR during the period of the refund application can be claimed. In addition, the application may include supplies or imports not included in a previous application as long as they relate to the same calendar year.

However, VAT cannot be reclaimed on amounts of VAT that have been incorrectly invoiced and amounts of VAT that have been invoiced in respect of goods dispatched to other Member States or exported outside the EU.

Where the applicant is partially exempt in their own Member State they will only receive a partial refund and the MSE will advise the MSR on the applicant's VAT reclaim status to enable only the correct proportion of VAT to be refunded. Details on the fields and the information that is required is set out in section 2 of Notice 723A.

The MSR must notify the applicant of the decision to approve or refuse the application within four months of the date they first received the application. If the MSR requires additional information in order to process the application, it can request this from the applicant, the applicant's tax authority, or a third party before the expiry of the four-month period.

The additional information must be provided by the person to whom the request is made within one month of receiving the request. Once the MSR has received the additional information it has two further months in which to notify its decision.

If further additional information is requested by the MSR the final deadline for making a decision can be extended up to a maximum of eight months from the date they received the application. Payment must be made within 10 working days following expiry of the appropriate decision deadline.

Where the claim is satisfactory the payment will be made in the MSR or, at the applicant's request, in any other Member State. In the latter case, any bank charges for the transfer will be deducted by the MSR from the amount to be paid to the applicant. If incorrect bank details are submitted by the applicant and they result in further bank charges being incurred these may also be deducted from the amount payable on the current or subsequent applications.

If an applicant discovers that it has made an error on an application, a corrected application can be submitted. The correction procedures allow existing lines on the application to be amended or deleted (by reducing to 'nil'), but do not allow new lines to be added. The correction procedure can also be used to amend incorrect bank details, email addresses etc. If an application is found to be incorrect any overpayment will be recovered, normally by deducting it from any refund due.

All Member States take a very serious view of incorrect applications. Refunds obtained on the basis of any incorrect application can be recovered, penalties and interest may be imposed and further refund applications suspended.

10.2.3 Applications by UK businesses to other Member States

In order to make a claim to another Member State a UK business must log onto its VAT Government Gateway and compile the claim. The applicant will need to have the VAT 4 "Certificate of Registration" and a copy of the last VAT return to hand and will need to follow the on-screen instructions. An activation PIN number will be mailed to the business address registered with HMRC within set time limits (currently 7-10 days). Once this is received they will then have 28 days from the date of the letter to activate the service.

In order to make a claim the UK business must be a taxable person registered for VAT in the UK or in the Isle of Man must meet all of the following conditions:

(a) they must not be registered, liable or eligible to be registered in the MSR; and
(b) they must not have any fixed establishment, seat of economic activity, place of business or other residence in the MSR; and
(c) during the refund period they must not have supplied any goods or services in the MSR with the exception of:
   (i) transport services and services ancillary to them; or
   (ii) any goods or services where VAT is payable by the person to whom the supply is made.

For a UK VAT group where the group has member companies in the MSR the refund scheme may only be used to claim VAT incurred by companies that are not established in and do not make supplies in the MSR.

Applications will be subjected to automated registration verifications by HMRC before being forwarded electronically to the MSR (and will only be forwarded to the MSR if these checks are satisfactory). If the checks are not satisfactory the application will be rejected by the electronic portal and the applicant will receive an appropriate error message.

In respect of VAT group registrations, the application will be forwarded in the name of the Representative Member. Where the application relates to VAT incurred by other group members, it may be accompanied by a covering note explaining that these companies are members of the same VAT group. This note can be sent using the 'attachment' facility for invoices and may reduce requests for additional information from the MSR. The time limits and claim thresholds are the same as those set out in section **10.2.2**.

10.2.4 Refunds in the UK for EU businesses

In addition to the rules set out in **10.2.2** and **10.2.3** there is no maximum limit for an individual claim to the UK, but there are minimum limits below which claims cannot be submitted. These are:

- £295 where the application covers less than a calendar year, but not less than three calendar months; and

- £35 where the application covers a calendar year or the remainder of a calendar year.

In context these limits mean where the claim exceeds £295 more than three months and less than 12 months must have elapsed and the claim must fall entirely within the relevant calendar year or if a shorter period only where a claim has already been made for an earlier period within that calendar year.

For claims between £35 and £295 the claim must be for a full calendar year or if for a shorter period ending on 31 December, where an earlier claim of at least £295 has already has been made in that calendar year.

£295 is approximately €400. The interim and annual limits can be checked on the TIC (Taxation & Information Communication) database on the Europa website at http://ec.europa.eu/taxation_customs/tic/.

In the UK VAT can be claimed on goods and services purchased during the refund period, and VAT on goods imported into the UK during the refund period except:
- amounts of VAT that have been incorrectly invoiced, or where VAT has been charged on the dispatch of goods to another Member State, or the export of goods outside the EU;
- VAT on the purchase of a motor car;
- VAT on goods and services used for business entertainment – however, VAT on entertainment for overseas customers may be reclaimed, but only if it is of a very basic nature;
- VAT on goods and services used for non-business activities; and
- 50% of the total VAT charged when hiring or leasing a motor car.

Applicants that are partially exempt in the MSE must only claim the proportion of VAT that relates to their taxable supplies. Where a Member State operates the 'pro-rata' system in respect of taxable and exempt supplies, and pro-rata rate changes from one year to the next, the applicant should submit a pro-rata adjustment through their own tax authority's electronic facility.

Details of the application and the process are provided in section 4 of Notice 723A.

10.3 Non-EU scheme

The scheme is for businesses established in a country which is not a Member State of the EU where goods or services have been purchased in the UK (or any other country) for example, if attending a trade fair. Businesses that are not registered for VAT in the UK cannot treat this VAT as input tax, but they may be able to use the scheme to reclaim VAT charged on imports into the UK or purchases of goods and services used in the UK.

Only businesses registered in a non-EU country can use the scheme and only where they are not:

- registered, liable or eligible to be registered for VAT in the UK - Notice 700/1: *Should I be registered for VAT?* explains these requirements and it can be obtained online[2] at or from the HMRC VAT Helpline on 0300 200 3700;
- have no place of business or other residence in the EU; and
- do not make any supplies in the UK (other than transport services related to the international carriage of goods, or services where VAT is payable by the person in the UK to whom the supply is made); and
- the applicant's own country allows similar concessions to UK traders in respect of its own turnover taxes. [The application will only be refused on these grounds if the applicant's own country has a scheme for refunding these taxes, but refuses to allow UK traders to use it].

10.3.1 Eligible goods and services

Not everything that the applicant has paid VAT on can be reclaimed. There is a long list of goods and services where VAT recovery is denied, these being:
- 'non-business' supplies. These are supplies made for private or non-economic reasons. However, if a supply covers both business and non-business use, VAT can be reclaimed on the business element of the supply;
- any supply used or to be used to make a supply in the United Kingdom for example hiring plant and equipment;
- the supply or importation of most ordinary business cars. Only 50% of the VAT incurred on the hire of lease of a car for mixed business and private purposes is allowed;
- certain second-hand goods, such as cars and antiques for which no tax invoice will be issued;
- business entertainment expenses. However, as an exception, VAT on entertainment for overseas customers may be reclaimed, but only if it is of a very basic nature;
- export of goods – but these will be zero-rated, provided the supplier has the necessary evidence;
- goods and services, such as hotel accommodation bought for resale which are for the direct benefit of travellers – termed a "Tour Operators' Margin Scheme supply"; and
- any supply used or to be used to make an exempt supply outside the United Kingdom. For this purpose an exempt supply is a supply described as exempt in Schedule 9 to the VAT Act 1994, whether or not the place of the supply is in the UK.

Where goods are imported into the UK VAT can be reclaimed provided there is no other VAT relief available at import. However, if, as a result of importing

---

[2]www.gov.uk/government/publications/vat-notice-7001-should-i-be-registered-for-vat/

the goods, they are used to make a supply in the UK the scheme cannot be used.

There is no maximum amount that can be claimed, but the UK has set minimum claim amounts that can be refunded. An application should cover any VAT incurred over a period of at least three months, but not more than the full prescribed year. When the application is for a period covering less than 12 months the total amount of VAT claimed must not be less than £130. The application can cover less than three months if this is all that remains of the prescribed year. In that case, or when the application is for the full 12 months of the prescribed year, the amount of VAT claimed must not be less than £16. Claims can also be made for items missed on earlier applications as long as they related to VAT charged in the year of the application.

The claim must be made no later than six months after the end of the 'prescribed year' in which the VAT was incurred. The prescribed year is the 12 months from 1 July to 30 June of the following calendar year, so the claim must be made by 31 December following that 30 June.

Applications

Applications for refund should be submitted on Form VAT 65A.[3] The Application must be completed in English, using block capitals, and sent with the **original** copy of all invoices included on the application to:

HM Revenue and Customs
Compliance Centres
VAT Overseas Repayment Unit
S1250
Benton Park View
Newcastle upon Tyne
NE98 1YX

When a new applicant submits their first application they must also include a certificate from the official authority in their own country showing that they are registered for business purposes in that country. When applying for the certificate, the applicant must ensure that it shows all the information that HMRC will need in order to process the refund application. For example, if the invoices are made out in a company's trading style, the certificate must show this as well as the name of the person registered.

The certificate must contain all of the following information and be an original certificate since a photocopy is not acceptable:
- the name, the address and official stamp of the authorising body; and
- the applicant's own name and address; and
- the nature of the business; and

---

[3]www.gov.uk/government/uploads/system/uploads/attachment_data/file/480833/VAT65A_11_15.pdf

RECOVERY OF VAT "CROSS BORDER"

- the business registration number.

Applicants can choose to use Form VAT 66A.[4] Each certificate is valid for 12 months from its date of issue and will cover any applications made during that year. Once the certificate has expired a new one will need to be sent to HMRC with the next application.

To reclaim the VAT paid the application must include correctly completed invoices, vouchers or receipts from the UK suppliers showing:
- an identifying number; and
- the supplier's name, address and VAT registration number; and
- the applicant's name and address; and
- details of goods or services supplied; and
- the date of supply; and
- the cost of the goods or services (excluding VAT); and
- the rate of VAT; and
- the amount of VAT charged.

If the value of a supply is £250 or less (including VAT), the invoice need only show:
- the supplier's name, address and VAT registration number; and
- the date of supply; and
- details of goods or services supplied; and
- the cost of the goods or services (including VAT); and
- the rate of VAT.

If claims are being made for goods imported into the UK the applicant must have the VAT copy of the import entry (Form C79) or other Customs documents showing the amount of VAT paid at importation. Originals of all invoices and import documents must be provided since copies are not acceptable.

The refund will be made within six months of HMRC having received a satisfactory application. Providing the application is satisfactory, the invoices showing the VAT charged will be returned as soon as the application is authorised for payment.

Full details of the claim methodology and process are provided in section 6 of Notice 723A.

---

[4] www.gov.uk/government/uploads/system/uploads/attachment_data/file/372666/vat66a.pdf

11 Intra-EU Transactions – Supplies of Services

11.1 Introduction

The EU VAT system is based on the "Destination principle", namely that the VAT should be finally paid to the government of the country in which the consumer who buys the goods lives – see Introduction in **Chapter 1**. So if company 'A' in the UK sells something to company 'B' in France, the VAT should be transferred from the UK to France. To achieve this, the transaction between the UK and France is exempt from VAT (zero-rated in UK law). Similarly, when a French company buys goods in another Member State, the VAT is payable in France under the Reverse Charge (for services) or Acquisition VAT (for goods).

However, for services, the full Destination system is not yet in place despite extensive changes designed to bring more and more supplies of services within the principle. Therefore, in the last five years the EC has implemented wholesale changes to the "Place of Supply of Services" (POS) rules for a wide range of services. The changes to the POS of services rules were implemented in a number of phases, the first being introduced in the VAT Place of Supply of Services Directive (EC Directive 2008/08/EC). These changes were agreed by all Member States as part of the VAT Package of legislation adopted in February 2008.

The widespread changes were staged to allow businesses time to accommodate them and amend their accounting systems etc. The first tranche of changes occurred on 1 January 2010 with the introduction of substantial changes to the "basic rule" or 'the general rule' for business to business ('B2B') supplies and a reduction in the number of exceptions to the general rule – see **11.2.1**. Further changes came into effect on 1 January 2011, 1 January 2013 and 1 January 2015. Any supply of services that falls outside of the general rules is treated as a supply within one of the "special rules".

Where the POS of services is in a Member State of the EU, that supply is subject to the VAT rules of that Member State and not those of any other country. For a UK supplier, if the POS is in another Member State, such supplies are said to be 'outside the scope' of UK VAT. Where the POS of services is outside the EU, that supply is made outside the EU and is therefore not liable to VAT in any Member State (although local taxes may apply). Such supplies are said to be 'outside the scope' of both UK and EU VAT.

However, as well as the two general rules for 'B2B' and 'B2C' supplies of services, because of the many and varied exceptions for different types of services, the complex POS rules now mean that either the supplier or the customer is liable to account for the VAT on the supply and potentially in the country where those supplies are "consumed" or otherwise termed "used and enjoyed". This largely depends upon the status of the recipient and whether they are receiving the services in a business capacity or for their own personal consumption either as a private individual or as "a non-taxable legal person".

Additionally, even though the supplier might still be the person responsible for accounting for the VAT due on the supply, they might have a liability to be registered for VAT in the Member State of consumption and account for the VAT to that tax authority. Furthermore, there are POS "use and enjoyment" rules that cater for B2B supplies used and enjoyed in or outside the EU, but the POS would, without the use and enjoyment rules, result in a distortion to the destination principle.

Underpinning all of this, however, is the fundamental need to understand the "place of belonging" rules that govern the place(s) from where the supplies are actually being made and are being received – see **11.1.2**. Therefore, suppliers in particular, but also recipients of services, can only determine whether any UK or EU VAT is due and by whom when they have correctly identified and understood all of the following:

- The nature of the supply. This is not always easy to determine so the Commission has provided guidance notes on the headings and definitions for different types of services, but Member States interpret the guidance as they see fit and there can be variations between Member States on what is actually being supplied, the place where it should be taxed and by whom. This can lead to distortions or 'double taxation' where more than one Member State demands the VAT is accounted for to their own Member State or no taxation – seen as a "VAT planning haven";
- The VAT status of the recipient i.e. a business or a "non-taxable legal person" (or a personal consumer);
- Whether the recipient, if a business, is buying the services for use in and by the business, or it is buying it for 'non-business' consumption, for example, a UK accountant preparing a personal tax return for a director;
- If a business, is it making "taxable supplies" in its own Member State or own country (if outside the EU), defined as being a "Relevant Business Person" – see **11.2.3**;
- If the recipient is a charity or a government department, a non-governmental organisation ("NGO"), or a pure holding company etc. and whether it is making supplies "by way of business" if its activities consist solely of fulfilling its charitable, governmental, NGO or passive investment activities;
- The place where the supplier and the recipient are established – see **11.1.3**;
- The establishment from which the services are supplied if the supplier has more than one establishment – see **11.1.6**;
- The establishment at which the services are consumed if the recipient has more than one establishment – see **11.1.6**; and
- If any "use and enjoyment" provision applies to the particular class of services.

Commentary on the B2B general rule is provided in **11.2.1** and on the B2C general rule in **11.2.2**. Further commentary on the exceptions to both rules and then on exceptions to the 'B2B' and 'B2C' general rules are provided in **11.2.5** to **11.7** below.

11.1.1 Nature of the supply

Deciding the nature of a service may be a difficult question of fact. Every transaction must be analysed to determine what the supplier and the recipient believe is actually being transacted. Contracts, agreements, heads of terms and the supplier's terms and conditions should be examined to see what is being supplied, how it is being "packaged" and how it is being delivered.

If a service consists of more than one element, for example, "long-distance learning" where there is 'on-line access' to teaching materials and physical delivery of course notes, textbooks etc. it might even be necessary to determine whether the supply is one of services with ancillary goods (the textbooks) or a physical product with ancillary access to learning materials and marking etc. Alternatively, when does education or training become consultancy work, especially if training is provided as part of the project?

Additionally, if the services consist of a "product" that can only be received by the recipient accessing it 'on-line' by clicking on a hyperlink or accessing the supplier's server or database and downloading it to their own server/computer, then it will fall within the complex rules for e-services and the **"Mini One Stop Shop"** or **"VAT-MOSS"** which require the supplier to register for VAT in a chosen Member State and charge and account for VAT applicable on all sales to private consumers throughout the EU using that VAT registration – see **11.3** below.

With regard to 'non-electronic' services, considerable difficulty can be encountered when determining the nature of the supply as found in a wide variety of transactions, including:
- cultural, artistic, sporting, scientific, educational, entertainment or similar activities;
- "admissions" to cultural, artistic, sporting, scientific, educational, entertainment or similar activities;
- sporting services;
- services "directly related to land";
- the intra-EU transport of goods and other movements of goods;
- passenger transport; and
- restaurant and catering services.

The sections that follow provide a comprehensive commentary on these and other supplies of services.

11.1.2 "Place of Belonging"

For the purposes of either making or receiving supplies of services a supplier and/or recipient belongs in a particular country when any of the following apply:
- they have a "business establishment" or some other "fixed establishment" in, for example, the UK and nowhere else;
- they have a business establishment in for example the UK and other fixed establishments in other countries, but the business establishment in the UK is "most directly connected" with making or receiving the supplies in question;
- they have a fixed establishment in for example the UK and a business establishment and/or fixed establishments overseas, but the UK establishment is most directly connected with making or receiving the supplies in question;
- they have no business or fixed establishment anywhere, but their "usual place of residence" is, for example, the UK.

11.1.3 Meaning of "business establishment"

The business establishment is the principal place of business and is usually the head office, headquarters or 'seat' from which the business is run. There can be only one such place which may be an office, showroom or factory. Increasingly, HMRC are taking the view that an agency in the UK acting for a non-UK business where it can bind its principal can effectively create a fixed establishment for UK VAT purposes for the business, but they are also stating that this does not create a permanent establishment for direct tax purposes – see **11.1.4**.

HMRC provide the following examples of business establishments in Notice 741: *Place of Supply of Services* (2010 edition, referred to in this chapter):
- a business has its headquarters in the UK and branches in France, Italy and Germany. Its business establishment is the headquarters in the UK; and
- a company is incorporated in the UK, but trades entirely from its head office in Bermuda. Its business establishment is the head office in Bermuda.

11.1.4 Meaning of "fixed establishment"

A fixed establishment is an establishment other than the business establishment, which has permanently present the "technical and human resources" necessary for providing or receiving services. A business may have several fixed establishments, which may include a branch of a business or an agency.

If it suits them tax authorities can seek to argue that a business (either when supplying services or when receiving services) has created a fixed establishment where a branch or agency is authorised to conclude contracts and to represent the business. It is essential that such branches or agents are prevented from doing these things if the business does not intend to create any fixed establishments outside of its business establishment.

In contrast, in the UK, HMRC provide the example of an overseas television company sending staff and equipment to the UK to film for a week, but where there is only a temporary presence of human and technical resources, as not creating a fixed establishment in the UK.

If, as well as the business establishment, there are establishments in more than one country, suppliers and recipients need to determine which one is most directly connected with a supply.

These matters can present serious problems where, for example, suppliers of 'IT' or pan-European auditing and accounting services provide services to the head office in, say, Geneva Switzerland, but for 'roll-out' to affiliates and branches across any of the 28 EU Member States and possibly outside the EU.

In such circumstances where is/are the place(s) most directly connected with the supply? Cases have gone as far as the CJEU as Member States fight to contest the position each seeking the revenue.

In the UK, in Notice 741A section 3.4.1 (2010 edn) HMRC has provided the following examples of what are deemed to be fixed establishments:
- an overseas business sets up a branch comprising staff and offices in the UK to provide services. The UK branch is a fixed establishment;
- a company with a business establishment overseas owns a property in the UK which it leases to tenants. The property does not in itself create a fixed establishment. However, if the company has UK offices and staff or appoints a UK agency to carry on its business by managing the property, this creates a fixed establishment in the UK;
- an overseas business contracts with UK customers to provide services. It has no human or technical resources in the UK and therefore sets up a UK subsidiary to act in its name to provide those services. The overseas business has a fixed establishment in the UK created by the agency of the subsidiary;
- a company is incorporated in the UK, but trades entirely overseas from its head office in the USA, which is its business establishment. The UK registered office is a fixed establishment;
- a UK company acts as the operating member of a consortium for offshore exploitation of oil or gas using a fixed production platform. The rig is a fixed establishment of the operating member.

11.1.5 Meaning of "usual place of residence"

If a limited company or other corporate body has neither a business establishment nor other fixed establishment in any country, its usual place of residence (in other words, its place of belonging) is where it is legally constituted.

INTRA-EU TRANSACTIONS – SUPPLY OF SERVICES

Individuals receiving supplies in a private capacity are treated as belonging in the country where they have their usual place of residence. An individual has only one usual place of residence at any point in time. Individuals are normally resident in the country where they have set up home with their family and are in full-time employment. They are not resident in a country they are only visiting as a tourist.

In Notice 741A section 3.5.1 HMRC provides the following examples of usual places of residence:
- the board of directors of a company incorporated in Bermuda, which has no business or fixed establishment anywhere in the world, meet from time to time in different countries, including the UK. The company belongs in Bermuda where it is incorporated;
- a person lives in the UK, but commutes to France daily for work. He belongs in the UK;
- overseas' forces personnel on a tour of duty in the UK live in rented accommodation with their families. They have homes overseas to which they periodically return on leave. They belong in the UK throughout their tour of duty.

HMRC say that for VAT purposes, persons who have not been granted a right or permission to remain in the UK should be treated as belonging in their country of origin. This will apply to, for example, asylum seekers and those entering the UK without permission.

In these circumstances, the country in which individuals have their usual or permanent place of residence can only reasonably be seen to be their country of origin unless and until they are granted the right to remain in the UK. Once an individual has been granted leave or permission to remain in the UK, they belong in the UK.

11.1.6 More than one place of establishment
If the supplier and/or the recipient have establishments in more than one country, it is essential to examine, **for every transaction,** the places at which establishment those supplies are made from or received at.

For each supply of services, the supplier and recipient are regarded as belonging in the country where the establishment most directly connected with that particular supply is located. Therefore, to be able to decide which establishment is most directly connected with the supply, all the facts must be examined and a judgment made, often on the balance of probabilities or according to the weight of evidence. These facts should take account of:
- for suppliers, the establishment from which the services are actually provided;
- for recipients, the establishment at which the services are actually consumed, effectively used or enjoyed;

- for both parties which establishment appears on the contracts, correspondence and invoices;
- for both parties the places where the directors or others who entered into the contract are permanently based; and
- for both parties at which establishment decisions are taken and controls are exercised over the performance of the contracts.

Despite all of the facts, even if the contractual position is different, normally it is the establishment actually providing or receiving the supply of services which is to be treated as the establishment most directly connected with the supply. In Notice 741A HMRC has provided the following examples to assist suppliers and recipients where there is more than one establishment.

Suppliers
- a company whose business establishment is in France contracts with a UK bank to supply French-speaking staff for the bank's international desk in London. The French company also has a fixed establishment in the UK created by a branch, which provides staff to other customers. The French establishment deals directly with the UK bank without any involvement of the UK branch. The staff are supplied by the French establishment; and
- an overseas business establishment contracts with private customers in the UK to provide information. The services are provided and invoiced by its UK branch. Customers' day-to-day contact is with the UK branch and they pay the UK branch. The services are actually supplied from the UK branch which is a fixed establishment.

Recipients
- a UK supplier contracts to supply advertising services. Its customer has its business establishment in Austria and a fixed establishment in the UK created by its branch. Although day-to-day contact on routine administrative matters is between the supplier and the UK branch, the Austrian establishment takes all artistic and other decisions about the advertising. The supplies are received at the overseas establishment;
- a UK accountant supplies accountancy services to a UK incorporated company which has its business establishment abroad. However, the services are received in connection with the company's UK tax obligations and therefore the UK fixed establishment, created by the registered office, receives the supply; and
- a customer has a business establishment in the UK and a fixed establishment in the USA created by its branch. The UK establishment contracts a UK company to provide staff to the USA branch. The supplier invoices the UK establishment and is paid by them. The services are most directly used by the USA branch and therefore are received at the overseas establishment.

11.1.7 Contradictory evidence

Despite all of the above guidance, sometimes suppliers can be utterly confused by the matrix of establishments presented by the recipient. In these

circumstances it is often helpful to take a 'step back' and consider the following:
- the clear use of the supplier's services at a particular establishment, for example, the lease of equipment for use at that establishment;
- taking instructions from a particular establishment; and
- the delivery of any 'products' (like a master tape) to a particular establishment.

11.1.8 Request for a "Non-Statutory Clearance" by HMRC

As a 'last resort', having conducted all of the above research and fact-finding, if suppliers have lingering doubts about the nature and place of supply of their services they should contact HMRC for further clarification.

This is because, if HMRC challenge the POS and determine that UK VAT is due on a supply of services where VAT has not been charged and brought to account by the supplier, HMRC's inclination will always be to assess for the VAT considered to have been lost. Furthermore, if suppliers have charged and accounted for VAT where the POS is properly outside the scope of UK VAT, then large overpayments can also result.

Example 1

A French company acted as an intermediary in a supply of services between suppliers of car parking and the suppliers' customers wishing to park their cars in relevant, economically-priced, car parks. Most of the car parking suppliers were established and the customers were resident in non-French places of belonging. The French company was paid a commission by the suppliers of the car parking, but also took deposits direct from the customers as advance payments for the actual car parking and these advances were in lieu of the commission chargeable (the advances were taken to secure payment of the commission due to the supplier as the non-French suppliers could have delayed payment of the commission or not made payment at all if the full payment for the car parking had been made to the suppliers in the first instance).

Because the advances were received directly from the customers, the French company considered it was supplying its own services to those customers in a 'B2C' capacity which contractually would have meant it found the car parks on behalf of the customers. However, in reality, in accordance with its Terms of Business it actually found for the car parks on behalf of the customers who wished to park their car parks and therefore the French company was acting in a 'B2B' capacity for the suppliers.

The fact that the supply of car parking is mostly a compulsory taxable supply in nearly all EU Member States did not mean that the French company was making a compulsory taxable supply of car parking itself. The description of the services as "car parking" was something of a misnomer and it was essential to examine what exactly was being supplied by the French company. Accordingly, the services were outside the scope of French VAT under the General Rule for B2B supplies – **see 11.2.1**

Example 2
The supplier was providing "spiritual readings" and "life counselling" services via the internet to private consumers outside the EU. He was treating the supplies as outside the scope of UK VAT as 'B2C' general rule service (see **11.2.2**). On examining the precise services being supplied, the closest heading of 'B2C' Relevant Services into which the services could be placed (see **11.4**) could have been said to be "the provision of information", but HMRC argued and the First Tier Tribunal (Tax Chamber) agreed, that the services could not fit within this or any other heading. Accordingly, the services were liable to UK VAT.

11.2 The General Rules

The distinction between supplies of services provided to businesses and to private consumers ensures that for the former the recipient accounts for any VAT due under the Reverse Charge (see **Chapter 12**) in their own Member State (or there is no reverse charge for a non-EU recipient) and for the latter it is the supplier, either in their own Member State, usually the Member State where they have their business establishment (see **11.1.2 to 11.1.6** above), in both cases subject to any variations for use and enjoyment within and outside the EU.

11.2.1 B2B General Rule

The general rule or default rule for a 'B2B' supply of services changed on 1 January 2010 to mean that the recipient, classed as a "Relevant Business Person" (see **11.2.3**) accounts for any VAT due on the supply under the Reverse Charge – see **12.3**. This rule applies to all cross-border B2B supplies whether the recipient is inside or outside the EU. The supply is not zero-rated or exempt, but is outside the scope of UK VAT.

The general rule attempts to prevent abuse or avoidance by the supplier, for example, charging VAT to the recipient and not accounting for the VAT to its own Member State and to remove the need for "mutual recovery" under the EU 8th and 13th Directives (see **Chapter 10**) by the recipient submitting a claim for refund of the VAT paid to the supplier from the supplier's Member State tax authority (the Member State of Refund).

A number of conditions must be present for the general rule to apply. These are:

- the recipient must be a business that qualifies as a Relevant Business Person – see **11.2.3**;
- the recipient must be using the services for the purposes of its own business; and
- the recipient must comply with various administrative matters such as when registered in an EU Member State providing a VAT number to the supplier (although this is not strictly necessary to treat the supply as outside the scope of UK VAT).

11.2.2 B2C General Rule

The general rule or default rule is that the POS is at the supplier's location, i.e. where he 'belongs' – see **11.1.2 - 11.1.6** above. Thus, 'B2C' supplies of services are still usually liable to VAT in the Member State where the supplier is based.

If the supplier has establishments both inside and outside the EU, for example in the UK and in Jersey or Guernsey or Gibraltar etc. or in more than one Member State, then it is vital to determine from which of those establishments the supplier is providing the services. This can be made more difficult where the supplier might have staff and resources in both/all establishments or where parts of the supplies are made or "assembled" using both/all establishments.

11.2.3 "Relevant Business Person"

Under VAT Act 1994 s.7A(4) a Relevant Business Person in relation to a supply of services supplied 'B2B' means the recipient is:

(a) a "taxable person" within the meaning of art. 9 of Directive 2006/112; or
(b) registered under VATA 1994; or
(c) identified for the purposes of VAT in accordance with the law of a Member State other than the UK; or
(d) registered in the Isle of Man under an Act of Tynwald for the purposes of any tax imposed by or under an Act of Tynwald which corresponds to VAT; and

the services are received by the person otherwise than wholly for private purposes.

Art 9 of Directive 2006/112 (the Principal VAT Directive) defines a "Taxable Person" as:

> 'Taxable person' shall mean any person who, independently, carries out in any place any economic activity, whatever the purpose or results of that activity.
>
> Any activity of producers, traders or persons supplying services, including mining and agricultural activities and activities of the professions, shall be regarded as 'economic activity'. The exploitation of tangible or intangible property for the purposes of obtaining income therefrom on a continuing basis shall in particular be regarded as an economic activity.
>
> In addition to the persons referred to in paragraph 1, any person who, on an occasional basis, supplies a new means of transport, which is dispatched or transported to the customer by the vendor or the customer, or on behalf of the vendor or the customer, to a destination outside the territory of a Member State but within the territory of the Community, shall be regarded as a taxable person.

If the recipient says they are registered for VAT in their own Member State (or another Member State) the supplier should ensure that the recipient is in fact VAT-registered through the normal checks, i.e. evidence of a valid VAT number.

If the recipient is not actually registered for VAT, so it is unable to provide a VAT number to the supplier, then the supplier must undertake normal due diligence checks of the recipient to satisfy themselves that the recipient is, in fact, a business and is buying the services for the purposes of their business. The supplier must check and validate such evidence as the recipient's Certificate of Incorporation and/or company number if it is a corporate body, their published annual accounts, their websites and internet presence, headed stationery, any publicly available data such as trade press and marketing information, and anything else that would lead to the conclusion that the recipient is actively carrying on a business.

The supplier must retain all the evidence they have gathered to prove to HMRC why they decided to not charge VAT on the supply if indeed this is the decision taken. The evidence must include the checks made on the EU "VIES" system where the recipient has quoted a VAT registration number – see section **9.3**. These registration details are also required to enable the supplier to complete an EC Sales List (ESL) for cross-border services supplied to EU VAT-registered recipients – see section **12.2.2**.

In the UK HMRC state that provided a charity or a Government department or NGO is making **some** supplies by way of business, the supplier can accept that the services being supplied are being made in all cases to a Relevant Business Person and can therefore be treated under the general 'B2B' rule.

For other recipients, identifying that the recipient is actually buying a service or services for a non-business purpose can be difficult especially where the services could quite easily be used in both business and private capacities such as legal and accounting services, for example, preparation of a director/shareholder's tax return.

Even where the recipient in its Member State might be prevented from reclaiming the Reverse Charge VAT as input tax, for example because it falls within any "business entertainment" heading, the supplier can still treat the supplies as outside the scope of VAT, quoting the recipient's own (or another) EU Member State VAT number, because the recipient is still buying the services for a business purpose such as sales and marketing.

If a business customer has an establishment in more than one Member State, the supplier must ascertain at which establishment the customer is receiving or using the supply. A supply may be ordered by one establishment, paid for by another, but supplied to a yet another establishment (or establishments).

A single contract may require supplies to be made to different establishments, e.g. branches or subsidiaries. The transaction is treated as several separate supplies, each made to the various establishments. These establishments may be in different Member States, outside the EU or in the same Member State as the supplier. Each creates different VAT requirements e.g. whether to charge VAT and what to include on EC Sales Lists.

INTRA-EU TRANSACTIONS – SUPPLY OF SERVICES

11.2.4 Special POS rules

As explained in **11.2.1.** and **11.2.2** the POS for a 'B2B' general rule service is the recipient's country and for a 'B2C' general rule service is the supplier's country. There are, however, a number of services where the general rules do not apply resulting in the supplies being taxed in the place of consumption, with the relevant revenue flowing to the tax authority in the recipient's Member State if used or consumed in an EU country. These special POS rules are explained in detail in **11.2.5** to **11.7** and cover:

- services supplied in connection with "immovable property" (land) – see **11.2.5**;
- passenger transport – see **11.2.6**;
- the 'short-term' and 'long-term' hiring of a 'means of transport' e.g. car hire – see **11.2.7**;
- the hiring of any goods other than a means of transport e.g. industrial plant, scaffolding for construction projects – see **11.2.8**;
- services supplied where they are performed such as cultural, artistic, sporting, scientific, educational, entertainment or similar activities (including fairs and exhibitions) and services that are "ancillary" to these services including the services of the organisers of such activities – see **11.2.9**;
- "admission" to cultural, artistic, sporting, scientific, educational, entertainment or similar events (including fairs and exhibitions) – see **11.2.10**;
- restaurant and catering services – see **11.2.11**;
- restaurant and catering services on board a ship, aircraft or train in connection with the transportation of passengers – see **11.2.12**;
- services within the scope of the "Tour Operators' Margin Scheme" (TOMS) – see **11.2.13**;
- the transportation of goods and the "intra-Community" (intra-EU) transport of goods – see **11.2.14**;
- "ancillary transport services" – see **11.2.15**;
- telecommunication services or radio or television broadcasting services and "Electronically Supplied Services" (ESS) – see **11.2.16**;
- "Mini One Stop Shop" or MOSS" – see **11.3**
- "intellectual-type" services and other "intangibles" – see **11.4** - such as:
    - transfers and assignments of copyright, patents, licences, trademarks and similar rights – **11.4.1**,
    - the acceptance of any obligation to refrain from pursuing or exercising (in whole or in part) any business activity or any rights within last bullet – **11.4.2**;
    - advertising services – **11.4.3**,
    - services of consultants, engineers, consultancy bureaux, lawyers, accountants, and similar services, data processing and provision of information, other than any services relating to land – **11.4.4**,

INTRA-EU TRANSACTIONS – SUPPLY OF SERVICES

- o banking, financial and insurance services (including reinsurance), other than the provision of safe deposit facilities – **11.4.5**,
- o the provision of access to, or transmission or distribution through:
  i. a natural gas system situated within the territory of a member State or any network connected to such a system, or
  ii. an electricity system, or
  iii. a network through which heat or cooling is supplied, and the provision of other directly linked services – **11.4.6**;
- o the supply of staff – **11.4.7**;
- o the letting on hire of goods other than means of transport – **11.4.8**; and
- o BTE services – **11.4.9**;
- "Emissions Allowances" – **11.5**;
- intermediaries' or agents' services – **11.6**; and
- valuation services and work on goods – **11.7**.

Additionally, there are "use and enjoyment" rules for a range of services that vary the POS to the place where the services are actually consumed. Use and enjoyment rules apply to a number of services including telecommunication services or radio or television broadcasting services, hire of goods and, from 2016, insurance repair services.

In the Summer Budget 2015, the UK Government announced that it would introduce a "use and enjoyment" provision to counter tax avoidance involving the provision of repair services, carried out under a contract of insurance, to insurers located outside the EU. The draft *VAT (Place of Supply of Services: Exceptions Relating to Supplies Made to Relevant Business Person) Order* 2016, was published for consultation and it explains the introduction of VAT use and enjoyment provisions for insurance repair services. HMRC invited comments to be received by 29 February 2016.

11.2.5 General exception for "land services"

Land-related services are deemed to be supplied where the land is situated. However, the services must relate directly to specific sites of land and do not include any services that only have an indirect connection with land, or if the land-related service is only an incidental part of a more comprehensive service.

'Land' includes all forms of land and property (growing crops, buildings, walls, fences, civil engineering works and other structures fixed permanently to the land or sea bed) and plant, machinery or equipment which is an installation or edifice in its own right (e.g. a refinery or fixed oil/gas production platform). Machinery installed in buildings other than as a fixture is normally not regarded as land but as goods.

Land includes:
- a specific part of the earth, on, above or below its surface, over which title or possession can be created;

- a building or construction fixed to or in the ground above or below sea level which cannot be easily dismantled or moved;
- an item making up part of a building or construction and without which it is incomplete, e.g. doors, windows, roofs, staircases and lifts; and
- equipment or machinery permanently installed in a building or construction that cannot be moved without destroying or altering the building or construction.

Therefore, a property includes buildings, civil engineering works, refineries, fixed production platforms, walls, fences or other structures fixed permanently to the land or sea bed, growing crops, trees, etc.

HMRC say that fixed North Sea oil rigs are regarded as land and are within the UK if within the territorial waters limit of twelve nautical miles. Additionally, HMRC deem the land in the Channel Tunnel to be within the UK as far as its mid-point.

Directly-related land services cover, mostly, construction, demolition and alteration of buildings and civil engineering works together with supplies by estate agents, auctioneers, architects, surveyors and engineers, *"and others"* – viewed as types of specialists dealing with land.

In fixing the POS the place where the land is situated is decisive not the place of belonging of the supplier or the recipient of the supply. Thus, if a UK architect advises a UK client about some land in France, the place of supply of the architect's services is France.

In VAT, the terminology used in the legislation dictates everything. The Tribunal, in the case of *Kenneth Richard Daunter (LON/2006/671)*, helped to clarify the meaning of the term 'land-related' where it involves professional services such as legal services supplied by a solicitor. The Appellant, a resident of Jersey, funded the purchase of a flat in the UK which was used by a different person. The Appellant entered into an agreement with the occupant that allowed them to remain in the property during their lifetime, after which vacant possession would revert to the Appellant. On the death of the occupant the Appellant took legal action against the deceased's estate to secure title to the property.

The Appellant argued that the services supplied by the solicitor were subject to the rules under the then Schedule 5 to the VAT Act 1994. That meant the place of supply was where the Appellant belonged, in Jersey. However, HMRC maintained that the place of supply was where the land was situated, the UK.

In dismissing the appeal the Tribunal concluded that, adopting the reasoning of the CJEU in *Rudi Heger GmbH (C-166/05)*, the property in question was a central and essential element and therefore the place of supply of the legal services was where the land was situated (the UK).

The Tribunal decided that the extant legislation using the words *"and others"* did not refer specifically to solicitors so such services came within *"others involved in matters relating to land"*.

The decision by the CJEU in the Rudi Heger case provided further clarification of the meaning of services related to land under what was Article 9(2)(a) of the Sixth Directive (now Article 47 VAT Directive 2006/112/EC).

Rudi Heger was a company established in Germany. In 1997 and 1998 it purchased fishing permits for the Gmunder Traun River in Austria from an Austrian company, Flyfishing Adventure GmbH. The permits gave the right to fish on certain stretches of the river during certain periods. Rudi Heger then resold the permits to customers across the EU.

Flyfishing Adventure GmbH invoiced Rudi Heger inclusive of Austrian VAT, which he then sought to recover via an 8th Directive refund claim. The Austrian authorities rejected the claim on the basis that the sale of the permits was a land-related supply under Article 9(2) (a) of the Sixth Directive, and so the VAT was incurred in making taxable supplies in Austria.

The CJEU went against the Opinion of the Advocate General (who opined that for place of supply purposes, supplies are only land-related where they involve physical or legal changes in land) and instead found that supplies of the rights to fish a section of river are land-related.

The following types of services are also deemed to be directly-related to supplies of land:
- the grant, assignment or surrender of any interest in or right over land e.g. leases, licences and tenancies;
- the grant, assignment or surrender of a personal right to call for or be granted any interest in or right over land;
- the grant, assignment or surrender of a licence to occupy land or any other contractual right exercisable over or in relation to land (including the provision of 'holiday accommodation', seasonal pitches for caravans and facilities at caravan parks for persons for whom such pitches are provided and pitches for tents and camping facilities); and
- the provision in a hotel, inn, boarding house or 'similar establishment' of sleeping accommodation or of accommodation in rooms which are provided in conjunction with sleeping accommodation or for the purpose of a supply of catering.

The POS of a right to services is the same as the place in which the supply of the services to which the right relates would be treated as made if made by the supplier of the right to the recipient of the right. The expression "right to services" in this context includes a reference to any right, option or priority with respect to the supply of services and to the supply of an interest deriving from any right to services.

INTRA-EU TRANSACTIONS – SUPPLY OF SERVICES

Because these rules do not apply where there is only an indirect connection to the land or the land-related service is merely an incidental component of a more comprehensive service it is essential to determine whether the fundamental supply is actually one of land or predominantly the land – reference the Rudi Heger CJEU case above.

'Holiday accommodation' includes any accommodation in a building, hut (including a beach hut or chalet), caravan, houseboat or tent which is advertised or held out as holiday accommodation or as suitable for holiday or leisure use. 'Similar establishment' includes premises in which there is provided furnished sleeping accommodation, whether with or without the provision of board or facilities for the preparation of food, which are used by, or held out as being suitable for use by, visitors or travellers.

According to the CJEU these POS rules also extend to the sale of 'timeshare' accommodation. The Court ruled that the taxpayer's supply, for which the enrolment, subscription and exchange fees were the consideration, was connected to the property in which the customer who wished to arrange an exchange had a right, and consequently was taxable by reference to the location of that property.

With effect from 1 January 2017 revised European legislation that will have "direct effect" in all Member States will introduce what the Commission hopes will be more certain definitions of supplies that are "land-related". Whilst the legislation is not yet implemented in the UK, HMRC have adopted it and are known to be already applying it as "policy". The Commission's guidance says:

> Services connected with immovable property shall include only those services that have a sufficiently direct connection with that property. Services shall be regarded as having a sufficiently direct connection with immovable property in the following cases:
> a. where they are derived from an immovable property and that property makes up a constituent element of the service and is central to, and essential for, the services supplied;
> b. where they are provided to, or directed towards, an immovable property, having as their object the legal or physical alteration of that property.
>
> Heads (a) and (b) above shall cover, in particular—
> (i) the drawing up of plans for a building or parts of a building designated for a particular plot of land regardless of whether or not the building is erected;
> (ii) the provision of on-site supervision or security services;
> (iii) the construction of a building on land, as well as construction and demolition work performed on a building or parts of a building;
> (iv) the construction of permanent structures on land, as well as construction and demolition work performed on permanent structures such as pipeline systems for gas, water, sewerage and the like;
> (v) work on land, including agricultural services such as tillage, sowing, watering and fertilisation;

INTRA-EU TRANSACTIONS – SUPPLY OF SERVICES

(vi) surveying and assessment of the risk and integrity of immovable property;

(vii) the valuation of immovable property, including where such service is needed for insurance purposes, to determine the value of a property as collateral for a loan or to assess risk and damages in disputes;

(viii) the leasing or letting of immovable property (other than for the provision of advertising), including the storage of goods for which a specific part of the property is assigned for the exclusive use of the customer;

(ix) the provision of accommodation in the hotel sector or in sectors with a similar function, such as holiday camps or sites developed for use as camping sites, including the right to stay in a specific place resulting from the conversion of timeshare usage rights and the like;

(x) the assignment or transfer of rights other than those covered by points (viii) and (ix) to use the whole or parts of an immovable property, including the licence to use part of a property, such as the granting of fishing and hunting rights or access to lounges in airports, or the use of an infrastructure for which tolls are charged, such as a bridge or tunnel;

(xi) the maintenance, renovation and repair of a building or parts of a building, including work such as cleaning, tiling, papering and parqueting;

(xii) the maintenance, renovation and repair of permanent structures such as pipeline systems for gas, water, sewerage and the like;

(xiii) the installation or assembly of machines or equipment which, upon installation or assembly, qualify as immovable property;

(xiv) the maintenance and repair, inspection and supervision of machines or equipment if those machines or equipment qualify as immovable property;

(xv) property management other than portfolio management of investments in real estate consisting of the operation of commercial, industrial or residential real estate by or on behalf of the owner of the property;

(xvi) intermediation in the sale, leasing or letting of immovable property and in the establishment or transfer of certain interests in immovable property or rights in rem over immovable property (whether or not treated as tangible property), other than intermediation in the provision of hotel accommodation or accommodation in sectors with a similar function, such as holiday camps or sites developed for use as camping sites, if the intermediary is acting in the name and on behalf of another person;

(xvii) legal services relating to the transfer of a title to immovable property, to the establishment or transfer of certain interests in immovable property or rights in rem over immovable property (whether or not treated as tangible property), such as notary work, or to the drawing up of a contract to sell or acquire immovable property, even if the underlying transaction resulting in the legal alteration of the property is not carried through.

The provision of land-related services does not extend to—

- the drawing up of plans for a building or parts of a building if not designated for a particular plot of land;
- the storage of goods in an immovable property if no specific part of the immovable property is assigned for the exclusive use of the customer;

- the provision of advertising, even if it involves the use of immovable property;
- intermediation in the provision of hotel accommodation or accommodation in sectors with a similar function, such as holiday camps or sites developed for use as camping sites, if the intermediary is acting in the name and on behalf of another person;
- the provision of a stand location at a fair or exhibition site together with other related services to enable the exhibitor to display items, such as the design of the stand, transport and storage of the items, the provision of machines, cable laying, insurance and advertising;
- the installation or assembly, the maintenance and repair, the inspection or the supervision of machines or equipment which is not, or does not become, part of the immovable property;
- portfolio management of investments in real estate;
- legal services other than those covered by point (xvii) above, connected to contracts, including advice given on the terms of a contract to transfer immovable property, or to enforce such a contract, or to prove the existence of such a contract, where such services are not specific to a transfer of a title on an immovable property.

Where equipment is put at the disposal of a customer with a view to carrying out work on immovable property, that transaction shall only be a land-related supply of services if the supplier assumes responsibility for the execution of the work. A supplier who provides the customer with equipment together with sufficient staff for its operation with a view to carrying out work shall be presumed to have assumed responsibility for the execution of that work. The presumption that the supplier has the responsibility for the execution of the work may be rebutted by any relevant means in fact or law.

Previously, in HMRC Brief 22/2012 HMRC announced changes to the POS for some specific supplies of land-related services as follows:
- stands at exhibitions and conferences;
- the storage of goods; and
- access to airport lounges.

11.2.5.1 Stands at exhibitions and conferences
In HMRC Brief 22/2012 HMRC announced a change in policy to state that stand space that is supplied *"with accompanying services as a package"* is no longer treated as a land-related service. Accompanying services provided as part of a package includes the design and erection of a temporary stand, security, power, telecommunications, and hire of machinery or publicity material.

11.2.5.2 Storage of goods
Also in HMRC Brief 22/2012 HMRC announced a change in policy to state that the "simple" storage of goods in an open warehouse or other open space by a provider of storage is not a land-related service and it is treated as falling

within the general POS rule. In such cases supplies to business customers who belong outside the UK are not liable to UK VAT as the supply falls under the B2B general rule – see **11.2.1**.

HMRC added that where the goods are stored in a *'specific area'* and the owner of the goods is granted *'exclusive use'* of this area then it is still a land-related supply. Further, if the customer is granted a licence to occupy the space or is granted a lease or tenancy over the space then it is also a land-related service.

The CJEU ruled in the case of *Minister Finansów v RR Donnelley Global Turnkey Solutions Poland sp. z o.o. (Case C-155/12) [2013] BVC 342* that to be land related the storage of the goods must, in principle, be considered to constitute the principal supply. All other ancillary supplies such as receiving the goods into warehouse, their placement, issuing, unloading and loading do not, in principle, constitute an end in themselves, but are transactions which enable the customers better to enjoy the principal service. However, the CJEU also ruled that the repackaging of the goods supplied in packaging in order to create individual sets, which is provided only to certain customers, constitutes an independent principal supply if that repackaging is not necessary to ensure better storage of the goods.

11.2.5.3 Access to airport lounges

From 2 August 2012 all supplies of access by passengers to airport lounges, for example "business class" passengers awaiting embarkation, became land-related services and taxable in the country where the airport lounge is situated. Therefore, VAT, if applicable, is due in the country where the airport lounge is located. No mention was made of railway companies' first class business lounges, such as the Eurostar although this ruling should still apply.

11.2.5.4 Non-UK suppliers of "land-related" services – extension to the Reverse Charge by UK "Relevant Business Persons"

The Reverse Charge is explained in more detail in section 12. However, to avoid non-UK suppliers of land-related services registering for VAT in the UK only to charge their UK VAT-registered customers with VAT that the VAT-registered customers reclaim as input tax, HMRC has introduced legislation under which the Reverse Charge is extended to such supplies.

Under VAT Act 1994 s.8(2) the extension to the Reverse Charge for land-related services applies where:
   (a) services are supplied by a person who **belongs** in a country other than the United Kingdom; and
   (b) the recipient is a Relevant Business Person who **belongs** in the United Kingdom; and
   (c) the place of supply of the services is **inside** the United Kingdom; and
   (d) the services fall within the scope of the 'B2B' cross-border supplies (set out in Part 1 and Part 2 of VAT Act 1994 Sch 4A – Place of Supply of Service, Special Rules); and

(e) the recipient is VAT-registered in the UK.
(the Reverse Charge does not apply to any services that are included in VAT Act 1994 Schedule 9 as being exempt from VAT in the UK).

Therefore, for the supply of land-related services to be subject to the Reverse Charge the recipient must be **both** a Relevant Business Person (see **11.2.3**) and **belong** in the UK (see **11.1.2 – 11.1.6**).

HMRC at the Non-Established Taxable Persons' Unit (NETPU) in Aberdeen have confirmed this treatment where they have stated in writing that for the extension to the Reverse Charge to apply to a supply of land-related services all the criteria listed above have to be present.

A "Non-Established Taxable Person" (NETP) is a business that is not normally resident in the UK, does not have a UK establishment and, in the case of a company, is not incorporated in the UK (Notice 700/1/2014, para. 9.1).

However, in Notice 741A the HMRC guidance seemingly ignores the criterion of the recipient having to belong in the UK for the extension to the Reverse Charge to apply and appears to concentrate only on the criterion of the customer being UK VAT registered.

Notice 741A (2010 edn) states at section 18.11.1

> The extension to the reverse charge applies if you are UK VAT-registered and receive B2B supplies of the services listed in paragraph 18.11 which are supplied in the UK where your supplier belongs outside the UK.

Under VAT Act 1994 s.8(2) where the recipient is a Relevant Business Person that belongs in the UK, and they are UK VAT-registered they must account for UK VAT under the Reverse Charge. However, at section 18.11.5 of Notice 741A HMRC state that an unregistered customer receiving such services supplied in the UK need not apply the Reverse Charge and the value of the Reverse Charge services do not count as taxable supplies for the purposes of determining whether they are liable to be registered as a taxable person.

Example
US company 1 ('US1') is developing new dwellings in the UK for sale. It is not established in the UK. It will be able to zero-rate the "first grant of a major interest" in the completed dwellings where it has "person constructing" status. A major interest is the grant of the "fee simple" which is held to be the freehold and a lease (in England) that exceeds 21 years (in Scotland 20 years). "Person constructing" status means that the developer has undertaken or commissioned the undertaking of the actual building construction services. The consideration for the freehold disposal or, if a lease, the premium or the first payment of rent, is zero-rated.

To be able to grant zero-rated major interests in the completed dwellings and reclaim the UK VAT it is incurring on such expenses as legal and professional fees on a timely basis, US1 registers for UK VAT.

As part of its corporate group, a second company, Guernsey Co (G), is contracted to provide the actual building services and invoices US1 for all goods and services of construction and installation. It also is not established in the UK, also has person constructing status because it is physically working on the building project and it can zero-rate its construction services as new dwellings are being built.

But, because US1 does not belong in the UK although it is UK VAT registered, G can also register for VAT in the UK and recover the VAT it incurs on the UK construction project. Conversely, if US1 actually had a UK establishment and belonged in the UK for VAT purposes (noting HMRC's policy of seeking to argue that non-UK companies can create fixed establishments in the UK (see **11.1.4**), G would be denied UK VAT registration and US1 would apply the Reverse Charge to G's services.

However, this could prove very costly for G because by not being VAT-registered it cannot reclaim the UK VAT it is incurring under a 'normal' UK VAT return process and can only do so, in this case, under the EC 13th Directive (see **Chapter 10**). Because the 13th Directive refund process is long-winded and cumbersome it can create serious cash flow delays. HMRC at the Overseas Repayments Unit will also examine the claims in great detail and have been known to refuse claims where the precise requirements for all suppliers' invoices or, for example, the "Certificate of Status" that is required to prove that the business is a bona fide enterprise registered with its own tax authority, are not met.

Conversely, where the recipient of the services is unregistered for VAT, for example because they are a small enterprise, or they are wholly exempt such as a finance or insurance business, or a welfare or healthcare business etc., the non-UK supplier is liable to become UK VAT-registered and account for VAT on the relevant services. Because of the "nil" VAT registration threshold for supplies of services made in the UK by non-UK established businesses, even small or "one-off" supplies of services will be caught as HMRC do not have any discretion to ignore such supplies.

The purpose behind this measure is that overseas businesses are not easy for HMRC to control because their affairs are largely outside of HMRC's scrutiny. In theory, this risk is eased with a nil threshold for registration. The benefit of the threshold was removed following the CJEU case of *Schmelz v Finanzamt Waldviertel (Case C-97/09) [2012] BVC 300*.

It can therefore be seen that considerable risk exists for non-UK suppliers of land-related services that are deemed to be made in the UK. Accordingly, extreme care must be taken to identify the supplies that are to be made, whether the recipient is actually established or belongs in the UK and their VAT status.

Only then can the supplier determine if UK VAT registration is required and the impact that non-registration would have on cash flow caused by the non-recovery of potentially large amounts of VAT or its long-delayed recovery.

INTRA-EU TRANSACTIONS – SUPPLY OF SERVICES

Additionally, there will always be the need for specialist advice and potentially the appointment of a UK VAT representative to manage everything on the supplier's behalf.

11.2.5.5 Legal land interests and Options To Tax

If the services supplied by the non-UK supplier involve the granting of an interest(s) in UK real estate and they have Opted To Tax their interest(s), then HMRC insist on the non-UK suppliers actually becoming UK VAT registered, irrespective of the sales revenue and whether or not the recipient belongs in the UK.

Example

Company 'A' established in non-EU country '1' grants a lease in a manufacturing plant to company 'B' established in non-EU country '2' and by virtue of having Opted To Tax that interest company A becomes UK VAT-registered (company A is required to Opt To Tax its interest because it bought the manufacturing plant from a vendor that charged it VAT on the purchase and, without exercising the Option To Tax, company A would have been unable to reclaim that VAT).

Company B then undertakes to 'toll-manufacture' pressings for company A using the manufacturing plant leased to it by company A. Because company A has exercised the Option To Tax and is UK VAT registered, although it does not belong in the UK, company A is required to account for VAT under the Reverse Charge on company B's toll-manufacturing services and company B is denied UK VAT registration.

This in turn results in company B having to seek the refund of the VAT on the lease rentals charged by company A from HMRC under the EC 13th Directive which can cause serious cash flow issues.

11.2.6 Special rule for "passenger transport services"

Passenger transport is deemed to be supplied in the country where the transport actually takes place irrespective of the supply being made 'B2B' or 'B2C' having regard (where more than one country is involved) to the proportion of distances covered in each country.

Therefore, where passenger transport takes place in the UK, the UK is the POS. To the extent that such transport takes place outside the UK, the POS is outside the UK. Additionally, journeys which begin and end in the same country, but take place partly outside that country, are treated as taking place wholly within that country provided the ship, aircraft or vehicle does not put in, land or stop (except in an emergency or involuntarily) in any other country and this applies even if the journey is part of a longer journey involving travel to or from another country.

Accordingly, if a journey involves travel through another Member State, the supply of passenger transport will be made in that Member State to the extent that the transport takes place there.

In Notice 744A HMRC provide the following examples for various passenger transport journeys:

INTRA-EU TRANSACTIONS – SUPPLY OF SERVICES

- where a ferry transports passengers from Northern Ireland to Scotland (or vice versa), the supply is treated as taking place wholly in the UK, even though part of the journey might take place in international, or Irish waters; or
- where a ferry transports passengers from Liverpool to Dublin the part of the journey that takes place within UK waters is zero-rated, the part of the journey outside UK waters is outside the scope of UK VAT; and
- where a coach transports passengers from Northern Ireland to France, crossing the Irish sea between Ireland and Wales the section of the journey that takes place transiting Ireland is deemed to take place wholly within the UK.

For transport services occurring outside the UK, in Notice 744A section 3.3 HMRC state:

If these occur in ...	then you may ...
other member states	have to register for VAT in those member states and account for VAT at the relevant rate accordingly. if you do not have an establishment in those member states, you may need to appoint a local tax representative to account for the VAT there on your behalf.
countries outside the EU	be liable to account for any tax in those countries that is applicable on these services.
in international airspace or waters	not have to account for any tax on that part of the supply in any country.

A pleasure cruise (including a cruise wholly or partly for education or training) is regarded as the transportation of passengers so services provided as part of such a cruise are treated as supplied in the same place as the transportation of the passengers.

If passenger transport services are bought and sold *"without material alteration"* i.e. in the same condition, *"for the direct benefit of a traveller"* then they are classed as *"Margin Scheme Supplies"* and fall within the "Tour Operators' Margin Scheme" (TOMS) – see **11.2.13**. In this case their POS is the country in which the supplier is established and if established in more than one country the establishment most directly connected with the supply – see **11.1.6**.

Even if the **only** supply made by the supplier is of bought and resold passenger transport, supplied without material alteration and for the direct benefit of a traveller, it will fall within the TOMS. These difficult concepts are explained by means of the following examples:

Example 1
Supplier buys in a coach transport service consisting of the coach with a driver and all fuel and where the coach company has undertaken all the repairs, servicing and bought the road fund licence etc. The supplier provides sightseeing trips for tourists using the bought-in coach transport. This is a TOMS supply with VAT accounted for in any positive profit margin made on the actual sightseeing trip i.e. excluding all

INTRA-EU TRANSACTIONS – SUPPLY OF SERVICES

overhead or office management costs. If the supplier also buys in the admissions to the place(s) of interest visited and resells them exactly as he has bought them, then the supply of the admissions is also a margin scheme supply.

Example 2
Taking the facts in Example 1, if the supplier simply hires the coach from the coach operator and employs its own driver and fuels the coach the supply of coach transport remains outside of TOMS and falls within the POS for passenger transport. If the tourists have to pay for the admission to the places of interest themselves then this is also not a TOMS supply and the supply of coach transport is a passenger transport service and zero-rated where the coach exceeds the minimum dimensions and seating numbers for such supplies. The admissions is a supply by the place of interest directly to the tourists.

Example 3
If the facts are the same as in Example 2 but the supplier also supplies the admissions (the "trip" or "excursion") then the admissions is a principal TOMS supply and that would bring the "in-house" supply of the coach transport (one made from the supplier's "own resources") also within TOMS and the TOMS calculations will apportion the supplies made and bring the relevant amounts of VAT on these supplies to account. See **11.2.13** for commentary on the TOMS.

11.2.7 Special rule for the "hiring of a means of transport"

The scope of the term "means of transport" is unclear. It has been held to include an ocean-going yacht hired for pleasure cruises and refrigerated trailers even though they do not have their own means of propulsion. A crane is not a means of transport, but railway wagons are.

HMRC state that a yacht is a means of transport even if it is to be used for racing and a train is a means of transport even where it may be leased to, for example, a transport museum. Hire of a means of transport also includes the hire of ships or aircraft under charter with or without a crew. HMRC also state that freight containers, 'static' caravans' and racing cars where the cars form part of a supply of sporting services, are not means of transport.

The POS for hiring out means of transport varies according the status of the hirer, whether they are a business or a private consumer.

11.2.7.1 "Short-term" and "long-term" hire
"Short-term" hire means hire of the transport for a continuous period not exceeding:
(a) 90 days if the means of transport is a boat, ship, barge etc. (a "vessel"); and
(b) 30 days for other types of transport e.g. cars, trucks, trains and aircraft.

"Long-term" hire is hire for any period over and above these limits.

It is essential to review the hire agreements or other contracts to decide whether the hire is short-term or long-term.

HMRC provides a table in Notice 741A for when hire is short-term and then becomes long-term, as follows:

When	if
Two or more separate contracts for the hire of the same means of transport follow each other with two days or less between them, the term of the first contract needs to be considered in order to decide whether the second term is short-term or long-term.	the two contracts together exceed 30 days (or 90 days for vessels) then the second and subsequent consecutive contracts are treated as long-term hires. If the first contract is genuinely of a short-term hire it will remain so.
there is a second separate contract for short-term hire between the same two parties.	that second separate hire contract relates to a different means of transport or the terms of the hire differ significantly, the contracts will need to be considered separately.
a short-term hire contract is extended.	that extension means that it exceeds the 30 or 90 day period the place of supply is determined by the long-term hire rule, unless it can be satisfactorily demonstrated that the circumstances leading to the events were outside the control of the parties involved.

11.2.7.2 'B2B' and 'B2C' short-term hire

A supply of services consisting of the "short-term" hiring of a means of transport is treated as made in the country in which the means of transport is actually put at the disposal of the person by whom it is hired. This means the place where the hirer takes actual control of the means of transport – but see **11.2.7.4** below for revised POS under the "Use and Enjoyment" rules.

For a Relevant Business Person (see **11.2.3**) the hire of a Means of Transport falling under the short-term hire time limits must account for VAT under the Reverse Charge (see **Chapter 12**) unless the Use and Enjoyment rules apply.

Subject to those countries' VAT registration rules, the supplier of a Means of Transport to a private consumer or non-taxable legal person ('B2C') must register for VAT in the countries where the hirer takes possession of the means of transport, and account for local country VAT on the hire.

Example
Hirers taking possession of a car in Northern Ireland to drive to Ireland will pay UK VAT on that car hire. If, however, the same customer only needs the car for the initial journey and a week later needs to hire the same or another car under a second hire agreement to return to Northern Ireland, and hires that car in the supplier's Dublin branch, Irish VAT is due on that hire.

If the hire is for the whole duration of the hirer's itinerary i.e. both journeys, the whole hire is liable to UK VAT as that is the only place where the car was put at the disposal of the hirer.

INTRA-EU TRANSACTIONS – SUPPLY OF SERVICES

Multi-national car hire companies etc. therefore need to maintain accurate records for the VAT liabilities of all car hire based on the depots from where the customers actually take possession of the cars – but also see **11.2.7.4** below for revised POS under the "Use and Enjoyment" rules.

11.2.7.3 'B2B' and 'B2C' long-term hire

Relevant Business Persons (see **11.2.3**) that hire a Means of Transport falling under the long-term hire time limits must also account for VAT under the Reverse Charge – but see **11.2.7.4** below for revised POS under the "Use and Enjoyment" rules.

Between 1 January 2010 and 31 December 2012 the long-term hire of a means of transport to a private consumer or non-taxable legal person ('B2C') was subject to the general rule for the POS for such supplies and was taxable in the supplier's Member State (or the Member State most directly connected with the supply if the supplier has more than one place of establishment – see **11.1.6**).

However, after 1 January 2013 the long-term hire of a means of transport supplied 'B2C' is liable to VAT where the customer "belongs" (see **11.1.2-11.1.6**) unless it was the long-term hire of a "pleasure boat". For pleasure boats the POS of a long term hire after 1 January 2013 is the place where the pleasure boat is *put at the disposal of the customer*, provided the supplier is hiring the pleasure boat from a business establishment or fixed establishment in that place of hire.

A pleasure boat is one that is designed or adapted for use for recreation or pleasure. This means it should not have any features that indicate a commercial design (such as a cargo hold, commercial fishing equipment, or the ability to convey large numbers of passengers) or enable permanent residential living. Pleasure boats include motor cruisers, powerboats or yachts either designed or adapted for use for recreation or pleasure.

Adaptation means to modify any vessel that becomes capable of use for pleasure or recreation such as strengthening it, or removing permanent sleeping accommodation etc. "Houseboats" of the kind moored on rivers etc. and designed for permanent residential living are not pleasure boats.

11.2.7.4 Additional rules for "use and enjoyment"

There are additional POS rules for all hires of any means of transport which are applied where the POS would be 'distorted' where the effective use and enjoyment of the means of transport was in the EU and the customer was established outside the EU or, conversely, when the use and enjoyment was outside the EU and the customer was in the EU. In these circumstances the POS is where the effective use and enjoyment takes place.

In order to decide whether the effective use and enjoyment rule applies the supplier needs to determine:

INTRA-EU TRANSACTIONS – SUPPLY OF SERVICES

1. the establishment from which they are supplying the services;
2. the place where the recipient belongs; and
3. the place where the services are effectively used and enjoyed.

For a UK supplier the rule does not apply where:

(a) the POS is the UK (because either the supplier or the recipient belongs in the UK) and the transport was effectively used and enjoyed in another EU Member State; or
(b) the POS is another EU Member State (because either the supplier or recipient belongs there) but the transport is effectively used and enjoyed in the UK.

Effective use and enjoyment is governed by the contract terms or terms of use of the transport. Therefore, any amount of use or proportion of use that takes place wholly outside the EU is outside the scope of UK and EU VAT. Suppliers must obtain and keep evidence to prove where the use and enjoyment actually takes place. This could be by vehicle mileage logs or ships' logs etc.

Conversely, where the POS would be outside the EU and any use and enjoyment takes place within the UK or within UK territorial waters, that use and enjoyment is liable to UK VAT. In Notice 741A HMRC have provided a liability matrix for such supplies, as follows:

If you	The POS of the hire is
hire out a means of transport where the place of supply is the UK which is used and enjoyed within the EU,	the UK
hire out a means of transport where the place of supply is the UK which is used and enjoyed outside the EU throughout the hiring period,	outside the EU
hire out a means of transport where the place of supply is the UK which is used and enjoyed partly within and partly outside the EU during the hiring period,	the UK to the extent that the transport is used and enjoyed in the EU
hire out a means of transport where the place of supply is outside the EU which is used and enjoyed within the UK for the whole duration of the hiring period,	the UK
hire out a means of transport where the place of supply is outside the EU which is used and enjoyed partly within the UK during the hiring period,	the UK to the extent that the transport is used and enjoyed in the UK

11.2.8 Special rule for the "hiring of any goods other than a means of transport"

The hire of goods other than a means of transport follow the general rules for 'B2B' and 'B2C' services and are taxed in the supplier's and customer's Member States respectively. However, where the POS would be 'distorted' because the effective use and enjoyment of the hire was in the EU and the customer was established outside the EU or, conversely, when the use and enjoyment was outside the EU and taxed as though in the EU the POS is where the effective use and enjoyment takes place.

In Notice 741A HMRC provide the following examples where the POS shifts to the place where the effective use and enjoyment actually takes place.

- a Canadian company hires out recording equipment to a UK private individual who uses the equipment in his UK home. The place of supply is the UK. This is because the goods are used and enjoyed in the UK and the place of supply would otherwise have been outside the EU;
- an Australian tourist hires a video camera from a UK provider during a visit to the UK. The place of supply is the UK. This is because the goods are used and enjoyed in the UK and the place of supply would otherwise have been outside the EU;
- a UK golf shop hires out a set of golf clubs to a UK customer for use on a holiday in the USA. The place of supply is outside the EU if the customer is able to demonstrate that the golf clubs are used and enjoyed only in the USA. This is because the goods are used and enjoyed outside the EU and the place of supply would otherwise have been the UK;
- a company belonging in Switzerland hires fax machines from a supplier in the USA. The fax machines are partly used and enjoyed at the Swiss company's London branch. The place of supply is the UK to the extent that the machines are used at the London branch. This is because the goods are used and enjoyed in the UK and the place of supply would otherwise have been outside the EU.

It is obvious from these examples that a UK supplier hiring goods to a tourist only visiting the UK can be quite certain that the use and enjoyment is wholly in the UK. However, if the goods are capable of being placed in luggage and the tourist is, say, from the US and is visiting a number of European countries before returning to London for his final few days before returning home, then, subject to satisfactory evidence, it is reasonable for the supplier to charge VAT only on the use and enjoyment that takes place whilst the tourist is visiting EU countries.

Evidence could be travel tickets etc. that show journeys to and from non-EU countries. However, the supplier might need to take a deposit for the VAT before the journeys begin and refund it on production of evidence supporting the non-EU visits when the hirer returns the goods at the end of the hire period. It is more probable that most suppliers will account for VAT on all hire as a prudent measure.

11.2.9 Special rule for "cultural, artistic, sporting, scientific, educational or entertainment services" and "ancillary services" relating to them – "Where Performed" services

Services covered by this section generally relate to a live event or physical activity. Careful consideration to the real nature of the services being supplied is vital as services of entertainment, sponsorship, or scientific performances e.g. a symposium, may fall under the general rule for 'B2B' services. There has been considerable transition in this arena with principle changes for services supplied 'B2B' from those supplied in a 'B2C' capacity.

Between 1 January 2010 and 31 December 2010 the supply both in a 'B2B' and a B2C capacity of *"cultural, artistic, sporting, scientific, educational or entertainment services, including fairs and exhibitions"* and *"ancillary services relating to such services, including services of organisers of such activities"* were all taxed where they were physically carried out.

However, after 1 January 2011 the POS for these services was differentiated between 'B2B' services which became taxable under the 'B2B' general rule (see **11.2.1**) and remained taxable where performed for 'B2C' supplies (see **11.2.2**). Therefore, suppliers of all of these types of services supplying them in a 'B2C' capacity are liable to be registered for VAT in the countries where the performances take place with 'one-off' performances also being caught.

Suppliers that resell these types of services, particularly educational services and services connected with conferences and meetings, together with supplies of accommodation and/or travel could be responsible for accounting for VAT under the Tour Operators' Margin Scheme (TOMS) where the services are bought for the *"direct benefit of the traveller"* and they are sold *"without material alteration"* – see **11.2.13**.

In VAT Notice 741A HMRC provide the following examples of the types of services that come within the headings for a 'B2C' "where performed" supply:
- services of sportspersons appearing in exhibition matches, races or other forms of competition;
- provision of race-prepared cars including the hire of the car and support services to ensure optimum maintenance and operation of the car throughout a series of races;
- scientific services of technicians carrying out tests or experiments in order to obtain data, provided the services were performed outside the UK even though the final compilation of results might have been carried out in the UK;
- services of an actor or singer, whether or not in front of a live audience;
- services relating to conferences or meetings;
- services of an oral interpreter at an event, such as a meeting;
- the right to participate in an exhibition or the provision of an undefined site for a stand at an exhibition – see **11.2.5** for examples of "defined sites";

INTRA-EU TRANSACTIONS – SUPPLY OF SERVICES

- services relating to a specific exhibition. This includes carpenters and electricians erecting and fitting out stands at exhibition venues; and
- educational and training services.

Additionally, in Notice 741A HMRC provide the following examples of services that are not deemed to be supplied where they are performed:

- services of sportspersons receiving sponsorship money as consideration for product endorsement or publicity appearances. These are advertising services rather than participation in a sporting event taxable under the general rules for 'B2B' and 'B2C' services – see **11.2.1** and **11.2.2**;
- written translation services or interpreters' services which do not take place at an event. These are consultancy service taxable under the general rules for 'B2B' and 'B2C' services – see **11.2.1** and **11.2.2**;
- the hire of goods without any additional services, even if the customer uses those goods at an exhibition or concert treated under the rules for such goods – see **11.2.8**.
- the provision of a defined site for a stand at an exhibition, which is land-related - see **11.2.5**.
- scientific services which include a recommendation or conclusion. These are services of consultancy or provision of information taxable under the 'B2B' and 'B2C' general rules (see **11.2.1** and **11.2.2**), or, if connected with oil/gas/mineral exploration or exploitation of specific sites of land or the seabed, they are land-related (see **11.2.5**); and
- veterinary services, taxable under the 'B2B' and 'B2C' general rules – see **11.2.1** and **11.2.2**.

11.2.9.1 "Pilot training" and "sailing tuition"

With regard to tuition in learning to pilot aircraft or sailing tuition, HMRC state that pilot training is treated as supplied wholly outside the UK provided the trainer aircraft leaves UK airspace and proceeds directly to a destination abroad, and at least 12 hours' training is provided at that place. HMRC also state that sailing tuition is treated as supplied wholly outside the UK provided all of the training is carried out on a vessel which clears UK territorial waters for a foreign destination. Additionally, the vessel must remain outside UK territorial waters for the whole of the period of training, except for the outward journey and inward return so long as these trips are directly from and to the UK.

11.2.9.2 Training performed in the UK for overseas governments

HMRC have granted an Extra-Statutory Concession (ESC) for training services provided to overseas governments for the purposes of their sovereign activities. Under the ESC such services are zero-rated in the UK provided:

- the services are used by the foreign or overseas government for the furtherance of its sovereign activities (that is not for business purposes), and

- the supplier obtains and retains a written statement from the foreign or overseas government concerned, or its accredited representative, certifying that the trainees are employed in furtherance of its sovereign activities.

The ESC, therefore, does not zero-rate the training of personnel from government owned industries or sponsored commercial organisations such as state airlines or nationalised industries. Additionally, zero-rating only applies to the supply of the actual training and does not extend to any associated services which are supplied separately, such as accommodation or transport.

'Foreign or overseas government' includes overseas government officials, public servants and members of organisations such as the armed forces, the police, the emergency services and similar bodies answerable to the government concerned.

The ESC only applies to services that would not be exempt under the VAT Act 1994 Schedule 9 Group 6. VAT Notice 701/30: *Education and vocational training* provides details of such services.

11.2.9.3 Exhibitions and trade shows

The phrase 'exhibition organiser' is a very general description. It covers a variety of services which are performed in different ways and it is important to establish the nature of the services being supplied, rather than relying on how the supply is described. For example, the exhibition organiser is likely to be supplying the stand sites, the actual visitor admission or advertising services (such as space in an event publication) whereas an agent acting for the exhibition organiser is more likely to be making all the arrangements for the event on the organiser's behalf. The legislation refers to these arrangement services as "ancillary services" – see **11.2.9.4**.

With effect from 1 January 2011 the POS of the exhibition or trade show by the organiser comes within the 'B2B' general rule if being supplied to a Relevant Business Person and is liable to VAT in the place where the event takes place if supplied as the organiser for the supplier's own event i.e. 'B2C'. HMRC has stated that where representative bodies assist exhibitors in their attendance at exhibitions and trade shows and provide a single package of various services which may include exhibition space obtained from the owner, consultancy, design, provision of displays, transport and stand construction, their services are supplied where they are physically carried out and from 1 January 2011 where the activities or events take place.

11.2.9.4 Ancillary services

Ancillary services include the services of organising the supply of the "Where Performed" services set out in **11.2.9.2** and **11.2.9.3**. The phrase "ancillary services" means any services that assist with the supply of the fundamental services such as arranging the fundamental services on the organiser's behalf.

Even simple things like providing cloakroom services at an event count as ancillary services. In Notice 741A HMRC state that such services include:
- the services of a co-ordinator in administering arrangements for a sporting event on behalf of a promoter; and
- the services of lighting or sound technicians at a concert. This also covers the hire of equipment included as part of the same supply; and
- the services relating to the admission to such events, for example a promoter who sells the tickets as well as arranging the theatrical content or publicising and promoting the concert or theatrical performance.

In practice, for all supplies made after 1 January 2011 this means that, say, if a French company supplies ancillary services to a UK ballet company, the place of supply of the French company's ancillary services is the UK, subject to the Reverse Charge by the UK customer. If the French company was involved in, say, the staging of the event, this would be taxable under the B2B general rule. Any supplies made in a B2C capacity would fall under that rule and the French company could be liable to UK VAT registration.

HMRC also state in Notice 741A that the following services are not ancillary services:
- a supply of advertising services to a sponsor by the promoter/owner of a sporting event; and
- the simple hiring of equipment for use at a concert, without the services of technicians or operators.

These services are treated under the 'B2B' and 'B2C' POS general rules – see **11.2.1** and **11.2.2**.

11.2.9.5 Valuation services and work on goods
The POS for a supply of services relating to working on another person's goods or of valuation services etc. is where the work is performed. B2B services mean the Relevant Business Person applies the Reverse Charge and for a B2C supply carried out in the EU the supplier is liable to be registered for VAT in the customer's Member State. Such services when carried out outside the EU are Outside the Scope of VAT – see **11.7**.

'Goods' include all forms of tangible moveable property, covering both finished commodities and raw materials, but do not include immoveable property such as permanently installed goods and fixtures.

Work carried out on goods is essentially any physical service carried out on another person's goods. HMRC provide the following examples in Notice 7451A section 8.5.2:
- processing, manufacturing or assembling;
- repairs, cleaning or restoration;
- alterations, calibrations, insulating, lacquering, painting, polishing, resetting (of jewellery), sharpening, varnishing, waterproofing; and

- nominations to stallions/covering (that is, attempting to secure the pregnancy of mares).

HMRC also provide the following examples of types of valuation services or work on goods:

- Services of a sub-contractor installing machinery supplied by another person.
- Simple valuation of goods by loss adjusters, average adjusters, motor assessors, surveyors and other experts in connection with an insurance proposal or claim. The final compilation of a related report in a different country from the goods will not change the place of supply from the country where valuation work is performed. However, where valuation forms only a part of your professional services your supplies are of consultancy.

Excluded services would include:

- work which is not mainly physical work performed on the goods themselves. For example, where inspection, is not 'work on goods'. It can be 'valuation', but only if that is the purpose of the inspection. However, such activities may form part of a consultancy service;
- testing and analysis of goods. The physical work simply provides data for the required analysis;
- valuation of, or work carried out on, land or property; and
- veterinary services.

11.2.10 Admission to Where Performed services

The POS for the supply of admission to "Where Performed" services as described in **11.2.9** in a 'B2C' capacity is always the place where they are performed. However, a 'B2B' supply to a Relevant Business Person of where performed services that do not include services relating to admissions is still subject to the 'B2B' general rule, with the recipient accounting for VAT under the Reverse Charge in their own Member State.

But, the supply of "admissions services" supplied 'B2B' after 1 January 2011 became liable to VAT under the Special rule and all suppliers must now register for VAT in the Member States where the admissions take place, subject of course to each Member State's VAT registration policy.

With effect from 1 January 2015, art 33a Regulation (EU) No 282/2011 provides that these rules apply to the supply of tickets granting access to an event by an intermediary acting in his own name, but on behalf of the organiser or by a taxable person, other than the organiser, acting on his own behalf. EC regulations outline the essential characteristics as *"right of admission to an event in exchange for a ticket or payment"* which includes a subscription, season ticket or periodic fee. In particular, this applies to shows, theatrical performances, circus performances, fairs, amusement parks, concerts, exhibitions and other similar cultural events, and sporting events such as matches and competitions.

11.2.11 Special rule for "restaurant and catering" services

Both 'B2B' and 'B2C' supplies of restaurant and catering services are treated as made in the country in which the services are physically carried out. Therefore, suppliers trading across the EU such as at airports or ferry terminals will require multiple EU VAT registrations.

11.2.12 Special rule for EU "on-board" restaurant and catering services

The POS of restaurant and catering services carried out on board a ship, aircraft or train in connection with the transportation of passengers during an "intra-EU passenger transport operation" is made in the country in which the "relevant point of departure" is located.

An "intra-EU passenger transport operation" is a passenger transport operation which, or so much of a passenger transport operation as:
(a) has as the first place at which passengers can embark a place which is within the EU;
(b) has as the last place at which passengers who embarked in a Member State can disembark at a place which is within the EU; and
(c) does not include a stop at a place which is not within the EU and at which passengers can embark or passengers who embarked in a Member State can disembark.

The "relevant point of departure" in relation to an intra-EU passenger transport operation, is the first place in the intra-EU passenger transport operation at which passengers can embark. The return stage of a return passenger transport operation is regarded as a separate passenger transport operation.

For this purpose:
(a) a return passenger transport operation is one which takes place in more than one country, but is expected to end in the country in which it begins; and
(b) the return stage of a return passenger transport operation is the part of it which ends in the country in which it began and begins with the last stop at a place at which there has not been a previous stop during it.

So, for example, UK VAT is due on the goods and services supplied on board a cross-channel ferry leaving the UK to go to France and French VAT is due on the goods and services for the return journey. It is vital therefore for the suppliers to ensure that pricing is reviewed to take account of the differing VAT rates in the Member States where the VAT becomes accountable. Additionally, any exchange rate differences will have to be factored into the pricing for international journeys. For the POS of goods sold on intra-EU transport see **9.18**.

11.2.13 Special rule for the "Tour Operators' Margin Scheme" (TOMS)

The Tour Operators' Margin Scheme (or the TOMS) is, perhaps, the most complex and the most widely misunderstood VAT legislation that befalls businesses.

The guidance provided here is literally a high-level overview of the TOMS and all affected businesses that might supply travel services or any of the other designated Margin Scheme supplies, even as an incidental part of their business, are advised to seek specialist advice since any misunderstanding in how the TOMS operates, probably leading to errors in VAT accounting or simply whether the business is caught by the TOMS, can lead to an exposure and a liability to HMRC. The liability can be by reclaiming VAT on expenditure that is non-recoverable or by a failure to account correctly for VAT on sales revenue.

11.2.13.1 Background to the TOMS

In essence the TOMS is a dispensation that enables businesses that fall within the TOMS to not have to register for VAT in every Member State in which "travellers" enjoy their "designated travel services". It is designed to alleviate VAT registration and to simplify VAT accounting such that all EU VAT that the supplier would be liable for under the General rule for 'B2C' supplies of travel services is accountable to the EU Member State in which they have established their business. If the supplier has more than one establishment then the POS is the establishment that is most directly connected with the supplies in question – see **11.1.6**.

If a business that would otherwise be caught by the TOMS is only established outside the EU, or decides to supply all travel services from an establishment that is outside the EU, then it is not liable for the TOMS. Non-EU businesses are therefore entirely outside the scope of the TOMS. So, currently, any EU business that wishes to avoid the TOMS can transfer its business to a non-EU establishment and supply all of its travel services from that establishment. However, the Commission is known to be considering changes to its effect in an attempt to ensure that non-EU businesses supplying travel services that are enjoyed within the EU are included.

The TOMS does not only apply to 'traditional' tour operators. The CJEU has confirmed that to make the application of the TOMS dependent upon whether a business was formally classified as a travel agent or tour operator would create distortion of competition.

Ancillary travel services which constitute *"a small proportion of the package price compared to accommodation"* would not lead to a hotelier falling within the provisions but where, in return for a package price, a hotelier habitually offers its customers travel to and from the hotel from distant pick-up points in addition to accommodation, such services cannot be treated as purely ancillary.

Under the scheme:
- The TOMS applies to travel services enjoyed within the UK, within the EU but outside the UK, and wholly outside the EU when supplied by a business established in the EU (for these purposes referring to the UK).
- VAT cannot be reclaimed on margin scheme supplies bought by the supplier for resale in the same state.
- VAT incurred on overheads outside the TOMS can be reclaimed in the normal way;
- A UK-based tour operator need only account for VAT on the margin, i.e. the difference between the amount received from customers (including any amounts paid on behalf of customers by third parties) and the amount paid to suppliers;
- VAT invoices cannot be issued for margin scheme supplies so business travellers can 'lose' the VAT they have paid to the supplier resulting in the "VAT" accounted for in the margin having to be absorbed in their businesses.
- "In-house" supplies supplied on their own are not subject to the TOMS and are taxed under the normal VAT rules.
- A mixture of in-house supplies and bought-in margin scheme supplies must all be accounted for within the TOMS, using the cost-based method or market value method approved by HMRC.

11.2.13.2 *Application of the TOMS*
The TOMS must be used by a person acting as a principal or undisclosed agent for:
- 'margin scheme supplies'; and
- 'margin scheme packages' i.e. single transactions which include one or more margin scheme supplies possibly with other types of supplies (e.g. in-house supplies).

'Margin scheme supplies' are those supplies which are:
- bought in for the purpose of the business, and
- supplied for the benefit of a 'traveller' without material alteration or further processing'

by a tour operator in an EU country in which he has established his business or has a fixed establishment.

The following are **always** treated as margin scheme supplies:
- accommodation;
- passenger transport;
- hire of means of transport;

- use of special lounges at airports;
- trips or excursions; and
- services of tour guides.

Other supplies meeting the above conditions may be treated as margin scheme supplies, but only if provided as part of a package with one or more of the supplies listed above. These include catering and theatre tickets.

'In-house' supplies are goods and services that are produced from the supplier's own resources such as owning the hotel or the coach transport or where a number of goods or services are bought in but they are "materially altered" when resold or "packaged" for sale to the consumer.

A 'traveller' is a person, including a business or local authority, who receives supplies of transport and/or accommodation, other than for the purpose of re-supply i.e. B2B supplies for consumption by the business itself are included. Currently, all supplies of travel services supplied for resale by another business ('B2B') are excluded from the TOMS and these are classed as 'wholesale supplies'.

The calculation of the "margin" on which VAT is to be accounted is currently based on averages using the business' annual accounts and provisional profit margins can be used for the current year calculations with adjustments made when the current year accounts are finalised.

In the UK tours that are enjoyed wholly within the EU are taxable at the standard rate and tours enjoyed wholly outside the EU are zero-rated. The TOMS calculations work out the VAT liability using the relative proportions of EU and non-EU tours plus the composition of "bought-in" and "in-house" supplies of margin scheme supplies.

11.2.13.3 EC intervention

The current application of the TOMS by a number of EU Member States was judged by the Commission and the CJEU to be in contravention of the Principal VAT Directive and Implementing Regulations for the TOMS. The Commission has announced a widespread review of the TOMS that, once finalised, will aim to rationalise the treatment of all TOMS supplies across all Member States. There is therefore a good deal of uncertainty in this area as Member States are still currently allowed to apply the TOMS as they always have done, but businesses can avail themselves of the CJEU's findings where they find this is to their own advantage.

The three key CJEU findings that conflict with current UK practice are:

(a) the TOMS should include wholesale supplies, i.e. travel services sold to tour operators for re-sale to the public;
(b) TOMS VAT must be computed on a transaction-by-transaction basis and not by reference to purchases and sales over a period of time; and

INTRA-EU TRANSACTIONS – SUPPLY OF SERVICES

(c) it is permissible in principle for TOMS VAT to be shown on an invoice to enable business customers to exercise their right to deduct input VAT if appropriate.

But, similarly to the changes where non-EU businesses that supply 'downloadable' products via the internet to EU private consumers have to register for VAT somewhere in the EU (see **11.3**), non-EU suppliers of TOMS services will probably be required to register somewhere in the EU following the Commission's review of the EU TOMS. However, there is yet no clear date for the Commission's publication of its review so the position is still in a state of flux.

Deciding whether a supply or supplies is actually within the TOMS can be very difficult as the following example demonstrates.

Example
Company 'A' buys in long-term accommodation from owners of property, most usually on licences to occupy terms. Company A then from its own resources adds a number of services such as housekeeping and broadband just as a hotel might do. Company A then sells 'long-stay accommodation' to the actual occupier who prefers to stay in a "home-from-home" rather than in a hotel. Some stays might last as long as six months or a year, for example, executives transferred from an overseas parent company to a UK affiliate, and the occupation can be by several employees of the same customer in successive periods. The question to answer is therefore:

> *Is the resale of the accommodation a TOMS supply sold in the same state i.e. without material alteration or is it a licence to occupy land or accommodation that is exempt or is it a supply that is liable to VAT because it is akin to "hotel accommodation or similar" with a reduced-value for the accommodation for stays in excess of 28 days' continuous duration?*

The answer will depend upon the precise terms of the lettings and how the services are advertised, packaged and provided to the customer. If reviewed by HMRC, they could rule that the supply is any one of:

1. a TOMS supply where the supplier might otherwise reclaim input tax (which is refused on margin scheme supplies); or
2. a TOMS supply where the supplies are materially altered such that they fall to be treated as "in-house supplies" and taxed outside of the margin (and input tax is allowable); or
3. an exempt licence to occupy which means that no input tax is reclaimable and no output tax is accountable (unless Company A has Opted To Tax the property); or
4. the supplies are of accommodation that is "similar" to hotel accommodation and hence taxable with a reduced-value for the accommodation for stays in excess of 28 continuous days.

In any event, for absolute certainty, the supplier should obtain a "Non-Statutory Clearance" from HMRC as the matters can be so complex. Armed with this, and provided every aspect of the business and the actual transactions are advised to HMRC in the Clearance application, HMRC, having provided the Clearance, ought to be prevented from raising assessments in the future, for example because of a Tax Tribunal or court decision (as far as one given by the CJEU) on similar transactions for other businesses.

11.2.14 Special rules for the transport of goods

The transport of goods or "freight" covers the transport of all of the following types of goods:
(a) goods/cargo;
(b) mail;
(c) documents;
(d) unaccompanied vehicles; and
(e) vehicles transported on ships which are charged at a 'driver accompanied' rate.

The POS of the transportation of goods for Relevant Business Persons (see **11.2.3**) falls under the 'B2B' general rule described in **11.2.1**. It does not matter where the goods being transported move from or to, or where any related service physically takes place.

For example (as per Notice 744B):

Customer is in-business in:	Place of supply of freight transportation and related service is:
France and goods move within France	France
Australia and the goods move from Australia to the UK with related transport services undertaken in France	Australia
United Kingdom and the goods move from Canada to China	United Kingdom
Holland and the goods move from Italy to Ireland where you supply a related transport service	Holland

However, HMRC realised that this change in law produced an unintended anomaly in the treatment of supplies wholly enjoyed outside the EU, which may also be taxed locally in the place of performance.

After recognising this, with effect from 15 March 2010, a supply of freight transport (or services closely associated with freight transport) which would otherwise be treated as supplied in the UK was treated as outside the scope of UK VAT if the use and enjoyment of the services was outside the EU. This administrative easement was a temporary measure, and with effect from 20 December 2012 it was put on a permanent footing.

HMRC state that transportation between EU member states that involves transiting a non-EU member state (for example Sweden to the UK via Norway) is to be treated as intra-EU transportation.

INTRA-EU TRANSACTIONS – SUPPLY OF SERVICES

For a subcontractor supplying freight transportation or related services to a main contractor, the POS is determined by the status of the immediate customer and not that of the ultimate customer of the main contractor.

For example, a French company moving goods from Italy to Ireland for a UK company will have a place of supply of freight transportation in the UK as that is where its customer belongs. The POS of services supplied by a firm sub-contracted to the French company to move these goods from Dover to Holyhead is France as that is where its own customer belongs.

For 'B2C' supplies of freight transport services the POS is the place varies as follows:
(a) When freight transportation is from a place within the EU to a third country/territory the POS is where the transportation is performed in proportion to the distances covered;
(b) When freight transportation is wholly within the EU, the POS is where the transportation begins; and
(c) the POS of related services takes place where they are physically performed.

For example (as per Notice 744B):

Non-business customer is in:	Place of supply of freight transportation and related service is:
France and goods move within France	France
Australia and the goods move from Australia to the UK with related transport services undertaken in France	Australia and the UK and any other country transited. The related transport services are supplied in France
United Kingdom and the goods move from Canada to the China	Canada, China and any other country transited
Holland and the goods move from Italy to Ireland where you supply a related transport service	Transport related service is supplied in Ireland

If the POS of freight transportation or ancillary services is the UK then the supply will be standard rated, except where:
- the supply is of transportation or related services connected with an import or export from the EU; or
- the actual movement of goods is from, to, or between the islands of the Azores or Madeira or the related service is physically performed on these islands (the Commission decided that freight transport services to and from the Azores and Madeira should be treated differently from other supplies of intra-EU freight transport); or
- the supply is of handling or storage of ship or aircraft cargo (in certain places),

when the liability will be zero-rated.

The UK VAT legislation zero-rates:
- the supply of transportation of goods from a place within to a place outside the EU and vice versa;
- the transport, handling and storage of goods, when they are supplied in connection with a journey from the place of importation to their destination either within the UK or within another Member State (to the extent that those services are supplied in the UK); and
- the transport, handling and storage of goods, when they are supplied in connection with a journey from their origin either within the UK or within another Member State to the place of export (to the extent that those services are supplied in the UK).

"Destination" means the furthest specified place in the UK or other Member State to which the goods are consigned at the time of importation. It is the place stated on the consignment note or any other document by means of which the goods are imported (the delivery terms). When that place is unknown, the destination is the place of importation.

"Origin" means the place from within the UK or other Member State from which the goods are first consigned for export. When that place is unknown, the origin is the place of exportation.

The handling and storage of ship and aircraft cargo may be zero-rated provided the service is physically performed in the UK at any facility such as in a port, on land adjacent to a port, in a customs and excise airport; or in a transit shed.

The detailed rules regarding the UK VAT liability of ancillary freight services treated as supplied in the UK are provided by HMRC in VAT Notice 744B.[1]

11.2.15 Ancillary transport services

Ancillary transport services include the following services when they relate to the transport of goods:
- loading, unloading or reloading;
- stowing;
- opening for inspection;
- cargo security services;
- preparing or amending bills of lading, air or sea-waybills and certificates of shipment;
- packing necessary for transportation; or
- storage.

The POS of B2B and B2C ancillary transport services fall under the rules set out in **11.2.14**. However, where the POS of services for the initial intermediary

---

[1] www.gov.uk/government/publications/vat-notice-744b-freight-transport-and-associated-services/

who arranges the freight transport services is the UK, the following services are zero-rated:
- the supply of space in a qualifying ship or aircraft;
- the supply of handling, storage or transportation of goods imported to or exported from the EU; and
- the supply of handling or storage services.

All other services they provide are standard-rated.

11.2.16 Special rule for "Broadcasting", "Telecommunication services" and "Electronic Services" ("Electronically Supplied Services") ("BTE" services)

The various parts of the VAT Package came into force over the period 2010 - 2015. The main changes came about in 2010 and included two general rules for the place of supply of services – see **11.2.1** and **11.2.2**. The final part of the VAT Package, concerning BTE services supplied to final consumers, came into force on 1 January 2015.

From 1 January 2015 all BTE services became taxable at the place where the customer belongs. In order to ensure the correct taxation of these services, EU and non-EU suppliers need to determine the status of their customer (a taxable or a non-taxable person) and the place (in which country of the EU or outside the EU) where that customer belongs.

The underlying reason for these changes was to bring the VAT treatment of these services in line with one of the main principles of VAT that, as a consumption tax, revenues should accrue to the Member State in which goods or services are consumed – see **Chapter 1**.

The Commission issued a Press Release in July 2014 in advance of the 2015 major changes, reproduced as follows:[2]

> **Questions & Answers: VAT changes from 2015**
> See also IP/14/758
>
> **Why was this change in VAT rules needed?**
> This change to the VAT rules will introduce more efficiency and fairness into taxation. By taxing at the place of consumption, there will be a level playing-field between all businesses supplying telecommunication, broadcasting and electronic services on a given market. The consumer will pay the same amount of tax regardless of where the supplier is located. This will simplify things for consumers, who will not have to work out where the supplier is established, and it will create fairer competition between domestic suppliers and those established in other EU countries. The level playing field aspect is particularly

---

[2] europa.eu/rapid/press-release_MEMO-14-448_en.htm

important for small businesses, which usually do not have resources to spend in VAT planning schemes.

The new rules will also ensure fairer revenue distribution between Member States. VAT is a consumption tax, and the new rules will ensure that taxation reflects where consumption takes place. This should boost tax revenues for most Member States: from now on, the VAT on purchases that their residents make will now go to their own treasury and not to a small number of low-tax Member States where e-giants have established themselves.

The EU is not the only jurisdiction that has decided to apply this principle. Other countries such as Norway or South Africa have decided to do the same, following OECD recommendations.

What type of transactions will be covered?
The change in place of supply rules concerns only digital services, being telecommunications, radio and television broadcasting and electronic services, supplied to private consumers. These can be, for example, phone or satellite TV subscriptions, downloadable software, songs or e-books. Any other e-commerce activity is not covered by the change. For instance, distance selling of physical goods or of other services that involve human intervention, even though the communication is done by email (i.e. legal services carried out at distance; education at distance involving assistance by the teacher) are not covered by the changes.

What has the Commission done to prepare?
In order to secure coherent and uniform application of the rules, and a smooth transition to the new system, the Commission has been working intensively with Member States and businesses to exchange information and points of view. The Commission took action to ensure efficient implementation in five main areas:

- Preparing and adopting the relevant legal framework, in particular implementing regulations to ensure coherent and consistent application of the new legislation;
- Providing for common understanding on the application of the new place-of-supply rules and on related obligations (MOSS);
- Ensuring the IT implementation of the MOSS;
- Clarifying the audit approach in the framework of the MOSS
- Informing and raising awareness among stakeholders: for this the commission organised seminars and conferences for taxpayers inside and outside of the EU.

The Commission will continue to monitor Member States' progress in implementing the mini-One Stop Shop, which should constitute a major step towards the simpler and more effective functioning of the Single Market. A web-portal is now available to allow taxpayers to check VAT rules in all Member States e.g. to know the various rates etc.

What have Member States done to prepare?
Member States are responsible for the transposition and application of the new EU rules on their territory. They have transposed the Directive into national law.

They have also set up the technical infrastructure and web portals that will enable their operators to comply and facilitate exchange of information with other Member States.

Member States have also the responsibility to inform taxpayers of the upcoming changes.

What do businesses need to do to prepare?
Businesses should get acquainted with the new rules and update their accounting system to ensure that all transactions are reported in the country where they should be. This is why the Commission published very detailed guidelines on the mini-One Stop Shop (MOSS) in 2013, and detailed explanatory notes in 2014. It is also taking part in communication events in Member States and outside the EU to explain the changes coming up and ensure businesses are aware and prepared.

What about small businesses that were previously exempt from VAT?
SME's that enjoy an exemption in their own country can retain it for services they sell to private consumers in their own Member State, provided that their Member State has opted for such a facility.

If they supply digital services to private consumers in other Member States, they will have to register in the mini One-Stop Shop because the VAT is due in another Member State. The MOSS has been made as simple and user-friendly as possible: it is fully electronic and it allows all businesses who opt for it to register, to declare and pay the VAT due in their own Member State, with the tax administration they know and in their own language. All communications will be by electronic means only.

How can compliance be ensured?
To reach their customers, businesses need to be visible online. If they are visible to customers in a country, they will also be visible to the tax administration of this country. On this basis, amongst other available tools, tax administrations will already have a good idea of which businesses to audit.

The Commission has worked with Member States to develop audit guidelines in order to ensure each plays their role in identifying where VAT is due. In addition EU legislation already provides for an extensive cooperation between tax administrations to assess and collect VAT.

Will this mean a rise in prices for these services in most Member States?
The change for consumers, if any, will be marginal. The basic price of the product remains the same, and then the VAT (calculated as a percentage of the basic price) may go up or down depending on where the consumer has been previously buying these services. For example, if a consumer has until now bought his/her software from a provider located in a Member State with a lower VAT rate than his/her own, then they will experience a small price difference (a few cents/percentage points). Conversely, if the VAT rate is lower where the consumer lives than where the supplier is based, there will be a small drop in the overall price. However, these are considered to be short-term effects. It is expected that in the longer term the new rules will increase market efficiency

and increase the number of suppliers and competition in general. This, in turn, should drive prices down. The new rules for e-services are exactly the same as with goods sold on a website, for which the VAT rate of the consumer is already applicable since many years.

Will this mean a loss in revenue for certain Member States where a large number of e-service providers are resident?
Taxation at the place of consumption is only logical for a consumption tax such as VAT. It may be the case that certain Member States with a low VAT rate may see their market share reduced as the advantage for companies to relocate to their territories for tax reasons is removed. However, a very long preparation period between the adoption of the Directive and its implementation has allowed any Member State in this position to prepare and adapt to the change. Moreover, there is a transitional period until end of 2019 during which the countries of establishment (i.e. where the supplier is based) will keep part of the revenue.

Shouldn't the One Stop Shop concept by extended to all e-commerce supplies (including distance sales)?
This was the initial proposal of the Commission in 2004, as the Commission is strongly in favour of a One Stop Shop, in particular for the distance sales of goods. The high level expert group on taxation of the digital economy made the same recommendation in its report of last May (see IP/14/604). However not all Member States accepted such a wide scope from the start. The application of a mini One Stop Shop may be an opportunity for Member States to experience the benefits of such a system, and may open the way for the wider application in the future."

For non-EU businesses supplying BTE services to private customers in the European Union, current rules already ensure taxation in the country where the customer belongs – see **11.3** supplies under MOSS.

Until the end of 2014, 'B2C' supplies by EU businesses were taxed in the country of the supplier. This meant that for supplies made to final consumers, businesses established in Member States applying lower VAT rates had a competitive advantage over businesses established in other Member States. The new rules of taxation based on the country where the customer belongs are designed to provide, as from 2015, a level playing field and also to ensure that the VAT receipts accrue to the Member State of consumption.

HMRC have published guidance on the changes that took place on 1 January 2015, which is available online.[3]

---

[3]www.gov.uk/vat-how-to-work-out-your-place-of-supply-of-services, and www.gov.uk/register-and-use-the-vat-mini-one-stop-shop

11.2.16.1 POS of Broadcasting, Telecommunications and Electronic (BTE) services – Effective Use and Enjoyment rules

The POS of BTE services varies according to where the services are actually used and enjoyed. Effective use and enjoyment takes place where the customer actually consumes the services (in practice this will be where the services are physically used) irrespective of contract, payment or beneficial interest.

This additional provision corrects instances of distortion which remain as a result of considering only where the provider and the customer belong. It would be distortive, for example, for supplies such as telecommunications services that are actually consumed outside the EU, to be subject to UK VAT. Equally, it would be distortive for there to be no EU VAT on such services where they are consumed in the UK.

Effective use and enjoyment is only a consideration when certain services made by a UK provider are consumed outside the EU or those services when supplied by a non-EU provider are consumed in the UK. When services are provided by an EU supplier and consumed in the UK, or provided by a UK supplier and consumed in another EU country, this provision will not apply. For example, the POS of telecommunications services is where they are used and enjoyed when supplied:

- by a UK provider to a UK customer or a non-business customer in another Member State, to the extent that effective use and enjoyment takes place outside the EU (such element being outside the scope of VAT), or
- by a non-EU provider to a UK customer or a non-business customer in another Member State, to the extent that effective use and enjoyment takes place in the UK (such element being subject to UK VAT).

Where only part of the supply is consumed in the UK the extent of use and enjoyment is often difficult to quantify. Suppliers should take a systematic and practical approach to avoid disputes with HMRC on the proportion of use within the UK. The method of apportionment could be by measured usage, internal management records showing inter-company recharges, percentage of business transactions at the specific location, proportion of telecommunications equipment, number of sites etc.

In its VAT Place of Supply Guidance Manual at VPOSS15300 HMRC provide the following examples of effective use and enjoyment for **telecommunications** services:

> Where telecommunications services are supplied by a business to another business, which use those services to supply its own customers, each supply must be looked at separately for place of supply purposes. At the same time it is important to remember that in determining whether the use and enjoyment

INTRA-EU TRANSACTIONS – SUPPLY OF SERVICES

provisions apply, you are looking to any use and enjoyment by the customer and not by the customer's customer.

Example 1
A UK telecommunications provider supplies telecommunications services to a telecommunications provider that belongs in the USA. The USA provider then supplies those services to a UK private customer. The USA provider receives the services in the USA and so the supply to the USA provider is outside the scope of UK and EC VAT. Those services are not used and enjoyed in the UK by the USA provider. However, the USA provider's onward supply is used and enjoyed by its UK private customer therefore the USA provider must register for VAT in the UK, subject to the normal registration rules.

Example 2
A UK telecommunications provider supplies telecommunications services to a telecommunications provider that belongs in the USA. The USA provider then re-supplies those services to its UK business customer. The USA provider receives the services in the USA and so they are outside the scope of UK and EC VAT. Those services are not used and enjoyed in the UK by the USA provider. The USA provider's onward supply is received by its UK business customer who accounts for VAT using the reverse charge procedure.

Example 3
A UK telecommunications provider supplies telecommunications services to a telecommunications provider that belongs in the USA. The USA provider then re-supplies those services to a USA business customer and that USA business customer partly uses that supply at its UK branch. The USA provider receives the services in the USA and so they are outside the scope of UK and EC VAT. Those services are not used and enjoyed in the UK by the USA provider. The USA provider's onward supply is received by its USA business customer and is also outside the scope. However, to the extent it is used and enjoyed in the UK, the UK branch accounts for VAT using the reverse charge procedure.

Telecommunications services supplied to travellers
Under these rules any telecommunications services used in the UK by customers belonging outside the EU are supplied in the UK. Telecommunications services are therefore subject to UK VAT when used in the UK by non-EU visitors. As an administrative measure HMRC will not seek to tax elements of telecommunications services used in the UK which are

- simply an incidental part of an established telephone contract or account held by a customer who belongs outside the EU
- used by a non EU temporary visitor, and
- HMRC are satisfied these conditions are not being abused.

In its VAT Place of Supply Guidance Manual at VPOSS15400 HMRC provide the following examples of effective use and enjoyment for **broadcasting** services:

INTRA-EU TRANSACTIONS – SUPPLY OF SERVICES

> Effective use and enjoyment of broadcasting services takes place where the customer actually consumes the broadcasting services irrespective of contract, payment or beneficial interest.
>
> The use and enjoyment rules apply in either of the following situations where
> (a) the place of supply would be the UK (because the supplier or the customer belongs in the UK) but the services are effectively used and enjoyed outside the EU, and
> (b) a supply would be outside the EU (because the supplier or the customer belonged outside the EU), but the service was effectively used and enjoyed in the UK.
>
> In these circumstances, the place of supply of the broadcasting services is where their effective use and enjoyment takes place. Where this is the UK, the services are subject to UK VAT.
>
> For example, a satellite TV company established in India supplies broadcasting to UK subscribers. The services are used and enjoyed in the UK and are subject to UK VAT.
>
> The use and enjoyment provisions apply where the EU VAT position would otherwise be distortive. Consequently, they do not apply where the place of supply is
> - the UK (because either the supplier or the customer belongs in the UK) and the service was effectively used and enjoyed in another Member State, or
> - the place of supply is in another Member State (because either the supplier or the customer belongs there) but the supply is effectively used and enjoyed in the UK.

In its VAT Place of Supply Guidance Manual at VPOSS15400 HMRC provide the following examples of effective use and enjoyment for **Electronically Supplied Services**:

> Effective use and enjoyment takes place where the customer actually consumes the electronically supplied services irrespective of contract, payment or beneficial interest.
>
> For electronically supplied services, the use and enjoyment provisions do not apply in any situation where the customer is a non-business customer. This is because most non-business customers are considered to use and enjoy the services in the same country in which they belong.
>
> The use and enjoyment rules apply in the following situations where
> - the supply is to another business (and not to a private individual or non-business organisation). The place of supply would be the UK (because the supplier or the customer belongs in the UK) but the services are effectively used and enjoyed outside the EU, and
> - the supply would be outside the EU (because the supplier or the customer belonged outside the EU), but the service was effectively used and enjoyed in the UK. The place of supply of the electronically supplied services is

where their effective use and enjoyment takes place and, where this is the UK, the services are subject to UK VAT.

Example 1

A UK business purchases digitised software from an Irish supplier for use only in its branch in the Channel Islands. Although the supply is received in the UK where the business belongs, it is used outside the EU and is outside the scope of UK (and EU) VAT.

Example 2

A USA business purchases web-hosting services for its international business, including its UK branch. Although the supply is received in the USA, to the extent that it is used in the UK, it is subject to UK VAT.

Example 3

A UK business purchases downloaded information from another UK business for use both in its UK headquarters and its Canadian branch. Although the supply is received in the UK, to the extent it is used in Canada, it is outside the scope of UK VAT. UK VAT is due only to the extent of use by the UK headquarters.

Examples of electronically supplied services not subject to use and enjoyment rules

The use and enjoyment rules apply in situations where the EU VAT position would otherwise be distortive. Consequently, they do not apply where the:

- supply is to a non-business customer, or
- the place of supply is the UK (because either the supplier or the customer belongs in the UK) and the service was effectively used and enjoyed in another Member State, or
- the place of supply is in another Member State (because either the supplier or the customer belongs there) but the supply is effectively used and enjoyed in the UK.

11.2.16.2 *Definition of 'telecommunications services'*

The Commission has defined telecommunications services as

> services relating to the transmission, emission or reception of signals, words, images and sounds or information of any nature by wire, radio, optical or other electromagnetic systems, including the related transfer or assignment of the right to use capacity for such transmission, emission or reception, with the inclusion of the provision of access to global information networks.

The Explanatory Notes issued by the Commission in supplementing the VAT Implementing Regulation ((EU) No 1042/2013) provide the following additional guidance of what telecommunication services really are:

(a) fixed and mobile telephone services for the transmission and switching of voice, data and video, including telephone services with an imaging component (videophone services);

(b) telephone services provided through the Internet, including voice over Internet Protocol (VoIP);

INTRA-EU TRANSACTIONS – SUPPLY OF SERVICES

(c) voice mail, call waiting, call forwarding, caller identification, three-way calling and other call management services;
(d) paging services;
(e) audiotext services;
(f) facsimile, telegraph and telex
(g) access to the Internet, including the World Wide Web;
(h) private network connections providing telecommunications links for the exclusive use of the client.

The Explanatory Notes specifically state that "electronically supplied services" and "radio and television broadcasting services" are not "telecommunications services".

11.2.16.3 Definition of "Broadcasting Services"

The Commission has defined 'Broadcasting services' as:

> services consisting of audio and audio-visual content, such as radio or television programmes which are provided to the general public via communications networks by and under the editorial responsibility of a media service provider, for simultaneous listening or viewing, on the basis of a programme schedule.

The Explanatory Notes issued by the Commission in supplementing the VAT Implementing Regulation ((EU) No 1042/2013) provide the following additional guidance of what broadcasting services include:

1. Broadcasting services shall include services consisting of audio and audio-visual content, such as radio or television programmes which are provided to the general public via communications networks by and under the editorial responsibility of a media service provider, for simultaneous listening or viewing, on the basis of a programme schedule.
2. Paragraph 1 shall cover, in particular, the following:
    a. radio or television programmes transmitted or retransmitted over a radio or television network;
    b. radio or television programmes distributed via the Internet or similar electronic network (IP streaming) if they are broadcast simultaneously to their being transmitted or retransmitted over a radio or television network.
3. Paragraph 1 shall not cover the following:
    a. telecommunications services;
    b. electronically supplied services;
    c. the provision of information about particular programmes on demand;
    d. the transfer of broadcasting or transmission rights;
    e. the leasing of technical equipment or facilities for use to receive a broadcast;
    f. radio or television programmes distribute via the Internet or similar electronic network (IP streaming), unless they are broadcast simultaneously over traditional radio or television networks

The definition agreed by the Council is relatively narrow and only covers services consisting of audio and audio-visual content provided by and under the editorial responsibility of a media service provider (where he has the effective control both over the selection of the programmes and over their organisation). Editorial responsibility does not necessarily imply any legal liability under national law for the content or the services provided to the general public.

In practice this means that a broadcaster who, for example provides premium sports channels and has the editorial responsibility over them is regarded as supplying broadcasting services. Such services could be subject to the reduced rate in certain Member States. However, if the right of access to the same channels is provided by a supplier who buys the right of access wholesale and then forwards the signals but has no editorial responsibility over the content provided, then this supplier will be regarded as supplying electronic services and the standard rate would apply in the Member State of supply.

The definition covers the distribution of radio and television programmes via electronic networks such as the Internet but only if they are broadcast for simultaneous listening or viewing. Where the audio or audio-visual content is not delivered in a synchronic way (at the same time) to the recipients (the general public) it would normally fall under the definition of electronic services.

At the same time it seems correct to include within the concept of simultaneous listening or viewing for the purpose of the broadcasting definition, listening or viewing which is quasi-simultaneous. Indeed, these services are normally available to the customer without the need to pay an additional fee for it.

Quasi-simultaneous listening or viewing would cover the following:

(1) Situations where a time lag occurs between the transmission and the reception of the broadcast due to technical reasons inherent in the transmission process or as a result of the connection;
(2) Situations where the customer is able to record for later listening or viewing, pause, forward or rewind the signal/programme;
(3) Situations where the customer is able to programme in advance that the particular audio or audio-visual content would be recorded at the time when it is broadcast for simultaneous listening or viewing. The recorded programme can then be listened to or viewed afterwards by the customer.

In any case quasi-simultaneous listening or viewing should only cover situations where the customer may influence within certain limits when he can listen to or view a program but without impacting the transmission of the signal itself.

Quasi-simultaneous listening or viewing should not cover cases where the customer can demand individually the program that he wants to watch from a list and he is paying a specific fee for this extra service.

11.2.16.4 Definition of "Electronic Services" or "Electronically Supplied Services" ("ESS")

The notion of *'e-commerce'* when commonly used covers various types of economic activity, including supplies of goods or services carried out over electronic systems such as the Internet. Not all of those activities are covered by the 2015 VAT changes. In particular the supply of goods (including distance selling) where use is made of electronic systems only to place the order, and the supply of services **other than** telecommunications, broadcasting and electronic services are not covered and these types of transactions are not included in the arrangements for the **"Mini One Stop Shop"** or **"MOSS"** – see **11.3**.

The Commission states in its Explanatory Notes accompanying the Implementing Regulation ((EU) No 1042/2013) that:

> "**Electronically supplied services**" (hereinafter "electronic services") "shall include services which are delivered over the Internet or an electronic network and the nature of which renders their supply essentially automated and involving minimal human intervention, and impossible to ensure in the absence of information technology.

The VAT Implementing Regulation lists all of the following types of supplies as coming within the definition of an ESS:

(1) the supply of digitised products generally, including software and changes to or upgrades of software;
(2) services providing or supporting a business or personal presence on an electronic network such as a website or a webpage;
(3) services automatically generated from a computer via the Internet or an electronic network, in response to specific data input by the recipient;
(4) the transfer for consideration of the right to put goods or services up for sale on an Internet site operating as an online market on which potential buyers make their bids by an automated procedure and on which the parties are notified of a sale by electronic mail automatically generated from a computer;
(5) Internet Service Packages (ISP) of information in which the telecommunications component forms an ancillary and subordinate part (i.e. packages going beyond mere Internet access and including other elements such as content pages giving access to news, weather or travel reports; playgrounds; website hosting; access to online debates etc.);
(6) Website hosting and webpage hosting;
(7) automated, online and distance maintenance of programmes;
(8) remote systems administration;
(9) online data warehousing where specific data is stored and retrieved electronically;
(10) online supply of on-demand disc space;
(11) accessing or downloading software (including procurement/accountancy programmes and anti-virus software) plus updates;
(12) software to block banner adverts showing, otherwise known as "Bannerblockers";
(13) download drivers, such as software that interfaces computers with peripheral equipment (such as printers);
(14) online automated installation of filters on websites;
(15) online automated installation of firewalls;

(16) accessing or downloading desktop themes;
(17) accessing or downloading photographic or pictorial images or screensavers;
(18) the digitised content of books and other electronic publications;
(19) subscription to online newspapers and journals;
(20) weblogs and website statistics;
(21) online news, traffic information and weather reports;
(22) online information generated automatically by software from specific data input by the customer, such as legal and financial data, (in particular such data as continually updated stock market data, in real time);
(23) the provision of advertising space including banner ads on a website/web page;
(24) use of search engines and Internet directories;
(25) accessing or downloading of music on to computers and mobile phones;
(26) accessing or downloading of jingles, excerpts, ringtones, or other sounds;
(27) accessing or downloading of films;
(28) downloading of games on to computers and mobile phones;
(29) accessing automated online games which are dependent on the Internet, or other similar electronic networks, where players are geographically remote from one another;
(30) receiving radio or television programmes distributed via a radio or television network, the Internet or similar electronic network for listening to or viewing programmes at the moment chosen by the user and at the user's individual request on the basis of a catalogue of programmes selected by the media service provider such as TV or video on demand;
(31) receiving radio or television programmes via the Internet or similar electronic network (IP streaming) unless the programmes are broadcast simultaneously over traditional radio and television networks;
(32) automated distance teaching dependent on the Internet or similar electronic network to function and the supply of which requires limited or no human intervention, including virtual classrooms, except where the Internet or similar electronic network is used as a tool simply for communication between the teacher and student;
(33) workbooks completed by pupils online and marked in an automated fashion without human intervention.

The Commission has stated however that all of the following types of services are not ESS:
(1) broadcasting services;
(2) telecommunications services;
(3) goods, where the order and processing is done electronically;
(4) CD-ROMs, floppy disks and similar tangible media;
(5) printed matter, such as books, newsletters, newspapers or journals;
(6) CDs and audio cassettes;
(7) video cassettes and DVDs;
(8) games on a CD-ROM;

(9) services of professionals such as lawyers and financial consultants, who advise clients by e-mail;
(10) teaching services, where the course content is delivered by a teacher over the Internet or an electronic network (namely via a remote link);
(11) offline physical repair services of computer equipment;
(12) offline data warehousing services;
(13) advertising services, in particular as in newspapers, on posters and on television;
(14) telephone helpdesk services;
(15) teaching services purely involving correspondence courses, such as postal courses;
(16) conventional auctioneers' services reliant on direct human intervention, irrespective of how bids are made;
(17) tickets to cultural, artistic, sporting, scientific, educational, entertainment or similar events booked online;
(18) accommodation, car-hire, restaurant services, passenger transport or similar services booked online.

The following definitions which are used in the Explanatory Notes also provide assistance when discussing the technological and technical nature of the BTE services:

'**Over the top**' services – services which can only be delivered thanks to a connection that is established via communication networks (*i.e.* an underlying telecommunications service is necessary) and therefore do not required the physical presence of the recipient at the location where the service is supplied.

'**Telecommunications networks**' are networks that can be used to transfer voice and data. They include but are not necessarily limited to cable networks, telecom networks and ISP (Internet Service Provider) networks. They should cover any facility which allows access to telecommunications, broadcasting or electronic services.

For VAT purposes the terms '**telecommunication networks**' and '**communication networks**' are interchangeable. '**Mobile networks**' (referred to in Article 24b(b)) is a wholly contained subset of telecommunications networks.

A '**fixed land line**' should cover elements that connect to a network which allows transmission and downloads (*e.g.* broadband, ethernet) and where there is a requirement for installation of hardware to send/receive a signal with a degree of permanence (not designed to be easily or frequently moved). It could cover therefore any type of cable used to transmit data to or from the premises (for example copper wire, fibre optic cable, broadband cable) and also a satellite when this requires the installation of a satellite dish at the premises.

A '**portal**' is any type of electronic shop, website or similar environment that offers electronic services directly to the consumer without diverting them to another supplier's website, portal etc. to conclude the transaction. Common examples of this include app stores, electronic marketplaces and websites offering e-services for sale.

An '**interface**' includes a portal but it is a wider concept. In computing it should be understand as a device or a program which allows two independent systems or the system or the end user to communicate.

11.2.16.5 *"Platforms", "portals" and "interfaces" etc.*

The Commission has clarified the position where a supplier might sell services via an 'on-line' platform, portal or interface such as the "Amazon Marketplace" or "eBay". The supply is only treated as pertinent to the supplier where that supplier acts in its own name and the platform etc. makes it clear from all terms and conditions and other contractual arrangements that the supplier is acting as a principal in the supply. The Commission states that for the supplier to be *"explicitly indicated as the supplier of those services"* the following conditions must be met:

(a) The invoice issued or made available by each taxable person taking part in the supply of the electronically supplied services must identify such services and the supplier thereof; and

(b) The bill or receipt issued or made available to the customer must identify the electronically supplied services and the supplier thereof.

For the purposes of this paragraph, a taxable person who, with regard to a supply of electronically supplied services, authorises the charge to the customer or the delivery of the services, or sets the general terms and conditions of the supply, shall not be permitted to explicitly indicate another person as the supplier of those services.

These rules extend to telephone services provided through the Internet including "Voice over Internet Protocol" (VoIP) supplied through a telecommunications network, or an interface or a portal such as a marketplace for applications.

However, these rules do not apply where suppliers only use payment processing websites such as "PayPal" and they do not take part in the supply of the relevant electronically supplied services or telephone services. In such circumstances the supplier is responsible for determining its own POS liabilities and accounting for VAT appropriately.

11.2.16.6 *Interpreting the rules*

HMRC has issued Guidance in a number of on-line briefing documents regarding the interpretation of these complex rules. Extracts of the latest Guidance (updated on 24 March 2015) are provided here: [4]

Defining 'electronically supplied'
This covers e-services which are automatically delivered over the internet, or an electronic network, where there is minimal or no human intervention. In practice, this can be either:

---

[4] www.gov.uk/government/publications/vat-supplying-digital-services-to-private-consumers/

INTRA-EU TRANSACTIONS – SUPPLY OF SERVICES

- where the sale of the digital content is entirely automatic e.g. a consumer clicks the 'Buy Now' button on a website and either:
    - the content downloads onto the consumer's device
    - the consumer receives an automated e-mail containing the content
- where the sale of the digital content is essentially automatic, and the small amount of manual process involved doesn't change the nature of the supply from an e-service

All 'e-services' that are 'electronically supplied' in the ways outlined above are 'digital services' and are covered by the rule changes.

Examples of electronic supplies and whether or not they are 'digital services'

Service	e-service	Electronically supplied?	Covered by the new rules
Pdf document manually emailed by seller	Yes	No	No
Pdf document automatically emailed by seller's system	Yes	Yes	Yes
Pdf document automatically downloaded from site	Yes	Yes	Yes
Stock photographs available for automatic download	Yes	Yes	Yes
Live webinar	No	No	No
Online course consisting of pre-recorded videos and downloadable pdfs	Yes	Yes	Yes
Online course consisting of pre-recorded videos and downloadable pdfs plus support from a live tutor	Yes	No	No
Individually commissioned content sent in digital form e.g., photographs, reports, medical results	Yes	No	No
Link to online content or download sent by manual email	Yes	Yes	Yes

Further information about what is and isn't a 'digital service' can be found on the European Commission's website and in particular the Annex, page 86, in the explanatory notes provides a list of digital services.

This is a fast-changing area. The above examples are illustrative and don't provide a comprehensive and definitive list of what is considered to be a digital service. If, after reading the detailed guidance that is available you are still unsure whether your supplies are 'digital services', please email: Vat2015.contact@hmrc.gsi.gov.uk.

Bundled or multiple supplies

Where a business supplies a consumer with a package of services, or goods and services, the business will have to decide whether the complete package should

INTRA-EU TRANSACTIONS – SUPPLY OF SERVICES

be considered and taxed as a single (bundled) supply, or multiple separate supplies, each element of which should be separately taxed. Examples of a bundled supply include:
- a technical journal with supplementary online content;
- a DVD with access to online streaming of content; and
- a music CD with digital download.

A digital supplier must apply the normal approach to bundled or package supplies. If the business supplies a physical product which is 'bundled' with a product that is accessed digitally (for example), the place of supply rule changes will only apply to the digital element of the supply.

Determining whether the customer is in business (a taxable person) or is a private consumer

If you supply digital services and your customer doesn't provide you with a VAT Registration Number (VRN) then you should treat it as a business to consumer supply and charge the VAT due in the customer's member state. If a customer is unable to supply a VRN but claims they are 'in business' but not VAT-registered because, for example, they are below their member state's VAT registration threshold, you can accept other evidence of your customer's business status e.g., a link to the customer's business website or other commercial documents.

It's your decision whether to accept alternative evidence that the customer is 'in business' and your customer can't require you to treat a supply as business to business if they haven't provided a valid VRN.

If you accept that your customer is in business, the supply doesn't come within the scope of these business to consumer arrangements. With a cross-border business to business supply the customer will be responsible for accounting for any VAT due to the tax authorities in their member state. You must complete and submit a quarterly European Community Sales List declaration to HM Revenue and Customs (HMRC). Other EU member state tax authorities are then able to request details of the database where these declarations are securely stored for taxpayer compliance and audit purposes.

Determining the place of supply and taxation

From 1 January 2015 the place of supply of cross-border digital services is the place where the consumer of that service is normally resident.

Place of supply 'presumptions'

To try to simplify the rules for some supplies of digital services the supplier can make a 'presumption' about the place where the supply is to be taxed. Where the presumptions apply, the business doesn't need to know in which country the consumer of the digital service resides. This in turn means that where a digital services supply is made through one of the locations below, the business supplying the service doesn't need to obtain any further evidence to justify in which member state the VAT is due.

Types of supplies covered by the presumption rule include where the digital service is supplied:

- through a telephone box, a telephone kiosk, a Wi-Fi hot spot, an internet café, a restaurant or a hotel lobby, VAT will be due in the member state where those places are actually located - so if a German tourist makes a call from a telephone box in France, VAT will be due in France;
- on board transport travelling between different countries in the EU - VAT will be due in the member state of departure e.g., if a ferry operator provides a Wi-Fi hotspot on board ship which is available to passengers for a fee, VAT will be due in the member state of departure and won't depend on a passenger's place of residence;
- through a consumer's telephone landline, VAT is due in the member state where the consumer's landline is located;
- through a mobile phone, the consumer location will be the member state country code of the SIM card - if a French resident downloads an app to their smartphone while on holiday in Italy, VAT will be due in France; and
- in the member state for the postal address where the decoder is located or the viewing card is sent - if a UK resident has a satellite television system in their Spanish holiday home, VAT will be due in Spain

Circumstances where the presumptions don't apply

Where the digital services are supplied other than in the circumstances listed above, the business making the supply must obtain and keep 2 pieces of non-contradictory information to support and evidence the member state where the customer is normally located.

Examples of the type of supporting evidence that tax authorities will accept include:
- the billing address of the customer;
- the Internet Protocol (IP) address of the device used by the customer;
- customer's bank details;
- the country code of SIM card used by the customer;
- the location of the customer's fixed land line through which the service is supplied; and
- other commercially relevant information (for example, product coding information which electronically links the sale to a particular jurisdiction).

*Businesses using payment service providers

A business which makes cross-border digital service supplies must obtain and keep 2 pieces of information to evidence where a consumer normally lives. This demonstrates that the correct rate of VAT has been charged and will be accounted for to the correct member state tax jurisdiction. For many micro and small businesses this requirement may be challenging. So, for micro and small businesses that use payment service providers, we suggest the following approach:
1. At the point of sale, ask the consumer to provide details of either their:
    - billing address, including the member state; or
    - telephone number, including the member state dialling code; and

2. When the consumer pays for the digital service, obtain from the payment service provider a notification advice containing the 2 digit country code of the consumer's member state of residence as listed in their records.

If the 2 pieces of information tally, that will be sufficient to define the consumer's location and you can record the details in your accounting records. However, if the information doesn't tally, you must contact the consumer and ask them to reconcile the discrepancy between the 2 pieces of information.

*[HMRC have in January 2016 relaxed these rules even further, only requiring a supplier to obtain one piece of evidence which can be on an "assumptive" basis].

Support for MOSS registered micro-businesses

UK micro-businesses, that are below the current UK VAT registration threshold and are registered for the "VAT Mini One Stop Shop" (VAT MOSS), may base their 'customer location' VAT taxation and accounting decisions on information provided to them by their payment service provider.

Place of supply of educational services

Applying the place of supply rules to educational services can sometimes be confusing, so the following examples are provided so that UK businesses can determine how they are to be considered and taxed.

Services provided by a person

Education, training, or a similar service delivered by a person over the internet or an electronic network (such as a webinar), isn't considered to be an electronically supplied service because an actual person is involved in the delivery. Consequently these services are not within the scope of the 2015 rules.

Services provided through automated learning

Automated learning doesn't involve any human involvement and is considered to be a digital service.

Educational examination services

The place of supply for educational examination services, for example, marking or assessing completed examination papers, will depend on whether or not the service requires or involves any human intervention. For example, where a student is required to complete and submit an online examination paper which is automatically checked and scored by computer, this is a digital service. However, if the service involves the completed examination paper being marked by an assessor, it won't be a 'digital service' covered by the new rules. The place of taxation will be the place where the service is performed.

The table below shows examples of typical supplies of business to consumer (B2C) education or examination services, and the place where the supply is to be taxed

Type of examination service	B2C rules from 1 January 2015
Admission to event (not an e-service)	Where event takes place
Distance learning using webinars/remote	Supplier's place of establishment

Type of examination service	B2C rules from 1 January 2015
tutors (not an e-service)	
Automated learning (no human involvement) (e-service)	Customer's address or residence
Examination services - human involvement	Education where performed
Examination services - automated	Customer's address or residence

VAT rates and obligations in other EU member states (EU VAT Web Portal)

For information about the VAT rates that apply to supplies of digital services in other EU member states, as well as any other obligations (e.g., VAT invoice requirements), businesses should refer to the tables in the European Commission's EU VAT Web Portal at: ec.europa.eu/taxation_customs/taxation/vat/how_vat_works/telecom/index_en.htm#national_rules.

Member state tax authorities are required to notify the Commission about any changes to their VAT rates or other obligations so businesses can rely on the accuracy of this published information.

All businesses will need to consider how charging for the foreign rate of VAT will impact on their prices. For example, the business will need to decide whether to charge a single price and to absorb the variable VAT rates. Alternatively, a business may decide to vary the price of its digital service products to reflect the different amounts of other member states' VAT due.

VAT accounting options for businesses supplying digital services to consumers

Apart from those businesses who sell digital services entirely through digital platforms or marketplaces who take on responsibility for accounting for the VAT due (see below) businesses must consider how they intend to account for the VAT on those supplies. Businesses will have to make one of the following choices and either register:

- to use the UK VAT Mini One Stop Shop (VAT MOSS) [see **11.3**] for VAT in every EU member state where you make digital supplies to consumers, and file returns and make payments to the tax authorities in each of those member states
- HMRC strongly recommends that you register for and use UK VAT MOSS. It makes accounting for VAT due in all the EU member states much easier.

If you are below the UK VAT registration threshold (currently £81,000) you can register for UK VAT to use the UK VAT MOSS. You can charge and account for VAT in respect of your EU cross-border B2C supplies but won't have to charge and account for VAT on your UK domestic supplies. In addition, you will also be able to reclaim any VAT charged on business expenses directly related to your cross-border digital service supplies.

Digital portals, platforms, gateways and marketplaces

If you supply e-services to consumers through an internet portal, gateway or marketplace, you need to determine whether you are making the supply to the consumer or to the platform operator. If the platform operator identifies you as

INTRA-EU TRANSACTIONS – SUPPLY OF SERVICES

the seller but sets the general terms and conditions, or authorises payment, or handles delivery/download of the digital service, the platform is considered to be supplying the consumer. They are therefore responsible for accounting for the VAT payment that is charged to the consumer.

Digital platforms and accounting for VAT
If you operate a digital platform through which third parties sell e-services you are liable to account for the VAT on those sales unless every one of the following conditions are met:

- the digital platform and everyone else involved in the supply must identify who the supplier is in their contractual arrangements
- the invoice, bill or sales receipt must identify that supplier and the service supplied
- the digital platform must not authorise the charge to the consumer
- the digital platform must not authorise the delivery
- the digital platform must not set the general terms and conditions of the sale
- If you do not meet all of these conditions, you must treat the sales of third party e-services as if they were your own and declare the VAT due.

If you do meet these conditions, the responsibility for accounting for the VAT moves back to the person who supplied you and you are providing intermediary services to that person.

How to contact HMRC to clarify your status
Because of these conditions the vast majority of digital platforms will be liable to account for the VAT on the third party sales. However, if you remain unsure about your responsibility, please contact HMRC's Non-Statutory Clearance Team for full guidance on non-statutory clearances.

Role of payment services
If your only role in the supply is to provide for the processing of payments you are not regarded as a digital platform and you do not have to account for the VAT.

More information
The legislation for this is Article 9A of Council Implementing Regulation 1042/2013 which, along with explanatory notes offer additional guidance on interpretation.

11.3 "Mini One Stop Shop" or "VAT MOSS" schemes

As explained in **11.2.16** the POS of BTE services changed on 1 January 2015 for supplies made to all recipients with B2B supplies to a Relevant Business Person (see **11.2.3**) being Reverse Charged by the recipient in its own Member State when the recipient is using those services for its business, but all 'B2C' supplies are now taxable in the customer's Member States which has resulted in revised VAT registration and VAT accounting provisions.

The supplier has the choice whether to register for VAT in each Member State where the consumers are accessing the Electronically Supplied Services (ESS),

INTRA-EU TRANSACTIONS – SUPPLY OF SERVICES

usually by downloading the particular service or product over the Internet by clicking into a hyperlink or accessing the supplier's websites.

The "VAT Mini One Stop Shop" or "VAT MOSS" scheme aims to ensure that VAT is accounted for in the Member States where ESS are consumed.

All BTE services that are consumed outside the EU are outside the scope of UK and all other EU VAT so it is vital that suppliers identify the places at which their private consumers or business recipients buying these services in a private or non-business capacity actually consume them i.e. use and enjoy them.

Because, under the VAT MOSS, the supplier must identify all the EU Member States in which the services are consumed, their business systems must be able to identify and recognise the places where the consumers actually download or otherwise access these services as errors in charging the consumers prices that cater for the correct amounts of VAT can be very costly, given the variations in the rates of VAT applicable across the 28 Member States for the same services.

The 'Mini One Stop Shop' is comprised of the **"Non-Union scheme"** (see **11.3.1**) and the **"Union scheme"** (see **11.3.2**). The VAT MOSS could well be a forerunner or a trial by the Commission (although not announced as such) of an EU-wide VAT return, where all supplies in all Member States are accounted for on one VAT return submitted to one EU Member State – see **Future of VAT in the EU** in section **1.4**.

The Non-Union MOSS is a modified version of the VAT Moss covering supplies of BTE services. The main difference is that the Union Scheme only covers the supply of e-services, but the non-EU VAT MOSS scheme also covers the supply of broadcasting and telecommunications services.

11.3.1 Non-Union MOSS

Up until 31 December 2014 non-EU suppliers of digital services ought to have registered for VAT in one Member State to account for all VAT on all supplies made to EU private consumers. Most non-EU suppliers chose to do this in a 'low-rate' jurisdiction such as Luxembourg and they used the "VAT on e-Services scheme" or "VoeS".

VoeS was replaced by the "Non-Union VAT MOSS" scheme and the VoeS website remained open to businesses already registered for VoeS so they could submit any missing returns. The VoeS scheme was effective for all BTE supplies made after 1 July 2003 and the non-Union MOSS is a modified version of VoeS covering supplies of BTE services.

The VoeS enabled such suppliers to:
(a) register electronically in one Member State; and
(b) declare electronically any EU tax due on a single return to the Member State of registration.

The Member State of registration distributes the VAT to the appropriate Member States in which the consumption actually occurs. Without the scheme, such persons have to register and account for VAT in each Member State where they make supplies. Such electronically-supplied services were already VATable when supplied by an EU person before 1 July 2003, but EU VAT is no longer chargeable on such supplies made outside the EU.

Member States' tax authorities partly seek to enforce the collection of VAT under the VoeS scheme using corporate governance. It is understood that they search for unregistered suppliers and e-mail such persons a notice of the need to register. The United States Government is understood to pressurise its businesses into complying with the taxation laws of other countries so the incidence of deliberately avoiding EU VAT registration is thought to be minimal.

There is no right to recover VAT incurred on expenses through this scheme and the only way for non-EU businesses to reclaim any EU VAT is through the Thirteenth VAT directive – see **Chapter 10**. A non-EU business that is already registered for the VOES scheme should have been provided with information to transfer the existing VAT registration to the VAT MOSS Scheme.

Records relating to VoeS returns are subject to VoeS rules and not VAT MOSS rules. Suppliers could only use the VoeS scheme to declare sales made before 1 January 2015 whilst existing UK VoeS registered businesses could choose to register for the non-Union MOSS scheme for sales after this date. From 1 January 2015, a non-EU business supplying BTE services to private individuals and non-business customers can register and use the non-Union MOSS online service in any Member State.

A business (or person) registering for the non-EU VAT MOSS should get an individual VAT identification number from the Member State in which it registers. This Member State is the "Member State of identification" (MSI) and once that Member State has obtained and validated the VAT MOSS registration details for a business, it should advise the other Member States, so that they know where the business should account for VAT on its 'B2C' e-services.

However, the Non-Union MOSS does not enable persons to set against the output tax due on the e-services any VAT incurred on costs and this has to be recovered under the 13th VAT directive (for non-EU suppliers) or under the 8th Directive for EU suppliers – see **Chapter 10**. Because these mechanisms are cumbersome and there can be extensive delays in obtaining refunds, businesses should consider the impact this has on their cash flow.

To use the Non-Union VAT MOSS scheme in the UK, suppliers must:
- be based outside of the EU;
- have no fixed or business establishments in the EU; and

- supply digital services to consumers in the EU.

To register for the Non-Union VAT MOSS scheme the non-EU supplier must create a Government Gateway account. Once they receive their user ID and password they can log in to HMRC Online Services to register for Non-Union VAT MOSS.

11.3.2 Accounting for Non-Union VAT MOSS

In order to account for VAT on the relevant supplies the non-EU supplier must complete on-line the Non-Union VAT MOSS returns which are used to declare VAT due on sales of digital services to consumers in the EU, including sales to UK consumers.

To submit the Non-Union Return the supplier can either:
- complete it online; or
- upload a completed Non-Union VAT MOSS Return template.[5]

The *VAT MOSS: Non-Union Return guide* explains how to do this.[6]

11.3.3 Union MOSS

To use the Union VAT MOSS scheme in the UK, the supplier must:
- be based in the UK, or be a non-EU business with a fixed establishment in the UK;
- be registered for UK VAT; and
- supply digital services to consumers in the EU.

If the supplier's business turnover is below the UK VAT registration threshold (currently £83,000 per annum) they must still register for UK VAT to use the Union VAT MOSS scheme. However, under the Union MOSS an EU business may register and use VAT MOSS in the Member State where it is established or in any other Member State.

If the UK Union VAT Moss is chosen suppliers must register for the scheme themselves as an agent is unable to register for them. However, once registered the supplier can appoint an agent to submit their VAT MOSS Returns.[7] The agent will need to sign up for the VAT MOSS for Agents online service.[8]

If the supplier is already registered for UK VAT they can log in to HMRC Online Services at **online.hmrc.gov.uk/login** to register for the Union VAT MOSS. The supplier will need to sign in with their existing Government Gateway user 'ID' and password, which will be the same one used to submit

---

[5] www.gov.uk/government/publications/vat-mini-one-stop-shop-non-union-return
[6] www.gov.uk/government/publications/vat-mini-one-stop-shop-non-union-return-guides
[7] www.gov.uk/appoint-tax-agent
[8] www.gov.uk/government/publications/vat-mini-one-stop-shop-agents-online-service

the periodic VAT Returns. HMRC explain that the user ID and password are the same as those set up for an organisation.

If the supplier doesn't already hold a Government Gateway account user ID and password, they can set this up when they register for UK VAT online.[9]

If the supplier has any fixed establishments in other EU Member States they must advise HMRC about these when registering for Union VAT MOSS. If they are already registered the supplier must advise HMRC about any new fixed establishments through your VAT MOSS account, in HMRC Online Services.

If the supplier's other UK taxable turnover is below the UK VAT threshold (currently £83,000) they will still need to:
- register for VAT before registering for Union VAT MOSS; and
- enter 'Digital Services' and select *'Supplies of Digital Services (below UK VAT threshold) under VAT MOSS arrangements'* - when asked to search for a business activity as part of the VAT registration application.

If the supplier only registers for UK VAT to use the Union VAT MOSS scheme, they only need to submit 'nil' VAT Returns.[10]

If the supplying business is part of a UK VAT group the group can register for UK Union VAT MOSS. The "Representative Member" must register using the group's UK VAT number. The representative member when registering for Union VAT MOSS must:
- state they are the representative member; and
- quote the VAT group's UK VAT registration number.

The Union VAT MOSS scheme can only be used to declare VAT on digital sales to consumers in countries where a business has no fixed or business establishment. Therefore, if any of the VAT group members have establishments or are based in other Member States, they can't include sales made in those countries on the group's UK Union VAT MOSS Return.

HMRC has invited suppliers who have questions on these matters to email them at **VAT2015.contact@hmrc.gsi.gov.uk** for advice.

Suppliers opting for the UK Union VAT Moss must register by the 10th day of the month after their first digital service sale. For example, if the first sale of digital services is on 8 July 2016, they must register by 10 August 2016. The VAT MOSS registration will be backdated to 8 July 2016, the date of the first sale. If the supplier has not been able to register by the deadline, they should email HMRC at the email address above for advice.

---

[9] online.hmrc.gov.uk/registration/organisation/moss/introduction
[10] www.gov.uk/vat-returns/fill-in-your-return.

Registration for VAT MOSS is optional, so suppliers can deregister if they no longer want to use the scheme. To deregister they need to log-in at **online.hmrc.gov.uk/login** and go to the VAT MOSS 'change registration details' section from the 'services you can use' page.

As the scheme runs on a quarterly basis, applicants need to tell HMRC that they wish to leave the scheme at least 15 days before the end of the quarter they wish to leave. For example, if they wish to deregister from 1 July, they must tell HMRC before 15 June. Once deregistered the supplier will be unable to re-join the scheme, in any Member State, for at least two calendar quarters. The supplier will need to wait until the first day of the calendar quarter after this period before re-joining the scheme.

By using the VAT MOSS, the business can make VAT declarations and payments, in respect of all EU supplies of services, to the tax authority in that one Member State.

11.3.3.1 *Accounting for Union VAT MOSS*

In the UK, a UK-established supplier of the affected e-services still declares his UK-related sales on his usual, non-VAT MOSS, UK VAT return. All other VAT applicable to all other EU Member States is accounted for on the VAT MOSS VAT return which is still submitted to HMRC, but HMRC distribute those VAT amounts to all the other tax authorities to whom the VAT is due to be paid.

When registering HMRC will automatically set the supplier up for the online VAT MOSS Return service. Suppliers need to log in at **online.hmrc.gov.uk/login** to send HMRC their VAT MOSS quarterly returns. The deadlines for the UK VAT Moss returns are:

- 20 April – for first quarter ending 31 March;
- 20 July – for second quarter ending 30 June;
- 20 October – for third quarter ending 30 September; and
- 20 January – for fourth quarter ending 31 December.

To submit a Union VAT MOSS Return the supplier can either:

- complete it online; or
- upload a completed Union VAT MOSS Return template. The *VAT MOSS: Union Return guide* explains how to do this.[11]

If the supplier has fixed establishments in other EU Member States, any digital sales made to consumers there must be declared in those countries as suppliers can only use the Union VAT MOSS scheme to declare sales to consumers in Member States where they have no fixed or business establishments.

---

[11] www.gov.uk/government/publications/vat-mini-one-stop-shop-union-return-guides

INTRA-EU TRANSACTIONS – SUPPLY OF SERVICES

If the supplier's UK Taxable turnover is below the UK VAT registration threshold (currently £83,000) they would not be liable to be VAT-registered in the UK (unless they voluntarily registered) so no UK VAT is due on their UK taxable sales. In this case as well as a VAT MOSS Return, they need to complete a nil UK VAT Return - guidance on how to complete and submit a UK VAT return is provided at **www.gov.uk/vat-returns/fill-in-your-return**.

It is vital that suppliers monitor their UK taxable turnover because if they exceed the UK VAT registration threshold, they must start accounting for VAT on UK sales. Consequently, If UK VAT is not accounted for at the correct time, HMRC may assess the tax due. HMRC information on how to calculate taxable turnover and when to register for UK VAT is provided online.[12] The current VAT registration thresholds are provided at **www.gov.uk/vat-registration-thresholds**.

Suppliers must pay HMRC the VAT due once each quarterly VAT MOSS Return has been submitted on-line. The deadlines for the quarterly payments are the same as the normal UK VAT return deadlines.

Each payment must reach HMRC on the last working day before the weekend or a bank holiday. HMRC has provided guidance on how to pay the MOSS VAT bill at **www.gov.uk/pay-vat/moss** for both the Union and Non-Union schemes.

It is important that for the Union scheme, the correct account is used and the payment reference is quoted. The payment reference is found:
- on the acknowledgement screen when the VAT MOSS Return is submitted; or
- by going to the 'customer communications' section of the VAT MOSS account in HMRC Online Services.

Union VAT MOSS liabilities cannot be paid together with UK VAT liabilities and they must be paid into HMRC's VAT MOSS account because HMRC needs to distribute non-UK VAT MOSS liabilities to all the other Member States into which digital services have been supplied.

If the VAT MOSS bill, or the full amount owing has not been paid on time, HMRC will send an email reminder 10 days after the payment is due. If the supplier has still not paid the VAT bill after the reminder has been sent, the supplier may have to make any further payments direct to the tax authority of the country(ies) concerned.

---

[12] www.gov.uk/vat-registration/calculate-turnover

INTRA-EU TRANSACTIONS – SUPPLY OF SERVICES

Guidance on how to correct any errors in previously submitted VAT MOSS returns is provided by HMRC online.[13] The record-keeping requirements for VAT MOSS are quite daunting and HMRC state in their guidance that records must be kept of:

- the member state where the sales were made - known as the "Member State of consumption";
- the date a service was supplied;
- the taxable amount, including the currency used;
- any increase or decrease of the taxable amount e.g. discounts;
- the VAT rate applied;
- the amount of VAT due and the currency used;
- payments received by the business - the dates and amounts;
- any payments on account received by the business for services before they were supplied;
- the information shown on any invoices issued;
- the customers' names - where known; and
- the information used to decide where a customer is based.

All of these records must be kept for **10 years** and if requested by HMRC the supplier must be able to send these details to HMRC electronically.

Suppliers who wish to reclaim the VAT paid on business expenses or purchases should do so on their UK VAT Returns instead of submitting nil returns as this VAT cannot be reclaimed on the VAT MOSS Returns.[14]

VAT incurred on business expenses in other EU Member States can only be reclaimed where it relates directly to VAT MOSS qualifying sales. In order to reclaim this VAT, suppliers must complete a cross-border VAT refund application.[15] The claim is made via the electronic portal.[16]

Details of VAT MOSS sales are not to be reported on EC Sales Lists[17] even though they are declared on the VAT MOSS Return.

If the supplier's UK taxable turnover is below the UK VAT registration threshold and the supplier has only registered for UK VAT to use VAT MOSS, they will not need to complete EC Sales Lists at all.

---

[13] www.gov.uk/guidance/register-and-use-the-vat-mini-one-stop-shop
[14] www.gov.uk/guidance/register-and-use-the-vat-mini-one-stop-shop#under-threshold-reclaim-vat-on-expenses
[15] www.gov.uk/guidance/vat-refunds-for-uk-businesses-buying-from-other-eu-countries
[16] online.hmrc.gov.uk/login?GAREASONCODE=-%201&GARESOURCEID=Common&GAURI=online.hmrc.gov.uk/home&Reason=-1&APPID=Common&URI=online.hmrc.gov.uk/home
[17] www.gov.uk/guidance/vat-how-to-report-your-eu-sales

11.3.4 Pricing services and VAT

Where suppliers charge a flat rate which is treated as a 'VAT inclusive' (or gross) price then they need to calculate what proportion of that price is VAT in order to be able to complete the Non Union VAT MOSS Returns or the Union VAT Moss Returns.

Example

Taking the example of the sale of an eBook (by the customer clicking into a hyperlink from a web page) for £10 including VAT, regardless of where the customer is based, the amount of VAT in the £10 will vary, depending on the VAT rate of the country where the customer is based.

To calculate the VAT due in the £10 the supplier must apply the relevant "VAT fraction" for the EU Member State concerned. Dividing the gross price by the relevant VAT fraction produces the amount of VAT contained within the price. Usually, if all products are liable to the same rate of VAT, the VAT fraction can be applied to the relevant VAT period's gross sales to arrive at the gross amount of VAT due on that period's sales.

The VAT fraction is calculated as:

(100 + VAT rate) ÷ VAT rate = VAT fraction

So for Sweden (VAT rate 25%) the VAT fraction would be (100 + 25) ÷ 25 = 5.

Therefore, for the sale of 12 eBooks costing £10 to customers in Sweden (VAT rate 25%), the total sales value is £120 and the VAT would be £120 ÷ 5 = £24.

As the VAT is £24, this means the VAT exclusive (or net) value of sales is £120 - £24 = £96.

Using the same example, if the same number of eBooks were sold in the UK the VAT due would be £20 because the standard-rate of VAT is currently 20%, which is a VAT fraction of 1/6th.

Therefore, suppliers must understand the effect VAT rates and VAT fractions will have on sales to multiple Member States and attempt to price the products accordingly. It might be possible for the products to bear different prices where they are advertised for download on different websites for example Amazon Sweden versus Amazon UK or are priced in different currencies e.g. Sterling and Sk/Euro.

Taxable sales of digital services to consumers based in territories of certain Member States may attract special VAT rates. If so, these sales must be declared on the VAT MOSS Returns on separate lines, against the relevant parent Member State (with the appropriate VAT rate shown). The VAT fractions will of course vary between products and Member States so again setting accurate prices is vital if losses are to be avoided. Appropriate VAT rates can be ascertained by visiting the EC's Europa website and by choosing the relevant country and type of services.[18]

Currency conversion can also create losses (or gains) according to the 'market rate' when the payments are cleared through the banks or on-line payment providers such as PayPal. Suppliers using the UK VAT Moss charging non-UK consumers in currency other than pound sterling and recording that currency in their business accounts must convert the amounts into sterling when entering the sales on the VAT MOSS quarterly returns.

The European Central Bank conversion rates, which are published on the last working day of each calendar quarter, must be used to achieve this. Details of the conversion rates for each quarter can be found by accessing **www.gov.uk/government/collections/vat-information-sheets**.

Alternatively, HMRC will allow business that automatically convert the foreign currency into sterling on their business accounts (using an agreed daily or other periodic rate) to use those figures when completing their quarterly VAT MOSS Return.

11.3.5 POS tables for Broadcasting, Telecommunications and Electronic (BTE) services

The following tables provided by the Europa website give an overview of the VAT POS and the liability for VAT of BTE services:

A Rules applicable until the end of 2014
A1 Supplies into or from the EU

Type of service transaction	VAT payable in ("place of supply")
Telecoms/broadcast/electronic services from: • outside the EU to a customer in the EU; or • inside the EU to a customer outside the EU	Country where customer belongs (has their main business or fixed premises, their permanent address or usually lives). In some cases, subject to a 'use and enjoyment' override

The effects of this are as follows:

A2 EU BUSINESSES supplying to:

Business or **consumer outside the EU**	Usually no EU VAT charged. But if the service is **effectively used & enjoyed** in an EU country, that country can decide to levy VAT.

A3 NON-EU BUSINESSES supplying to:

Business in the EU	No VAT charged. Customer must account for the tax (reverse-charge mechanism).

---

[18] ec.europa.eu/taxation_customs/tic/public/vatRates/vatrates.html

INTRA-EU TRANSACTIONS – SUPPLY OF SERVICES

Consumer in the EU - telecoms or broadcasting services	Must charge VAT in the EU country where the service is effectively used and enjoyed.
Consumer in the EU - electronic services	Must charge VAT in the EU country where that consumer belongs (is registered, has their permanent address or usually lives)

A4   Supplies between EU countries

Type of service transaction	VAT payable in ("place of supply")
Telecoms/broadcast/electronic services supplied *within* the EU	B2B – EU country where the customer belongs B2C – EU country where the supplier belongs

B   Rules applicable as from 2015

From 1 January 2015, telecommunications, broadcasting and electronic services will always be taxed in the country where the customer belongs* – regardless of whether the customer is a business or consumer – regardless of whether the supplier based in the EU or outside

* *For a business (taxable person) = either the country where it is registered or the country where it has fixed premises receiving the service.*
* *For a consumer (non-taxable person) = the country where they are registered, have their permanent address or usually live.*

The effects of this are as follows:

B1   EU BUSINESSES supplying to:

Business in another EU country	No VAT charged. Customer must account for the tax (reverse-charge mechanism).
Consumer in another EU country	Must charge VAT in the EU country where the customer belongs (not where the business is based). Example: a Polish customer downloading an App on his mobile phone from a Finnish supplier. The Finnish company must charge the customer Polish VAT. MOSS available.
Business or consumer outside the EU	No EU VAT charged. Example: a Hungarian company sells an anti-virus program to be downloaded through its website to businesses or private individuals in Australia. No VAT but if the service is effectively used & enjoyed in an EU country that country can decide to levy VAT (option for Member States).

B2   NON-EU BUSINESSES supplying to:

Business in the EU	No VAT charged. Customer must account for the tax (reverse-charge mechanism).

INTRA-EU TRANSACTIONS – SUPPLY OF SERVICES

Consumer in the EU (telecoms, broadcasting or electronic services) — Must charge VAT in the EU country where the customer belongs.
Example: a person living in Barcelona pays a US company for access to American TV channels. The US company must charge the customer Spanish VAT. MOSS available

The Commission has provided a guide to the 2015 changes for micro-businesses[19] (reproduced here):

> **Basic summary information for micro businesses on 2015 EU VAT**
> In accordance with the rules that entered into force on 1 January 2015 all suppliers delivering cross border electronic services to final consumers have to account for VAT in Member States where their customer are located. In order to simplify obligations linked with those supplies a Mini One Stop Shop (MOSS) is offered as an option to avoid registration in several countries.
>
> Micro businesses will find below the most basic information needed in order to correctly fulfil their EU VAT obligations. It should be seen as a starting point for those who are for the first time supplying electronic services in another Member State.
>
> **What is the definition of electronically supplied services?**
> 'Electronically supplied services' include services which are delivered over the Internet or an electronic network and the nature of which renders their supply essentially automated and involving minimal human intervention, and impossible to ensure in the absence of information technology.
>
> Examples of what is and what is not an electronically supplied service are to be found in the Explanatory Notes on 2015 EU VAT changes on pages 83, 85 to 88 in three tables named Annex II, Article 7 and Annex I on the European Commission webpage see
>
> ec.europa.eu/taxation_customs/resources/documents/taxation/vat/how_vat_w orks/telecom/explanatory_notes_2015_en.pdf
>
> In the same document on page 11 (point 1.3) you can find which supplies are not covered by 2015 EU VAT changes.
>
> **What are the rates that should be applied to electronically supplied services in all Member States?**
> See table with applicable VAT rates on pages 4 and 5 of
>
> ec.europa.eu/taxation_customs/resources/documents/taxation/vat/how_vat_w orks/telecom/instructions_report.pdf
>
> **Additional information:**
> All VAT rates, provided and monitored by national administrations, can be verified via ec.europa.eu/taxation_customs/tic/

---

[19] ec.europa.eu/taxation_customs/resources/documents/taxation/vat/how_vat_work s/telecom/information_microbusinesses_euvat_2015.pdf

Which Member States oblige businesses to issue an invoice for B2C supplies?

See table, on pages 4 and 5 of the document at

ec.europa.eu/taxation_customs/resources/documents/taxation/vat/how_vat_w orks/telecom/instructions_report.pdf

Where can more information on national rules relevant for suppliers of electronic services be found?

At ec.europa.eu/taxation_customs/taxation/vat/how_vat_works/telecom/index en.htm (information on selected national VAT rules) there is a report which provides more information on national rules relevant for suppliers of electronic services. After opening the report some users may need to enable content in order to search effectively for information. In practice one may need to click on the field [Enable Content] which normally is to be found on the opening page of the report close to top left corner. In order to see all the types of information included in the report one should click on the field where word [All] is written.

What is the mini One Stop Shop (MOSS) and what are my obligations under the MOSS?

The MOSS is a system that will allow taxable persons supplying telecommunication, broadcasting and electronic services to non-taxable persons in Member States in which they do not have an establishment to account for the VAT due on those supplies via a web portal in the Member State in which they are identified. More detailed information is included in the MOSS guidelines, which can be found at

ec.europa.eu/taxation_customs/resources/documents/taxation/vat/how_vat_w orks/telecom/one-stop-shop-guidelines_en.pdf

All the information that are provided above (and much more) is to be found on the EU webpage at

ec.europa.eu/taxation_customs/taxation/vat/how_vat_works/telecom/index_e n.htm

One Stop Shop and Audit guidelines for 2015

A practical guide has been prepared in order to provide a better understanding of EU legislation relating to the mini One Stop Shop, as well as of the functional and technical specifications of the special schemes, as adopted by the Standing Committee on Administrative Cooperation (SCAC) - see

ec.europa.eu/taxation_customs/resources/documents/taxation/vat/how_vat_w orks/telecom/one-stop-shop-guidelines_en.pdf

This guide is complemented by additional guidelines available in all EU official languages, Russian, Chinese -and Japanese) on the audit of the mini One Stop Shop and IT information related to a suggested standard audit file for MOSS (mentioned in the additional guidelines under d)) – see ec.europa.eu/taxation_customs/resources/documents/taxation/vat/how_vat_w orks/telecom/one-stop_add_guidelines_en.pdf

INTRA-EU TRANSACTIONS – SUPPLY OF SERVICES

C Legislation before and after 1 January 2015
Sales to final consumers – overview

RULES until 31/12/2014 Telecommunications, broadcasting & electronic services[1]			
Services supplied by/to	EU consumer in EU country 1	EU consumer in EU country 2	Non-EU consumer[3]
EU supplier (EU country 1)	Taxable in EU country 1	Taxable in EU country 1	No EU VAT
EU supplier (EU country 2)	Taxable in EU country 2	Taxable in EU country 2	No EU VAT
Non-EU supplier	Taxable in EU country 1[2]	Taxable in EU country 2[2]	No EU VAT

(1) One-time registration (MOSS) available for electronic services.
(2) Taxable in country of effective use & enjoyment, if this is not the country where the customer belongs.
(3) Unless used in a country that applies the effective use & enjoyment rules.

RULES from 2015 Telecommunications, broadcasting & electronic services			
Services supplied by/to	EU consumer in EU country 1	EU consumer in EU country 2	Non-EU consumer[2]
EU supplier (EU country 1)	Taxable in EU country 1	Taxable in EU country 2[1]	No EU VAT
EU supplier (EU country 2)	Taxable in EU country 1[1]	Taxable in EU country 2	No EU VAT
Non-EU supplier	Taxable in EU country 1[1]	Taxable in EU country 2[1]	No EU VAT

(1) One-time registration (MOSS) available.
(2) Unless used in a country that applies the effective use & enjoyment rules.

Changes to one-time registration scheme (MOSS) from 2015

Online declaration/payment For supplies to consumers, both EU and non-EU businesses can use a **web portal** in the EU country where they are VAT-registered to declare and pay the VAT due in their customer's EU country.

11.4 Specific exception for 'B2C' "intellectual-type" services and other "intangibles"

Specific rules apply for "intangible services" supplied to private consumers resident in non-EU countries. The common feature of such services is that their place of performance can be indeterminate or variable and they are easily undertaken in a different place to where a supplier has established a business.

Where such intangible services (other than, with effect from 1 January 2015, broadcasting, telecommunications and electronically supplied services (see section 11.2.16) are supplied to a customer who is not a "Relevant Business Person" and belongs in a country which is not a Member State (other than the Isle of Man) the place of supply is where the customer belongs.

From 1 January 2015 the place of supply and therefore the place of taxation is deemed to be, for a public authority or a government department etc., the place where its central functions of its administration are carried out. However, if the body has other places where a sufficient degree of permanence and sufficient human and technical resources are present to enable it to receive and use the services in question, then that place can also be treated as the place of taxation. It would then be necessary to determine the place most appropriate to the use and enjoyment.

In the case of a private person the place where they usually reside, unless there is evidence that they have an alternative "permanent address" and use the services there, is to be taken as the place of taxation.

The following headings cover a range of services that can be treated as supplied at the customer's place of belonging and whilst they appear to be fairly self-explanatory, often taxpayers and HMRC (in the UK) form opposing views on what exactly is being supplied and whether the relevant services fit within a relevant heading. The headings are not all-encompassing so if a service or services cannot fit within a particular heading, it might fit into an alternative heading and still be tax-shifted to the customer's country.

It is essential therefore that suppliers identify the precise nature of the service in question and take a view on whichever heading might be most suitable. If a service cannot fit into any of the headings (or HMRC object to the VAT treatment applied) the service will fall to be excluded from the enabling legislation and be taxable resulting in an exposure to VAT that has not been costed by the supplier and which is usually not recoverable from the customer.

These headings cover:
- Transfers and assignments of copyright, patents, licences, trademarks and similar rights – **11.4.1**.
- The acceptance of any obligation to refrain from pursuing or exercising (in whole or in part) any business activity or any rights relating to an intangible service – **11.4.2**.
- Advertising services – **11.4.3**.
- Services of consultants, engineers, consultancy bureaux, lawyers, accountants and other similar services; data processing; and the provision of information – **11.4.4**.
- Banking, financial and insurance services (including reinsurance), other than the provision of safe deposit facilities – **11.4.5**.
- The provision of access to, and of transport or transmission through, natural gas and electricity distribution systems and the provision of other directly linked services – **11.4.6**.
- The supply of staff – **11.4.7**.

- The letting on hire of goods other than means of transport (subject to use and enjoyment provisions) – **11.4.8**.
- Additionally, the supplies of BTE services (**"Relevant Services"**) made to private consumers are also briefly mentioned in this section although full details are provided in other sections of this book, these being Telecommunication services, Radio and television broadcasting services and Electronically supplied services (all subject to use and enjoyment provisions) – **11.4.9**.
- Emissions Allowances – **11.5**.
- Agency services – **11.6**.
- Valuations services and work on goods – **11.7**.

Where a supply of relevant services would otherwise be regarded as made in the UK, but the effective use and enjoyment of those services is outside the EU, the supply is to be treated as taking place in that country to the extent of its actual use and enjoyment.

Alternatively, where a supply of relevant services would otherwise be regarded as taking place outside the EU, but the effective use and enjoyment of those services is in the UK, the supply is to be treated as taking place in the UK to the extent of its actual use and enjoyment.

11.4.1 Transfers and assignments of copyright, patents, licences, trademarks and similar rights.

HMRC describe "similar rights" as intellectual property rights which are capable of being legally enforced with the payments for these intellectual rights often known as 'royalties'. They can be made on a regular and continuing basis or take the form of a single, one-off fee. HMRC state that services which do not involve intellectual property are not covered even though they may be described as a right or licence.

In Notice 741A HMRC state the following types of services are included in this heading:
- the granting of a licence to use computer software;
- the transfer of permission to use a logo; and
- the granting of a right by a photographer for one of his photographs to be published in a magazine article. This includes material which is digitally downloaded to the customer.

HMRC state that none of the following types of services can be included:
- the supply of individual shares in goods, for example an animal or yacht, even though certain rights may be included in the supply;
- the supply of a right to obtain reduced rates for admission to conferences and meetings as well as similar discounts on facilities available to members of clubs, associations or societies in return for a subscription;

- the supply of the right to occupy land or property including hotel accommodation; and
- the granting of a right to a future supply of a service. The place of supply of that right will be the same place as the underlying supply to which the right relates. This will be the case even in situations where the right is never exercised. A right to services includes a reference to any right, option or priority with respect to the supply of services and to the supply of an interest deriving from any right to services.

11.4.2 The acceptance of any obligation to refrain from pursuing or exercising (in whole or in part) any business activity or any rights relating to an intangible service

In Notice 741A HMRC state this heading covers entering into agreements not to pursue or undertake any business activity and refraining from exercising, or relinquishing, those rights providing the following examples:
- the vendor of a business accepting an undertaking not to compete with the purchaser; and
- agreement by the owner of a trademark to refrain from using it.

11.4.3 Advertising services

HMRC say that this heading covers all services of a person publicising another person's name or products with a view to encouraging their sale including supplies of advertising services in the established media, for example, of radio or television advertising time; of the right to place an advertisement on a hoarding; or of advertising space in any publication. Newer promotional methods such as an entry in a telephone enquiry directory or advertising space in any electronic location are covered.

Advertising services include operations involving the distribution or supply of goods either free or at a reduced price; the organisation of publicity events for promotional or publicity campaign purposes.

11.4.4 Services of consultants, engineers, consultancy bureaux, lawyers, accountants and other similar services; data processing; and the provision of information

This heading covers a wide range of services of different natures including those provided by consultants, engineers, consultancy bureaux, lawyers and accountants as well as other services which are similar to them. Data processing services and the provision of information are also included. It does not matter how supplies of these services are delivered to a customer, which may be by electronic transmission, courier or mail. However, all services relating to land and property are excluded from this heading with the place of supply always treated as the place where the land is situated.

The courts have given the expression "consultancy" a wide meaning, and consultancy can include advisory services. In a case decided in 2003

(Mohammed (t/a The Indian Palmist) v C & E Comrs (2003) the Tribunal stated that the term "consultants" should be construed as referring to members of the "liberal professions". This means that the consultant and the profession in which he/she practises must:

> have a marked intellectual character, require a high level qualification, and be subject to clear and strict professional regulation

In the case of *Sumitomo Mitsui Banking Corporation Europe Ltd v Revenue and Customs Commissioners (2009)* the Tribunal accepted HMRC's view of the distinction between management and consultancy, namely that:

> the defining features of the principal and habitual activities of consultants were that they were advisory and carried out in an independent manner, in the sense that the activities were not an integral and ongoing part of managerial activities...

Moreover the Tribunal ruled in the case of *Gabbitas Educational Consultants Ltd v Revenue and Customs Commissioners (2009)* that:

> organisational and administrative services or the provision of practical advice were not services that a consultant would principally and habitually supply.

It is therefore vital to ensure that when the phrase "consultancy" is used, there is more than habitual processing of management information or managing data etc. (as opposed to the processing of data or the provision of information – see **11.4.4.5** and **11.4.4.6**).

11.4.4.1 Consultants and consultancy bureaux

In Notice 741A HMRC state that services of consultants and consultancy bureaux cover the normal services of experts in all professional areas who act in an accepted professional or advisory capacity, providing the following examples:

- research and development;
- market research;
- written translation services or interpreters' services which do not take place at an event, such as interpreting services for a telephone conference - see section 8 for oral interpreting at an event;
- testing and analysis of goods (for example, drugs, chemicals and domestic electrical appliances). The essential nature of such services is analysis by experts who use the results of the testing to reach a professional conclusion, such as whether goods meet specified standards;
- writing scientific reports;
- production of customised ('bespoke' or 'specific') computer software, excluding digitally downloaded software, as well as the services of adapting existing packages. However, some 'off-the-shelf' software packages are treated as supplies of goods; and
- software maintenance involving upgrades, advice and resolving any problems. The place of performance is not relevant as solutions may be provided by telephone conversations, remote links or attending a

mainframe site. However, a contract for simply maintaining computer hardware relates to work on goods.

HMRC state that the following types of services are excluded from this heading:
- services of consultants and consultancy bureaux that relate to specific land or property;
- supplies described as management services, unless they can be shown to be essentially of consultancy services (however, such services may fall within other headings;
- clerical or secretarial services, the provision of office facilities and archiving services; and
- services provided by a consultant which are outside the supplier's remit.

11.4.4.2 *Engineers*

HMRC state that to be included in this heading the engineers should usually possess formal qualifications. Services of engineers cover engineering design or consultancy services. The services must be of a type expected of an expert or professional. Examples are:
- the provision of intellectual engineering advice or design. This includes overseeing the resultant physical work, provided that any such supervision is merely to ensure that the design or other advice is properly implemented; and
- services of engineers/technicians within the entertainment industry. This covers editors and sound engineers producing an edit master from which copies can be made (films, videos, compact discs or audio tapes) as well as those who exercise a degree of artistic control or influence over material.

Some excluded services are:
- services of surveyors and consultants consisting primarily of work such as design, surveying, site supervision or valuation where these directly relate to land or property; and
- services carried out by an engineer which consist wholly or mainly of physical work on goods, including their installation.

11.4.4.3 *Lawyers and accountants*

Services of lawyers and accountants include services normally provided by lawyers, accountants, solicitors, barristers or auditors in their professional capacities, except where those services directly relate to land or property.

HMRC provide the following examples of included services in Notice 741A:
- legal and accountancy services in the general administration or winding up of a deceased's estate even if that estate includes land or property. Such supplies are not made to beneficiaries but to the estate. This is seen as whoever is appointed executor or administrator, although they may also be a beneficiary; and
- services described as management services, the essential nature of which comprise accountancy or legal services.

The following examples are provided by HMRC as excluded services:
- services consisting primarily of work which directly relates to land or property, such as:
  - property management;
  - conveyancing; and
  - obtaining planning consent;
- a claim of ownership over a particular piece of land or property; and
- clerical or secretarial services, which includes the keeping of financial records.

Also, in a case called *Fairplay Ltd v Revenue and Customs Commissioners (2007)* the supply of a complete payroll service, comprising the payment of wages, the administration, calculation and payment of tax and NI contributions, and the issuing of wage slips was held to fall outside this heading.

11.4.4.4 "Similar services"

The phrase "similar services" can cause a good degree of confusion and debate over what types of services that are similar in nature to the above types of services and therefore included in this heading.

HMRC blandly state that similar services include services which are similar to those normally provided by consultants, consultancy bureaux, engineers, lawyers, and accountants providing the following examples:
- services of loss adjusters and assessors in assessing the validity of claims (except when these services relate to land). Such services may include examination of goods to establish a value for damage or deterioration as well as negotiating a settlement amount;
- services of surveyors, providing opinions which do not relate to specific sites;
- architects' services where there is no specific site of land;
- design services;
- services of specialists or technicians which are essentially creative or artistic in nature; and
- services of film directors or producers, where their services are not of rights included in **11.4.1** above.

HMRC state that the following types of services are excluded from "similar services":
- services provided by architects and surveyors which directly relate to land or property. This includes surveying, site supervision, conveyancing, valuation and obtaining planning consent; and
- loss adjusting services in relation to claims on land or property and services provided by a loss adjuster which are simply the valuation of goods.

11.4.4.5 *"Data processing"*
Data processing is described as the application of programmed instructions on existing data which results in the production of required information. Rather than expand on this definition by providing examples of what are data processing services, in Notice 741A HMRC provides the following examples of services that are not data processing:
- services which simply include an element of data processing. Where this is simply required for a contract to be completed, the nature of the actual contracted services determines which place of supply rule applies;
- processing data from seismic surveys where the computer analysis relates to a specified area of land or seabed; and
- simple re-formatting where there is no change to the meaning of the content.

11.4.4.6 *"Provision of information"*
HMRC state that the "Provision of information" covers the supplying of knowledge of any type and in any form including facts, data, figures and other material. HMRC provides the following examples in Notice 741A:
- tourist information;
- weather forecasts;
- information supplied by a private enquiry agent;
- telephone helpdesk services (such as for computer software);
- satellite, navigational and location services; and
- provision of online information.

HMRC also provide the following examples of excluded services:
- the delivery or transmission of another person's information by whatever means; and
- information relating to specific land or property.

11.4.5 Banking, financial and insurance services (including reinsurance), other than the provision of safe deposit facilities

This heading covers all banking, financial and insurance services many of which are exempt when made in the UK. Examples of services included are:
- granting of mortgages and loans – selling debts;
- the storage of gold bullion or gold coins by a bank or a dealer in gold who is a subsidiary of a bank;
- the sale of securities as principal;
- the sale of unallocated precious metals,[20] or of unallocated precious metal coins;[21]
- debt collection services;

---

[20] Gold, silver, platinum, palladium, rhodium, ruthenium, osmium and iridium
[21] Goods are unallocated if they remain an unidentifiable part of a larger stock of goods held by the supplier

- portfolio management services;
- the provision of insurance or reinsurance;
- the supply of financial futures and financial options;
- trustee services; and
- commodity brokers' services of arranging transactions in futures and options.

Excludes services include:
- services of physical safe custody other than those included above; and
- rent collection services.

11.4.5.1 "Securities"

Details of the VAT liability of dealing is securities is provided in VAT Notice 701/49: *Finance*.

In summary, however, the issue of securities such as shares, bonds, loan notes, debentures etc., are not supplies for VAT purposes when the purpose of that issue is to raise capital. This includes the issue of units or shares in an investment fund. Conversely, transactions in securities that are already in existence are exempt when they are sold or transferred in the course of a business activity and the normal partial exemption rules apply.

Where securities are sold by UK suppliers and the place where the purchaser belongs cannot be determined, the supplier can apply a special rule, known as the **'easement'**. The rules for determining the Place of Supply are given in Notice 701/49 at section 6.16 and are:

If:
- your place of belonging is the UK; and
- you sell securities to a customer; and
- you cannot identify your customer or their place of belonging

you may
- treat the supply as being in the UK and exempt; or
- use the place of belonging of a nominee account for the purchaser to determine the place of supply; or
- use a special rule known as 'the easement'. This works by using the following tests in sequential order:

(a) Where the place of transaction, that is the relevant security exchange, is known then a sale transacted:
- in the UK is treated as made to a person belonging in the UK and exempt;
- in any other EU Member State is treated as made to a taxable person belonging in that Member State, and is outside the scope of UK VAT, but without recovery of your related input tax; and
- outside the EU is treated as made to a person belonging outside the EU and is outside the scope of UK VAT. You can recover related input tax subject to normal rules.

(b) Where the place of the transaction is not known
- then the place of supply is deemed to be a place where the security is listed.

(c) Where the place of transaction is not known and the security is not listed or is listed on both a EU and non-EU exchange
- then the place of supply is deemed to be the place where the last known broker in the transaction 'belongs'.

11.4.6 The provision of access to, and transport or transmission through, natural gas and electricity distribution systems and the provision of other directly linked services

This heading covers supplies of services which allow access to, and actual use of, the distribution networks. The distribution systems are the transmission networks of pipelines, cables and interconnectors, which enable the national and international transport of gas and electricity to be carried out. They provide the essential link between producers and consumers of natural gas and electricity within Europe. Also included are 'directly linked' services. These are services which, although not directly involving use of the systems, are clearly an adjunct to such usage. In Notice 741A HMRC provide the following examples of included and excluded services for this heading.

Included services:
- use of the gas National Transmission System;
- use of the National Grid;
- provision of data on network usage;
- storage of gas within the natural gas distribution system; and
- services involving injection of gas into the system.

Excluded services
- balancing and imbalance charges;
- contract termination payments;
- fees/subscriptions for membership of regulatory or trade bodies; and
- brokerage fees.

11.4.7 Supplies of staff

A supply of staff is when the company or entity that employs the staff members allows them to work under the general control and guidance of another party as if they become employees of that other party. However, the supply of staff must be distinguished from supplies of other services which the employee's own employer makes by using the staff to supply that other service. Here, this is not a supply of staff even if the cost is calculated on an hourly rate.

Therefore, when a supplier uses employees to provide whatever service they are contracted to supply (under a contract for services) to a customer, it is not a supply of staff by the supplier but a supply of other services.

In Notice 741A HMRC provide the following examples of included and excluded services.

Included services:
- a supply (which may be described as a 'secondment', 'transfer' or 'placement') of e.g. a typist to a customer and that typist comes under their general control and direction as an employee;
- the supply, secondment, loan, hire, lease or transfer as principals of personnel for a consideration by bodies such as employment and recruitment businesses, agencies or bureaux; and
- the transfer for a fee by a sports club of a professional sportsman who has a contract of service with the club, such as a professional footballer.

Excluded services:
- The supply by a freelancer or other person of a **specific service or services** under a contract for services. The place of supply will depend on the nature of the services provided;
- Supplies by employment or recruitment businesses or agencies, of making arrangements for the supply of staff between other parties; and
- a company employing typists supplies **typing services** under a specific typing assignment for a third party using those typists.

11.4.8 The letting on hire of goods

This heading covers the letting on hire, or leasing, of all goods other than those which are a means of transport – see **11.2.7**. Goods include all forms of moveable property but exclude land and property or equipment and machinery installed as a fixture. However, this heading excludes supplies of the letting on hire or leasing of goods where the services of an operator or technician are included. In such cases the place of supply of such services depends on the nature of the services provided.

Examples of included and excluded services are provided by HMRC in Notice 741A as follows:

Included services:
- The hire of mobile telephone handsets;
- The hire of freight containers;
- The hire of computer and office equipment; and
- The hire of exhibition stand furniture and equipment without any other services.

Excluded services:
- The hire of exhibition stand space – see **11.2.5.1**; and
- The hire of a means of transport – including the leasing or hiring out of cars – see **11.2.7**.

11.4.8.1 *"Use and enjoyment" of goods on hire*

Just as for the supply of goods on hire to Relevant Business Persons (see **11.2.3**) there are additional use and enjoyment rules for determining the Place of Supply when they hired to private consumers in a B2C supply – see **11.2.8**.

Effective use and enjoyment means that the Place of Supply is the place where the goods are put at the disposal of the customer and they actually use the goods in that place. If this place is in the EU even though the customer might normally be resident outside the EU the supply becomes liable to UK and EU VAT according to the place from where the supplier suppliers the hire i.e. the place where they are established or from a fixed establishment if in another place – see **11.1.2 – 11.1.6**.

11.4.8.2 *"Freight containers"*

There are special rules for the export of freight containers from the UK to a place outside the EU. Such freight containers which are exported from the EU are zero-rated whether they are supplied on hire or by outright sale – see Notice 703/1.[22]

11.4.9 BTE services

BTE services cover supplies of Broadcasting, Telecommunications and Electronic services. Full details of these definitions and HMRC's interpretation of included and excluded services are provided in sections **11.2.16.2 – 11.2.16.4**.

Just as for supplies made to Relevant Business Persons (see **11.2.3**) there are additional use and enjoyment rules for determining the Place of Supply when they are supplied to private consumers in a 'B2C' supply.

Details of the rules relating to the effective use and enjoyment of BTE services is provided in section **11.2.16.1** and a summary of the Place of Supply rules is provided in the Tables in **11.3.5**. Effective use and enjoyment means that the Place of Supply is the place where the services are actually consumed rather than the place where the customer might normally be resident. See **11.1.2 – 11.1.6** for an explanation of the meaning of places of establishment and residence.

11.5 "Emissions Allowances"

Emissions allowances or 'carbon credits' are issued by governments under various schemes designed to cut carbon emissions by businesses. Emissions allowances under the "EU Emissions Trading Scheme" (EU ETS), and instruments representing emission reductions, carbon credits, and certificates that identify that the production of energy has been generated from renewable sources include, but are not limited to, "Certified Emissions Reductions"

---

[22] www.gov.uk/government/publications/vat-notice-7031-supply-of-freight-containers-for-export-or-removal-from-the-uk/

(CERs), "Renewal Obligation Certificates" (ROCs), "Emission Reduction Units" (ERUs), "Levy Exemption Certificates" (LECs), "Assigned Amount Units" (AAUs), "EU Allowances" (EUAs), "Renewable Energy Certificates" and "Verified Emission Reductions" (VERs).

Where certificates or instruments are sold with goods or services they will usually be viewed as incidental or ancillary to the main supply. An example of this is where a guarantee of origin is issued to customers purchasing electricity that certifies the electricity was generated from renewable sources.

Emissions Allowances are transacted across Europe (and wider afield) and the activity has been the subject of major VAT fraud within "Missing Trader Intra-Community" (or MTIC) fraud. With effect from 1 November 2010 the reverse charge has been applied to emissions allowances supplied in the UK and the zero rate for such supplies was withdrawn.

B2B supplies of trading in emissions allowances or instruments are subject to the B2B general rule. From 2010 'B2C' supplies of such services supplied by a UK supplier to a customer belonging outside the EU have been treated as supplied where the customer belongs.

11.6 Agency services ("intermediary services")

HMRC define as "intermediaries" persons or businesses that act as a third party in arranging, or even simply facilitating, the making of supplies. An intermediary arranges supplies between two other parties, being a supplier and that supplier's customer. Intermediaries may be referred to as 'brokers', 'buying' or 'selling' agents, 'go-betweens', 'commissionaires' or 'agents acting in their own name', deemed to be undisclosed agents. Payments for the intermediary's services are often described as 'commission'.

An intermediary's customer is the person to whom they supply their intermediary services and this can be either the supplier or the recipient of the arranged supply, and in some cases, may even be both parties.

The POS of an intermediary's services is the place where the underlying arranged supply is made and will differ according to supplies made to Relevant Business Persons ('B2B' supplies– see **11.2.3**) and private consumers ('B2C' supplies – **see 11.2.2**).

The supply of 'B2B' intermediary services is treated as supplied in the recipient's country under the rules set out in **11.2.1** with the recipient accounting for VAT under the Reverse Charge where they are established and registered for VAT in another EU Member State.

When intermediary services are supplied to a person who is not a Relevant Business Person the POS is the place where the underlying service is made regardless of whether the intermediary is acting for the supplier or the customer.

For B2C supplies, the CJEU ruled in the case of *Staatssecretaris van Financien v Lipjes (Case C-68/03)*, that a supply by a Dutch business of arranging the sale of a yacht by a French boatyard to a Dutch purchaser was made in France because that was the place where the underlying supply, i.e. the sale of the boat, took place.

In the UK the Tax Tribunal ruled in a case called *The Finest Golf Clubs of the World Ltd v HMRC (2005) VAT Decision 19347* that the Place of Supply of arranging for persons to play golf at golf courses outside the UK was outside the scope of UK VAT, being at the places where the golf clubs were located.

11.7 Valuations services and "work on goods"

"Work on goods" includes any services that render a process or an application to those goods – see **11.2.9.5**. An example could be an 'IT' firm repairing computers and laptops etc. or providing a valuation to the owner or to their insurance company in cases of claims for damage under the insurance policy.

With effect from 1 January 2010 all such services when provided to a private consumer are treated as supplied where the supplier is established. Therefore, all supplies under this heading are liable to VAT if any where the services are carried out.

INTRA-EU TRANSACTIONS – SUPPLY OF SERVICES

12 Tax invoices, Reverse Charge and Reverse Charge EC Sales Lists

12.1 Introduction

Normally, the supplier of a service is the person who must account to the tax authorities for any VAT due on the supply. However, in certain situations, it is the customer who must account for any VAT due.

This book deals with both international trade of goods and cross-border supplies of services. The introduction to trade in international services (see sections **11.1** and **11.2.1**) set out the background to the cross-border treatment of a 'B2B' supply of services.

For a supply of services made 'intra-EU' to a Relevant Business Person (see **11.2.3**) in another EU Member State the VAT liability is governed by:
- the place of belonging of the supplier – see **11.1.2 – 11.1.6**;
- the place of belonging of the customer – see **11.1.2 – 11.1.6**;
- the VAT status of the recipient i.e. are they a Relevant Business Person – see **11.2.1**;
- whether the Relevant Business Person is VAT-registered in another Member State from that of the supplier; and
- whether the Relevant Business Person makes use of a VAT number that is not issued by the same EU Member State as that issued to the supplier.

12.2 Sales

Where the recipient provides to the supplier a valid EU Member State VAT number (that is issued by a different Member State to that issued to the supplier) and the supplier quotes that VAT number on its tax invoice and the supplier also inserts into the tax invoice the legend required by EC Council Directive 2006/112/EC Art 226 (11(a) informing the recipient that the services are subject to the Reverse Charge in the Member State that issued the VAT number, then the services are Outside the Scope of VAT in the supplier's Member State and are liable to VAT in the recipient's Member State under the Reverse Charge.

The invoice legend can be fairly straightforward, along the lines of *"Services liable to Reverse Charge"* or *"Recipient to account for VAT under the Reverse Charge"*.

The Reverse Charge applies to almost all 'B2B' supplies of services except those of a description in VAT Act 1994, Schedule 9 (Exemptions).

Suppliers can verify recipients' VAT numbers using the EC's on-line database at ec.europa.eu/taxation_customs/vies/

TAX INVOICE AND REVERSE CHARGE

12.2.1 UK VAT invoices for Sales to EU Customers

The obligation to provide a VAT invoice for intra-EU supplies is covered by VAT Regulations 1995, regulation 13(1)(b). The details which must be shown on the invoice are listed in VAT Regulations 1995, regulation 14(2):

> 14(2) Save as the Commissioners may otherwise allow, where a registered person provides a person in another member State with a VAT invoice or any document that refers to a VAT invoice and is intended to amend it, he must ensure that it states thereon the following particulars-
> (a) the information specified in sub-paragraphs (a) to (e) (g) (j) (m) (n) and (o) of paragraph (1) above;
> (b) the letters 'GB' as a prefix to his registration number,
> (c) the registration number, if any, of the recipient of the supply of goods or services and which registration number, if any, shall contain the alphabetical code of the member State in which that recipient is registered,
> (d) the gross amount payable, excluding VAT,
> (e) where the supply is of a new means of transport (as defined in section 95 of the Act) a description sufficient to identify it as such,
> (f) for each description, the quantity of the goods or the extent of the services, and where a positive rate of VAT is chargeable, the rate of VAT and the amount payable, excluding VAT, expressed in sterling, and
> (g) where the supply of goods is a taxable supply, the information as specified in sub paragraph (l) of paragraph 1; and
> (h) where the supply is an exempt or zero-rated supply, a relevant reference or any indication that the supply is exempt or zero-rated as appropriate.

The alphabetical codes of the EU Member State in which the recipient is registered are provided in section **9.2**.

12.2.2 Reverse Charge EC Sales Lists ("ESLs")

In addition to "normal VAT accounting" and the issue of the tax invoices in the correct format EC Directive 2008/117/EC requires all suppliers of cross-border services to complete and submit on a periodic basis Reverse Charge EC Sales Lists ("Statements") to show the VAT numbers of the recipients to whom cross-border services have been supplied and the relevant values of the supplies. In other EU countries the forms are referred to as **'recapitulative statements'** or **'summary statements'**.

ESLs in respect of services are not required for:
- supplies which are exempt from VAT according to the rules in the Member State where the supply takes place;
- business-to-business supplies where the recipient is not VAT registered; and
- business-to-customer supplies.

Information on ESLs is provided in Section **9.21.2**.

12.2.3 Agreement with VAT returns

HMRC conduct specific Assurance visits to businesses that are required to account for VAT under the Reverse Charge and to submit EC Sales Statements.

The transactions entered on VAT returns that declare intra-EU Dispatches of goods and intra-EU sales of services should match the entries on the EC Sales Lists, both for goods and for services.

Additionally, particularly because of widespread tax fraud, EU Member States routinely follow-up with their counterpart tax authorities to check that Reverse Charge VAT has been accounted for where a recipient's VAT number has appeared on a supplier's EC Sales List.

12.3 Purchases or "imported services"

In the UK as in all other EU Member States, Relevant Business Persons who are VAT-registered and who have provided their VAT number to an EU supplier must account for Reverse Charge VAT on the value of the "imported services" as though the supplies had been supplied within the UK.

Additionally, however, the Relevant Business Person must also account for Reverse Charge VAT on all supplies of imported services bought from 'non-UK' suppliers, not just those who are VAT-registered in other EU Member States.

Therefore, the Reverse Charge applies to all imported services irrespective of the places from where the services are delivered, if from a non-UK supplier, and whether the suppliers are registered for VAT in another EU Member State. There is an exception for services that, if supplied from within the UK, would be exempt under VAT Act 1994, Sch 9 where the Reverse Charge is not required.

Additionally, the Reverse Charge applies to Relevant Business Persons who happen, in the UK, to not be registered for VAT because, for example, their UK Taxable Turnover is below the VAT registration threshold. In this case the unregistered business or natural person must review the annual value of Reverse Chargeable imported services to identify whether they ought to become VAT-registered simply to account for the Reverse Charge VAT.

A further complication arises with regards to any business or person who imports services and his business falls to be treated as 'partially exempt' for VAT purposes, for example, an Independent Financial Advisor (IFA). Where a business is partially exempt and it falls outside of specified *de-minimis* limits for the amounts of VAT that can still be reclaimed despite the business making some exempt supplies, it can only reclaim the proportion that relates to taxable supplies. Therefore, the equivalent amount of output tax accounted for under the Reverse Charge can only be reclaimed where the particular services are imported (bought for) and used for the purposes of the recipient's taxable activities.

This use has to be measured by either the Partial Exemption "Standard Method" (which applies the ratio of taxable income to taxable plus exempt income and applies that ratio to the costs and the VAT incurred in the business in a broad approximation of 'use') or an allocation of costs under a Special Method, which can be by any means that provides an acceptable (to HMRC) recovery. A Special Method could be based on "headcount", "transaction count", timesheet" or another "sectorisation" attribution of overhead costs that the business can identify and apply to the VAT-bearing costs.

However, whichever partial exemption method is used it must produce a **"fair and reasonable"** attribution of input VAT to taxable and to exempt supplies, and it must also be capable of being audited without undue difficulty by HMRC.

Sometimes services might also be imported by a Relevant Business Person for 'non-business' or 'private purposes' such as a company director having work done on his own home or by a Tour Operator where the VAT cannot be reclaimed under the TOMS (see **11.2.13**) or a Second-hand Margin Scheme where VAT cannot be reclaimed because VAT is accounted for on any profit margin made. In such cases the "input tax" on the Reverse Charge cannot be recovered from HMRC.

12.3.1 Accounting for Reverse Charges

The Reverse Charge VAT is accounted for to HMRC on the VAT return covering the period in which the tax point for the imported services falls. Therefore, to be able to account for Reverse Charge VAT it is essential to understand when the tax point falls.

For a "One off" supply of services the time of supply and therefore the tax point is the earlier of the time when the service is completed or when it is paid for.

For a continuous supply of services the time of supply is the end of the periods in respect of which payments are made or invoices issued, to the extent covered by the payment or invoice as follows:

(a) where a payment is made at a time which is earlier than the end of the period to which it relates, the time of supply is the time of payment;
(b) where a payment is made which is not made in respect of any identified period, the time of supply is the time of payment;
(c) where a payment is received in respect of services the time of supply is the time of payment;
(d) where the supply commences before 1 January and continues after 31 December of any year, and

i. during that year no invoice is issued in respect of a period, and
ii. no payment is made in respect of the supply,

the time of supply is 31 December of that year to the extent that the recipient has received the benefit of those services.

These rules apply so that the time when VAT is accounted for on such supplies corresponds with the dates on which supplies are reported on EU Sales Statements.

Value for Reverse Charge

The value of the services treated as made by the Relevant Business Person is taken to be:

(a) an amount that is equal to the consideration in money (if the consideration for which the services were in fact supplied to him was a consideration in money); or
(b) an amount in money that is equivalent to the consideration (if the consideration for which the services were in fact supplied to him was a consideration which did not, or did not wholly, consist of money).

Where a transaction has been transacted in a different currency to that used by the tax authority the recipient should use a recognised exchange rate, ideally one published by a central bank, to calculate the equivalent values for Reverse Charges.

12.3.2 Reverse Charge VAT not accounted for

Where the Relevant Business Person does not account for the Reverse Charge VAT but they are able to recover exactly the same amount as input tax (i.e. the person is treated as "fully taxable" (see **12.3**) and the input tax in question is also not restricted specifically under other legislation relating to "blocked goods" and "blocked services" as in the TOMS or a Second-hand Margin Scheme, the application of the Reverse Charge would seem, at first sight, to be a pointless exercise.

Looking at this Advocate-General Sharpston advising the CJEU stated in the case of *Ecotrade SpA v Agenzia Entrate Ufficio Genova 3 (Case C-95/07)*:

> Where there is no risk of any loss in tax revenue, the principle of neutrality requires that VAT returns which have been erroneously completed can be adjusted. There is no such risk where liability and the right to deduct cancel each other out.

However, she added that:

> Appropriate and proportionate penalties may none the less be imposed for failure to declare transactions correctly.

Where the equivalent amount of VAT can be reclaimed as input tax it is included in Box 4 of the same VAT return in which the Reverse Charge Output VAT is declared in Box 1.

TAX INVOICE AND REVERSE CHARGE

The net values of the Reverse Charge services must be included in Boxes 6 and 7 of the VAT return (net being the amount actually charged by the supplier before the addition of the Reverse Charge output tax by the recipient).

13 "Best Practice" and Planning

Businesses trading internationally have to manage considerable risk regarding the delivery of the goods and payment for them. The ancillary, but vital, issues regarding import duty and import VAT can result in serious expense for the business if not understood and controlled. A simple means of understanding, and therefore managing, the taxation risk of international trade is for a business to constantly ask itself *"so what does that mean?"* with regards to the movement of the goods both into and out of the EU and intra-EU.

That question can identify potential issues, for example, *"Am I the 'Importer of Record' and liable to pay Customs import duty and import VAT?"* As with most taxation issues, planning for transactions can remove potential issues and improve others. Businesses are recommended to consider the following questions before embarking on particular international trades.

Similarly, the plethora of POS of services rules means that businesses must take exceptional care when determining the potential liability to VAT on international services.

13.1 Imports

1. What are the Incoterms? – are they suitable to both seller and buyer?
2. Who is the "importer of record"?
3. What is the correct classification for the goods being imported?
4. Are the goods subject to any preference or Anti-Dumping Duty?
5. What is the lowest possible valuation?
6. Who classifies and values the goods? – an agent or the business?
7. Can I save money by bringing this function "in-house"?
8. Are the goods eligible for relief from import duty?
9. Am I trans-shipping the goods to another Member State?
10. Do I need a licence to import the goods?
11. Are they subject to any quota? (limits on the units and values imported)
12. How is the import duty and import VAT paid?
13. Should I have a duty and VAT deferment account?
14. What should be the value of the guarantee?
15. Is the business eligible to use Simplified Import VAT Accounting (SIVA)?
16. If a VAT group registration, do all subsidiary members obtain copies of the Import VAT Certificate (C79)?
17. Do I need other evidence of VAT paid at import to claim input tax on the VAT return?
18. Have I received all available shipping documents etc.?
19. Are my Terms of Business robust, i.e. do I have an exposure to trading fluidity?
20. Are my accounting records able to recognise imports as distinct from Arrivals?
21. Are my VAT return procedures capable of reporting the imports correctly?

BEST PRACTICE AND PLANNING

22. Are the "goods inward" staff trained sufficiently to cope with imports?
23. Do I need to seek advice on any aspect of my international trade matters?

13.2 Exports
1. What are the Incoterms? – are they suitable to both seller and buyer?
2. Who is responsible for insurance and carriage?
3. Are my Terms of Business robust, i.e. do I have an exposure to trading fluidity?
4. Do I need a licence to export the goods?
5. Is it a direct or an indirect export?
6. If indirect, who is responsible for organising the freight forwarding?
7. Can I save money by bringing this function "in-house"?
8. How will I ensure I receive copies of all documents to evidence the export?
9. Have I received all available shipping documents etc.?
10. How can I ensure the evidence of export is obtained within the stipulated time limits?
11. Are the goods subject to any preference, for example exports to Turkey?
12. Are my accounting records able to recognise exports as distinct from Dispatches?
13. Are my VAT return procedures capable of reporting the exports correctly?
14. Are the export department staff trained sufficiently to cope with exports?
15. Do I need to seek advice on any aspect of my international trade matters?

13.3 Arrivals
1. What are the Incoterms? – are they suitable to both seller and buyer?
2. Who is responsible for insurance and carriage?
3. Are my Terms of Business robust, i.e. do I have an exposure to trading fluidity?
4. Have I received all available shipping documents etc.?
5. Have I provided my (up-to-date) VAT registration number to all my suppliers in other Member States?
6. Is the removal of the goods under the "normal" intra-EU trade VAT rules?
7. If not "normal" is the removal one of:
    7.1. "Triangulation"?
    7.2. Supplied and assembled goods?
    7.3. Call-off stock?
    7.4. Consignment stock?
    7.5. Process or incorporation goods?
    7.6. Excise goods?
    7.7. Sale or return goods?
    7.8. Samples?
    7.9. Goods sent for testing?
8. Are my accounting records able to recognise Arrival transactions?
9. Is the business liable to account for Acquisition VAT?

BEST PRACTICE AND PLANNING

10. Are my accounting records able to recognise Arrivals as distinct from imports?
11. Are my VAT return procedures capable of reporting the Arrivals correctly?
12. Is the business liable to complete Intrastat Arrival SSDs?
13. Are the "goods inward" staff trained sufficiently to cope with Arrivals?
14. Do my Arrivals SSDs agree with the corresponding VAT returns?
15. Do I need to seek advice on the VAT issues of my Intra-EC trade?

13.4 Dispatches

1. What are the Incoterms? Are they suitable to both seller and buyer?
2. Is it a direct or indirect removal?
3. If indirect, who is responsible for organising the freight forwarding?
4. Who is responsible for insurance and carriage?
5. Are my Terms of Business robust, i.e. do I have an exposure to trading fluidity?
6. Have I received all available shipping documents etc.?
7. Will the goods be removed within the stipulated time limits?
8. Should I take a deposit from the customer for the VAT?
9. Is it a B2B or a B2C removal?
10. Have I obtained (up-to-date) VAT registration numbers of all my customers in other Member States?
11. Is the removal of the goods under the "normal" intra-EC trade VAT rules?
12. If not "normal" is the removal one of:
    12.1. "Triangulation" and chain transactions?
    12.2. Transfer of own goods?
    12.3. Temporary movements?
    12.4. Supplied and assembled goods?
    12.5. Call-off stock?
    12.6. Consignment stock?
    12.7. Process or incorporation goods?
    12.8. Distance selling?
    12.9. Excise goods?
    12.10. Sale or return goods?
    12.11. Samples?
    12.12. Goods sent for testing?
13. Is the business liable to register for VAT in the Member State of Arrival to account for Acquisition VAT and onward taxable supplies of the goods in that country?
14. If Distance selling, should I be registered for VAT in the Member State of Arrival (where the goods are delivered)?
15. Should I register in advance of exceeding the relevant country threshold?
16. Are my accounting records able to recognise Despatches as distinct from exports?

BEST PRACTICE AND PLANNING

17. Are my VAT return procedures capable of reporting the Despatches correctly?
18. Is the business liable to complete Intrastat Dispatch SSDs?
19. Are the export department staff trained sufficiently to cope with Dispatches?
20. Do my Dispatches SSDs agree with the corresponding VAT returns?
21. Do I need to seek advice on the VAT issues of my Intra-EU trade?

13.5 International services

It is vital to consider all of the following points associated with the supply of services 'cross-border'.

1. What is the nature of the service – is it subject to a special POS rule?
2. Is the customer a business or a private consumer?
3. If the customer is a Relevant Business Person are they using the services for their business?
4. If so, has the customer supplied a valid EU VAT number and is this annotated on the supplier's sales invoice?
5. If the supplier has more than one place of establishment from which place are the services supplied?
6. In which country(ies) is the customer established or if a private person resident?
7. If they have more than one place of establishment or residence in which place are they using and consuming the services?
8. Is there an effective use and enjoyment 'tax-shift' that applies to the services?
9. Is there a liability to be registered for VAT in another EU Member State e.g. admissions services for events?
10. Are the products being sold being 'downloaded' and if so is there a liability to account for VAT under the MOSS?
11. Are services received from outside the UK Reverse Charged? If so, can all of the Reverse Charge VAT be reclaimed as input tax?
12. Are EC Sales Lists completed for services Reverse Charged by recipients in other EU Member States?
13. Is VAT being incurred in other Member States? If so, is this the correct position and can it be reclaimed under the EC 8th or 13th VAT Directive?

13.6 Summary

No list of questions can ever be comprehensive as international trade constantly highlights unique trading circumstances. Advice on all aspects of international trade can be obtained from UKTI at **www.ukti.gov.uk** and from the Department of Business, Innovation and Skills at **www.bis.gov.uk**, as well as HMRC at www.hmrc.gov.uk and UK Trade Info at **www.uktradeinfo.com**.

The following paragraphs summarise the content in this book, but readers are advised to seek professional assistance where they consider they require help with the import duty, import VAT and intra-EU VAT requirements of international trade.

13.6.1 Imports
VAT is charged and payable on the importation of goods into the EU from all third countries/territories, unless any special relief can be claimed such as customs or excise warehousing or certain customs-approved regimes such as inward processing relief or Community Transit arrangements. All VAT due on the imported goods must normally either be paid at the time of importation or deferred with any import duty, where deferment has been approved by HMRC. VAT paid on the importation of goods can be claimed as input tax, subject to the normal rules.

13.6.2 Exports
Where the evidence to demonstrate the physical removal of the goods from the UK is obtained, exports from the EU are zero-rated. It is vital that the supplier obtains all of the applicable evidence of export within the stipulated time limits or the goods will be deemed to be standard-rated.

13.6.3 Intra-EU supplies of goods
Supplies of goods to a customer registered for VAT in another Member State can be zero-rated provided:
- the supplier obtains and quotes on their sales invoice the customer's VAT registration number; and
- the goods are physically removed from the Member State of Dispatch; and
- the supplier obtains satisfactory proof of removal from the Member State of Dispatch.

The customer then accounts for VAT ("Acquisition tax") at the appropriate rate on the goods in the Member State of Arrival.

If the conditions cannot be met, VAT must be charged by the supplier in the country of origin at the rate applicable to the goods in that country.

Additionally:
- VAT must also be charged on supplies of goods to non-registered customers in other Member States, but where the supply is one of Distance Selling, the supplier must consider the need to register and account for VAT in the customer(s) country(ies) subject to the calendar year values of all goods dispatched to those Member States;
- special rules apply to the transfer of an entity's of own goods to another Member State;
- special rules apply to goods installed or assembled at the customer's premises;
- special rules apply to New Means of Transport;
- special rules apply to the Dispatch of goods to non-taxable customers in other Member States, that are subject to excise duty; and

- there are special rules for 'Triangulation' i.e. where a chain of supplies of goods involves three parties and, instead of goods physically passing from one party to the next, they are delivered from the first party to the last party in the chain.

13.6.4 Declarations

Suppliers and customers must ensure that their primary accounting records and their VAT records can identify and report all of the following transactions:
- the importation of goods from third countries/territories;
- the Arrival of goods from other Member States;
- the export of goods to third countries/territories; and
- the Dispatch of goods to other Member States.

Additionally:
- VAT returns (form VAT 100);
- Dispatch SSDs (Intrastat);
- Arrival SSDs (Intrastat);
- Delivery Terms (Intrastat); and
- EC Sales Lists (ESLs)

must all be capable of being completed and submitted without error.

Where goods are transferred to another Member State, the entity removing the goods must keep a Register of Own Movements to support these transfers.

13.6.5 International services

The exact nature of the services or other products being supplied must be determined to ensure compliance with both the VAT position in the UK and in the countries where the services are deemed to be supplied/received or otherwise consumed. This requires a comprehensive review of the services/products and all contracts, agreements and Terms of Business to ascertain the supply position.

Where required, local country VAT registration must be followed up as soon as a liability to be registered is identified. In cases of doubt advice should be sought from specialist VAT and Indirect Tax Consultants or other legal advisers. If there is any lingering doubt as to the Place of Supply or the VAT liability of a service, an application to HMRC (and any other Tax Authority) should be considered.

Because the VAT issues for supplies of services supplied cross-border are constantly changing and Tax Authorities consistently challenge the VAT position adopted by businesses, suppliers should seek to remain up to date on all matters relating to their businesses.

Appendix A: Terms of Trade

Using the correct "Incoterms®"

The term, Incoterms, is an abbreviation for International Commercial Terms and define the responsibilities of sellers and buyers for the delivery of goods under sales contracts for domestic and international trade. They are published by the International Chamber of Commerce (ICC) at http://www.iccwbo.org and are widely used in international commercial transactions.

Incoterms provide a common set of rules to clarify responsibilities of sellers and buyers for the delivery of goods under sales contracts. They apportion transportation costs and responsibilities associated with the delivery of goods between buyers (importers) and sellers (exporters) and reflect modern-day transportation practices. Incoterms significantly reduce misunderstandings among traders and thereby minimise trade disputes and litigation.

RULES FOR ANY MODE OR MODES OF TRANSPORT

EXW Ex Works

"Ex Works" means that the seller delivers when it places the goods at the disposal of the buyer at the seller's premises or at another named place (i.e. works, factory, warehouse, etc.). The seller does not need to load the goods on any collecting vehicle, nor does it need to clear the goods for export, where such clearance is applicable.

FCA Free Carrier

"Free Carrier" means that the seller delivers the goods to the carrier or another person nominated by the buyer at the seller's premises or another named place. The parties are well advised to specify as clearly as possible the point within the named place of delivery, as the risk passes to the buyer at that point.

CPT Carriage Paid To

"Carriage Paid To" means that the seller delivers the goods to the carrier or another person nominated by the seller at an agreed place (if any such place is agreed between parties) and that the seller must contract for and pay the costs of carriage necessary to bring the goods to the named place of destination.

CIP Carriage And Insurance Paid To

"Carriage and Insurance Paid to" means that the seller delivers the goods to the carrier or another person nominated by the seller at an agreed place (if any such place is agreed between parties) and that the seller must contract for and pay the costs of carriage necessary to bring the goods to the named place of destination.

The seller also contracts for insurance cover against the buyer's risk of loss of or damage to the goods during the carriage. The buyer should note that under CIP the seller is required to obtain insurance only on minimum cover. Should the buyer wish to have more insurance protection, it will need either to agree as much expressly with the seller or to make its own extra insurance arrangements."

DAT Delivered At Terminal
"Delivered at Terminal" means that the seller delivers when the goods, once unloaded from the arriving means of transport, are placed at the disposal of the buyer at a named terminal at the named port or place of destination.

"Terminal" includes a place, whether covered or not, such as a quay, warehouse, container yard or road, rail or air cargo terminal. The seller bears all risks involved in bringing the goods to and unloading them at the terminal at the named port or place of destination.

DAP Delivered At Place
"Delivered at Place" means that the seller delivers when the goods are placed at the disposal of the buyer on the arriving means of transport ready for unloading at the named place of destination. The seller bears all risks involved in bringing the goods to the named place.

DDP Delivered Duty Paid
"Delivered Duty Paid" means that the seller delivers the goods when the goods are placed at the disposal of the buyer, cleared for import on the arriving means of transport ready for unloading at the named place of destination. The seller bears all the costs and risks involved in bringing the goods to the place of destination and has an obligation to clear the goods not only for export but also for import, to pay any duty for both export and import and to carry out all customs formalities.

RULES FOR SEA AND INLAND WATERWAY TRANSPORT
FAS Free Alongside Ship
"Free Alongside Ship" means that the seller delivers when the goods are placed alongside the vessel (e.g. on a quay or a barge) nominated by the buyer at the named port of shipment. The risk of loss of or damage to the goods passes when the goods are alongside the ship, and the buyer bears all costs from that moment onwards.

FOB Free On Board
"Free On Board" means that the seller delivers the goods on board the vessel nominated by the buyer at the named port of shipment or procures the goods already so delivered. The risk of loss of or damage to the goods passes when

the goods are on board the vessel, and the buyer bears all costs from that moment onwards.

CFR Cost and Freight
"Cost and Freight" means that the seller delivers the goods on board the vessel or procures the goods already so delivered. The risk of loss of or damage to the goods passes when the goods are on board the vessel. The seller must contract for and pay the costs and freight necessary to bring the goods to the named port of destination.

CIF Cost, Insurance and Freight
"Cost, Insurance and Freight" means that the seller delivers the goods on board the vessel or procures the goods already so delivered. The risk of loss of or damage to the goods passes when the goods are on board the vessel. The seller must contract for and pay the costs and freight necessary to bring the goods to the named port of destination.

The seller also contracts for insurance cover against the buyer's risk of loss of or damage to the goods during the carriage. The buyer should note that under CIF the seller is required to obtain insurance only on minimum cover. Should the buyer wish to have more insurance protection, it will need either to agree as much expressly with the seller or to make its own extra insurance arrangements.

Further information on international trade and help for importers and exporters can be found at:
- The International Chambers of Commerce website – www.iccwbo.org/
- The Department for UK Trade and Investment (UKTI) – www.gov.uk/government/organisations/uk-trade-investment
- The department for Business, Innovation and Skills (UKBIS) – www.gov.uk/government/organisations/department-for-business-innovation-skills

Appendix B: Useful addresses

HM Revenue and Customs addresses:
Banking Operations
Central Deferment Office
6th Floor North West
Alexander House
21 Victoria Avenue
Southend-on-Sea
Essex SS99 1AA

Telephone:
01702 36 7425/7429/7431/7450
Fax: 01702 366091

National Clearance Hub
Ralli Quays
3 Stanley Street
Salford M60 9HL

Fax: 0800 496 0699
Email: NCHCIE@hmrc.gsi.gov.uk
and NCHLAP@hmrc.gsi.gov.uk

National Duty Repayment Centre
Priory Court
St John's Road
Dover CT17 9SH
Telephone: 03000 582687
Fax: 03000 583027
Email: ndrcenquiries@hmrc.gsi.gov.uk

National Import Reliefs Unit (NIRU)
Abbey House
Head Street
Enniskillen
County Fermanagh
Northern Ireland
BT74 7JL

Telephone: 02866 344 557
Fax: 0286 344 571
Email: niru@hmrc.gov.uk

National Rejected Imports Team
Excise and International Trade
Sapphire Plaza
Reading
RG1 4TE

Non-Established Taxable Persons Unit (NETPU)
Ruby House
8 Ruby Place
Aberdeen AB10 1ZP

Personal Transport Unit (PTU)
Priory Court
St John's Road
Dover CT17 9SH

Phone: 01304 664171
Fax: 01304 664179

Custom House
Post Clearance Amendments
Ralli Quays
3 Stanley Street
Salford M60 9HL

Telephone: 03000 588453
Fax: 03000 588462
Email: nchcie@hmrc.gsi.gov.uk

SIVA Approvals Team
Ruby House
8 Ruby Place
Aberdeen AB10 1ZP

VAT Central Unit, Microfilm Section
8th Floor, Alexander House
Victoria Avenue
Southend-on-Sea
SS99 1AU

VAT Overseas Repayment Unit
S1250
Benton Park View
Newcastle upon Tyne
NE98 1YX

APPENDIX B: USEFUL ADDRESSES

The Department of Business, Innovation and Skills
Overseas Trade Division
1 Victoria Street
London SW1H 0ET

London Chamber of Commerce and Industry
33 Queen Street
London EC4R 1AP
Phone: 020 7248 4444

British Forces Liaison
Customs and Immigration
Germany
BFPO40

SBA Customs
RAF Akrotiri
BFPO57

Glossary

Term	Description
Anti-Dumping Duty	A customs duty on imports providing a protection against the dumping of goods in the EU at prices substantially lower than the normal value.
Acquisitions	Goods arrived in the UK from other EU countries
Acquisition VAT	Goods purchased from a VAT-registered business in another EU country and removed to the UK. VAT in the UK may be applicable on the acquisition of the goods. This is recovered as input tax on the same VAT return, subject to the normal rules for reclaiming input tax.
Agent	A person appointed to represent another in their dealings with HMRC. Legal representation may be either direct or indirect.
Authorised operator	A trader authorised by HMRC to operate one or all of export simplified procedures (SDP and LCP) and/or a DEP. It also includes an exporter or third party allowed to make full export declarations to CHIEF.
ATA carnet	ATA stands for 'Admission Temporaire – Temporary admission'. The carnets are multi-sheet documents issued by Chambers of Commerce, with the backing of an international guarantee chain, to facilitate the temporary export and re-import of all kinds of goods.
A.TR documents	Certificates used to show that goods are entitled to preferential rates of duty in Turkey.
CAP	Common Agricultural Policy
CFSP (Customs Freight Simplified Procedures)	Simplified procedure for the importation of third country goods including the simplified declaration procedure and local clearance procedure.
CHIEF	Customs Handling of Import and Export Freight. The Customs entry processing computer system.
CIE	Customs input of entries to CHIEF.
CMR	Convention Merchandises Routiers – a movement document.

GLOSSARY

Clear/clearance — The clearance of a declaration occurs when HMRC have accepted and formally released the goods for export.

Common Transit — Used to describe community Transit movements to, from or via EFTA countries.

Community — Member States of the European Union.

Community Transit — A system of controlling the movement of certain goods across the territory of the EC and that of other signatories to the Transit Convention.

Compensating Products — All products obtained from processing operations.

Compensatory interest — Interest charged when certain TA/IP goods are diverted to Free Circulation

Countervailing duty — A customs duty on goods which have received government subsidies in the originating or exporting country.

CPC (Customs Procedure Code) — A 7-digit code used on SAD/C88 declarations to identify the type of procedure for which the goods are being entered and from which they came. Details of CPCs can be found in The Tariff.

Customs charges — An indirect tax that provides protection for Union Industries raised on import goods. This includes duty, agricultural charges and other import charges provided for under CAP. It does not include Excise duty or VAT.

Customs duty — An indirect tax that provides protection for Community industry. Raised on imported goods, it does not include excise duty or VAT.

Customs procedure — Release for free circulation, Community Transit (Notice 750), Customs Warehousing (Notice 232) IP (Notice 221), Processing under Customs Control (PCC) (Notice 237), TA relief (Notice 200), Outward Processing Relief (OPR) (Notice 235), Exportation (Notice 275).

Customs procedure with economic impact — These are: customs warehousing – inward processing – processing under customs control – temporary Admission, and – outward processing.

GLOSSARY

Customs Procedure Code (CPC)	A 7 digit code used on entries on import, export and warehouse declarations, to identify the type of procedure for which the goods are entered and from which they came. Details of CPCs can be found in Volume 3 of the Tariff.
Customs warehouse	A system or place authorised by customs for the storage of non-Community goods under duty and/or VAT suspension – see Notice 232.
Declarant	The person legally responsible for the accuracy of the information given in the declaration the authenticity of the documents which relate to it and, compliance with all the obligations relating to the entry of the goods under the procedure concerned.
Declaration	A declaration made in the appropriate form to customs indicating the intention of the declaration to declare goods to the export procedure.
Departure Message	Where the vessel/aircraft/vehicle directly leaves the UK (and the EC) a 'Goods Departed' message must be sent to CHIEF to confirm that the goods actually departed. The departure message should advise the date/time, freight location and transport details. UCR, mode of transport and flag code, are also necessary.
Dispatches	Goods removed from one Member State to another Member State.
Direct Exporter	For Customs purposes, refers to goods exported directly from the UK to a third country/territory.
Distance sales	Where a business in one Member State sells and ships goods directly to consumers in another Member State, e.g. by internet or mail-order sales.
Drawback goods	Goods subject to a claim for the drawback of duty paid.
DTI	Direct Trader Input to CHIEF
EC	European Commission
EU	European Union
EFTA	European Free Trade Association. A group of countries

GLOSSARY

	comprising Iceland, Norway and the Swiss Confederation.
End Use	Arrangements which allow certain imported goods to be declared to free circulation in the Union at a reduced or 'nil' rate of duty, provided they are put to a prescribed use under Customs control. (See Notice 770 for full details).
Enhanced Remote Transit Shed	Approved premises outside of a port or airport where goods having the status of goods in temporary storage may be stored under HMRC' supervision.
Excise Warehouse	A warehouse approved for the deposit of goods subject to excise duty see Tax warehouse.
Exports	The movement of goods to a destination outside the EU (Customs and/or VAT) territory.
EORI	Economic Operator Reference Information
Euro (€)	European currency unit
Excise duty	A duty chargeable, in addition to any customs duty that may be due, on the goods listed in The Tariff, Volume 1 Part 12 paragraph 12.1.
Free Circulation	Goods imported from outside the EU are in free circulation when:- all the import formalities have been complied with; and- all import duties, levies and equivalent charges payable have been paid and have not been wholly or partly refunded. Goods that originate in the Union are also in free circulation.
Free Zone	**No longer authorised in the UK.** They were designated areas into which non-community goods may be moved and remain without payment of import duty and/or VAT otherwise due at importation.
HMRC	HM Revenue & Customs.
ICD	An ICD is an approved (inland) location where goods can be declared to HMRC and be brought under Customs control.

GLOSSARY

Imports	Goods brought into the EU from a third country/territory
Import VAT	When goods are imported into the UK from outside the EU, VAT is normally due at the same rate as on a supply of those goods in the UK.
Indirect export	For UK Customs purposes, refers to goods declared in the UK leaving the EU via another Member State.
Input Tax	Input tax is the VAT paid or payable by taxable persons on goods or services supplied to them (or acquired by them from another Member State) used or to be used for the purposes of their business.
IPR (Inward Processing Relief)	A customs procedure providing import duty relief for goods imported into the EU or removed from a customs warehouse, for process and export outside the Union. See Notice 221.
Member State	A Member State of the European Union.
Non-Community Countries - also known as 'third countries.	Countries which are not members of the European Union.
Non-Community goods	Goods which are not of Union origin or imported goods which have not been released into free circulation.
OPR (Outward Process Relief)	Allows temporarily export of Union goods for processing or repair, and re-importation of the compensating products with total or partial relief from import duties. See Notice 235.
Output Tax	The VAT charged by the supplier to the customer on their sales.
Processing	Any operation which changes the condition of imported goods. This includes both the manufacture and assembly of goods.
PCC (Processing under Customs Control)	A system of import duty relief for goods imported or transferred from another customs regime for processing into products on which less or no duty is payable - see Notice 237.

GLOSSARY

Person established in the Community
In the case of a natural person, any person who is normally resident there.
In the case of a legal person or an association of persons, any person that has, in the Community:
- its registered office
- its central headquarters, or
- a permanent business establishment.

Person established outside the Community
In the case of a natural person, any person who is not normally resident there.
In the case of a legal person or an association of persons, any person that has, outside the Community:
- its registered office
- its central headquarters or,
- a permanent business establishment.

Place of supply
The country in which a supply of goods or services is deemed to be liable for VAT purposes.

Pre-entry
Notification to customs of the intention to export the goods by the submission of an entry.

Preference
Arrangements which allow reduced or nil rates of customs duties to be claimed on eligible goods imported from certain non-Community countries.

Removal
The transfer of goods from one Member State to another usually by the owner.

Single administrative document (SAD/C88)
Document used throughout the EU for making import/export declarations – the UK version is Form SAD/C88.

Special Territory
A territory within the EU for customs purposes but outside for fiscal (VAT) purposes.

Supply
Selling or otherwise providing goods or services, including barter and some free provision.

Supply of goods
When exclusive ownership of goods passes from one person to another.

Supply VAT
VAT payable on the supply of goods or services – also see Output Tax.

GLOSSARY

'TA' goods	'Temporary Admission' goods
Tariff	The Integrated Tariff of The United Kingdom.
Taxable Person	Any business entity that buys or sells goods or services and (in the UK definition) is required to be registered for VAT - this includes individuals, partnerships, companies, clubs, associations and charities. The EU definition is a person or legal entity that is in business and makes supplies of a consistent value and permanence.
Taxable supplies	All goods and services sold or otherwise supplied by a taxable person which are liable to VAT at the standard, reduced or zero rate.
Tax point or "time of supply"	The date when VAT has to be accounted for - for goods, this is usually when they are despatched to the customer or when they take them away; for services, this is usually when the service is performed.
Tax Warehouse	An authorised place where goods subject to excise duty are produced, processed, held, received or despatched under duty suspension arrangements by an authorised warehouse keeper in the course of his business and includes excise warehouses, registered premises, distilleries and refineries.
Third country/territory	Any country that is outside the Customs Territory of the EU.
TI relief	Temporary Admission a customs procedure which allows goods to be used in the Union without payment of duty or VAT under certain conditions and re-exported afterwards in the same state as they were in at import.
TIR	Transports International Routiers, a system involving the issue to road haulier of carnets which allow loaded vehicles to cross national frontiers with minimum customs formalities.
Union Goods	Goods which are:(a) entirely obtained or produced in the Customs territory of the Union, without the addition of goods from third countries or territories that are not

GLOSSARY

	part of the Customs territory of the Union,(b) imported from countries or territories not forming part of the Customs territory of the Union which have been released for free circulation in a Member State; obtained or produced in the Customs territory of the Union either wholly from those referred to at (b) or partly from (a) and (b).
VAT	Value Added Tax
VATA 1994	VAT Act 1994

GLOSSARY

Index

A.TR documents 408

Acquisition VAT 6, 13, 107, 108, 237, 238, 253-266, 284, 398, 408

Acquisitions 13, 238

ad valorem duty 69, 85

AEOC status 16

AEOS status 17

aerodrome 21

agents
  clearing 91
  customs 16, 32
  export 191
  freight forwarding 18
  import 172
  shipping 36
  UK 180

air-waybills 202

Akrotiri 254, 407

Aland Islands 10

alcohol and tobacco 129
  excise duty 150
  from other Member States 151
  gifts 148
  intra-UK movements 199
  Special Territories 152

Andorra 10, 53

animals
  scientific research, for 120

Anti-Dumping Duty 408

antiques 65, 95, 96, 121

Arrivals 238

ATA carnets 194, 195, 408

Authorised Economic Operator ... 1, 15

Automated Import System (AIS) 20

Azores 10, 11

Balearic Islands 10, 11

Best Practice 397

bills of lading 165, 202

blood-grouping reagents 121

British Forces Post Office (BFPO) 224

British Sovereign Base Areas ... 9, 11

business to business (B2B) 303

business to consumer (B2C) 359, 361
  supplies 248

Call-off stocks 268

Canary Islands 10, 36

capital goods 122

carbon credits *See* emissions allowances

Certificate of Entitlement 267

Certificate of Status 323

CFSP 39, 408

change of residence relief 143

Channel Islands ....
  .... 10-14, 36, 142, 150, 206

chemical and biological substances
  .... 119, 123
  Chemical Abstracts Service 27

CHIEF ....
  ...38, 39, 88, 191-195, 206, 408-410

CIM 209

Classification
  commodities, of 24

clearance 408

CMR 202, 243, 408

collectors' items 65, 94, 95-97

commercial samples 125

Commercial Samples Relief 126

TRADING PLACES 417

INDEX

Common Agricultural Policy.......... .... 7, 44, 153, 408
Community Customs Code 17, 19, 78, 206, 279
Community Customs Duty........... 7
Community Customs Tariff.... 9, 10
Community goods 36, 153, 194, 409
Community Systems Providers National Transit simplification31
Community Transit...... 36, 194, 409
Community Transit procedure 31,36
computer software 95, 99
consignment stocks 268
consolidation cargo 207
Continental shelf goods 102
Convention International des Marchandises par Chemin de Fer .... See CIM
Convention Merchandises Routiers .... See CMR
Convention on International Trade in Endangered Species of Wild Fauna and Flora (CITES) 34
courier and fast parcel operators 246
currency adjustments................... 89
Customs
   Civil Evasion Penalties (CCEPs)..183
   Civil Penalties (CCP)......................184
Customs Authority.......................... 6
Customs debt 13, 14, 67, 94, 133, 167, 169
Customs Freight Simplified Procedures .... See CFSP
Customs Handling Imports Exports and Freight....See CHIEF
Customs Handling of Import and Export Freight (CHIEF) 24, 35

Customs Procedure Code 26, 37, 56, 58, 125, 131, 151-155, 195, 197, 199, 409
Customs Territory 9-14, 19, 36, 42, 206, 414
customs warehouse.......................... ....31, 44, 60, 92, 106-110, 181, 412
Customs-approved procedures....... ....42, 43, 91
declarant..41
declaration...................................409
   hard copy 35
decorations and awards 126
Deferment Approval Number (DAN) 170
Department for Business, Innovation and Skills..............187
Despatches 6, 13, 238
disabled people............131, 132, 133
distance selling 151, 152, 248, 249, 274
duty deferment................................ ....13, 39, 40, 170-174, 269
duty/tax free goods....................129
duty/tax-free shops.....................235
EC Sales Lists 239, 272, 273, 392
EFTA countries ..28, 29, 31, 194, 408
electricity 133
emissions allowances...................387
End Use Relief 49, 53, 112
endangered species..........33, 63, 149
Enhanced Remote Transit Sheds.45
Entry Price System 85
Entry Processing Unit....................94
Entry Summary Declaration (ENS) 20
EORI number 14, 15, 155, 175, 176, 178

INDEX

ESL Correction sheet 273
establishment
   business 306
   fixed 306
Establishments and residence ... *See* Fixed establishment and Permanent establishment
EU 8th Directive 311, 365
EU 13th Directive 311, 323, 324
EU *acquis* 11
EU Customs Union 126
EU Emissions Trading Scheme .. 387
EU Member States ....
   .... 8, 142, 213, 240, 252
EU TARIC (TARiff Integre Communautaire) 25
EU trader 6
European Free Trade Area 153
Eurozone 13
excise goods 198
Excise Movement Control System (EMCS) 35, 199
Excise Territory 10, 12
Export Administrative Document 206
exports
   by rail 209
   charities 226
   computer software 235
   Customs procedures relating to .. 191
   direct 189
   Government Departments 218
   hydrocarbon oils 234
   indirect 190
   machine tools 225
   motor vehicles 230
   sale or return goods 216
   time limits 211
   to overseas person 216
   types of 213
External Temporary storage Facility (ETSF) 45

Faroe Islands 9
Fixed establishment 7, 306
Floating Production Storage and Offloading (FPSO) vessels 224
fodder and feeding stuffs 134
food and plants 130
Forms
   101 274
   BFG 414 254
   C&E 941 156
   C&E941A 156
   C&E1179 182
   C&E 1331 157
   C18 176
   C79 .... 15, 55, 101,175, 178, 182, 302
   C79 15
   C105A 91
   C105B 91
   C109A 91
   C220 178
   C259 176
   C273 191
   C285 .... 168, 170
   C1314 152
   C1331 234
   C1600 (goods arrived from non-EU countries) 32
   C1600A (presentation of Third Country Goods) 31
   CN22 .... 140, 146, 147, 170
   CN23 .... 140, 146, 147, 170
   SAD/C88 .... 36, 66, 234, 413
   VAT 65A 301
   VAT 66A 301
   VAT 101B 273
   VAT 407 228
   VAT 410 232
   VAT 411 .... 251, 253
   VAT 415 253
   VAT 436 .... 233, 234
   VAT 908 176
   VX302 252
   W5 176
   W5D 176
   W6 176
   W6D 176
   W20 176
   W50 176

INDEX

free zone 44
freight containers 74, 75, 220
French Guiana 10, 36
frozen round sets 85
fruit and vegetables 83, 85, 91
fuel and lubricants 133
GATT Agreement 69
General Valuation Registration Unit 91
Gibraltar 10
gold 130, 163, 278
goods
    for use by a charity 134
    imported for onward dispatch 134
    imported for testing 136
    inherited 137
    war graves, related to 137
    works of art 141
Goods Departed Messages 201
goods imported free of charge 86
groupage 207, 245
Guadeloupe 10, 36
Heligoland 11
Hong Kong 150
hydrocarbon oils 95
import
    VAT reliefs
        aircraft ground and security equipment 119
        animals
            scientific research, for 120
        antiques 121
        blood grouping, tissue typing and therapeutic substances 121
        capital goods 122
        chemical and biological substances 123
        commercial samples 124
        decorations and awards 126
        duty/tax free goods 129
        food and plants 130
        medical equipment
            donated 127

Import Control System (ICS) 19, 20, 35
import duty 4, 119
    relief 127
    RGR 152
import procedures 23
import VAT 4, 7, 13
    accounting 19
    deferment 18
    recovery of 175
    RGR 153
importation methods
    air 21
    Channel Tunnel 22
    Northern Ireland land boundary .. 22
    pipeline 22
    Post Office 23
    sea 22
imported replacement products .. 93
Incoterms 89, 266, 403
input tax 13, 14
intellectual property 94
intermediary services 363, 388
Internal Temporary storage Facility (ITSF) 45
International Collaboration (Defence) Arrangements 217
intra-EU Dispatches 187
intra-EU trading 5, 237
    arrivals and acquisitions 256
    call-off stocks 268
    consignment stocks 268
    distance selling 248
    excise goods 268
    new means of transport 250
    non-taxable persons 248
    supplies to diplomats and "international organisations" .. 266
    temporary movement of goods ... 260
Intrastat 276
Intrastat Territory 10
invoices(tax invoices) ....
    77, 83, 90, 144, 159, 177-180, 189,

209, 248, 260, 272, 279, 298, 301, 302, 309, 323, 338, 370, 391- 394
UK VAT invoices 392
Inward Processing Relief ....
.... 49, 93, 152, 155, 412
Irish land boundary 41, 282
Isle of Man 10, 11, 12
machine tools 225
Madeira 10, 11
marriage relief 161
Martinique 10, 36
medical equipment 127
medical schools 122, 123
Member State ....
.... 1, 9, 56, 143, 241, 246, 412
Member State of identification (MSI) 365
Merchandise In Baggage (MIB) ..46, 179, 197
Mini One Stop Shop ....
.... *also see* VAT MOSS
non-Union scheme 364
Union scheme 366
Ministry of Defence 122, 212, 217
Monaco 9, 11, 12
Mount Athos 10, 11, 36
Movement Reference Number (MRN) 20, 206
museums and galleries 140
Mutual Assistance 238
National Advice Service ....
.... 128, 133, 137, 140, 146
National Export System (NES) ...35, 192
National Import Reliefs Unit ....
.... 124, 131, 140, 157, 163
NATO 267
natural gas 133
NCTS 194

New Community Transit System (NCTS) 35
New Computerised Transit System 29, 31, 194
New Means of Transport 250
New Zealand 83, 150
Non-Union goods 29, 45
Northern Cyprus 11
Office of First Entry (OoFE) 20
Offices of Subsequent Entry (OoSE), ... 20
oil and gas rigs and continental shelf 224
onward supply relief .. 103, 106, 116
output tax 13
Outward Process Relief ....
.... 49, 57, 93, 412
Outward Processing Relief 92
overseas authorities 212, 216
overseas person 7, 8
packings 134
Parcelforce ... 146, 169, 208, 246, 283
Permanent establishment 7, 8
personal allowances 129, 156
Personal Export Scheme 231, 232
place of belonging 8
place of export 8
place of import 8
place of introduction 87, 89
place of residence 8
Place of supply (POS) rules 303,314
accountants 381
admission to events 335
advertising 379
agency services 388
banking, financial and insurance services 383
Broadcasting, Telecommunication and Electronic services (BTE) ..344
broadcasting services *352*

INDEX

e-commerce 353
effective use and enjoyment 348
platforms, portals and interfaces .. 357
telecommunications 351
BTE services 387
consultants 379
consultants and consultancy bureaux 380
cultural, artistic, sporting, scientific, educational or entertainment services 331
data processing 383
emissions allowances 387
energy and fuel distribution networks 385
engineers 381
hiring of a means of transport 326
hiring of any goods other than a means of transport 329
intangibles 376
intellectual property rights 378
intermediary services 388
land services
    airport lounges 321
    general exception 315
    option to tax 324
    reverse charge 321
    stands at exhibitions and conferences 320
    storage of goods 320
lawyers 381
letting on hire of goods 386
passenger transport services 324
provision of information 383
restaurant and catering 336
restaurant and catering: 336
supply of staff 385
Tour Operators' Margin Scheme . 337
transport of goods
    ancillary transport services 343
    transport of goods 341
    valuation services 389
    work on goods 389
place of supply of services 8, 94, 306, 315
plants and fresh produce 33, 34
pleasurecraft 141, 142, 143
Post Office 19, 23

Postponed Accounting System ... 41, 178
pre-entry 413
preference 413
printed matter 163
private gifts 146
Procedure for Electronic Application for Certificates (PEACH) 34
Processing under Customs Control 412
Processing Under Customs Control 49, 52
proof of export 201
racehorses 95, 212, 217
rate of exchange 90, 92, 253, 259
Recovery of VAT
    EU Scheme
        Member State of Establishment ... 295
        Member State of Refund 295
    EU Scheme 295
    non-EU Scheme 299
Registered Excise and Dealers ... 268
rejected imports 49, 59, 182
Relevant Business Person 7, 8, 304, 311, 312, 315, 321, 322, 327, 333, 335, 363, 394, 395
removal 413
rented or leased goods 87
research laboratories 120, 122, 123, 124, 145
Retail Export Scheme 226, 228
Returned Goods Relief ... 49, 53, 152
Reunion 10, 36
Reverse Charge 8, 94, 260-262, 273, 311, 313, 321-328, 335, 388, 391-394
    accounting for 394
    not accounted for 395
Road Tanker Wagons 234

INDEX

Royal Mail 146, 149, 169, 208, 283
royalties and licence fees.. 74-76, 94
Rural Payments Agency (RPA)...34
SAD/C88 43
Sailaway boat scheme.................233
sale or return exports...................216
sale or return terms.............223, 270
Samples..271
San Marino 10, 12, 53
Schengen Agreement...................141
science projects............................145
scientific instruments..................145
sea-waybills..................................202
second-hand goods 64
security, customs debts 172
Ships and aircraft stores 221
Simplified Import VAT Accounting......................See SIVA
Simplified Procedure Values.......85
Singapore......................................150
Single administrative document (SAD/C88) 413
Single Market...................................1
......., 5, 12, 180, 237, 244, 259, 262
SIVA 19
software ...... See computer software
special situations reliefs 61
Standard Exchange System (SES)57
Statistical Supplementary Declarations 239
stolen and lost goods 61, 215, 282
Summary Declaration......14, 20, 31, 32, 36, 37, 40, 43, 183, 195, 196
Supplies of services (intra-EU)..303
  business establishment................306
  fixed establishment........................306
  general rules
    B2B..311

B2C..312
  more than one place of establishment............................308
  nature of supply 305
  non-statutory clearance 310
  place of belonging 306
  usual place of residence.............307
supply and install contracts 215
surcharges......................................89
TA relief 63, 64, 66, 67, 157
Tariff ....
... 9, 37, 97, 117, 163, 409, 411, 414
  classification........................24, 25, 51
tax point 414
taxable person 6, 56, 175, 414
temporary admission.....49, 63, 64, 140, 143, 156, 194, 234, 261, 413
Temporary Admission (TA) regime..138
temporary importation 8
temporary storage..........................
.... 30, 33, 36, 43, 278, 410
third country/territory..13, 39, 126, 137, 142, 153, 179, 213, 225, 409
time limits
  for exporting goods......................211
  for removing the goods from the UK
   243
time of supply ....
... 211, 212, 219, 228, 229, 243, 414
TIR.................................194, 414
tools of trade................. 122, 138, 159
Tour Operators' Margin Scheme (TOMS) 337
Trade Control and Expert System (TRACES) 34
trade statistics.... 38, 69, 71, 117, 276
Trader Unique Reference Number 14
Transit Sheds 45
transport costs 87, 88, 89, 258

INDEX

Transports International Routiers .... *See* TIR
triangulation 153, 264
UK Border Agency 149, 191
UK Trade and Investment 187
uncleared goods 22
Union Customs Code (UCC) 17, 49
universities 123
unregistered importers 170
US visiting forces 156
used goods 86
valuation declaration 80, 91
valuation methods
  "fall-back" method 69, 85
  cost of producing the goods 69, 84
  selling price of goods in the EC 69, 82
  transaction value 6
  .... 9, 70, 74, 77, 78, 85, 87
  value of identical goods 69, 81
  value of similar goods 69, 81
valuing goods for customs duty. 69
VAT Certificates ... 15, 170, 178, 182
VAT Directives
  Directive 77/388/EEC 4, 6, 268
  Directive 2006/112/EC 4, 6
VAT Gap 237, 238
VAT group 169, 178, 219

VAT MOSS 361-370
  accounting for non-Union VAT ... 366
  accounting for Union VAT 368
  BTE services 372
  pricing services 371
  Return 372
VAT
  principles 4
  registration number 14, 15, 228, 240, 241, 242, 262, 265, 273
  return ... 13, 14, 170, 241, 265, 272, 275
  Territory 9, 36
  zero-rating 187, 188, 201, 209
Vatican 11
veterinary products 34
VIES system 240
visiting forces
  motor vehicles 156
  NATO 154
  US 154
visitors to the UK 156
visual and auditory materials ....
  .... 119, 162
warehousekeepers ....
  .... 32, 106, 170, 198, 199
warehousing 41, 44, 64, 66
works of art 64, 65, 94-97
World Trade Organisation "Valuation Agreement" 69
zero-rated articles 163